Darwin's Con

MW00633772

Darwin's Conjecture

*The Search for General Principles of
Social and Economic Evolution*

GEOFFREY M. HODGSON
AND THORBJØRN KNUDSEN

The University of Chicago Press

CHICAGO AND LONDON

The University of Chicago Press, Chicago 60637
The University of Chicago Press, Ltd., London
© 2010 by The University of Chicago
All rights reserved. Published 2010.
Paperback edition 2012
Printed in the United States of America

21 20 19 18 17 16 15 14 13 12   2 3 4 5 6

ISBN-13: 978-0-226-34690-8 (cloth)
ISBN-10: 0-226-34690-0 (cloth)
ISBN-13: 978-0-226-00578-2 (paper)
ISBN-10: 0-226-00578-x (paper)

Library of Congress Cataloging-in-Publication Data
Hodgson, Geoffrey Martin, 1946–
    Darwin's conjecture : the search for general principles of social and economic
evolution / Geoffrey M. Hodgson and Thorbjørn Knudsen.
        p.   cm.
    Includes biographical references and index.
    ISBN-13: 978-0-226-34690-8 (hardcover : alk. paper)
    ISBN-10: 0-226-34690-0 (hardcover : alk. paper)
        1. Social Darwinism.   2. Social evolution.   3. Natural selection—Social
    aspects.   I. Knudsen, Thorbjørn.   II. Title.
    HM631.H634 2010
    303.4—dc22   2010009308

Contents

Preface

Although the idea of generalizing core Darwinian principles to social evolution is well over a century old, ours is the first book-length, systematic treatment of the topic. Despite the celebrated power of Darwin's ideas, it is remarkable that they have had relatively little impact on the social sciences. The adoption of Darwinism by social scientists has been thwarted by numerous misinterpretations and misunderstandings, several of which we hope to remove in this volume. And Darwinism is not simply an option. We hold that there is no known alternative to Darwinism as a general framework with which to analyze the evolution of social and economic systems.

The core Darwinian principles involve variation, selection, and inheritance (or replication). The claim that Darwinism applies to social evolution must rest on a clear picture of what these concepts mean. Otherwise, the arguments and counterarguments become lost in a fog. Consequently, much of this work is devoted to clarifying concepts and refining definitions at a fairly abstract level.

The importance of these preliminaries should not be underestimated. While we refer to some empirical cases, this work is largely conceptual—and necessarily so. The disposing of major misconceptions and the provision of clear definitions of the general elements and mechanisms of Darwinian evolution are ground-clearing preconditions for both middle-range theory and more extensive empirical research. The primary aim of this book is to show that the core Darwinian mechanisms of variation, selection, and replication apply to social entities and processes, and we give some examples of how they pertain to business and other social phenomena.

Our goal is to provide a guide for future research, not to develop models of immediate empirical application. Darwinism as such provides no single model or axiomatic system. Instead, it is a metatheoretical framework that stimulates further inquiry and provides a repository for contingent auxiliary theories and models. This book remains largely at the metatheoretical level. We use some empirical illustrations and show how the work of some other leading theorists slots into this rubric. But the construction of a new Darwinian theoretical system capable of generating powerful predictive models to rival established alternatives in the social sciences is a long way off. As with the application of Darwinian principles to biology, the first and principal achievement is to build a conceptual engine that is capable of guiding specific inquiry into detailed causal mechanisms. The secondary process—of showing how these principles operated in specific contexts and in particular ways—required a century of detailed empirical and experimental study before Darwinism triumphed in the 1940s. The task of applying Darwinism to the social sciences is much younger and has far to go.

The compelling logic of Darwinism is that it addresses the evolution of all aspects of living systems, including human intentionality and social structures. Much social science takes one or both factors as given. The promise of Darwinism is that it may help explain socioeconomic phenomena better than existing theory and, eventually, generate novel testable predictions concerning socioeconomic phenomena. Although our work does not yet fulfill this promise, we believe that this book is a vital step in the right direction.

Evolutionary theory tackles highly complex phenomena. There is no simple explanation of why some organizations prosper and others fail. Just as *fitness* acts as a placeholder for multiple specific and detailed phenomena in the natural world, specific explanations of organizational success or failure are varied and context specific. Their full elaboration requires immense further detailed work that is beyond the scope of this volume. Instead, this book provides a conceptual framework for understanding evolution in human societies. Empirical investigation must be guided by some classificatory and conceptual scaffolding. As Darwin himself wrote: "Without the making of theories I am convinced there would be no observation" (Darwin 1887, 2:315).

We make a further step forward in dealing with the seemingly enduring and apparently intractable problem of the equivalent "genetics" of social evolution. For over thirty years, the term *meme* has been used as a vague placeholder in this context, without much further investigation of how social and cultural entities actually replicate.

Genes hold and pass on information, in the broad and basic sense of some encoded means of generating conditional dispositions that can be transmitted to other entities and cause a response. We regard the storing and replication of information as central to social evolution as well. Hence, our general framework focuses on other informational mechanisms at the social level.

Here, the concept of habit is crucial. Habits are essential psychological mechanisms in learning and skill development (Dewey 1922). They are the individual building blocks of customs, routines, and all higher-level social replicators in organizations. Habits and routines are persistent, they replicate, and they contain ready-made solutions to frequently occurring problems. Their persistence means that organizational evolution often stubbornly resists corporate or government initiatives.

We also stress the importance of the distinction between replicators and interactors. Without this, it is impossible to tackle the thorny proposition of whether social evolution is "Lamarckian." More important, and more constructive, the identification of social replicators leads to further questions concerning the generation of complexity in social evolution and important transitions in the mode of replication in the evolution of human society. Our approach highlights the importance of social organization over and beyond previous evolutionary work in the social sciences.

We fully acknowledge our debt to others in the development of this work. Prominent among these are Richard Nelson and Sidney Winter (1982) in economics and Robert Boyd and Peter Richerson (1985) in anthropology. Their many inspiring works have had a major impact in bringing evolutionary ideas into the social sciences and have spawned a large number of theoretical and empirical studies.

Yet, with Nelson and Winter (1982), the Darwinian principles are implicit rather than explicit. We make explicit their use of Darwinian principles, and develop these as a general theoretical framework for evolutionary economists. Boyd and Richerson concentrate on one social and cultural level only, and they sidestep the important philosophical task of defining and elucidating the core Darwinian concepts in a generalizable manner. Also, our timescale is shorter. Apart from the early stages of cultural and linguistic evolution, our analytic framework for social evolution relates to the last few thousand years. While there have been enormous social and economic developments in this period, there has been very little change in the human gene pool. Recent and dramatic socioeconomic evolution is, thus, not driven by genetic changes. Our framework is designed to operate even when genetic changes do not take place. Despite the inspirational achievements of all these authors, gaps remain to be filled.

It is hoped that, through a future combination of our conceptual schema with detailed empirical investigation, an alternative to the existing, more static mainstream approaches in economics and other social sciences will develop more fully. Darwinism might then have as great an impact on the social sciences as it has had on the biological.

Acknowledgments

For illuminating discussions and comments, we wish to thank Richie Adelstein, Howard Aldrich, Robert Aunger, Amitai Aviram, Christian Barrère, Markus Becker, Marion Blute, Guido Bünstorf, Werner Callebaut, Uwe Cantner, Michael Christensen, Jean-Philippe Colin, Christian Cordes, Peter Corning, James F. Crow, Simon Deakin, Jerker Denrell, Denise Dollimore, Robin Dunbar, Christoph Engel, David Gindis, Ian Gough, Kevin Greene, David Hull, Elias Khalil, Janet Landa, Arturo Lara, Dan Levinthal, John Linarelli, Ed Lorenz, Pavel Luksha, Tage Koed Madsen, James March, J. Stanley Metcalfe, Joel Mokyr, Richard Nelson, John Nightingale, John Pepper, Peter Richerson, W. Garry Runciman, Itai Sened, Kim Sterelny, Nils Stieglitz, Jan-Willem Stoelhorst, Viktor Vanberg, John van Whye, Jack Vromen, Richard Webb, Katja Wegner, David Sloan Wilson, Sidney Winter, Ulrich Witt, and many others, including several anonymous referees.

Chapter 2 adapts Geoffrey M. Hodgson and Thorbjørn Knudsen, "Why We Need a Generalized Darwinism, and Why a Generalized Darwinism Is Not Enough," *Journal of Economic Behavior and Organization* 61, no. 1 (September 2006): 1–19. Copyright © 2006, with permission from Elsevier. Chapters 4, 5, and 6 make use of and revise material from Geoffrey M. Hodgson and Thorbjørn Knudsen, "Dismantling Lamarckism: Why Descriptions of Socio-Economic Evolution as Lamarckian Are Misleading," *Journal of Evolutionary Economics* 16, no. 4 (October 2006): 343–66; "The Nature and Units of Social Selection," *Journal of Evolutionary Economics* 16, no. 5 (December 2006): 477–89; and "Information, Complexity and Generative Replication," *Biology and Philosophy* 43, no. 1 (2008): 47–65; copyright © Springer Science and Business Media; used with kind permission of Springer Science and Business Media. We are grateful for permission from the publishers to use this material.

Finally, we thank our families for tolerating our enthusiasm for, and intense discussions of, evolutionary ideas.

CHAPTER ONE

Introduction: The Challenge of Darwinism for the Social Sciences

Nothing I have said is intrinsically a matter of biological analogy, it is a matter of evolutionary logic. Evolutionary theory is a manner of reasoning in its own right quite independently of the use made of it by biologists. They simply got there first.

J. STANLEY METCALFE, (1998)

Empirical evidence is usually too malleable to be very decisive in conceptual revolutions. . . . Initial acceptance of fundamentally new ideas leans more heavily on the increased coherence which the view brings to our general world picture.

DAVID L. HULL, (1978)

Darwinian ideas are widely celebrated in biology. But human society also evolves. Could Darwinian principles also apply to the evolution of social entities? Just as organisms compete for scarce resources, businesses, states, and other organizations do likewise. They adapt and change. Some fail; others prosper. Organizations learn and pass on information. Are these not broadly Darwinian processes?

Several thinkers have suggested that social evolution could be partly understood in Darwinian terms. But a full and systematic account has so far been lacking. Elucidation of the Darwinian conceptual framework is one of the most important unfulfilled promises on the agenda of institutional and evolutionary economics. It is our aim to move this project forward and to help stimulate its further development.

Darwin's theory has been battered but never beaten. For much of the twentieth century, talk of applying Darwinism in the social sciences was curtailed. Even today, many social scientists approach Darwinism with trepidation. Writers have held that, while Darwinism is important in biology, it does not apply to human society. This book takes a different view. It explains how Darwinian principles also apply to social evolution and why prominent objections to their use are unwarranted.[1] This chapter looks at the historical background to generalizing the Darwinian approach and provides an outline of the book as a whole.

While the advantages of a unifying evolutionary theory should be obvious, there are reasons to be cautious about an approach that spans social and biological evolution. The most important relates to the legacy of reckless generalization and oversimplification in the social sciences. Perhaps because of "physics envy" (Mirowski 1989), economists have been inclined to search for the scientific Holy Grail of explanation in terms of a few general concepts and equations. Incautious enthusiasm for such catchall concepts as *utility maximization* and *transaction costs* is evidence of this tendency. The problem with overgeneralized explanations is that they become all-embracing and impossible to falsify and lead to a neglect of vital differences of context and detail.[2]

One of us has written a full-scale account of how economics and sociology were diverted from historical and cultural specificities in their search for a unifying grand theory of everything (Hodgson 2001a). Does the idea of generalizing Darwinian principles not fall into the same trap? Should social scientists forget such an ambitious idea and, instead, dig deep into empirical detail?

As explained elsewhere (Hodgson 2001a), the dangers of reckless overgeneralization do not mean that generalizations should be avoided when they are appropriate. Indeed, to some extent, general frameworks and principles are unavoidable. Without classifications and communalities, no empirical work would be possible. Good theoretical frameworks are precursors to appropriate empirical classification. Theories in the social sciences should embrace appropriate generalizations without neglecting important specificities of detail and context. We require guiding theories that are sensitive to historical and other specificities.

There have been many attempts to establish general theories or frame-

---

1. Generally, we use the term *social* in an inclusive sense, to include business and other phenomena studied by economists as well as social structures. Occasionally, we use *socioeconomic* as an alternative but equally inclusive term.

2. In 1904, Max Weber (1949, 72–80) wrote that "the most general laws" are "the least valuable" because, "the more comprehensive their scope," the more they "lead away" from the task of explaining the particular phenomenon in question. Ernest Nagel's (1961, 575) "principle of the inverse variation of extension with intension" similarly alleges that there is a trade-off between the generality and the informative content of a theory. Oliver Williamson (1995, 33) has likewise conceded: "There is nonetheless a grave problem with broad, elastic and plausible concepts—of which 'transaction costs' is one and 'power' is another—in that they lend themselves to *ex post* rationalization. Concepts that explain everything explain nothing."

works in the social sciences. Prominent among these is the Walrasian theory of general economic equilibrium (Walras 1874; Arrow and Debreu 1954). But among the deficiencies of this approach are its limited treatments of interactions between agents and of the dynamic phenomena of individual learning and development. General equilibrium analysis does not capture the innovativeness and restlessness of modern economies (Nelson and Winter 1982; Metcalfe 1998; Beinhocker 2006). Another approach that claims to offer an alternative general framework is game theory (Gintis 2007), but questions have been raised about its strong assumptions concerning information and rationality and its capacity to embrace novelty and complex phenomena (Kirman 1993, 2005; Bicchieri 1994; Hargreaves Heap and Varoufakis 1995; Hodgson 2007a).

Like the social sciences, biology addresses systems of immense complexity. Specificities are vital, but that does not mean that general principles cannot be established. Darwinism is a model here. It can neither explain nor predict everything. Instead, it provides an overarching theoretical framework in which explanations of specificities and contingencies must be placed. This involves theorizing on multiple levels (Hodgson 2001a, chap. 21). A grand theory of this type is necessary to organize the empirical quest and to accommodate all the differences of specific mechanism and detail. The pursuit of this type of grand theory, far from abandoning empirical material, gives it full scope and power.

We suggest that generalized Darwinism could become the backbone of a unified evolutionary framework for the social and behavioral sciences. Many of the details must await further research, and at this stage we can provide only a limited number of empirical illustrations. The main contribution of this volume is to clarify the conceptual framework, to probe its potential, and to prepare the ground for this venture. Long overdue in the Age of Darwin, its time has now come.

1.1. DARWIN'S TRIUMPH

On his mission to explain evolution, Charles Darwin gathered masses of empirical material. His theory of evolution was not the result of armchair introspection but the outcome of a theoretically guided and persistent interrogation of the facts. Although aspects of his argument can be modeled mathematically and we have powerful formulations such as the Price Equation, Darwinian evolution cannot be modeled fully with simple and universal equations akin to those in physics.

Darwin's classic 1859 *On the Origin of Species* became the foundation of modern evolutionary biology. His ideas attracted much attention because of their suggestion that humankind was not of divine origin but descended from apes. But this proposition was neither original nor his major achievement. Indeed, Darwin postponed discussion of human evolution to the 1871 *Descent of Man*. Instead, his supreme triumph was to propose connected mechanisms of evolution that relied on materialist causes and effects, rather than regarding evolution as a product of design or as some mysteriously predestined process toward improvement or perfection. In short, Darwin advanced evolutionary science by building a theory in which cause and effect both have material substance and are subject to scientific inquiry. His triumph was to create a theoretical framework to help explain the causal processes of the evolution of astoundingly complex phenomena with recourse to neither predestination nor design.

Darwin often expressed ignorance about the detailed mechanisms involved, and several of his speculations at this level have proved wrong. He knew nothing about genes or DNA, and their discovery, as well as the crucial fusion of Darwinian theory with Mendelian genetics, had to wait until the twentieth century. Nevertheless, he laid out the core, overarching principles of variation, inheritance, and selection that are now recognized as essential to the understanding of the evolution of species and the complex marvels of nature.

This scientific triumph was quite different from others, such as in physics. With Newton's laws of motion, for example, it is possible to predict with impressive degrees of accuracy the motions of the planets or the journey of a space vehicle to the moon. No such precise predictions are possible with Darwin's theory. Although some Darwinian biologists have discerned trajectories in evolution, these remain controversial, and the strength in Darwinism lies in its powers of explaining observed facts, rather than predicting any future evolutionary outcome.

Crucially, as Darwin acknowledged, his theory of natural selection is inadequate to explain specific phenomena *on its own*. This core theory cannot entirely account for the fact, for instance, that some birds have colorful plumage and others are gray or brown. Some auxiliary explanations are required to explain these divergent outcomes. Darwin himself pointed to these, and some are special cases of his general principle of selection. Bright plumage is explained by the specific mechanism of *sexual* selection. Duller plumage is explained by the specific advantages of camouflage and the avoidance of predators. These two mechanisms work against each other: bright plumage has the opposite effect to camouflage, and neither is universal. The principle of selection relies on specific auxiliary theories or special cases in order to complete the explanation of the phenomena in question.

Accordingly, the general evolutionary principles of variation, inheritance, and selection do not provide a complete theory in the manner of those of Isaac Newton or Albert Einstein in physics. Instead, Darwin provides an overarching theory, in which other, special assumptions and auxiliary theories must be placed. This theoretical framework is a major stepping-stone for the sciences of evolving, complex phenomena. At the same time, Darwinism obliges us to focus on those detailed mechanisms in order to identify the causal mechanisms or "algorithms" that generate complex outcomes (Dennett 1995). Darwin was one of the first and most profound theorists of complexity.

1.2. THE GENERALIZATION OF DARWINISM TO SOCIAL EVOLUTION

Given this achievement, the possibility emerges of applying Darwinian ideas to other complex evolving systems, outside biology. Darwin himself left further clues. In *The Origin of Species*, for example, he briefly considered the possibility that natural selection operates on the elements of language (see Darwin 1859, 422–23). In 1869, the German economist Hugo Thiel sent him his 1868 pamphlet *Über landwirtschaftliche Genossenschaften* (On agricultural cooperatives). Thiel crudely interpreted Darwin's theory as supporting individual competition in the economic sphere. He did not consider the selection of cooperatives or other firms as entities. In his immediate response, Darwin politely expressed interest in the application of his ideas to "moral and social questions." He wrote modestly: "It did not occur to me formerly that my views could be extended to such widely different and most important subjects" (Darwin 1887, 3:113).[3]

But Darwin had already hinted at the possibility of some such applications in the *Origin*. In *The Descent of Man*, he again conjectured that natural selection operates on the elements of language (see Darwin 1871, 1:59–61,

---

3. To what extent did Darwin understand or endorse Thiel's argument? He wrote in his autobiography: "During my whole life I have been singularly incapable of mastering any language." In his letters, he admitted to reading German "very slowly" and "so badly." And, while he taught himself some German and read some biological texts in that language, he still allowed: "Though I can read descriptive books . . . pretty easily, when any reasoning comes in, I find German excessively difficult to understand" (Darwin 1887, 1:32, 2:278, 319, 279). The extent to which he appreciated the details of Thiel's argument and its crude and inadequate depiction of Darwinian principles is a mystery.

106).[4] Therein, he described attempts by Walter Bagehot to apply Darwinian principles to political evolution as "remarkable" (162n).[5] He also proposed that tribal groups with moral and other propensities that served the common good would be favored by natural selection (162–66). In effect, he suggested that selection could operate on ethical principles. He thus endorsed a version of group selection and hinted at the natural selection of institutions as well as the natural selection of individuals.[6] However, these were no more than hints, and Darwin never attempted to apply his ideas systematically to socioeconomic evolution.[7]

Darwin's brief conjecture that his core principles might apply to other evolving systems outside the biological sphere did not imply that explanations of social (or other) phenomena had to be reduced to biological entities. On the contrary, Darwin suggested that the principles of variation, selection, and inheritance have a broader applicability and are not confined to biology. This conjecture was very different from the reductionist proposal that social phenomena can be entirely explained in biological terms.

A few years after the publication of *The Origin of Species*, several scholars followed Darwin's hints that the principles of selection, variation, and inheritance may have a wider relevance than to biological organisms alone, in-

4. No doubt Darwin was encouraged by his friend Charles Lyell's (1863, chap. 23) claim that languages and dialects were related by descent from common origins and were subject to a "struggle for existence" and processes of "selection." Lyell believed that languages evolved, but he was equivocal on the question of organic and human evolution by natural selection.

5. Bagehot's essays appeared in the *Fortnightly Review* from 1867 to 1869 and were later republished in book form (see Bagehot 1872).

6. But Darwin neglected some possible further extensions of group selection arguments in the social sphere. In 1872, he wrote to the German law professor Heinrich Fick and acknowledged his argument that military recruitment leads to the death of the fitter individuals. He added that trade unionism undermined individual incentives (Weikart 1995, 1998). He did not consider group selection and efficiency-enhancing arguments for cooperation in this context (Campbell 1994). Generally, the idea of group selection remained underdeveloped in Darwin's work. Much later, after criticism of the work of Vero Copner Wynne-Edwards (1962), it fell out of favor (Williams 1966; Dawkins 1976). Its importance in the social domain was inadequately appreciated until the end of the twentieth century (Boyd and Richerson 1985; Hodgson 1993; Campbell 1994; Sober and Wilson 1998; Bergstrom 2002, 2003; Henrich 2004; Wilson 2002; Bowles 2006; Wilson and Wilson 2007).

7. In 1873, Darwin thanked Karl Marx for sending him a copy of *Capital* and noted its contribution to "the deep and important subject of political economy." However, the pages of this volume in Darwin's library in his house in Kent remained uncut (Colp 1974). The idea that Marx went so far as to ask permission from Darwin to dedicate a volume of *Capital* to him turns out to be a myth (Feuer 1975; Fay 1978; Colp 1982). In relation to Adam Smith, there is evidence in his notebooks that Darwin read *The Theory of Moral Sentiments* but none that he read *The Wealth of Nations* (Gruber 1974; Vorzimmer 1977). Generally, references to social, political, or economic evolution are rare in Darwin's works and correspondence.

cluding to the evolution of human society. We have already mentioned that
Bagehot (1872) applied the principles of selection and inheritance to ideas
and political institutions. Subsequently, William James (1880) considered
the natural selection of ideas in human learning and in the development of
science. He was among the first to consider an evolutionary epistemology.[8]
James (1880, 441) opened his essay with the observation of a "remarkable
parallel . . . between the facts of social evolution on the one hand, and of
zoölogical evolution as expounded by Mr. Darwin on the other." But his
discussion was largely confined to the selection of ideas in the heads of
individuals.

Samuel Alexander (1892) and Benjamin Kidd (1894) also wrote on the
natural selection of ethical principles. Albeit limited in robustness and
scope, their works were exceptional in bringing the Darwinian principle
of selection into the social domain and considering units of selection other
than individuals alone. These early precedents show that the idea of generalizing Darwinism to other evolving systems, outside biology and including
human society, was taken on board by a number of influential thinkers
from the 1870s to the 1890s.[9]

While several writers believed that Darwinian principles could be applied to social phenomena, they applied them loosely and incompletely.
Hence, Bagehot's emphasis was broadly on the struggle between nations,
not on a process of selection involving well-specified additional social units
or structures. He considered the role of imitation and the "cake of custom"
but did not identify particular institutions as units of selection. Similarly,
Sidney Webb (1889, 53) insisted that "the units selected are not individuals
but societies." But he was also unclear of the mechanisms of selection, other
than to allude to the competitive struggle between nations for access to raw
materials and for supremacy in world markets.

Kidd (1894, 43) suggested a process whereby the selection of human "societies" was driven by "the survivals of the fittest." But he did not clearly
establish any notion that social structures were themselves subject to selection processes. In the same year, Henry Drummond (1894) saw Darwinian
evolution in human society, but he did not examine the selection process in

---

8. Evolutionary epistemology was later rediscovered and developed by Popper (1972) and
Campbell (1974).

9. Remarkably, in 1898, the American philosopher Charles Sanders Peirce proposed that the
laws of nature themselves evolve (Peirce 1992). This idea is being further developed by physicists
today, involving the mind-blowing argument that key physical constants take the values they do
because alternative universes in which the constants took different values failed to survive (Smolin
1997).

more detail. These writers failed to consider the natural selection of social structures or institutions or to address the problems involved in establishing levels of selection above the individual human actor. When they applied Darwinian selection, it was loosely to individuals or collections of individuals. In seeing individuals as units of selection, it was widely accepted that the selected traits might also be conducive to the harmony and the survival of groups or nations. But this did not establish a viable concept of selection at the group level or higher.

Accordingly, these early extensions of Darwinian principles to social evolution failed to establish the social units of replication and selection, other than to refer imprecisely to societies or groups. It was not explained why human social evolution involved anything more than the selection of individuals. After all, the selection advantage of one group over another may result simply from the selection advantages of the members of the more adapted group. In this case, group (or social) selection amounts to nothing more than individual selection. Without a supplementary explanation, such notions of social evolution dissolve into simply the evolution and selection of human individuals.

Several prominent accounts in the 1890s of Darwinian evolution in human society shared this limitation. The then prominent analyses of Otto Ammon (1895), Georges Vacher de Lapouge (1896, 1897), and Carlos Closson (1896a, 1896b) addressed individual selection, not the selection of social units. The writings of Ammon and Lapouge were preoccupied with explanations of social phenomena in terms of the alleged racial characteristics of individuals. Even when Lapouge and Closson emphasized the term *social selection*, they meant the selection of ethnically defined individuals in the context of their social environment.

For these and many other writers at that time, the quality of human civilization depended principally on the biologically determined capacities of the human individuals within it. Accordingly, the prominent thinker Alfred Marshall (1923, 260) could write: "Economic institutions are the products of human nature and cannot change much faster than human nature changes."

1.3. EARLY RECOGNITIONS OF SOCIAL UNITS OF REPLICATION OR SELECTION

In the 1890s, and independently of each other, two writers first clearly formulated the notion that there were social units of selection, irreducible to individuals, to which Darwinian principles might apply. The first of these was the Scottish philosopher David George Ritchie. Like Alexander—with whom he corresponded—Ritchie saw that Darwinian selection could be applied to the evolution of ethical ideas. But he went further than that.

In *Darwinism and Politics* (1889), Ritchie held that, in human societies, "language and social institutions make it possible to transmit experience quite independently of the continuity of race." In other words, cultural transmission functioned alongside, and in addition to, what today we describe as *genetic inheritance*.[10] Ritchie argued: "An individual or a nation may do more for mankind by handing on ideas and a great example than by leaving numerous offspring" (59). This is a far-reaching claim.

In the second edition of *Darwinism and Politics* (1891), Ritchie added a new essay: "Natural Selection and the History of Institutions." It offered one of the earliest coherent arguments that Darwinian principles of variation, inheritance, and selection applied to the evolution of both social institutions and organisms. Ritchie saw language and institutions as social mechanisms through which adaptations and knowledge can be inherited. He wrote of a struggle between "institutions, languages, ideas" (139) as well as a struggle between individuals. But he warned that, although Darwinian principles applied to social evolution, they must always be used carefully and with meticulous acknowledgment of differences in the mechanisms involved.

Later, Ritchie (1896) developed these ideas in more depth. Although he regarded biology as a better source of ideas for the social sciences than physics or chemistry, he repeatedly warned against the casual and uncritical use of biological terms in the social context. He argued that there was not simply a process of struggle in society between individuals but also one between different "social organisms," including the family, social organizations, nations, and so on. This second level of struggle vastly complicated the processes of social evolution and selection. For instance, as Ritchie pointed out, one individual might simultaneously belong to several social units or institutions. Accordingly, different processes of selection at a social level might conflict with each other as well as with the natural selection of individuals.

Ritchie noted that natural and social evolution differed in other respects. For instance, selection in the natural world works through the death of the unfit. In contrast, in the social sphere, it is not simply through "the slow and deadly process of natural selection that the various elements in our

10. George Henry Lewes (1879) and Henry Drummond (1894) also suggested this idea.

civilization have been produced, preserved, and diffused." He argued that, in social evolution, "a great many habits are due to imitation and not to instinct, *i.e.*, they are transmitted in the *social inheritance* of the race, and are not dependent on *heredity*, in the biological sense" (1896, 168–69).

Ritchie established imitation as an important element of cultural transmission and outlined what is today known as a theory of *dual inheritance*, according to which cultural and genetic evolution take separate but interdependent trajectories. Here is his description of a separate cultural inheritance track: "the *habit* may be changed without the extinction of the *race* . . . customs and institutions may perish without the necessary destruction of the race that practiced them" and "customs and institutions may be handed on from race to race, and may long survive the race from whom they originated" (1896, 170). Cultural inheritance and biological inheritance were governed by different processes even to the point where the life span of the social units of selection could be entirely noncoextensive with the lives of the human individuals who sustained them.

While carefully acknowledging important differences between evolution in nature and society, Ritchie still regarded the theory of selection as being applicable to the social domain. Despite detailed differences of evolutionary mechanism, the "range" of Darwinian theory could be extended from the biological to the social sphere. In a prescient passage, Ritchie (1896, 170–71) wrote: "But in asserting that human society presents many phenomena that cannot be accounted for by natural selection in its purely biological sense, I am not denying the truth of the theory, but rather extending its range. There is going on a 'natural selection' of ideas, customs, institutions, irrespective of the natural selection of individuals and of races." This is a pathbreaking recognition that Darwinian principles could be applied to social evolution and to nonbiological units of replication or selection. The idea of "extending [the] range" of Darwinian principles to outside the biological sphere tallies with what was many years later described by Richard Dawkins (1983) as *universal Darwinism*. The work of Ritchie and others shows that the idea of generalizing Darwinian principles was established in the nineteenth century rather than the twentieth.[11]

Ritchie's key innovation was to recognize that the units of replication or selection could be social entities such as customs and institutions, rather

11. We prefer the term *generalized Darwinism*. Dawkins's (1983) *universal Darwinism* can misleadingly suggest that Darwinism covers *everything* or has "universal validity" (Dawkins 1976, 205). As explained below, Darwinian principles apply to complex population systems only, notwithstanding that these systems cover a highly varied set of phenomena.

than individuals alone. This is possibly the first explicit appearance of the idea of a natural selection of institutions or social structures in the English language. There were several earlier applications of natural selection to social phenomena, but none of them so clearly made institutions the explicit units of selection.

The second scholar to write of institutions as units of selection was Thorstein Veblen. The British zoologist and philosopher Conwy Lloyd Morgan may have stimulated Veblen's thinking in this area, along with James, Peirce, and others.[12] By 1896, Morgan had accepted the arguments of August Weismann (1893) that acquired characters could not be inherited in the biological sphere. Rejecting Lamarck in favor of Weismann, he then asked, If human beings had evolved only slightly in genetic terms, then *what* had evolved in the last millennium or so when human achievements had been transformed beyond measure? His answer to the puzzle was as follows:

> Evolution *has been transferred from the organism to the environment*. There must be increment somewhere, otherwise evolution is impossible. In social evolution on this view, the increment is by storage in the social environment to which each new generation adapts itself, with no increased native power of adaptation. In the written record, in social traditions, in the manifold inventions which make scientific and industrial progress possible, in the products of art, and the recorded examples of noble lives, we have an environment which is at the same time the product of mental evolution, and affords the condition of the development of each individual mind to-day. . . . [T]his transference of evolution from the individual to the environment may leave the *faculty* of the race at a standstill, while the *achievements* of the race are progressing by leaps and bounds. (Morgan 1896, 340)

He thus established the possibility of social evolution having a substance and a pace that was reducible neither to individuals nor to their biological attributes. Over and beyond the passive environment of biotic selection, information and knowledge involved a level of inheritance in their own right. Morgan argued that human biotic and mental capacities could not evolve so rapidly as to account for the evolution of human civilization.[13]

---

12. Circumstantial evidence exists that Veblen came into contact with Morgan in Chicago in 1896 (Dorfman 1934; Hodgson 2004a). In any case, Veblen's idea of the natural selection of institutions dates from this time, and he was later to cite Morgan in his work.

13. Morgan (1923) went on to contribute to the development of the philosophical idea of emergent properties. Emergentist philosophy itself reached its zenith in the 1920s, before positivist currents in philosophy swept it aside. It was not until the 1960s that emergentist ideas began to revive. Arguably, an emergentist philosophy is necessary to sustain a theory of evolution on multiple levels, including the social level (Blitz 1992; Hodgson 2004a; Okasha 2006).

As for Veblen, in a book review of a work by Antonio Labriola, he saw in the author's Marxism the doctrine that the "economic exigencies" of the industrial process "afford the definitive test of fitness in the adaptation of all human institutions by a process of selective elimination of the economically unfit" (1897, 390). But these were Veblen's words, not Labriola's. Veblen made the additional and substantial theoretical leap of applying the principle of selection to institutions and not merely to individuals or groups.

For Veblen, the institutional structure of society was not merely "the social environment," as Morgan had put it. Veblen indicated that the social environment consisted of institutional elements that were themselves, like organisms, subject to evolutionary processes of selection. Darwinism was interpreted not narrowly, in terms of individuals being selected in a fixed environment, but more broadly, in terms of individuals being selected in an environment that is changed in its interaction with those creative individuals. As Veblen put it: "The economic life history of the individual is a cumulative process of adaptation of means to ends that cumulatively change as the process goes on, both the agent and his environment being at any point the outcome of the last process." He concluded: "An evolutionary economics must be a theory of a process of cultural growth as determined by the economic interest, a theory of a cumulative sequence of economic institutions stated in terms of the process itself" (1898, 391, 393).

In a key passage in *The Theory of the Leisure Class*, Veblen (1899, 188) declared:

> The life of man in society, just like the life of other species, is a struggle for existence, and therefore it is a process of selective adaptation. The evolution of social structure has been a process of natural selection of institutions. The progress which has been and is being made in human institutions and in human character may be set down, broadly, to a natural selection of the fittest habits of thought and to a process of enforced adaptation of individuals to an environment which has progressively changed with the growth of community and with the changing institutions under which men have lived. Institutions are not only themselves the result of a selective and adaptive process which shapes the prevailing or dominant types of spiritual attitude and aptitudes; they are at the same time special methods of life and human relations, and are therefore in their turn efficient factors of selection. So that the changing institutions in their turn make for a further selection of individuals endowed with the fittest temperament, and a further adaptation of individual temperament and habits to the changing environment through the formation of new institutions.

It was no accident that Darwin's phrases *natural selection* and *struggle for existence* appeared in this passage. Veblen wrote also in the same work of "the law of natural selection, as applied to human institutions" (207). He became the second writer after the publication of *The Origin of Species* to apply Darwin's principle of selection to the evolution of institutions. The decisive implication was that Darwinism could be applied to human society without necessarily reducing explanations of social phenomena to individual psychology or biology. As Veblen (1909, 300) wrote: "If . . . men universally acted not on the conventional grounds and values afforded by the fabric of institutions, but solely and directly on the grounds and values afforded by the unconventionalised propensities and aptitudes of hereditary human nature, then there would be no institutions and no culture." He thus suggested that, if social or economic phenomena were determined exclusively by biological factors, then the concepts of institution and culture would be redundant. Culture and institutions are irreducible to biological factors alone. Veblen thus broke decisively from biological reductionism.

Ritchie and Veblen died in 1903 and 1929, respectively. Their thinking was ahead of its time, and few of their contemporaries and followers pursued further the research agenda of extending Darwinian principles to social evolution, except for neglected figures such as Albert G. Keller (1915). All three of these thinkers made great strides toward realizing Darwin's conjecture, but they also left a number of critical issues unaddressed. Despite rare extensions of Darwinian principles to the social sphere, it took much of the twentieth century before these issues again became priorities for social scientists.[14]

1.4. THE REJECTION OF DARWINISM

By the start of the First World War, the uncompleted project to apply Darwinian principles rigorously to social evolution was in deep trouble. At that time, Darwinian ideas in biology were widely criticized by biologists. While Darwin had become famous for providing scientific accreditation for the idea of human evolution from other species, his core theoretical ideas were poorly understood and found relatively few devotees (Bowler 1983, 1988). Darwin himself had no adequate explanation of the sources of variation in individuals or of the mechanisms of inheritance.

Critics of Darwin complained that natural selection could account for neither the origins of variations nor the presumed speed of evolution. Dar-

---

14. Other early extensions of Darwinian principles to social evolution include Petr Kropotkin (1902), James Mark Baldwin (1909), F. Stuart Chapin (1913), and Herbert William Conn (1914).

win's attempts to deal with these problems resulted in successive editions of *Origin* that were increasingly Lamarckian, in the sense of admitting the possible inheritance of acquired characters.

From the 1860s to the 1880s, support grew among biologists for Lamarckian doctrines. A strong group of Lamarckian biologists emerged in the United States under the leadership of Edward Drinker Cope and Alpheus Hyatt (Pfeifer 1965; Richardson and Kane 1988). On the whole, the American Lamarckians were vitalists, believing in the "life force" as the driver behind evolution. (But, notably, this doctrine is not found in Lamarck's own writings.)

Another challenge to Darwin's theory came from Sir William Thomson (later Lord Kelvin) in the 1860s. Using the classical laws of heat production and radiation, he calculated that the Earth had existed for a few million years. This was not enough time for the evolution of life and complex organic species to take place by natural selection. Unto his death, Darwin regarded this as the most serious objection to his theory. But Lord Kelvin was in error. He had neglected the heating effects of radioactive decay. Scientists now believe that the Earth has existed for about five billion years.

Further objections to Darwin's theory emerged. For example, it was argued that any favorable mutation in a population would be overwhelmed and diluted through the interbreeding of organisms; a beneficial mutation would not endure for long enough to be favored by natural selection (Jenkin 1867; Bennett 1870). The critics assumed that each offspring blended in some near-medial proportion the characteristics of its parents. We now know this assumption to be false. Blending inheritance can maintain variation as long as a large enough source of hereditable dissimilarity exists. But, as a result of the Jenkin-Bennett criticism, Darwin was again forced to put more stress on the envisaged possibility of a Lamarckian inheritance of acquired characters, although he never abandoned his central principle of natural selection. In contrast, Herbert Spencer (1893) regarded the Jenkin-Bennett argument as one of the decisive objections to natural selection as a primary explanation of evolution.

Even Darwin's closest followers, Alfred Russel Wallace and Thomas Henry Huxley, had misgivings about his theory of selection. Wallace (1870) thought that natural selection could not explain the evolution of the highly complex human mind and turned to spiritualism for an answer. Having earned the nickname "Darwin's bulldog" for his forceful defense of Darwin, Huxley nevertheless was unconvinced that natural selection was the principal evolutionary mechanism (Kottler 1985). He also gave less emphasis than Darwin to the importance of adaptation. As Michael Ruse (1979, 223) put it: "But, for all his emotional identification with Darwin, Huxley put evolution first and natural selection second." Also unlike Darwin, Huxley (1894, vol. 9) rejected the idea that Darwinian principles could apply to social evolution.

Samuel Butler (1878) published an influential attack on Darwin's theory, arguing that natural selection could not account for the evolution of complex organisms. Quoting from secondhand sources rather than Lamarck himself, Butler developed a version of "Lamarckism" in which both "want or desire" and "inherited memory" aided the evolutionary process. Proposing that Darwinism reduced human beings to purposeless machines, he attempted to restore teleological causation to biology.

It eluded Butler that Darwin had attempted to explain human intentionality, not to belittle it. Yet this criticism of Darwin became popular. George Bernard Shaw (1921) repeated it in the famous preface to *Back to Methuselah*. Butler's idiosyncratic doctrine that memory is inherited by offspring from parents would today find few adherents. But some of his other views survive. Many share his mistaken notion that Lamarck saw changes to organisms as resulting from their own volition. Also repeated today is the false idea that Darwin's theory of natural selection depends on a view that human beings are purposeless automata.

Partly because of the perceived limitations of Darwin's theory, and partly because his "synthetic philosophy" explicitly covered several disciplines (including biology, psychology, sociology, and ethics), Spencer overshadowed Darwin in the period 1880–1900, and Darwinism was in partial eclipse in the scientific community. The particular emphasis on natural selection, and other detailed features of Darwin's theory, had a restricted influence, even among scientists who embraced the general idea of evolution (Allen 1968; Bowler 1983, 1988; Sanderson 1990). Evolutionary discourse was, instead, dominated by Spencerian and other ideas of automatic progress or development, with the causal mechanisms inadequately explained.

The publication of August Weismann's (1893) critique of the doctrine of acquired character inheritance turned the tide against Lamarckism and Spencerism in biology, but perceived problems with Darwinism remained. Even the emergence of Mendelian genetics in the early years of the twentieth century did not immediately rescue Darwinism. Indeed, Mendelian genetics and mechanisms such as mutation (De Vries 1909) were seen as alternatives rather than complements to Darwin's ideas. It was not until the 1940s that the synthesis between Mendelian genetics and Darwinism was achieved.

To be extended to the social sciences, Darwinian ideas had to overcome the resistance of strong intellectual traditions that either minimized the application of common principles to both biology and the social sciences or saw those principles as being non-Darwinian in nature. The influential sociologist Émile Durkheim excluded both biological and psychological explanations from his theory. Karl Marx and Frederick Engels found "dialectics" in both nature and human society, but they declared that the scope of Darwinism was confined to biology (Singer 1999; Hodgson 2006a).

In the surge of nationalism before and during the First World War, phrases such as Spencer's *survival of the fittest* and Darwin's *struggle for existence* were given nationalist and racist associations. Vaguely Darwinian ideas were also bandied about to justify or illustrate all sorts of contradictory social and political stances, including nationalism, militarism, imperialism, free trade, individualism, socialism, and even pacifism (Himmelfarb 1959, 407).

In several countries, including Britain and the United States, there was a widespread repugnance among intellectuals toward the use of seemingly biological language to justify imperialism, nationalism, or war. These sentiments were fueled by the antagonism between the rival imperialist powers and the carnage of the First World War. Attempts to explain national or ethnic attributes in biological terms were rejected, and the very use of biological concepts or metaphors in the social sciences was shunned. For many, because of its biological associations, the very word *evolution* became taboo. This was the beginning of the "dark age" for evolutionism in the social sciences: "During this time evolutionism was severely criticized and came to be regarded as an outmoded approach that self-respecting scholars should no longer take seriously. . . . [E]ven the word 'evolution' came to be uttered at serious risk to one's intellectual reputation" (Sanderson 1990, 2). Even before the war, in a book that originally appeared in German in 1911, Joseph Schumpeter (1934, 57) wrote: "The evolutionary idea is now discredited in our field." Perhaps this mood explains why by 1908 Thorstein Veblen had changed the subtitle of his famous and reprinted *Theory of the Leisure Class* from *An Economic Study in the Evolution of Institutions* to *An Economic Study of Institutions*.[15]

The American philosopher and pacifist Ralph Barton Perry (1918) attacked notions of racial superiority and the idea that conflict was natural

15. But Schumpeter later revived his use of the word *evolution*. And Veblen's commitment to the application of Darwinian ideas to the social sphere remained undiminished.

and beneficial. He also rejected all associations between biology and the social sciences. Darwinism was accused of a circularity of logic and a "strong tendency to favor the cruder and more violent forms of struggle, as being more unmistakably biological" (145).

But the use of the term *social Darwinism* was very rare, and—despite modern folklore—it was not then applied to Herbert Spencer or William Graham Sumner. Before the 1940s, the term was generally but infrequently used by leftist critics to describe a militarist, racist, or competitive individualist position that they opposed.[16]

A few years later, Talcott Parsons (see Parsons 1932, 325; and Parsons 1934, 524)—who was to become the most influential American sociologist of the twentieth century—conjured the demon of *social Darwinism* to help fix the supposed boundaries of good and bad sociology. He extended the usage of the term from its previous ideological associations to also include anyone who believed in the application of Darwinian concepts of variation and selection to social evolution. With this changed meaning, *social Darwinism* was applied, not only to doctrines of race struggle or war, but also to any application of Darwinism or related biological ideas to the study of human society.

In 1944, during the Nazi genocide and the Second World War, Hofstadter published the classic *Social Darwinism in American Thought*. For Hofstadter, social Darwinism was found in the use of key phrases such as *natural selection, struggle for existence*, and *survival of the fittest*. The term *social Darwinism* was used, not only as a general description of abuses of biology by the Nazis and others, but also as a means of sustaining the established separation between the social sciences and biology. This separation was also aided by the enduring influence of Marx and Durkheim in the social sciences.

The degree to which the tide had turned against Darwinian ideas can be judged by considering Veblen's institutionalist followers in the interwar period. Veblen himself remained enormously influential. But even his closest followers were quick to abandon his Darwinian project. Veblen's student Wesley Mitchell (1936, xlix) rejected Darwinism. The leading institutionalist, John R. Commons (1897, 1924, 1934), saw Darwinian principles as inappropriate when applied to economics. Clarence Ayres (1932, 95)—who emerged as the de facto leader of American institutionalism after the Second

---

16. There is now a huge literature on social Darwinism, and aspects of its meaning and history are still under dispute. See, e.g., Bannister (1979), Jones (1980), Bellomy (1984), and Hodgson (2004b, 2006a).

World War—declared that Darwinism was generally flawed and outmoded (Jones 1995; Hodgson 2004a).

Overall, this severe and widespread reaction against Darwinism in the social sciences helps explain much of the lasting resistance to the project of generalizing Darwinism in this sphere. This resistance has been fueled by stubbornly enduring misunderstandings concerning the nature of Darwinism itself.

1.5. SLOW REVIVAL AND STUBBORN RESISTANCE

In the hostile intellectual environment of the 1930s and 1940s, the idea of Darwinian social evolution lay mostly dormant and undeveloped, until it began to be revived after the Second World War.

The famous archaeologist V. Gordon Childe (1951, 175–79) loosely considered both social institutions and technological innovations as units of selection. In his little book *Natural Selection of Political Forces*, Adolf A. Berle[17] (1950, 17) proposed: "There exists a law of selection of political forces somewhat analogous to the law of selection of species in the world of biology." Selection would change the frequencies of competing, organized political forces (e.g., socialism vs. liberalism). Berle's book was favorably reviewed as an exposition of familiar ideas with an unfamiliar vocabulary—and then quickly forgotten.

Around this time, there was also a brief flurry of interest in Darwinian ideas in economics when Armen Alchian (1950) and Milton Friedman (1953) wrote briefly and without much in-depth analysis of the "natural selection" of firms in a competitive market. Alchian's arguments were met by a powerfully skeptical article by Edith Penrose (1952). Later, Sidney Winter (1964) argued at length that Friedman's conclusions could be drawn from an evolutionary and competitive process under very special conditions only. However, for both sides, this debate was mostly about the usefulness or otherwise of Darwinian analogies, not whether Darwinian principles could be applied more broadly to social or economic evolution.

In a classic essay that provides an enduring stimulus, Donald T. Campbell (1965, 24) argued that the appropriate template for social evolution is not biotic evolution but a more general process of evolution "for which

---

17. Berle and Means (1932) had previously used the term *evolution* to describe the historical development of corporate systems and the supporting legal institutions. But they did not explicitly characterize selection processes or elaborate on the details.

organic evolution is but one instance." He emphasized the core Darwinian principles of "variation and selective retention" and argued that they apply to social as well as biotic evolution. Relevant in this process is not only variation between individuals but also variation between organizations. And selection can be both haphazard and deliberate.[18]

Particularly after the publication of Richard Nelson and Sidney Winter's (1982) hugely influential book and allied works by Kenneth Boulding (1981), Friedrich Hayek (1967, 1988), and others, *evolution* became a voguish word in economics and other social sciences.[19] *Evolutionary economics* became a fashionable label. But, generally, this did not signal any enthusiasm for the explicit application of Darwinian principles to social or economic evolution.

For example, Nelson and Winter (1982) mentioned Darwin only once in their book, preferring instead to describe their approach as *Lamarckian*. Ironically, however, the Darwinian principles of variation, inheritance, and selection are clearly manifest in their volume. They have inspired an entire generation of researchers deploying these core Darwinian principles in their work—but many dare not speak their name.

Although he embraced Darwinism more than others, Hayek (1973, 22–23) belittled its significance for his evolutionary theory: "Those eighteenth-century moral philosophers and the historical schools of law and language might well be described . . . as Darwinians before Darwin. . . . A nineteenth-century social theorist who needed Darwin to teach him the idea of evolution was not worth his salt." This underestimates the importance of the specific contribution of Darwin, especially in terms of the principle of selection.[20]

Despite the huge revival of evolutionary economics, many of its devo-

---

18. Campbell's (1965) essay remains essential reading, but its message is not yet fully absorbed in the literature. For example, Lawson (2003) proposes a "PVRS [population-variation-retention-selection] model" of evolution as a novelty.

19. Tilly's (1975) classic account of the evolution of European states evokes several Darwinian themes. But only recently have political scientists begun to discuss evolutionary ideas more openly (John 1999; Thelen 2004).

20. Hayek (1973, 23) hinted at generalized evolutionary principles. He distinguished between "the selection of individuals" and "that of institutions and practices" and between "the selection of innate . . . [and] culturally transmitted capacities of individuals." He thus differentiated between the selection of biological and social entities and then proposed that "the basic conception of evolution is still the same in both fields." But to complete the picture he should have highlighted that (according to his own account) "selection" is central to this "basic conception of evolution" and then acknowledged that the fully fledged principle of selection does not predate Darwin, unlike the vaguely defined "idea of evolution."

tees remain skeptical about whether Darwinian ideas have any relevance to their field. Many retain evolutionary claims for their theory but reject Darwinism as inappropriate. Some wrongly equate Darwinism with narrowly individualistic, selfish, or anticooperative ideas that were not promoted by Darwin himself. Other critics address particular versions of Darwinism that claim that evolution is always a progressive or optimizing process. The critics then conclude that Darwinism is inappropriate in the social domain. They seem unaware of Darwin's (1871, 1:166) own words: "We are apt to look at progress as the normal rule in human society; but history refutes this." Darwin similarly insisted to Charles Lyell on 11 October 1859: "The theory of Natural Selection . . . implies no necessary tendency to progression" (Darwin 1887, 2:210). Despite this rejection of the inevitability of progress, Darwin believed that his evolutionary principles could be applied to human society.

The extent to which some social scientists have been immunized against Darwinism can be gauged by the hysterical reaction in some quarters against the rise of sociobiology in the 1970s, particularly after the publication of two books by Edward O. Wilson (1975, 1978). The Sociobiology Study Group of Science for the People entered the fray, declaring immediately that Wilson had opened the door to racism and other doctrines that it explicitly associated with social Darwinism (Allen et al. 1976). Wilson's views were caricatured as an attempt to explain all social phenomena in biological terms, whereas Wilson (1978, 153) in fact admitted some space for other explanations and declared that human "social evolution is obviously more cultural than genetic."

Whatever the validity or otherwise of Wilson's detailed views, it is clear that he has been misunderstood as an extreme biological reductionist. Wilson (1975, 1978) himself rejected the label *social Darwinism*. There is no evidence that he is a racist or a fascist. Furthermore, his passionate environmentalism does not align him with exponents of unbridled capitalist competition. The critical attack by social scientists on sociobiology provides abundant evidence of misquotation and gross misrepresentation, motivated by a deeply ingrained resistance to any incursion of Darwinian ideas into the social domain (Segerstråle 2000; Vandermassen 2005).

If Wilson is charged with the application of Darwinian ideas to social phenomena, then he stands condemned, along with Bagehot, Baldwin, Kropotkin, Ritchie, Veblen, and many modern writers who have also applied Darwinian principles of variation, selection, and inheritance to social or economic change. Alternatively, if he is charged with claiming to explain human social phenomena *entirely* in biological terms, then he must be acquitted, partly on the grounds of his explicit and repeated claims to the contrary. But, if he is charged with exaggerating the possibility of using biology to explain human behavior, then there remains a case against him to be answered.

The evidence for the prosecution would involve the earlier claim that sociobiology predicts common behavioral patterns in tribal societies on the basis of shared human genes. But, despite the existence of several important universal features of all known societies (Brown 1991; Schwartz 1994), there is still enormous variation between cultures. Wilson (1998, 174) later admitted: "To a degree that may prove discomforting to a diehard hereditarian, cultures have dispersed widely in their evolution under the epigenetic rules so far studied."

Although the idea of generalizing core Darwinian principles in the social sciences has a long history, it has not proved popular. Resistance to abstract Darwinian ideas probably results from a general wariness on the part of social scientists of the importation of concepts from biology (Degler 1991), rather than from any adequately detailed critique of the proposal for a generalized Darwinism. Dismissals are typically brief. Some have centered on the true but irrelevant claim that the detailed mechanisms of social and biological evolution are very different. We explain why such critiques are off target below.

Some critics mistakenly conflate universal Darwinism with "genetic reductionism" or "ultra-Darwinism."[21] Although Dawkins is responsible for the term *universal Darwinism* and he is also associated with a gene-centered view of biological evolution, the idea of generalizing Darwinism is logically independent of whether a gene-centered view is appropriate in biology. Furthermore, generalized Darwinism does not claim that social or economic phenomena can be adequately and entirely explained in biological terms. It is not a version of biological reductionism.

Sometimes even Dawkins departs from the gene-centered view. In the final chapter of *The Selfish Gene*, he proposed the "meme" as a replicator and unit of selection at the cultural level. The genes no longer rule the roost alone: ideas or memes also compete among one another for survival.

---

21. Rose (1997) has a long chapter entitled "Universal Darwinism?" that very briefly (175–76) mentions memes and "neural Darwinism" (Edelman 1987), dismisses them without effective criticism, and then devotes its remaining twenty pages to biological issues that have no relevance to the claim that core Darwinian principles can be generalized to cover social entities and social evolution.

His argument that Darwinism consisted of general and powerful principles pulled Dawkins away from an exclusive stress on the gene as the unit of selection.

In two powerful essays, David Hull (1980, 1981) explored these tensions in Dawkins's work. He showed that, "in spite of himself" (Depew and Weber 1995, 384), Dawkins had implicitly endorsed the idea of selection on multiple levels, including the social as well as the biological. Dawkins (1983, 422) himself admitted: "It is also arguable that today selection operates on several levels, for instance the levels of the gene and the species or lineage, and perhaps some unit of cultural transmission." An important point here is that Dawkins's attempt to generalize Darwinism to the social and cultural domain led uncharacteristically but unavoidably to the nonreductionist proposition that selection processes operate on multiple levels.

Contrary to some critiques, the idea of generalizing Darwinism has little to do with biological metaphors or analogies. Instead of analogies, which are typically inexact and sometimes treacherous, generalized Darwinism relies on the claim of common abstract features in both the social and the biological world; it is essentially a contention of a degree of *ontological communality* at a high level of abstraction and not at the level of detail.[22] This communality is captured by concepts such as replication and selection, which are defined as precisely and as meaningfully as possible but in a general and abstract sense.

What is the difference between analogy and generalization? Analogies take phenomena and processes in one domain as reference points for the study of similar phenomena or processes in another domain. Differences are regarded as disanalogies. Social evolution is clearly disanalogous to genetic evolution because of the very different entities and mechanisms of replication. By contrast, for example, the Keynesian "circular flow of income" may have some features analogous to those of hydraulic mechanisms, as illustrated by the famous Phillips Machine, which simulates money flows through water in transparent tubes (Barr 1988). Some theories of the business cycle use the analogy of a pendulum and deploy similar differential equations. These analogical claims are different from generalizations.

Generalization in science starts from a deliberately copious array of different phenomena and processes, without giving analytic priority to any of them. Where possible, scientists adduce shared principles. Given that the

22. Note that levels of abstraction are different in meaning from ontological levels. The former are levels within theories, the latter levels in the structures of reality. On Darwinian ontological commitments, see also Beinhocker (2006) and Stoelhorst (2008).

entities and processes involved are very different, these common principles will be fairly abstract and will not reflect detailed mechanisms unique to any particular domain. The very triumph of successful generalization is in the face of real and acknowledged differences at the level of detail.

For example, the laws of motion in physics apply equally to planets, rockets, and billiard balls, despite huge differences of size, composition, and shape. We can generalize across these domains because, at an abstract level, the same principles apply to all the phenomena, despite major differences in their features. In biology, and in the social sciences, the phenomena are so complex that scientists supplement general principles by auxiliary and particular explanations, thus differentiating these sciences from physics (Mayr 1985).

Critics of generalized Darwinism have often failed to distinguish between analogy and generalization, different levels of abstraction, and different domains of similarity or dissimilarity (Cordes 2006). The claim that social evolution and biological evolution are different at the level of detail is important and true but, ultimately, irrelevant to the project of generalizing Darwinism. Generalizing Darwinism does not rely on the mistaken idea that the mechanisms of evolution in the social and the biological worlds are similar in a substantive sense.

But the resistance to Darwinism in the social sciences cannot be entirely explained in terms of the misunderstandings of opponents. The basic argument, which has been sustained now for a century and a half, is that the core Darwinian principles of variation, inheritance, and selection apply to social as well as biological phenomena. Darwinism in biology has made major breakthroughs. But an adequate refinement of *general* Darwinian concepts such as selection, replication, and inheritance—in terms that could be applied to social or economic evolution without forcing it into a biological mold—has been lacking, at least until the final years of the twentieth century.[23] We subject them here to further refinement. The development of a generalized Darwinism has been hindered by internal underdevelopment as well as strong external resistance.

1.6. LOOKING FORWARD FROM THE PAST

The earlier literature cited above reveals several uncompleted tasks. First, absent in this literature were rigorous definitions of the core concepts of a

---

23. Notably Hull (1988), Sterelny, Smith, and Dickison (1996), Godfrey-Smith (2000b), Price (1995), and Sperber (2000). These contributions are discussed in later chapters.

generalized Darwinism, including variation, selection, and replication. Generally, mechanisms of selection were not discussed in much detail. Building on recent literature, we propose refinements and clarifications concerning these key concepts and mechanisms.

Among these we establish the importance of the distinction between replicator and interactor. Originally, Dawkins (1982) distinguished between replicators and their "vehicles," where the genes are the replicators and the organisms their vehicles. Later writers, after David Hull (1980), often prefer the term *interactor* to *vehicle*, stressing not only the cohesive nature of the replicator-carrying unit but also the importance of its interaction with its environment.

Following Robert Brandon (1996, 125), the distinction between replicators and interactors "is best seen as a generalization of the traditional genotype-phenotype distinction." Earlier writers discussed above failed to distinguish between the relatively cohesive entity that is actually being selected (the *phenotypes* or *interactors*) and the entities that replicate differentially as a result of selection (the *genotypes* or *replicators*). We offer refined definitions of these concepts in chapters 4, 6 and 7 below.[24]

Another important characteristic of our argument is that it is not confined to a basic and ubiquitous cultural level of individual behavioral imitation: it also addresses the social institutions found in more complex human societies. We consider the nature of sociality and identify social units of replication or selection. Many of even the most sophisticated attempts to apply Darwinism to cultural evolution—including the work in dual inheritance or gene-culture "coevolution" by Robert Boyd and Peter Richerson (1985) and William Durham (1991)—regard ideas as the units of selection at the cultural level. Cultural evolution reduces to the selection sets of ideas, beliefs, or preferences on a single level. Little connection is made to the vast literature in social theory on social structures, roles, positions, and institutions. These are reducible neither to individuals nor to their ideas.

What makes an entity social and more than a common attribute of a number of individuals? Because of structured interactive relations between individuals, properties emerge at the social level that are irreducible to indi-

---

24. Some colleagues working in this area have proposed alternative terms to *replicator*, by including *instructor* and *codex*. While these have their merits, we see little benefit and some demerit in departing from a word that has now become well established in the philosophy of biology. Furthermore, the notion of "replicator dynamics" is now widely utilized in economic theory. We are unaware of any serious alternative to the term *interactor*. Hence, we follow Hull and what is now a conventional view in adopting the replicator-interactor terminology.

viduals alone. These involve social structures (generally relations between individuals) and sometimes social positions (with specific roles—e.g., sales manager or president—that are irreducible to the properties of their incumbents).

Despite earlier important statements of the "natural selection of institutions," the concept of social structure has hitherto been inadequately incorporated in a Darwinian evolutionary framework. Remarkably little progress has been made to date in identifying what social institutions or structures are units of replication or selection. We must either follow up the hints of Ritchie, Veblen, and others in a more rigorous manner or show that such social units of replication or selection are unviable. Ducking the issue is unacceptable.[25]

Recent careful analytic work on group selection is relevant here.[26] This establishes the special conditions under which groups may emerge as units of selection in biological as well as social evolution. But pointing to groups as possible units of selection is not enough. It must be shown that groups are sufficiently cohesive to be selected and differentially replicated as entities. Furthermore, the factors that give rise to relatively cohesive groups themselves must be explained.

Clearly, human sociality involves more than the anthill or the beehive. In particular, it relies on language and culture, with intersubjective interpretations of intention and meaning (Bogdan 2000). These complex causal interactions are the basis of emergent social properties. These must be described, analyzed, and placed within a theory of social evolution. To establish the essence of human sociality and place it in an evolutionary framework, an intensive and detailed dialogue must be created between evolutionary and social theory.

Our aim is to consolidate the suggestions of Ritchie (1896), Veblen (1899), and Keller (1915) concerning social units of selection, but with the significant additional benefit of modern developments in social theory, sociology,

25. On the concept of social structure, see Kontopoulos (1993), Archer (1995), and Weissman (2000). Fracchia and Lewontin (1999) argue that Darwinism does not apply to social evolution. They claim that theories of cultural evolution lack an adequate concept of social structure, treating populations rather as aggregates. But they do not show that a Darwinian approach to social evolution would necessarily exclude an adequate treatment of social structures. A multilevel Darwinian approach (with group selection) would require a notion of social structure to explain how groups or structured populations are maintained.

26. For discussions of group selection, see Boyd and Richerson (1985), Hodgson (1993), Campbell (1994), Sober and Wilson (1998), Bergstrom (2002, 2003), Wilson (2002), Henrich (2004), Okasha (2006), Wilson and Wilson (2007), and chapter 7 below.

Replication

Produces copies of replicators that are similar to the original; the original is causally implicated in the copying and provides necessary information.

Examples:
Copying of genes, prions, habits, routines, or customs.

Generative Replication

Replication involving copying of construction mechanisms (or "programs") that are similar to the original.

Examples:
Copying of genes, habits, routines, or customs.

Diffusion

Differential adoption of replicators by host organizations or organisms.

Examples:
Adoption of copied habits, routines, or customs, by existing firm or other organization.

Selection

Subset selection

Environmental interaction and variation in fitness cause differential elimination of entities.

Examples:
Death of organisms, bankruptcy of firms, industry exit of firms.

Successor selection

Interaction of a population with its environment and variations in individual fitness lead to novel entities and differential replication of replicators such as genes, habits, routines, and customs.

Examples:
Replication of genes among offspring, spin-offs where new firms copy routines from their parent firms, secession of states.

Drift

Alteration of the frequencies of particular replicators in a population through replication, interactor birth or death, or other processes where the frequency outcomes are unrelated to fitness.

Examples:
As with subset and successor selection, but probability of replication does not depend on fitness.

FIGURE 1.1. Darwinian evolutionary processes in nature and society.

One of the aims of chapter 7 is to refine the definition of *interactor*. When group selection occurs, the groups are interactors. A review of group selection and the interactor concept leads to a methodology for establishing multiple levels of selection. This leads to an account in chapter 8 of some of the major informational transitions in social evolution, including the emergence of language, custom, law, and institutionalized science and technology.

While separate chapters are devoted to selection and replication, no single chapter has variation as its primary theme. This is not because we regard the existence and sources of variation as unimportant. On the contrary, understanding the roles and sources of novelty and innovation in social evolution is one of the most important tasks ahead. The reason why it has no separate chapter is that, among the Darwinian trinity of variation, selection, and inheritance, variation is the easiest of the three concepts to define in general terms. Yet, by contrast, at a less abstract and more detailed level, and especially in the social sciences, innovation and novelty are among the most difficult phenomena to explain.

The development of the Darwinian conceptual framework in a manner that can be applied to social and economic evolution is the principal aim of this work. In the final chapter, we summarize our outline of a Darwinian conceptual framework for the social sciences and set out an agenda for future research.

CHAPTER TWO

Generalizing Darwinism

In sum, natural selection and evolution should not be viewed as concepts developed for the specific purposes of biology and possibly appropriable for the specific purposes of economics, but rather as elements of the framework of a new conceptual structure that biology, economics and other social sciences can comfortably share.

SIDNEY G. WINTER, (1987)

What is *evolution*? Etymologically, like the word *development*, *evolution* derives from the Latin verb *volvere*. This means "to roll," but it can refer more broadly to the general idea of motion. The companion verbs *evolvere* and *revolvere* are more explicit, respectively denoting forward and backward motion, as in the unrolling and rolling up of a scroll. The word *evolution* therefore derives from the Latin word associated with a specifically directional and predestined activity; the scroll is unrolled to reveal that which is already written within.

In this spirit, the word *evolution* was first applied to natural phenomena by the German biologist Albrecht von Haller in 1744. He used the word to characterize embryological development as the augmentation and expansion of a preformed miniature adult organism, a common idea in the seventeenth and eighteenth centuries. Indeed, in biology, the idea of preformation, where the embryo is deemed to contain in microcosm the form of its future development, lasted well into the nineteenth century, being embraced explicitly by Herbert Spencer, and subtly affecting Charles Darwin's thought (Richards 1992).

Spencer did much more than Darwin to popularize the term *evolution*. In the first edition of *The Origin of Species*, Darwin did not use this word and wrote *evolved* only once. Subsequently, he infrequently used the term *evolution*, but, on the whole, he preferred phrases like *descent with modification*. Hence, no Darwinian copyright can be imposed on the word *evolution*. Today, *evolution* is used in a number of senses, and there is little basis on which to claim that any one usage has greater legitimacy. Attempts to give *evolution* some narrower and sharper meaning, whether Darwinian or otherwise, are unwarranted.

Instead of starting from the vague and fruitlessly contested word *evolution*, we prefer to commence from the types of phenomena involved. We refer to a broad class of systems, involving populations of entities and all feasible manifestations of development and change. We then show, under some minimal conditions, that ongoing change in such systems is inevitably Darwinian in the sense that it must involve Darwin's central principles of variation, inheritance, and selection.

We show in later chapters that this central argument can resist a number of objections. For instance, some authors point to the theory of self-organization and suggest that it is an alternative to Darwinian selection. Others point to human intentionality and claim that it is inconsistent with the "blind" processes of Darwinism. Others regard Lamarckism and Darwinism as rivals, seeing social evolution as an exemplification of the former rather than the latter.

We argue that all these objections are mistaken, one way or another. Processes of self-organization are very important in nature and society. Human intentionality and choice are distinctive and should not be ignored. Many propose that the Lamarckian inheritance of acquired characters occurs in social evolution. But none of these propositions rules out Darwinism. On the contrary, all accounts must heed Darwinian principles to complete their explanations.

Clearly, the detailed mechanisms of change are often very different, both within and between different types of systems, in nature and in human society, but again, as argued below, this does not undermine a generalized Darwinian analysis.

Much progress in broadly defined *evolutionary* thinking in the last three hundred years has involved the insight that complex outcomes are not necessarily the result of deliberate design, by humans or by God. Such a theme is found in the writings of Bernard Mandeville, David Hume, Adam Smith, and Carl Menger, as Friedrich Hayek (1973, 1988) and others have discussed extensively. All these writers pointed to the emergence of undesigned social orders and institutions that resulted from individual interactions.

This was a highly significant but incomplete step. Writers such as Mandeville and Smith did not explain how the individuals and their dispositions had themselves evolved, and they gave only limited insights into why particular undesigned outcomes would survive longer than others and could, thereby, be copied or imitated. Darwin (1859) filled these gaps with his principle of selection. Humans who were more adapted to their environment would have a survival advantage over others.

While Mandeville, Hume, Smith, and Menger had shown how undesigned social orders and institutions can emerge, Darwinism helps show how some but not all of them might survive. The principle of selection helps explain adaptedness[1] and survival, without assuming that the capacities to adapt and survive are given or decreed by a divine creator. Partly for this reason, Darwin made a big step ahead of Mandeville, Hume, and Smith.[2]

This chapter is divided into four further sections. Section 2.2 describes the broad type of evolutionary system that we are required to explain and shows why Darwinian principles are unavoidable in dealing with such systems. Section 2.3 gives the other side of the coin. While Darwinian principles are always necessary to explain complex evolving population systems, they are never sufficient on their own. Attention to specific, detailed mechanisms is always required. Section 2.4 summarizes the importance of a generalized Darwinism for the social sciences. Section 2.5 concludes the chapter.

2.1. COMPLEX POPULATION SYSTEMS AND THE INEVITABILITY OF DARWINISM

What kind of systems are we required to explain? Rather than simple, mechanical phenomena, the objects of our discussion are complex systems, at least in the sense that they involve a variety of entities that interact with one another. Such complex systems produce some outcomes that are not willed by any individual entity and have properties that do not correspond to any individual entity taken alone.

Still retaining a high degree of generality, we can add some further details to this picture. The complex systems considered here involve populations of

---

1. Following a convention in biology, *adaptedness* refers to the fitness of a trait (or trait complex) in a specific environment. By contrast, *adaptation* often denotes the process by which a set of entities of a particular type becomes adapted in terms of its evolutionary history. Thus, in its present use, *adaptedness* relates to the features of organisms; *adaptation* refers to the process by which a population becomes adapted. A second meaning of *adaptation* is the process of phenotypic adjustment of the characteristics of an individual entity in a given environment. This latter use is commonly employed in economics and organization theory but not in biology.

2. As Dennett (1995, 28–33) points out, Hume had a "close encounter" with a selection-driven theory of evolution in his *Dialogues*, but he neither developed it nor took it seriously. As noted in the preceding chapter, Hayek (1973, 22–23) belittled the significance of Darwin's advance over these predecessors.

entities of specific types. Members of each type are similar in key respects, but, within each type, there is some degree of variation owing to genesis, circumstances, or both. Ernst Mayr (1976, 1982) famously describes such "population thinking." Diversity in a population is underlined, rather than overlooked with an exclusive focus on averages or representative types.

Entities within these populations have limited capacities to absorb some materials and energy from a sector of their environment in some manner of consumption, and they are able to process some information about their environment attained by the use of some sensory mechanisms. Beyond that, we do not need to go into further detail about their cognitive and informational capacities just yet. These entities may or may not have a developed brain or memory. They may or may not be capable of reflecting on their circumstances and imagining past or future behaviors. Our characterization includes bacteria, birds, and human beings.

Some further elements are necessary to complete the picture. All these entities are mortal and degradable, and they need to consume materials and energy in order to survive or minimize degradation. However, because they do not have access to all environmental resources at once, they face an omnipresent problem of *local and immediate scarcity*.[3] These circumstances present specific problems that must be solved to minimize degradation and raise the chances of survival. In short, these entities are engaged in a *struggle for existence*, to use the term adopted by Darwin (1859, 62-63).

Finally, we assume some capacity to retain and pass on to others workable solutions to problems faced in the struggle for existence. Examples include tools and technological know-how. Retaining such problem solutions or adaptations means avoiding the risks and labor of learning them anew. Given that the entities in the population are mortal and degradable, there are also good reasons to assume that some capacity exists to pass on to others information about such workable solutions.

This is the basis of the Darwinian *principle of inheritance*. This term refers to a broad class of replication mechanisms, including *diffusion* and *descent*

---

3. The concept of scarcity is widely assumed by economists but rarely defined or discussed in detail. When Robbins (1932) described economics as the science of choice under scarcity, he defined *scarcity* loosely as a condition under which a resource is "limited." But there is a big difference between global or absolute scarcity and scarcity in a local and immediate sense. Many resources are globally limited. But useful resources such as skill, trust, and honor do not face the same constraints. Nevertheless, all organisms and agents face the problem of scarcity in an immediate sense, referring to the relevant cost of obtaining and processing resources, even if plentiful. Such immediate scarcity is universal in complex population systems.

(Mayr 1991), by which information concerning adaptations is passed on or copied through time.

In sum, a complex population system involves populations of nonidentical (intentional or nonintentional) entities that face locally scarce resources and problems of survival. Some adaptive solutions to such problems are retained through time and can be passed to other entities. Examples of such complex population systems are plentiful both in nature and in human society. They include every biological species, from amoebas to humans. They would include self-replicating automata, of the type discussed by John von Neumann (1966) or appearing in the 2004 movie *I, Robot* starring Will Smith. In addition, and importantly for the social scientist, they include human organizations such as business firms, as long as these organizations are cohesive entities with a capacity to retain and replicate problem solutions.[4]

Having sketched in broad terms the type of evolutionary system we are considering, we now come to the crucial step in the argument: an adequate explanation of the evolution of such a system *must* involve the three Darwinian principles of variation, inheritance, and selection.[5] These are the broad Darwinian theoretical requirements that advance a unifying treatment of evolutionary dynamics across empirical domains (Page and Nowak 2002).[6] They do not themselves provide all the necessary details, but, nevertheless, they must be honored. Otherwise, the explanation of evolution will be inadequate.

Consider the three Darwinian principles in turn. Each principle is an explanatory requirement. First, there must be some explanation of how variety is generated and replenished in a population. In biological systems, the answers—established since Darwin's death—involve genetic recombination and mutations. By contrast, the evolution of social institutions in-

4. Others may prefer to describe replicating social entities more broadly as *memes* (Dawkins 1976). But the choice of label does not affect our general argument here.

5. Conceptions of Darwinism, and how Darwinians have presented its message, have themselves evolved since 1859 (Hull 1985; Depew and Weber 1995; Keller 2002). Nevertheless, the three core principles of variation, inheritance, and selection have endured. They are prominent in the long final paragraph of the *Origin* (Darwin 1859). These core principles long predated and existed independently of the 1940s synthesis of Darwinism with Mendelian genetics and the discovery of the structure of DNA in 1953. A generalized Darwinism essentially invokes the three core principles, not these auxiliary developments. But this does not deny that other processes (such as drift or self-organization) are important in particular circumstances.

6. We use the terms *variation, inheritance* (or *replication*), and *selection*. These are similar in meaning to the terms *mutation, reproduction,* and *selection* advanced in recent influential work on unifying evolutionary dynamics (Page and Nowak 2002).

volves innovation, imitation, planning, and other mechanisms very different from the detailed processes found in biology (Aldrich and Ruef 2006). The general problem of the existence and replenishment of variety remains a vital question for evolutionary research in the social and technological domain (Nelson 1991; Metcalfe 1998; Saviotti 1996). Innovations are a common source of new variation, but the determinants of such novelties are not fully understood (Witt 2009a, 2009b).

Second, there must be an explanation of how useful information concerning solutions to particular adaptive problems is retained and passed on. This requirement follows directly from the broad nature of the complex population system that we are required to explain, in which there must be some mechanism by which adaptive solutions are copied and acquired. In biology, these mechanisms often involve genes and DNA. In social evolution, we can include the replication of habits, customs, rules, and routines, all of which may carry solutions to adaptive problems (see, e.g., Veblen 1899, 1919; Keller 1915; Nelson and Winter 1982; Hayek 1988; Postrel and Rumelt 1992; and Hodgson 2003c). There must be some mechanism that ensures that some such solutions (embodied in habits, routines, or whatever) endure and replicate; otherwise, the continuing retention of useful knowledge would be impossible (Vanberg 1994a).

Third, and not least, there must be an explanation of the fact that entities differ in their longevity and fecundity. In given contexts, some entities are more adapted than others, some survive longer than others, and some are more successful in producing offspring or copies of themselves. Here, the *principle of selection* comes in. As elaborated in chapter 5 below, selection involves an anterior set of entities, each interacting with its environment and somehow being transformed into a posterior set where all members of the posterior set are sufficiently similar to some members of the anterior set and where the resulting frequencies of posterior entities are correlated positively to some degree to their fitness in the environmental context. Through selection, a set of entities—a population—will gradually adapt in response to the criteria defined by an environmental factor. Thus, in a cold environment, the proportion of mammals with more fat or long fur is likely to increase.

The principle of selection is different from the principle of variation. The latter is the requirement for some explanation of the sources and replenishments of variety. Variety can sometimes be generated by apparently random processes, including drift, without the operation of selection.

Drift involves replication, but the outcomes are unrelated to fitness. It is a process in which solutions that are passed on to the next generation constitute a sample of the currently available solutions, which are uncorrelated with fitness or efficiency. In nature, genetic drift is a process in which gene frequencies in the next generation are unsystematic or random samples of the present gene pool. In industry evolution, drift would govern the evolutionary process if investors laid their bets with no regard to past or expected performance. But empirical studies portray industry evolution as a selection process in which there is some significant correlation between firm properties and survival, even if the properties involved are complex and multidimensional (Audretsch 1991; Audretsch and Mahmood 1994, 1995; Suarez and Utterback 1995; Agarwal and Gort 1996; Klepper 2002b).[7]

Typically, a "dominant design" gradually emerges through a selection process (Utterback and Abernathy 1975; Tushman and Anderson 1986; Klepper and Graddy 1990; Klepper 1997; Nelson and Winter 2002). Firms whose products exemplify the dominant design are thriving, while firms that are producing something else are ailing. The weeding out of firms that are unable to meet customer preferences is a very common example of selection in the social and economic domain.

Selection refers to the mechanisms that bring about the survival of some variations rather than others, often reducing variety. Even when both variety creation and selection involve human agency, as is often the case in the human domain, the two processes are quite different. Innovation is about the creation of new variations; selection is about how those variations are tested in the real world. For example, innovating firms create new design variants, while customers provide differential rewards.

Outcomes of a selection process are necessarily neither moral nor just. And there is no requirement that outcomes of a selection process are necessarily optimal or improvements on their precursors. Insofar as these outcomes relate to fitness or efficiency, it is fitness relative to the given environment and efficiency that is tolerable rather than optimal. The Price formulation relates selection to fitness, but it does not require that fitness be optimal or desirable. Darwinism does not assume that selection brings about globally efficient or (near) optimal outcomes, and, in certain instances, selection can even lead to systematic errors (Hodgson 1993; Hull 2001a). There can be local and inferior adaptive peaks, or path dependence can limit innova-

---

7. On the other hand, some studies in specific contexts have revealed no systematic relation between apparent fitness and survival (Singh 1975). We do not claim that such a relation is universal. Industry evolution is often haphazard, and properties conducive to survival are typically opaque.

tion possibilities (David 1985; Arthur 1989; Levinthal 1997). There is no reason to believe that the special requirements needed to asymptote global efficiency are generally prevalent in nature or society (Winter 1964, 1971; Gould 2002).

While selection does not necessarily lead to optimality, it is, nevertheless, a vital part of Darwinian theory. Without the principle of selection, we have no way of explaining systematic changes such as moth populations changing color or industries varying dominant designs. The selection process systematically alters the composition of a population because entities receive differential feedback from environmental interaction.

It is necessary to explain why some members of a species have greater chances of survival and procreation. The move from the natural to the social world does not undermine this point. Even if there is no mortal struggle between rival product designs, business organizations, customs, or institutions, some explanation is required of why some enjoy greater longevity than others, why some are imitated more than others, and why some diminish and decline. Any such explanation must come under the general rubric of *selection*, as defined above.

Darwin's principles of variation, inheritance, and selection are required to explain not only evolution within populations but also the origins of those populations themselves. Overall, as long as there is a population with imperfect inheritance of characteristics, not all individuals having the same potential to survive, then Darwinian evolution will occur.

2.2. BUT WHY THE CORE DARWINIAN PRINCIPLES ARE NOT ENOUGH

Complex population systems are found in both nature and the human social world. Explanations of their evolution involve shared Darwinian principles. It is not that social evolution is *analogous* to evolution in the natural world; it is that, at a high level of abstraction, social and biological evolution both require these general principles. In this sense, social evolution *is* Darwinian.

Does this ignore the big differences between the mechanisms of social and biological evolution? Of course, they are hugely dissimilar in all sorts of details (Gould 1996; Fracchia and Lewontin 1999; Wimsatt 1999; Nelson 2006, 2007b). Nothing in the social domain corresponds closely to DNA or sexual recombination. Social units such as routines and institutions can change much more rapidly than human DNA, and they replicate by very different mechanisms. As Alfred Kroeber (1948, 260) pointed out, cultural evolution involves branches that sometimes recombine or "reticulate," and he claimed that this was a key difference with biological evolution. But Darwinism is more general and is not tied to these particulars.[8]

But all detailed differences are important. While the biological and the social are different levels of the same world, the detailed ontology of (say) genes is different from the detailed ontology of (say) the immune system, and both are very different from the detailed ontology of the human social world. A generalized Darwinism proposes that, despite these real and severe ontological differences at the level of detail, there are, nevertheless, also common ontological features at an abstract level. Precisely because it abstracts from detailed ontological differences, a generalized Darwinism cannot explain everything.

To say that two sets of phenomena are similar in general terms does not imply that they are similar in detailed respects. Mice and elephants are both mammals, but they differ greatly in size, behavior, and life span. Steam engines and internal combustion engines are very different in their mechanics and performance, but they are both carbon-fueled heat engines subject to the laws of thermodynamics. Many different objects are subject to Newton's laws of motion.

Not only do natural and social evolution differ greatly in their details, but also detailed mechanisms differ greatly *within* the biological world. Biological organisms differ enormously in size, life span, and reproductive fertility. Some species are social, others not. Not all biological replication is sexual, biparental, or via DNA. Haploid and diploid organisms have single and paired chromosomes, respectively, and their mechanisms of reproduction differ in many ways. An even more fundamental difference is between prokaryotes (no cell nucleus) and eukaryotes (nucleated). The reproduction and selection of immunities and neural patterns involve very different processes, and these, in turn, are different from replication and selection of DNA, but all of these are subject to Darwinian principles (Edelman 1987; Darden and Cain 1989; Plotkin 1994; Hull, Langman, and Glenn 2001). As well as through seeds, some plants can reproduce by lateral root sprouts or suckers, cloning a similar and independent plant with identical DNA. Generally, replication among invertebrates is very different from that among vertebrates. And so on.

8. In fact, biological reticulation can occur through genetic (sexual) recombination or natural or (humanly) deliberate hybridization (Sneath 2000). And not all biological evolution is slower than social evolution: some bacteria evolve quickly, and very rapid biological replication and mutation can occur with viruses.

The differences in mechanism *within* the biological world are as impressive in some ways as the differences between the biological and the social. Accordingly, the generalization of the Darwinian principles within biology yields propositions of significance far beyond biology itself, encompassing the very different and itself intrinsically diverse world of social evolution. As David Hull (1988, 403) puts it: "The amount of increased generality needed to accommodate the full range of biological phenomena turns out to be extensive enough to include social and conceptual evolution as well."

The ongoing attempts of evolutionary biologists to understand the variety within the natural world offer a lesson for the evolutionary social scientist. It is not to copy slavishly all ideas from the biological to the social domain. It is, instead, to appreciate the evolving panorama of evolutionary theory in its attempts to explore and understand this complexity while retaining Darwin's three general principles at the core. The issues are far from settled in evolutionary biology (Stadler, Stadler, and Wagner 2001), but there is a consensus on the centrality of the Darwinian principles of variation, inheritance, and selection.

A recent account of the evolution of evolutionary thought in biology points to an expanded synthesis with the principles of variation, selection, and inheritance as common core concepts (Kutschera and Niklas 2004). These are minimal principles that are common to Darwin's own work and the elaborated synthetic theory. The concepts have been refined and now rest on solid mathematical description. Our argument implies that these three principles are minimal conditions for a theory of evolution.

Given that Darwinian principles operate at a relatively high degree of generality, they cannot themselves provide an account of all the details, in either the social or the biological sphere. They do not provide a complete theory of everything, from cells to human society. Darwinism provides an overarching framework of explanation, but without claiming to explain every aspect or detail. As noted in the preceding chapter, explanations additional to natural selection are always required to explain any evolved phenomenon, such as why some birds have dull, and others colorful, plumage. Insisting that evolution was always dependent on its specific mechanisms or context, Darwin (1859, 314) declared: "I believe in no fixed law of development."

Accordingly, the transfer of Darwinian principles from biological to social evolution does not imply that the detailed mechanisms of selection, variation, and inheritance are similar. On the contrary, the important differences between and within the two spheres suggest that the details are very different, and there are bound to be many detailed mechanisms in the social world that are not found in biology. Consequently, the application of general Darwinian principles cannot do all the explanatory work for the social scientist. Darwinism alone is not enough. But the insufficiency of a theoretical approach does not itself deny its necessity. Darwinism is insufficient, but we have argued above that it is also necessary at an abstract and general level. The very generality of Darwinism hints at a multiple-level mode of theorizing in complex population systems (Hodgson 2001a).[9]

The Darwinian framework has a high degree of generality, and it always requires specific auxiliary explanations. But these auxiliary arguments must be logically compatible with general Darwinian principles. The metatheoretical framework of Darwinism provides a way of inspiring, framing, and organizing these explanations as well as providing key concepts and pointing to particular analytic methods (Darden and Cain 1989; Blute 1997; Hodgson 2001a). A case in point is the centrality of the Darwinian principles of variation and selection in evolutionary theories of economic and cultural change (Nelson and Winter 1982, 2002; Boyd and Richerson 1985; Hannan and Freeman 1989; Durham 1991; Aldrich 1999).

This does not overlook the important differences between the specific mechanisms of evolution in biology and in society. On the contrary, Darwinism always requires further explanations of the particular mechanisms that occur in specific cases. In any relevant domain, it points to a combination of overarching general principles and much more specific and detailed explanations as a means of understanding evolution in complex systems. Indeed, it is the only general framework that has been devised to deal with the complex population systems that have been described above. Darwinism here is unavoidable.

The three core Darwinian principles are necessary, but also insufficient, for a complete theory of evolution in any domain. An important consequence of this observation is the possibility of supporting or refuting claims relating to specific hypotheses about the way the core principles are actually expressed in nature or society. For example, Lamarckism involves a specific

9. As criticized in the following chapter, Witt (1997, 489) holds that the "theory of self-organization . . . provides an abstract, general description of evolutionary processes." Note here that Witt's proclamation of such a "general description" is vulnerable to his own objection (to a generalized Darwinism) that such generalities ignore the vital differences between the natural and the social worlds. He (wrongly) regards this objection to be crucial evidence against a generalized Darwinism but fails to deploy it against his favored general theory of self-organization. Not only is self-organization present in both society and nature, but also the core Darwinian principles apply at an abstract level to both domains.

hypothesis about inheritance, macromutation is a specific hypothesis about the generation of variation, and group selection is a specific hypothesis about the selection mechanism. The first two have been rebutted in biology, while there is empirical support for group selection in some contexts. It is, here, important to understand that a number of auxiliary hypotheses are consistent with the minimal principles of evolution. In our view, this is a strong case for advancing systematic empirical studies of social evolution on the basis of common principles.

2.3. GENERALIZED DARWINISM—ITS RELEVANCE AND IMPORTANCE

Appropriate generalization is at the core of all scientific endeavors. However, generalization should not go so far as to become vacuous. We believe that a generalized Darwinism sustains important propositions and modes of analysis that have application and relevance to evolution in human societies.[10]

Darwinism, for instance, establishes the role of variety in the evolution of complex population systems. There are vital lessons here for social scientists. In pursuit of tractable models, economists have often aggregated, averaged, or assumed away variety. But to neglect variation in complex population systems is to overlook their evolutionary fuel. This point has been made by evolutionary economists in attempts to remedy defects in mainstream models (Metcalfe 1988, 1998; Nelson 1991; Foster and Metcalfe 2001). We also know from system simulations that the incorporation of variation is often crucial (Allen and McGlade 1987a, 1987b). Darwinian "population thinking" thus provides an important imperative for empirical and theoretical research. Within fully fledged evolving systems, variation among populations of firms or other entities must be fully acknowledged rather than assumed away or ignored.

There are a number of advantages of a general analysis of selection processes that builds on core Darwinian principles. Generalized Darwinism provides a focus for inquiry and enables a more systematic accumulation of

10. Generalizing Darwinism does not mean adopting all Darwin's ideas. Darwin's (1859, 1868) work also contained erroneous specific hypotheses relating to biological evolution (e.g., Lamarckian inheritance and pangenesis). Some might prefer a term different from *generalized Darwinism* (e.g., *expanded synthesis*, as suggested by Kutschera and Niklas [2004]), but we use it because the three principles of variation, inheritance, and selection originate from and are central to Darwin's work.

knowledge pertaining to a wider array of selection processes. As we elaborate in chapter 5, it offers a broad definition of *selection* within which we can classify and compare different types of selection processes. Furthermore, as Hull, Langman, and Glenn (2001) demonstrate, a generalized Darwinism can lead to comparative analyses of selection processes across empirical domains. In turn, such empirical comparisons can lead to further revisions and refinements of our understanding of general selection principles.

The application of Darwinian ideas to social phenomena has important implications concerning the rationality and psyche of human agents. Properties of human agents must be susceptible to causal explanation and be consistent with general Darwinian principles and our understanding of human evolution (James 1890; Dewey 1910; Veblen 1914; Richards 1987; Mesoudi, Whiten, and Dunbar 2006).

Consider human rationality. Darwin (1974, 84, 115) wrote in 1856: "Men are called 'creatures of reason,' more appropriately they would be *'creatures of habit.'*" Although he did not elaborate further, we can draw out some of the implications within a generalized Darwinism.

Darwinian evolution involves the development, retention, and selection of information concerning adaptive solutions to survival problems faced by entities in their environment. Questions naturally arise concerning the nature and material substrate of these adaptive solutions. The biologist and philosopher Ernst Mayr (1988) developed the concept of "program-based behavior" involving sets of conditional, rule-like dispositions, linked together into what he termed *programs*. Instincts and biological genotypes incorporate programs. Human ideas, habits, and customs can also have program-like qualities.

Darwinism constantly raises questions of causality and requires explanations of origin. This applies to the dispositional programs behind human behavior. Instead of simply assuming that agents hold beliefs and preferences, the paradigm of program-based behavior requires an explanation of their evolutionary emergence, through both natural selection and individual development. Evolution involves both the adaptation of programs to changing circumstances and the elimination of other programs through selection.

The conventional rational actor model in the social sciences simply sets out assumptions that are consistent with a set of behaviors. By contrast, the paradigm of program-based behavior focuses on the explanation of the dispositions behind any act. The concept of the program can be subdivided between programs that do and do not involve deliberation or conscious prefiguration. The paradigm of program-based behavior has been applied to economics by Viktor Vanberg (2002, 2004) and has strong similarities with

John Holland's (1995) theory of adaptive agents. This paradigm is more adequate than a primary focus on rationality and beliefs. The related concept of habit—as a particular form of a program—has also been revisited and refined in this evolutionary context, as we shall elaborate in later chapters.[11]

A generalized Darwinism provides a framework in which particular evolutionary patterns and mechanisms can readily be considered. One example is the wider use of Niles Eldredge's and Stephen Jay Gould's (1977) concept of "punctuated equilibria." Within biology, this concept has attracted some criticism and debate (Somit and Peterson 1992). Some scholars have wrongly misinterpreted it as a challenge to core Darwinian principles. Instead, a viable concept of punctuated equilibria posits that, under specific conditions, Darwinian evolutionary processes can sometimes dramatically accelerate and that the whole system can shift relatively rapidly from one chaotic attractor to another.

A number of authors have applied the concept of punctuated equilibria to social, organizational, institutional, political, cultural, economic, and technological evolution (see, among others, Miller and Friesen 1980; Tushman and Romanelli 1985; Collins 1988; Krasner 1988; Hannan and Freeman 1989; Mokyr 1990b; Gersick 1991; Gowdy 1993; Aoki 2001). The viability of this concept in specific circumstances depends on not only a reconciliation with the framework of generalized Darwinism but also an examination of the specific mechanisms of replication and selection that have the potential to generate such dramatic shifts in the pattern of evolution.

Darwinism focuses our attention on the possible mechanisms through which variety is preserved and created. It is remarkable that two of the most important mechanisms identified by Darwin (1859) and retained in modern biology depend on locational considerations. First, the migration of a group to another area with a different physical environment and, second, the use or creation of different niches remain two of the most important mechanisms explaining speciation. Related ideas would seem to transfer directly to the social or economic domain, for example, with the creation of new products or industries in different geographic and institutional contexts. In these cases, the new environment and the (relative) isolation of a group from the majority create new opportunities for variation.

As the population becomes subdivided into (relatively) isolated subsets, small mutations can have bigger overall effects on the population as a whole.

11. Recent neuroscientific and robotic research underlines the importance of modular programs over all-purpose information processors (Reeke and Sporns 1993; Arkin 1998; O'Reilly and Munakata 2000; Sperber 2005).

Furthermore, the different environments require different fitness characteristics for survival. New species may emerge as a result of physical separation or the demands of different environments. These arguments apply equally to human institutions and biological organisms. They particularly apply to the evolution of languages and all sorts of customs. In such cases, the foremost mechanism is often geographic separation; relative isolation leads to subdivision and, often, the creation of new languages.

In addition, there is now a growing literature on how firms perform differently in different contexts, such as under different regulatory regimes or among different types of financial institutions (Whitley 1999; Amable 2000, 2003; Aoki 2001; Hall and Soskice 2001; Boyer 2005; Kenworthy 2006; Barnett 2008; Gagliardi 2009).

The examples offered above indicate how the framework of a generalized Darwinism can be helpful in organizing and promoting specific research programs in the social domain. A generalized Darwinism helps us focus on specific mechanisms, particularly concerning replication, selection, and the sources of variation. Applied rigorously, it forces authors to be specific and precise in defining units of analysis. It also obliges analysts to be historical because, no matter what the exact setup or units of analyses are, such an evolutionary analysis directs attention to processes going back into the past, their built-in tendencies to persist (through replication), and how the present is created through multiple variations on the past. In that sense, all social scientists relying on this framework will be forced to take history into account (Mokyr 1996).

By itself, a generalized Darwinism is insufficient to provide a complete answer, but it provides a general framework in which additional and context-specific explanations can be placed. Its further usefulness depends on additional and extensive work. Despite several earlier and partial starts, the research program is still in its infancy.

2.4. GENERALIZING DARWINISM: A SUMMARY AND CONCLUSION

To repeat: a generalized Darwinism does not assume that the detailed mechanisms of social and biological evolution are similar. They are certainly not. The mechanisms of selection and replication are also very different between different entities *within* the biological domain. Consequently, we should expect considerable evolutionary differences (*a*) between nature and society and (*b*) within society itself. Instead of detailed similarity, the idea of generalizing Darwinism depends on a degree of ontological communality at a fairly high level of abstraction. This communality is captured by the broad idea of a complex population system and the formulation of general concepts of selection and replication.

Proposals for a generalized Darwinism are also unaffected by the claim that Darwinism or the principles of selection, inheritance, and variation are inadequate to explain social evolution. They are definitely inadequate. They are also insufficient to explain detailed outcomes in the biological sphere. In both cases, auxiliary principles are required. However, none of this undermines the validity of generalization at an abstract level. Insufficiency does not amount to invalidity. Furthermore, given the existence of complex population systems in both nature and society, a generalized Darwinism is the only overarching framework that we have for placing detailed specific mechanisms.

Given these rebuttals, how could one criticize the idea of generalizing Darwinism? Critics could argue that the ontology of complex population systems does not apply to socioeconomic evolution. Alternatively, they could attempt to show that explanations of complex population systems do not require the Darwinian principles of variation, inheritance, or selection. Finally, they could apply the rigorous definitions of *variation, inheritance,* and *selection* to socioeconomic phenomena and show that the outcomes are not particularly meaningful or useful. The idea of generalizing Darwinism is not immune to criticism, but previous critiques have generally been misconceived or misplaced.

We hypothesize that much of the resistance to the idea of generalizing Darwinism to include social evolution stems from social scientists' ingrained suspicion of ideas from biology. Students in the social sciences are often warned against social Darwinism and explaining human behavior in terms of genes. Not only are the issues more complex than the students are usually told, but also the idea of generalizing Darwinism has nothing to do with standard (and often dubious) accounts by social scientists of social Darwinism, sociobiology, or genetic reductionism. Our project should not be confused with these.

Strangely, many opponents of a generalized Darwinism have something in common with the reductionists they likewise eschew. Gene-centered theorists, biological reductionists, and those evolutionary economists who resist a generalized Darwinism all deny the existence of replicators at the social level. An adequately formulated generalized Darwinism sustains replication and selection on multiple levels and resists rather than endorses biological reductionism.

On the other hand, the idea of generalizing Darwinism to socioeconomic

evolution challenges the long-standing idea among social scientists that social and biological phenomena should be completely partitioned and that
social scientists have little to learn from biology. A generalized Darwinism
is consistent with the idea that human society is embedded in the natural
world and depends on it for its survival.

We also suggest that a generalized Darwinism sustains important, non-
vacuous propositions that are highly relevant to the evolution of human
societies. It systematizes the process of empirical inquiry and organizes detailed knowledge pertaining to a wide variety of evolutionary processes.

Furthermore, Darwinian ideas have important implications for social
scientists concerning the rationality and the psyche of human agents. Assumptions concerning human agents must be consistent with our understanding of human evolution. Darwinian evolution involves the development, retention, and selection of information concerning adaptive solutions
to survival problems faced by organisms in their environment. Darwinism
constantly raises questions of causality and requires explanations of origin. This applies in particular to the dispositional programs behind human
thought and behavior.

While Darwinism by itself is insufficient to provide full answers, it provides a general framework in which additional and context-specific explanations can be placed (Hull 1973). It is a general metatheoretical framework rather than a complete context-specific theory. But, as long as we
are addressing a population of replicating entities, social evolution *must* be
Darwinian, whether or not self-organization, human intentionality, and
Lamarckian inheritance are involved. As long as there is a population of
replicating entities with varying capacities to survive, then Darwinian evolution will occur.

On the other hand, the theory is falsifiable. It would not apply if there
were no population variation, no information inheritance, or no selection.[12]
That is, Darwinian principles would not apply to a world without variation,
scarcity, differential fitness, or the differential replication of key information as described above. Furthermore, Darwinism depends on the empiri-
cally falsifiable proposition that selection—which is related to fitness—is a
principal mechanism of change. Darwinism is neither strictly universal nor
unfalsifiable.

12. Although it seems obvious that variation, inheritance, and selection are present in social
evolution, these conditions are sometimes downplayed. For example, some evolutionary psychologists claim that culture is evoked rather than replicated. And some evolutionary economists claim
that selection is unimportant.

CHAPTER THREE

Rivals and Rebuttals

> That evolution is a core concept in biology does not mean that it is an inherently biological concept. Evolution can happen in other domains providing that conditions for an evolutionary process are in place. Thus, as economists applying evolutionary tools to economic phenomena, we can learn from the debates on evolutionary biology in order to understand better the logical status of concepts such as fitness, adaptation and unit of selection without in any sense needing to absorb the associated biological context.
>
> J. STANLEY METCALFE, (1998)

There are a number of objections to the idea of generalizing Darwinism. These arguments are mostly hindering scientific progress, and we address them before engaging in the constructive development of our argument.

Successive authors have argued over the years that Darwinian principles are inappropriate to the social domain because they downplay human intentionality or treat evolutionary processes as entirely blind. A related argument is that Darwinian selection is inappropriate in the social domain because selection therein is artificial rather than natural. These objections are based on misunderstandings concerning the nature of Darwinism.

Some recent authors have suggested that the idea of self-organization— where complex outcomes emerge in nature or society without an overall plan or design—provides an alternative general theory of evolution in both domains. On the contrary, while self-organization is extremely important, it cannot itself provide an adequate explanation of the evolution of complex population systems.

Another idea has recently surfaced. This is the "continuity hypothesis," according to which human social evolution emerged from and is embedded in the constraints shaped by evolution in nature (Witt 2003, 2004; Cordes 2006). This is a rather obvious statement of fact. But the continuity hypothesis is promoted as an alternative to Darwinism in the social domain.

Another perceived rival to Darwinism is Lamarckism. We devote an entire chapter to this doctrine because of its enduring influence in the social sciences and because its dissection helps us understand some essential details of Darwinian evolution. In chapter 4, it is argued that, if Lamarckian inheritance did occur, it would require Darwinian principles to explain its role and place in the evolutionary scheme.

3.1. CAN DARWINISM COPE WITH INTENTIONALITY?

An enduring mischaracterization of the Darwinian account of evolution is that it is blind (Commons 1924; Penrose 1952). Specifically, some authors interpret this alleged blindness within the Darwinian picture of evolution as a depiction of organisms, including humans, with little conception of what they are doing or where they are going.

On the contrary, Darwin did not treat humans as if they were incapable of self-reflection, reason, foresight, purpose, or planning. Furthermore, such attributes are neither irrelevant nor entirely absent in the nonhuman animal world. As Darwin (1859, 208) wrote: "A little dose . . . of judgment or reason often comes into play, even in animals very low in the scale of nature." As he repeated the point elsewhere: "Animals possess some power of reasoning. Animals may constantly be seen to pause, deliberate and resolve" (Darwin 1871, 1:46). He believed that animals had limited powers of reasoning, and he neither belittled those powers nor denied them in humans.

But Darwinism does not take intentionality as given. It holds that intentionality and other human mental capacities must have evolved from similar but less developed attributes among our prehuman ancestors. It insists that intentionality must be explained rather than simply taken for granted. Intentionality is an evolved property. As Claes Andersson (2008, 232) puts it: "The extraordinary explanatory force of Darwinism is due to its ability to explain purpose without assuming purpose *a priori*."

But many social scientists are used to taking these human mental capacities as given. The separation of the social sciences from biology for much of the twentieth century (Degler 1991) has sustained resistance to Darwinian attempts to break down this separation. This is a huge drawback.[1]

Notwithstanding the reality and importance of intentionality, there are some senses in which evolution can be blind. With self-organization, spontaneous order, or Darwinian selection, complex design emerges without a seeing designer (Vanberg 2004). This does not mean that individual agents or organisms within a system are necessarily unable to prefigure or plan

---

1. It is a question of scientific inquiry as to what degree mental capacities are explained in terms of nurture or nature. While there is evidence of genetic influence on the ability to form forward-looking expectations (McClearn et al. 1997), a full explanation of mental capacities would involve both (within-brain) cognitive processes and human interaction within social structures.

their own actions. It is simply that they do not plan or predict the overall outcome with others, and it is often very difficult for them to do so. This does not mean that human intentionality and its effects can be neglected.

Donald T. Campbell (1987) argues that any effective capacity for foresight or prescience must be based on tried and tested knowledge; otherwise, we have no grounds to presume its effectiveness. Accordingly, when genuine innovations are launched, we are unable to assess the probability of their success or failure—a well-established empirical fact (Klepper and Graddy 1990; Nelson and Winter 2002). In this sense, innovations are blind. Again, this does not undermine the reality or importance of human deliberation, intention, foresight, or creativity.

Hence, the term *blind* in this context has several meanings. Only one of them depicts humans as lacking in deliberation or foresight, and this is wrongly associated with Darwinism. Given these ambiguities and misunderstandings, we prefer to drop the term *blind* in this context. Terms such as *undesigned* or *unforeseen* are less open to misinterpretation.

Such misunderstandings have been exacerbated by some Darwinians. For example, Richard Dawkins (1976, x) famously claimed: "We are survival machines—robot vehicles blindly programmed to preserve the selfish molecules known as genes." Clearly, he uses metaphors to make a point. But he does little to compensate for their misleading connotations. He admits that humans have *consciousness* and *purpose,* but with minimal exploration of the meaning of these terms. Dawkins further weakens the meaning of human purposefulness by repeatedly ascribing intentionality to the genes. In his rhetoric, genes are purposeful, but humans are mere machines. Hence, the concept of intentionality is undermined. While Darwin was more careful, the reckless use of language by some Darwinians—even if only intended as metaphor—has further reinforced the mistaken impression that Darwinism denies human intentionality.

Again the separation of the social sciences from biology is part of the problem. Intentions and beliefs are central to the understanding of human agency in the social sciences. By contrast, natural scientists often focus on dispositions and behaviors, with little consideration of the mental deliberations of the organism. Even if this were adequate in the natural world, knowledge and beliefs become much more important in the study of human society. To a unique extent, humans attribute thoughts and intentions to others in their social interactions. Social scientists are aware of this, but their frequent error is to take human mental capacities, beliefs, or preferences for granted, rather than considering them evolving phenomena requiring explanation. They detach mind and belief from nature. On the other hand, many people educated exclusively in the natural sciences have an inadequate appreciation of the role of belief, intention, and intersubjectivity in human society.

In a related vein, some authors reject the application of Darwinism to the social sphere because it involves natural selection, whereas, by contrast, social evolution involves "artificial selection." The American institutional economist John R. Commons repeated this view (see Commons 1897, 90; Commons 1924, 376; and Commons 1934, 45, 120, 636-38, 657-58, 713), and it has its modern supporters. As Commons was aware, it was Darwin himself who established the distinction between natural and artificial (or "methodical") selection. Employing familiar examples such as pigeon breeding, Darwin used artificial selection to convince his readers that descent with modification was possible and, thereby, to introduce the concept of natural selection. Note the irony. Darwin used artificial selection to introduce the concept of natural selection. He emphasized the similarity between the two forms of selection, while several social scientists regard them as antithetical.

With artificial selection, humans manipulate the criteria or environment of selection; the selection process is under the control of a human agent. But artificial selection is not an *alternative* to natural selection. Darwin did not propose that artificial and natural selection are mutually exclusive. As Darwin's friend George Romanes (1893, 296) wrote: "The proved capabilities of artificial selection furnish, in its best conceivable form, what is called an argument *a fortiori* in favor of natural selection."

Crucially, the humans doing the selecting are also a product of natural evolution. The dispositions, aims, and criteria that they use in artificially selecting natural specimens or social rules are also themselves the products of cognitive and cultural evolution (Copeland 1936). The phenomenon of humans selecting between outcomes or possibilities is important and real, but their preferences and choices must also be explained as far as possible.

When artificial selection does take place, it is not the end of the story. Different institutions or societies in which artificial selection is involved sometimes compete against each other. Hence, some additional processes of evolutionary selection may be involved. Sometimes, despite human intentions, some institutions will survive, while others do not. Natural events or other forces may influence the selection result. Any outcome of artificial selection must be tested in the environment. Artificial selection cannot replace or demote a broader concept of evolutionary selection in human society. Some compartmentalizations of artificial from natural selection elevate intentionality to something distinct and separate from the multiple causal linkages of nature. Intentions are real and have effects. Nevertheless, intentions themselves are caused and must be explained.

In the social sciences, it is often still taken for granted that the existence of human intentionality is sufficient to explain human action, without probing the causes behind intentions themselves. Darwinism does not deny belief, choice, purposeful behavior, or foresight: it simply asserts that they too are caused and worthy of explanation. Indeed, Darwinism can help explain how agents formulate and revise goals, how agents generate new alternatives, and why goal-directed behavior very often leads to failure.

3.3. IS THE THEORY OF SELF-ORGANIZATION AN ALTERNATIVE TO DARWINISM?

Is there any alternative general evolutionary theoretical framework? Some evolutionary economists have proposed that—instead of Darwinism—the theory of self-organization can fill this role.[2] *Self-organization* can be defined as the capacity of a system to determine its own structure on the basis of the functional interactions of its components (Misteli 2001, 181). That is, self-organization is a process by which interacting elements in a system give rise to an ordered pattern or outcome that is intended by no element or outside agent (Anderson 2002). Snowflakes and other forms of crystallization are very well-known examples of self-organization in nature. Examples of self-organization in living systems include the formation and movement of swarms of bees and flocks of birds. We can observe intricate patterns of interactions as a school of fish snakes upstream in the river.[3]

The existence of self-organized outcomes shows that we do not always have to look for a designer to explain their emergence. This counters the

2. For example, John Foster (1997) proposes that the theory of self-organization provides a sufficient, general basis for evolutionary thinking in economics, and Ulrich Witt (1997, 489) argues that it "provides an abstract, general description of evolutionary processes."

3. The theory of endosymbiosis proposes that life itself emerged through cellular networking and cooperation (Margulis and Sagan 2001).

mistaken view that all social phenomena are the result of conscious design. Many complex and efficacious human institutions such as language and much of common law are not the outcome of a supreme plan. A classical example of self-organization in the social world comes from economics. Economists point to markets as self-organizing and see Adam Smith's "invisible hand" as a precursor of this idea.

Accepting its importance in nature, is self-organization *sufficient* to explain the origin of species and all complex biological phenomena? The answer is no. Darwin's principle of selection is also required.

Consider the role of self-organization in living systems. At a very fundamental level, the self-organization of chemical hypercycles is thought to explain the emergence of life. Emergent chemical hypercycles provide the feedback necessary for the emergence of self-reproducing metabolic networks. In the absence of emergent hypercycles, there would be no positive feedback for growth, implying that metabolic networks would simply die out (Eigen and Schuster 1979; Kauffman 1993; Hofbauer and Sigmund 1998). Once self-reproducing metabolic networks have emerged, however, a selection process is required for these entities to continue to increase in complexity. This is one of the major findings in the hypercycle literature.

An often-cited example of self-organization in biology is the ribosome: when the parts are introduced, the structure snaps into place. But the shapes of the components that fit together are the result of past selection; some parts fail to self-assemble when structure-altering mutations are introduced. Self-organization depends on both anterior and posterior processes of selection.

In fact, leading proponents of self-organization in biology do not see it as an alternative to natural selection. Stuart Kauffman (1993) made a powerful argument that natural selection alone cannot explain the origin of complex organisms. Systems involving nonlinear interactions constitute a large number of possible states, most having little survival value. Kauffman argued that processes of self-organization channel systems into more restrictive possibilities by way of positive feedback. But Kauffman further argued that selection sustains organisms at a level of complexity beyond that explained by the principles of self-organization in isolation.

Self-organization may be necessary to explain the emergence of a number of complex phenomena, such as the formation of new species in nature (Stewart 2003). But, in the absence of selection, there is little chance of the development of increasingly complex structures. Thus, Kauffman (1993, 465) saw self-organization and selection, not as alternatives, but as a "natural marriage." He and several other pioneers of self-organization theory do not present their argument as an alternative to Darwinian theory. Jeffrey Wicken (1987) wrote of "extending the Darwinian paradigm," not exterminating it. David Depew and Bruce Weber (1995) considered "Darwinism evolving," not Darwinism abandoned. Weber and Depew (1996, 51) wrote: "The very concept of natural selection should be reconceived in terms that bring out its dynamical relationships with chance and self-organization. In our view, Kauffman's recent work, as expressed in *The Origins of Order* [1993], does just this." What is involved here is a revision and extension of natural selection theory, not its negation. Kauffman (1995, 8) himself called for a "revision of the Darwinian worldview," not its abandonment. As he also related: "I have tried to take steps toward characterizing the interaction of selection and self-organization. . . . Evolution is not just 'chance caught on the wing.' It is not just a tinkering of the ad hoc, of bricolage, of contraption. It is emergent order honored and honed by selection" (1993, 644).

Kauffman's (2000) later work on self-organization reinforces this point. Once self-organized systems and subsystems emerge, natural selection acts on these self-organized structures once they emerge. Far from being an alternative to natural selection, self-organization requires it in order to determine which self-organized units survive. Accordingly, other self-organization theorists, such as the biologist Scott Camazine and his colleagues, similarly recognize that self-organization complements rather than displacing the "orthodoxy" of natural selection. Echoing Kauffman, Camazine et al. (2001, 89) write: "There is no contradiction or competition between self-organization and natural selection. Instead, it is a *cooperative 'marriage'* in which self-organization allows tremendous economy in the amount of information that natural selection needs to encode in the genome. In this way, the study of self-organization in biological systems promotes orthodox evolutionary explanation, not heresy." Consequently, evolutionary economists who propose that self-organization theory is an alternative to Darwinian principles are at variance with their prominent mentors in self-organization theory. Leading theorists of self-organization recognize that natural selection is required at some point in the explanation. Otherwise there is a gaping hole in the argument.

An exclusive focus on self-organization would concentrate on the development of the entity, neglecting its interactions with its environment, and providing no adequate explanation of how the entity comes to be adapted to survive in this environment (Cziko 1995). The mistake is to concentrate entirely on internal development and evolution from within, even to the extent of defining *evolution* in these narrow and unwarranted terms.[4]

On the contrary, in biology, neither individuals, species, nor ecosystems are entirely self-transforming. Evolution takes place within *open* systems involving both endogenously and exogenously stimulated change. Generally, evolution takes place through both internal changes and interactions with the (possibly changing) environment.

Often, the environment changes because of migrations and intrusions from another region. As already observed by Darwin (1859), isolation mechanisms have important effects on the evolutionary path of ecosystems. Isolation gives new variation time to evolve slowly but generally reduces the level of new variation that is being produced. The breakdown of isolation mechanisms increases the level of variation present in a population, sometimes leading to the overcoming of system rigidities.

In biology, much change in a given area is due to the introduction from other regions of existing species, which then interact with their new neighbors and affect the course of evolution. Exogenous shocks, such as meteor impacts and climate change, are also believed to have had a major influence, leading to the extinction of some species and the expansion of others.

Likewise, in social evolution, exogenously stimulated change is sometimes of great importance. Exogenous shocks sometimes overcome the rigidity of the system. Many historical examples illustrate this, such as the seventeenth-century revolutions in England being sparked by forces from Scotland and elsewhere. The arrival of American warships in Tokyo Bay led to the Meiji Restoration of 1868 and the abrupt transition of Japan from a feudal to a Western-inspired capitalist society. The occupation of Japan and Germany by American and Allied troops in 1945 also led to major institutional changes. The course of institutional evolution was altered by the intrusion of new forces across the boundaries of the system, as in many other cases of institutional transformation being promoted by invasion or other forces from outside.

---

4. Witt (2003, 13) has repeatedly defined *evolution* as "the self-transformation over time of a system." This echoes similar and equally confined conceptions of evolution as primarily a system changing according to its own internal logic (Marx 1976, 90–92) or "from within" (Schumpeter 1934, 64), among others. Nevertheless, Witt's emphasis on the creation of novelty is entirely consistent with a Darwinian approach, especially when external as well as internal stimuli for creativity are taken into account and a necessary selection process to weed out useless novelties is added. Indeed, without some process of selection, Witt cannot explain why some novelties prove fruitful and others are dropped.

On its own, self-organization theory can adequately explain neither the current adaptedness nor the process of adaptation to the environment. It also leaves unexplained the effects of environmental change on a population of entities. In biology, self-organization is insufficient to address the contingent nature of life and the basic problem of survival and reproduction. Self-organization explains neither the characteristics of the elements that interact to create the emergent order nor how the emergent order adapts and survives in the broader environment. It leaves out two necessary processes of selection: that which led to the original population of (interacting) elements and that which led to the survival of the particular emergent order.

The leading biologist Theodosius Dobzhansky (1962, 16) wrote: "No theory of evolution which leaves the phenomenon of adaptedness an unexplained mystery can be acceptable." Some theory of adaptation and survival is essential. Lacking such an account, self-organization is highly inadequate as a general evolutionary theory. Gary Cziko (1995, 323) similarly argued: "The laws of physics acting on nonliving entities can lead to spontaneous complexity, but nothing in these laws can guarantee *adapted* complexity of the type seen in living organisms. . . . Of all the complex systems and structures that may self-organize due to the forces of nature, there can be no assurance that all or any of them will be of use for the survival and reproduction of living organisms." In other words, self-organization does not address the survival potential of a self-organized system. Self-organization may help us understand the emergence of pattern and order, but it cannot account for the survival of the emergent order itself, especially when compared with rival entities or organisms.

At this stage, it is useful to distinguish the concepts of ontogeny and phylogeny. In biology, *ontogeny* refers to the growth and development of single organisms from embryo to adult. In this case, changes in the genotype are irrelevant to the explanation. Similarly, self-organization involves an ontogenetic evolutionary process, in that it addresses the development of a particular organism or structure and not necessarily the constituent elements.

This does not rule out the possibility that ontogeny can also involve the natural selection of entities *within* the organism. For example, the growth of many organisms involves the natural selection of immunities, neural patterns, and (often beneficial) bacteria in their gut (Edelman 1987; Plotkin 1994; Hull, Langman, and Glenn 2001). Likewise, the ontogenetic growth of a firm may involve the internal selection of individuals. Hence, some self-organizing processes involve some (phylogenetic) selection of constituent components of the emerging structure.

But self-organization does not *necessarily* involve selection or phylogeny. *Phylogeny* relates to the evolutionary history of a sizable related group of organisms, such as a species. It refers to the evolution of a whole population among which selection occurs. As a result of selection, the gene pool in the whole population changes. Natural selection is *always* phylogenetic as well as ontogenetic, in that it addresses the evolution of whole populations of organisms or structures as well as the development of individual organisms. Ontogeny *may* but does not necessarily incorporate phylogeny, but phylogeny *always* incorporates ontogeny. The two concepts differ in their generality; ontogeny is necessarily an aspect of phylogeny, but the reverse is untrue.[5]

From the point of view of the overall evolutionary process, complete evolutionary descriptions require a phylogenetic account of the selection of ontogenetically developing units. Hence, self-organization cannot provide a complete evolutionary theory even when it is important (and, perhaps, essential). This must involve phylogeny as well as ontogeny. If we are confined to ontogeny, then our description of the evolutionary process does not address the differential survival and fecundity of different (self-organized) structures or organisms. Self-organization cannot replace selection.

Self-organization means that complex structures can emerge without design, but these structures are themselves subject to evolutionary selection. Some will survive longer and be more influential than others: selection will operate. We regard these issues as vital for social evolution. Conscious choices, competitive pressures, market forces, or environmental constraints operate on habits, customs, technologies, institutions, and even whole economies. Many of these contain self-organized structures, but this neither precludes nor demotes the role of selection.

Self-organization does not stand up as a general theory of evolution because it is not universal within complex population systems. It alerts us

5. The status of phylogeny vs. ontogeny has triggered the famous evo-devo dispute in biology (Gilbert, Opitz, and Raff 1996; Baguñà and Garcia-Fernàndez 2003). A number of developmental biologists call for a new synthesis of evolutionary biology and developmental biology (an evo-devo synthesis) because "macroevolutionary questions are not seen as being soluble by population genetics, and the developmental actions of genes involved with growth and cell specification are seen as being critical for the formation of higher taxa" (Gilbert, Opitz, and Raff 1996, 357). This emphasizes ontogeny more than other accounts that accent phylogeny. But, whatever their relative importance (which is largely a matter for empirical inquiry), the evolution of populations always involves both phylogeny and ontogeny (Stadler, Stadler, and Wagner 2001). Given this, the generalized Darwinian framework can accommodate any outcome of this dispute over relative importance.

to the possibility that order can emerge from the interaction of elements. While it is vital to the explanation of some evolved phenomena, it is not a general process. It offers little in terms of explanation, particularly of adaptation or survival. It is no alternative to Darwinism, but a useful complementary concept that aids understanding of complex systems spanning multiple levels of organization. The challenge, then, is to understand how selection and replication shape the dynamics of systems where self-organization is present.

3.4. FROM CONTINUITY TO DISCONTINUITY?

The "doctrine of continuity" formulated by Thomas Henry Huxley and the more recent continuity hypothesis advanced by Ulrich Witt both address the relation between the natural and the human worlds. To avoid confusion, we need to clarify them both. Furthermore, while one is a core idea in Darwinism, the other is mistakenly presented as Darwinism's rival. Our position is that both these ideas are valid enhancements of Darwinism, particularly when applied to human evolution.

In a paper of 1874 (see Huxley 1894, 1:236–37), Huxley explained the doctrine of continuity as the Darwinian view that evolution cannot make huge leaps and that phenomena such as human consciousness are preceded by lower degrees of deliberation and awareness in our prehuman ancestors.[6] He argued that no "complex natural phenomenon comes into existence suddenly . . . without being preceded by simpler modifications" and that this applied in particular to human consciousness: "In the individual man, consciousness grows from a dim glimmer to its full light, whether we consider the infant advancing in years, or the adult emerging from slumber and swoon." Furthermore: "The lower animals possess, though less developed, that part of the brain which . . . [is] the organ of consciousness in man." They also "have a consciousness which, more or less distinctly, foreshadows our own" (1894:236–37). Huxley argued that important evolutionary developments—such as sight and consciousness—are always foreshadowed by earlier evolutionary outcomes and adaptations. The doctrine

---

6. It is a common misunderstanding that continuity is a contrast to rapid change. Rapid change depends on the timescale of the relevant dynamics. If the process is fast enough, then a continuous process may look like a discontinuity to the human observer. Note that Huxley's doctrine can accommodate periods of relatively fast evolutionary change. Even with punctuated equilibria (Eldredge and Gould 1977; Gould 2002), relatively rapid evolutionary changes take place over many thousands of years and involve numerous small and discrete causal steps.

of continuity insists that all evolutionary developments must be the result of a material and causal evolutionary process. Genes give rise to other genes, organisms give rise to other organisms, and species give rise to other species (Hull 1976, 174). Similarly, habits give rise to other habits, institutions give rise to other institutions, and technological paradigms give rise to other technological paradigms. Darwinism characterizes selection processes in terms of continuity by descent.

Witt's (2003, 2004) continuity hypothesis was coined in apparent ignorance of Huxley's doctrine of continuity. Witt's (2004, 131–32) continuity hypothesis proposes that natural evolution has "shaped the ground, and still defines the constraints, for man-made, or cultural, evolution . . . not withstanding that the mechanisms and regularities of cultural evolution differ from those of natural evolution. The historical process of economic evolution can be conceived as emerging from, and being embedded in, the constraints shaped by evolution in nature." We fully agree with this broad hypothesis. Indeed, we cannot imagine how it could be false. It is a *fact* that all aspects of human social evolution emerge from and are embedded in "the constraints shaped by evolution in nature."[7]

Witt's valid idea predates Darwin and modern evolutionary theory. For example, Auguste Comte (1853, 2:112) wrote: "Biology will be seen to afford the starting point of all social speculation in accordance with the analysis of the social faculties of Man and the organic conditions which determine its character." Since Darwin, the idea that the natural world shapes and conditions the social has become commonplace, even among social scientists. We cannot think of a reputable contemporary social scientist who believes otherwise.[8]

Our differences lie elsewhere. We hold that the abstract Darwinian principles of variation, selection, and inheritance are not confined to the biological domain. In contrast, Witt claims that cultural evolution is driven by different mechanisms and principles than biological evolution. He therefore questions the relevance of the principles of variation, selection, and inheritance for understanding cultural evolution.

Such a view would have difficulty dealing with the fact that several human biological characteristics, such as large brains, small jaws, menstrua-

7. Witt's definition neither excludes nor endorses the proposition that cultural evolution can be explained entirely in genetic terms. In practice, he eschews such reductionism, as do we.

8. Cordes (2006, 531) sees the continuity hypothesis as negating Darwinian principles in social evolution. But nothing in Witt's (2003, 2004) or Cordes's (2006) definitions of the continuity hypothesis implies such a rejection.

tion, and lactose tolerance, have emerged through a Darwinian process of coevolution of interacting biological and social levels (Durham 1991; Dunbar 1993, 1998; Wills 1993; Deacon 1997; Ehrlich 2000; Wrangham 2009). It would require drawing a sharp line between the biological and the social domains in cases where such a division is difficult to establish. On the contrary, biological evolution is sometimes channeled by culture. Because the biological and the social are so deeply entwined, it is difficult to confine powerful general principles to one domain alone. Ironically, by contrast, Witt ends up defending a good measure of discontinuity rather than continuity.

Rather than denying the broad application of Darwinian principles, we can sometimes separate the dynamics according to the involved timescales. Many social processes, such as industry evolution, operate on much shorter timescales than some processes in nature. In analyzing industry evolution, we can, therefore, safely ignore biological evolution even though such changes can very slightly affect the human gene pool. However, when we consider how production methods can promote the epidemiological spread of salmonella and other bacteria, it is clear that evolutionary processes in nature and society are sometimes interacting in an enhanced manner. The influence of human production on climate change is another case in point. The study of interacting evolutionary processes in nature and society is of primary importance for advancing the evolutionary program.

3.5. CONCLUSION

The arguments in this chapter expose several misunderstandings and demonstrate that several purported rivals to Darwinism are not rivals at all. On the contrary, Darwinian principles are required even when self-organization or artificial selection occurs. *Self-organization* refers to the development of a single entity and does not deal adequately with adaptation and selection in populations of multiple entities. Artificial selection of rules or institutions may result from the actions of governments or law courts, as Commons (1924, 1934) explained. But other modes of institutional selection occur, including by competition, conquest, or war. Furthermore, even when artificial selection occurs, the principles, dispositions, and preferences of the agents doing the selecting also require explanation (Copeland 1936).

Another false claim is that Darwinism denies or downplays intentionality. Intentionality, and the capacity to prefigure in the mind the consequences of actions or events, is much more developed in humans than in other species and must, therefore, be highlighted in a Darwinian account of the evolution of human social phenomena. There is nothing in Darwinian principles that excludes such an emphasis.

We also think that it is confusing to think of Darwinian evolution as blind. We prefer more precise descriptions, such as those concerning the uncertainty of actions in a complex environment, the emergence of un-designed phenomena, and the existence of unintended consequences.

Finally, we have considered notions of continuity between the social and the natural worlds. Huxley's doctrine of continuity is a central tenet of Darwinism. Witt's continuity hypothesis proclaims in similar terms that the social is grounded in the natural, but it is strangely combined with a strong reluctance to extend Darwinian principles to the social domain.

CHAPTER FOUR

The Lamarckian Confusion

Let us fix the Lamarckian evolutionary process well in our minds.

GEORGE BERNARD SHAW, (1921)

Cultural evolution is commonly said to be Lamarckian rather than Darwinian, but there has been surprisingly little effort to work out a precise theory of its principles.

JOHN MAYNARD SMITH, (1988)

This chapter criticizes misleading depictions of social evolution as Lamarckian and shows that Lamarckism is not an alternative to Darwinism. But it also has a constructive agenda. Because accounts of Lamarckism in social evolution evoke social learning, we take the opportunity to address this concept in box 4.1. Also, because Lamarckism typically involves claims concerning inheritance, it obliges us to clarify this concept. This, in turn, establishes the importance of the distinction between genotype and phenotype—and the more general distinction between replicator and interactor. This general distinction turns out to be of vital importance in the understanding of social evolution, even when the issue of Lamarckism has been left behind.

Consequently, empirical applications of Darwinian principles must identify relevant replicators and interactors. We specify individual habits and organizational routines as primary examples of replicators. Surpassing the vague term *meme* gives more precise guidance for future empirical work.

4.1. SOME PRELIMINARIES

Since the theoretical and experimental work of August Weismann (1893), Lamarckism has been generally excluded in modern biology because there is no apparent mechanism by which the acquired characters of an earthly organism can be transferred to its genotype.[1]

---

1. There is a minority view among biologists that the inheritance of acquired characters may be possible in a restricted set of circumstances, such as the transfer of acquired immunities from

BOX 4.1 *Cultural transmission and social learning*

Cultural transmission involves the replication of habits where individuals are instructed by parents, teachers, or drill sergeants. Such replication from individual to individual is a fundamental process in the evolution of culture (Boyd and Richerson 1985; Durham 1991; Dunbar, Knight, and Power 1999; Richerson and Boyd 2004). Individuals acquire habits of language, social norms, taboos, role conceptions, personality types, and professional skills from parents (vertical transmission) and other teachers (horizontal transmission). Boyd and Richerson (1985, 40) reviewed empirical evidence in support of this view:

1. Laboratory experiments show that humans learn from others with great facility. Social learning theorists have shown in some detail how an individual can acquire a very large cultural repertoire.
2. Studies of socialization in more naturalistic settings have shown that child-rearing patterns are correlated with behavioral variations in children.
3. A large body of psychometric and sociometric studies measuring correlations among offspring, genetic parents, and various classes of potential cultural parents; provides ample evidence of cultural transmission despite an inevitable tendency for the effects of genetic, cultural, and environmental variation to be confounded.
4. Historians, sociologists, and anthropologists have found a number of striking examples of cultural inertia, situations in which cultural ancestry is important in changed situations or traditional cultural differences persist in similar environments.

More recent theoretical and experimental studies of social learning (including Mesoudi and Whiten 2003; Schotter and Sopher 2003; McElreath et al. 2005; Kirby, Cornish, and Smith 2008) have vastly expanded our understanding of these processes. We have a richer knowledge of the role of such factors as hierarchy and cognitive framing in the transmission of information from individual to individual.

mother to child (Steele 1979; Ho and Saunders 1984; Jablonka, Lachmann, and Lamb 1992; Steele et al. 1998; Gottlieb 2001). And, although there is evidence of epigenetic inheritance (Pennisi 2008), it is debatable whether it can be described as Lamarckian (because the environment affects gene expression rather than genes themselves). We entirely abstain from evaluating these arguments in biology, and our argument here would be unaffected by either their validity or their falsehood. The imaginary journey below to Planet Lamarck is a thought experiment, asking the question, *If* Lamarckian inheritance existed, what would be involved? It does not mean that we believe in the possibility of Lamarckian inheritance in biological organisms on Earth. And, concerning life on other real planets, we have insufficient knowledge to form an opinion.

By contrast, prominent economists and other social scientists, including Jack Hirshleifer (1977), Herbert Simon (1981), William McKelvey (1982), Richard Nelson and Sidney Winter (1982), Robert Boyd and Peter Richerson (1985), Friedrich Hayek (1988), and Arthur Robson (1995), have described social or economic evolution as Lamarckian. A dispute within organization science over the extent to which firm routines can adapt is often described as a contest between Darwinian and Lamarckian conceptions of organizational change (Usher and Evans 1996).[2]

According to van de Ven and Poole (1995), the Darwinian evolution of organizations means that traits are inherited through intergenerational processes, whereas Lamarckian evolution means that traits can be acquired within the lifetime of an organization through learning and imitation. It is surprising to see that many works actually agree with this distinction and promote Lamarckian evolution over Darwinian (Hedlund 1994; Helfat 1994; Metcalfe 1994; Rosenberg 1992), without much consideration of the nature of either form of evolution.

Unfortunately, the precise meaning of *Lamarckism*, and the relation of Lamarckism to Darwinism, is often unclear. Critics of this Lamarckian terminology are few, among them David Hull (1982, 1988). John Wilkins (2001) portrays *Lamarckism* as an ambiguous term with three different meanings:

- The *first* meaning of *Lamarckism* is the notion that acquired characters can or will be inherited. Jean Baptiste de Lamarck strongly promoted this idea, but it was not original to him.[3] We discuss this notion of Lamarckism extensively below.
- A *second* strong theme in the writings of Lamarck—which he developed rather than originated—is that evolution leads to greater complexity. Although later Lamarckians such as Herbert Spencer took up this idea, it has today grown beyond its Lamarckian associations.

2. To add further confusion, Reydon and Scholz (2009) have recently argued that the work of McKelvey (1982) and Hannan and Freeman (1989) is not Darwinian because it lacks an adequate explanation of organizational diversity. If true, this would mean, not that this work was un-Darwinian, but simply that the Darwinian account was incomplete. Incomplete Darwinism does not disqualify the label *Darwinian*: it means that more work must be done within the Darwinian framework. For the label *Darwinian* to be unwarranted, the approach would have to be incompatible with Darwinism. This is not the case. See also Lemos (2009).

3. Lamarck (1984, 113) himself believed in the stronger version of this thesis, that *all* acquired characters are inherited: "All the acquisitions and losses wrought . . . through the influence of the environment . . . are preserved by reproduction to the new individuals."

• A *third* use of the label *Lamarckian* entails an emphasis on will, choice, or volition in the process of evolutionary change. Many Lamarckians have invoked such concepts to explain the development of acquired characteristics (e.g., Butler 1878). But Lamarck himself emphasized neither will nor volition, and their association with Lamarck originates from his hostile critic Georges Cuvier (Boesiger 1974; Burkhardt 1977; Lamarck 1984).

The third meaning—that Larmarckism entails an emphasis on will, choice, or volition in the process of evolutionary change—is acceptable and does not exclude Darwinism. Although human mental capacities are more highly developed, most living organisms anticipate, choose, and strive for prefigured goals. These intentional factors play a role in biological as well as social evolution. The nature and sophistication of these cognitive mechanisms has an enormous bearing on adaptation and survival in the evolutionary process. This was a theme in Darwin's own writings, and it has been developed by Darwinian biologists (Mayr 1960; Waddington 1969, 1976; Corning 1983).

It is when these anticipative and purposive capacities are assumed to have somehow appeared without cause and independently of an evolutionary process that the third meaning becomes problematic. Yet this extraordinary version of the third meaning is as far from Lamarck himself as one could imagine.

In its uncontroversial form, the third meaning acquires more bite when it is combined with the first meaning: volition thus becomes part of the mechanism by which new characteristics are developed and acquired. The third meaning says nothing about inheritance, which is the key element in the first meaning.[4]

The volitional acquisition of characteristics is often contrasted to the allegedly blind or random mutations in some versions of Darwinism. However, Darwin himself never wrote of *random* mutations, and, in principle, core Darwinian principles are broad enough to accommodate both contrasting accounts. Furthermore, volition and randomness are neither mutually exclusive (think of the stock market) nor strictly necessary for Darwinian evolution to occur.

We accept the possibility, in the social if not the biological sphere, that

---

4. In her defense of the description of cultural evolution as Lamarckian, Kronfeldner (2007) emphasizes the third meaning, in the sense of problem solving leading to directed variation. She ignores the inheritance and evolution of these problem-solving capacities.

some (social) phenotypes (or interactors) can affect their (social) genotypes (or replicators), just as firms can alter their routines in the Winter (1971) and Nelson and Winter (1982) models. Our argument below addresses problems in the other part of the argument, concerning the inheritance of acquired characters. Hence, the controversy surrounding the label *Lamarckian* centers mostly on the first meaning.

Contrary to a widespread view, Lamarckism and Darwinism are not mutually exclusive. This is confirmed by inspection of the following definitions of these terms:

- *Darwinism* is a general theoretical framework for understanding evolution in complex population systems, involving the inheritance of replicator instructions by individual units, a variation of replicators and interactors, and a process of selection of the interactors in a population.
- *Lamarckism* is a doctrine admitting the possibility of the (genotypic/ replicator-to-replicator) inheritance of acquired (phenotypic/interactor) characters by individual organisms or entities in evolutionary processes.
- *Weismannism* (or neo-Darwinism)[5] is a doctrine denying the possibility of the (genotypic/replicator-to-replicator) inheritance of acquired (phenotypic/interactor) characters by individual organisms or entities in evolutionary processes.

In two independently drafted papers (Hodgson 2001b; Knudsen 2001), we asked whether social evolution is Lamarckian or Darwinian. We held that Darwin's principles of variation, selection, and inheritance apply to both biological and socioeconomic entities. But we also accepted a Lamarckian possibility in social evolution, regarding the issue as a matter of empirical inquiry. We left the question of the extent of Lamarckism in social evolution open. In the present chapter, we go further, by considering the conceptual limits to Lamarckian social evolution in more depth.

Key phenomena such as learning allow the development and transmission to subsequent generations of adaptations much more rapidly among

---

5. Note that this is only one of three or more meanings of this confused term that are currently in use. As here, *neo-Darwinism* has been taken to refer to a Darwinism modified by Weismann's work and the denial of the inheritance of acquired characteristics. But it is also used elsewhere to refer to the "neo-Darwinian synthesis" of Darwinism and Mendelian genetics in the 1930s and 1940s. More recently, it has been used to refer to "gene-centered" versions of Darwinism developed by Williams (1966), Dawkins (1976), and others. The moral here is that the term *neo-Darwinism* should be used very sparingly at most and, even then, always clearly defined.

humans than among other species. We fully accept that cultural transmission occurs in human societies and is much more important there than in other species. Human culture is unique in its nature, dimensions, and significance.

But such observations do not themselves justify the label *Lamarckian*. Lamarckism involves the *inheritance* of acquired characteristics. *Inheritance* means more than merely "passed on." If it were merely the latter, then the spread of a virus among members of any species would be evidence of Lamarckism. No biologist regards such commonplace epidemiological contagion as Lamarckian. The concept of inheritance is invested with a different meaning: it must involve the transmission of crucial information from one genotype (or replicator) to another. That is why the genotype-phenotype (or replicator-interactor) distinction is essential to any full definition and explanation of a Lamarckian process. Those who think otherwise are challenged to provide a definition of *Lamarckism* that uses the concept of inheritance in a sense that excludes contagion.

In biology, the genotype is the complete genetic coding of an organism, consisting of instructions to help guide its growth and development. Most of these instructions depend on environmental triggers or stimuli. The phenotype is its actual form and character, including its behavioral propensities and capabilities. Each individual phenotype develops according to the instructions in its genotype and the influence of environmental conditions, including interactions with other organisms. The genotype-phenotype distinction is a case of the more general distinction between the replicator and the interactor (Brandon 1996). In later chapters, we refine the general concepts of replicator and interactor and apply them to social evolution.

Genes are not the only replicators, even in the biological sphere. Following others, we propose that replicators exist at the social level as well as the biological. Candidates include ideas, memes, habits, and routines. The possibility of Lamarckism at the social level hinges on the existence or otherwise of two mechanisms: one that encodes acquired characteristics in the replicator and another that conveys the acquired characteristics from one social replicator to another. We examine this possibility below.

The remainder of this chapter is structured as follows. Section 4.2 concerns biological evolution and the theoretical reasons why any Lamarckian transmission must, in practice, be limited (if, indeed, it exists at all) in any biological system. Several of these theoretical reasons turn out to have a applicability beyond biology alone. The significance of the genotype-phenotype and replicator-interactor distinctions is also established. We show this by a visit to an imaginary planet where Lamarckian transmission does exist among its biological species. This sets the stage for the discussion of social evolution in section 4.3. Some possible social replicators are considered, with a view to exploring possible distinctions between replicator and interactor at the social level. We then consider the possibility of, and limits to, Lamarckian transmission in social evolution. Section 4.4 concludes the discussion of Lamarckism. Section 4.5 underlines the importance of the replicator-interactor distinction for the constructive arguments in this book.

4.2. PROBLEMS ON PLANET LAMARCK

To explore further the theoretical limits to Lamarckism, we consider the viability of a hypothetical inheritance system on Planet Lamarck. We later explain the significance of this discussion for social evolution on Planet Earth. The first humans to explore Planet Lamarck were a group of evolutionary economists and organization theorists.[6] They observed the reproduction of several species, including a giraffe-like organism. They noted that, with each generation, some characteristics were further exaggerated. With the giraffes, for example, each generation would give rise to offspring with a longer neck, resulting in a discernible increase in neck length through the giraffe lineage, from generation to generation.

One evolutionary economist quoted Joseph Schumpeter (1934, 64) and argued that this evolutionary process seemed to operate in the giraffe species as if "from within." But her colleagues pointed out that the increase in neck length occurred in an environment where the giraffes depended on sustenance and were reaching for the uppermost leaves in the trees and that the impact of the environment should not, therefore, be ignored. They persuaded each other that biological evolution on this planet was, in fact, Lamarckian and similar in its essentials to the Lamarckian processes of social and cultural evolution that they had analyzed in human society on Earth. Accordingly, they named the planet Lamarck.

In their report on the biological evolution of organisms on Planet Lamarck, the social scientists included the diagram reproduced in figure 4.1. Their account of the evolution of organisms on the planet noted the individual developmental process of each organism from O_i to $O_i{}'$ in each generation i, subject to environmental influences E_i. The offspring in the

---

6. Our lawyers have urged us to state that any resemblance to any living evolutionary economist or organization theorist is purely coincidental.

	Generation 1	Generation 2	Generation 3
Environment	E_1	E_2	E_3
Organism	$O_1 \rightarrow \quad O_1' \rightarrow$	$O_2 \rightarrow \quad O_2' \rightarrow$	$O_3 \rightarrow \quad O_3' \rightarrow$

FIGURE 4.1. A process of evolution (or contagion?).

next generation inherited and started with the acquired characteristics of O_i' in the form O_{i+1}, and these were, in turn, developed and augmented into O_{i+1}'. This process was then repeated indefinitely. The observers proposed that this was formally similar to their Lamarckian models of learning processes in human organizations and cultures on Earth, where, in each discrete stage, knowledge K_i builds on and develops to K_i' while adapting and testing in environmental conditions E_i, and this knowledge is accumulated and transmitted onto the next stage.

The social scientists added a caveat in their report that they did not have training in biology and that it would be necessary for a group of evolutionary biologists to explore Planet Lamarck in order to confirm their observations and results. The evolutionary biologists on Earth were very critical of the report. They asked, How could it be possible for a characteristic acquired in the development of one organism to be passed on to the next generation? The next generation is not a mere photocopy of its predecessor, so what mechanism could account for the transmission of these characteristics from generation to generation?

In addition, the evolutionary biologists on Earth pointed out that the model portrayed in figure 4.1 cannot distinguish between genuine inheritance and more superficial infection or contagion. This distinction again depends on attention to the mechanisms of inheritance that were treated inadequately.

The critics also objected that this picture of inheritance on Planet Lamarck does not explain why acquired improvements are favored over acquired impairments or injuries. If an organism becomes aged or infirm or is injured or mutilated, then no reason is given why these impairments are not immediately passed on to the offspring. Presumably, these characteristics would also be apparent at their birth. So newborn giraffes would not only have necks as long as their parents but also inherit any rheumatism, diminished virility, and failing eyesight.

In their application for a research grant to finance a second exploration of Planet Lamarck, the evolutionary biologists hypothesized that, for these reasons, it was unlikely that all acquired characters would be inherited.

They also set out a framework using the biological concepts of genotype and phenotype. They noted in particular that the evolutionary economists had made little use of these key concepts but that they were necessary to sustain an adequate account of evolution on Planet Lamarck—or Lamarckian evolution elsewhere, if, indeed, it existed. They also noted that other theorists of social or cultural evolution, including enthusiasts of memes, had either failed to mention the genotype-phenotype distinction in that context or failed to reach a consensus regarding the identification and consistent specification of the meme genotype or the meme phenotype (Dawkins 1976; Blackmore 1999).[7]

Pouring more skepticism on the claims of the memeticists and other social scientists, the evolutionary biologists cited a paper by the philosopher of biology David Hull (1982) arguing that memetic evolution cannot be Lamarckian but must be Darwinian. According to Hull (1982, 278): "Social learning is not an instance of the inheritance of acquired characters." For him, it is more like epidemiological infection or contagion. He thus rejects the notion that Lamarckian transmission is involved. For Hull (1982, 309), the inheritance of acquired ideas or memes is not an instance of the inheritance of acquired characters because ideas and memes are analogous to genes, not characteristics: "In order for sociocultural evolution to be Lamarckian in a metaphorical sense, conceptual genotypes must be distinguishable from conceptual phenotypes and the two must be related in appropriate ways." If we make this important distinction, and if we choose to treat memes or ideas as genotypes, then the spreading of ideas or memes is like the spreading of genes and does not necessarily involve the inheritance of acquired characters.

To appreciate that social learning and cultural transmission are more than the contagious spread of ideas, we should consider notions of information storage and replication. Consequently, we must consider the possibility of meaningful social genotypes (or replicators). For Hull, the transmission of ideas or memes is more like the spread of genotypes than the acquisition of characteristics. If we deny this by regarding the genotype-phenotype distinction as unwarranted, then we have no way of distinguishing between acquired character inheritance and contagion.[8]

In emphasizing the importance of the genotype-phenotype (replicator-

7. The *Journal of Memetics* announced its own demise in 2005 and included a number of obituaries for the troublesome concept of a meme.

8. In the next chapter, we discuss the concept of diffusion, which is especially important at the social level. By definition, diffusion is more than contagion because it involves one interactor copying the replicators of another. It is a form of inheritance, but it is defined in terms of replica-

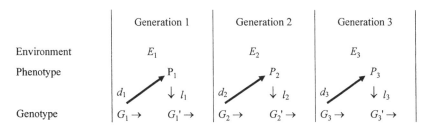

FIGURE 4.2. An expanded evolutionary schema with Lamarckian inheritance.

interactor) distinction, the evolutionary biologists expanded the crude evolutionary picture in figure 4.1 into the more sophisticated presentation in figure 4.2. In both cases, for clarity the diagram omits a selection effect in order to focus on Lamarckian inheritance. Selection would operate at the population level: entities with less fit phenotypes would exit the population, and the distribution of genotypes would change. New entities would enter via replication, with the more fit phenotypes leaving more replicas than the less fit. This would further alter the distribution of genotypes. In the presence of a fairly stable environment and a replication process that reliably transmitted genotypes between generations, the population would slowly and systematically adapt to that environment. The biologists knew all this, but, following good scientific practice, they wanted to examine the effect of Lamarckian inheritance in isolation.

Figure 4.2 illustrates the supposed inheritance process on Planet Lamarck, with its reported inheritance of acquired characters.[9] The variables G_i and G_i' refer to the genotypes of organism i in a lineage of organisms. P_i refers to the developed phenotype. In order to keep the presentation simple, we have not distinguished between stages of phenotypic development. It must be emphasized that phenotypic development is an outcome of both the genotype and the environment. In the construction of a more complete evolutionary theory, developmental process must be brought fully into the picture.

The first organism has a genotype G_1 that instructs its development d_1 (denoted by a thicker arrow) into phenotype P_1. This phenotype reflects environmental conditions E_1 as well as genotypic characteristics G_1. Somehow,

tors rather than (acquired) characters. Neither contagion nor diffusion is necessarily a Lamarckian process.

9. Similar multilevel transmission diagrams can be found in Boyd and Richerson (1985) and Durham (1991) and are now in widespread use in the literature.

through a process of Lamarckian transmission l_1 (denoted by a downward-pointing arrow), some or all of the characteristics of this phenotype are encoded in the same organism's genotype, so G_1 transforms into G_1'. Of course, such Lamarckian transmission l is minimal or absent at the biological level on Earth. But, on Planet Lamarck, we can consider the possibility that a fraction of information might be transferred with an organism from phenotype to genotype. Some or all of this information might be transferred in process l.

Next, through mating or whatever, replication occurs. So the information in genotype G_1' is passed on to the next generation in the form of genotype G_2. The same process repeats in this and subsequent generations. By the time we have reached the third generation, the genotypic outcome G_3' carries information gathered from its ancestral genotypes, including some accumulated phenotypic information encoded in genotypes, reflecting previous environmental conditions E_1, E_2, and E_3.

The evolutionary biologists noted that, without the conceptual distinction between genotype and phenotype, the phenotype and genotype rows in figure 4.2 would be conflated into a single row, and the characteristically Lamarckian process l would disappear from the picture. Accordingly, claims that (biological or social) evolution is Lamarckian, whether valid or not, depend on a clear distinction between genotype and phenotype (or replicator and interactor) in order to be adequately meaningful. Few previous advocates of Lamarckian social evolution have paid sufficient attention to this point. This is curious because the very existence of Lamarckian transmission turns on this distinction (Hull 1982, 1988, 2000; Aunger 2002).

Some Lamarckians have denied that developments such as the growth of a giraffe's neck must result from genotypic instructions. It is here that the third, volitional interpretation of Lamarckism is sometimes invoked. But, even if the giraffe could use its own willpower to stretch its neck, we would then have to explain why it has a disposition to act purposefully in this manner. The cause and evolutionary origin of this volitional propensity would itself have to be explained. No answer to this question is available except for a Darwinian one, in which such a willful propensity somehow gives the giraffe a fitness advantage and is, thus, favored by natural selection. But this argument also requires that the volitional propensity is itself genetically encoded. Consequently, the propensity to stretch the neck again derives from the biological genotype.

Lamarck (1984, 113) himself argued that "a more frequent and continuous use of any organ gradually strengthens, develops and enlarges that organ . . . while the permanent disuse of an organ imperceptibly weakens and deteriorates it." This famous Lamarckian principle of "use and disuse" does not help matters either. Again, we must search for a causal explanation, why the use of an organ leads to enlargement or strengthening and disuse to diminution. For these processes to occur in a systematic way, there must be a mechanism in the body that reacts to use or disuse and causes such strengthening or weakening. This mechanism must be inherited and, thus, must be an outcome of the genotype. Hence, Lamarck's principle of use and disuse cannot escape the requirement that the outcomes derive from instructions in the genotype played out in specific environmental conditions.

In systems without Lamarckian inheritance, the environment affects the distribution of genotypes solely through a process of selection on the expressed phenotypic properties (traits) present in the whole population. Some phenotypes are less adapted than others to a given environment. Given a systematic relation between genotypes and phenotypes, the gene pool can, thus, change from generation to generation as a result of selection (Price 1995). Selection occurs on Planet Lamarck, but it is relatively less important in the explanation of the evolution of the genotype. Hence, Lamarckians such as Herbert Spencer gave relatively less emphasis to selection in their evolutionary theory.

In their grant application, the evolutionary biologists elaborated the following theoretical argument. The *inheritance* of acquired characters must be distinguished from something akin to epidemiological infection or contagion, where one phenotype influences a second phenotype without corresponding changes in the second genotype. The propensity to grow a longish neck must be encoded in the genotype of the newborn giraffe. Especially with Lamarckian transmission, this genotypic inheritance mechanism is necessary to avoid newborn giraffes having necks as long as their parents'. Instead, these offspring inherit a genotypic propensity to grow long necks. This genotypic propensity is passed from generation to generation.

But there is nothing specifically Lamarckian about the inheritance of a propensity to grow a long neck. Giraffes on Earth inherit such a propensity, without Lamarckian meddling with their DNA. For Lamarckian inheritance to occur, the longer necks of the parents must further *enhance* the propensity to grow a long neck that is encoded in their genotype, and this *enhanced genotypic propensity* must then be passed on to the genotype of the parents' offspring. Hence, Lamarckian replication must involve the following two essential stages:

L1. Although its genotype already contains instructions to develop a particular characteristic (such as a long neck), this realized phenotypic outcome somehow causes *an amplification of these genotypic instructions,* to enhance this characteristic even further.

L2. Through reproduction, the instructions that favor this *additional* development are also passed on to the next generation.

Compare these points with Hull's (2000, 55–56) definition of *Lamarckism*:

> Inheritance is Lamarckian if the environment changes the phenotype of an organism in such a way that this organism is better adapted to the environmental factor that produced this change. This phenotypic change must then be transmitted somehow to the genetic material so that it can be passed on to the offspring of the organism through reproduction. These offspring then are born with this acquired characteristic more highly developed or with a strong tendency to produce this characteristic more highly developed. Lamarckian inheritance is the literal inheritance of acquired characteristics. The transmission must be genetic, and the relevant effect must be phenotypic.

Hull's formulation is close to ours.[10]

A key element in both stage L2 and Hull's statement requires further emphasis. The Lamarckian "inheritance of acquired characteristics" must mean more than the mere inheritance of the capacity to grow a long neck. The genotypic instructions that lead to the realization of this outcome must somehow lead to the amplification of those instructions. Lamarckian organisms must have genotypes that provide positive feedback on the genotypic instructions that promote this growth.

Having clarified the meaning of *Lamarckian inheritance*, the evolutionary biologists explained why they were skeptical that such a process of inheritance existed. They identified some dangers in excessive feedback from phenotype to genotype. Given that particular environmental cues trigger only a subset of a large range of phenotypic possibilities, an organism represents only one of the adaptive outcomes that are possible given its genotype. The genotype carries the accumulated wisdom of past generations, in many environments. To preserve this valuable heritage, this genotypic baseline

---

10. By insisting that "Lamarckian transmission must be genetic," Hull seems to immediately rule out the possibility that (literal?) Lamarckian transmission can exist with social and other replicators that are not genes. Rather than excluding the possibility of Lamarckian social evolution by an act of definition at the outset, we prefer to explore the possibility with social replicators. Despite her differences with Hull, Kronfeldner (2007) replicates his questionable and imprecise usage of the terms *literal* and *metaphoric* in this context, where they refer respectively to genetic and nongenetic inheritance.

must not adjust too rapidly in response to current phenotypic outcomes.[11] Accordingly, Lamarckian inheritance would somehow have to preserve much of the genetic material that is not actually expressed in the current phenotype. Hence, Lamarckian inheritance cannot be so strong that it distorts or overwhelms this legacy.

In a Lamarckian process of inheritance, genetic instructions must be altered to correspond to previous phenotypic change through a mechanism of back translation. Back translation of an acquired trait requires an accurate identification and modification of the genes that correspond to this and only this trait, such as a long neck. Error in back translation of an acquired long neck might instead promote a smaller neck or larger feet.

It is difficult to conceive of such a reliable process, especially with modern knowledge of the complexities of genetic coding and expression (Stumpf et al. 2008). Such a process presumes that the environment acts like an expert computer software redesigner, understanding the complex interconnections between each piece of coding, and knowing which instructions to preserve and which to modify. It must anticipate how the environment interferes with genetic instructions as the new organism develops from embryo to maturity. Such a degree of detailed, complicated, and fortuitous reprogramming is very unlikely to happen in the haphazard and undesigned turmoil of nature. Readily solving the problem of back-translating phenotypic traits to genetic information requires a one-to-one mapping of phenotype onto genotype. No such mapping is known in biology or elsewhere.[12]

Another problem concerns the very meaning of an acquired character. The evolutionary biologists pointed out that, logically, there were two entirely different types of acquired characters, depending on whether it (i) resulted or (ii) did not result from instructions in the genotype. In the first case, there is nothing specifically Lamarckian about a character resulting from its genotypic coding. As argued above, *Lamarckism* must refer to the additional process by which the genotype somehow encodes the enhanced characteristic so that the next generation does not have to start developing from the same starting point.

In the second case, the acquired character does not result from instructions in the genotype. Neither can it result from (unintentional or inten-

11. See Maynard Smith and Szathmáry (1999) and Knudsen (2001, 2002b). DNA has a remarkable mechanism for limiting mutations. Consisting of two strands, one can be checked against the other by an enzyme and, if necessary, repaired by other enzymes.

12. Some biological research suggests that the mapping of phenotype onto genotype is many-to-one or even many-to-many (Stadler, Stadler, and Wagner 2001).

tional) behavior in the organism because behavioral dispositions can themselves be genetically inherited. The remaining possibilities are degradations due to environmental interactions, including accidental impacts. Unfortunately, most accidental impacts result in injuries. Hence, prominent cases of acquired characteristics include injuries and other impairments. But, for species to evolve, the effects of such deleterious acquired characters must be restricted. To provide a complete explanation, we need to account for the existence of sufficiently tight limits that disallow the inheritance of useless and injurious characters. The only possible explanation for the evolution of the limits necessary to filter the many useless and injurious characteristics is natural selection. Accordingly, Lamarckism depends on the Darwinian principle of selection in order to explain why any disastrous propensity to inherit acquired impairments does not prevail. As Richard Dawkins (1986, 300) argues: "The Lamarckian theory can explain adaptive improvement in evolution only by, as it were, riding on the back of the Darwinian theory." If Lamarckism is valid in any particular domain, it depends on Darwinian mechanisms of selection for evolutionary guidance.

Lamarckian inheritance requires natural selection for guidance; hence, it must not overreach the effects of natural selection. We know that natural selection works very slowly and erratically and, therefore, that the generational effects of any Lamarckian inheritance, with its strong injurious bias, must be small by comparison.

Consider the possibility that there is competition on Planet Lamarck between Lamarckian and non-Lamarckian species. For Lamarckian inheritance to prevail, it must bestow an advantage. The most obvious advantage would be the encoding and replication of fortuitous adaptations to a given environment (assuming that the inheritance of impairments could somehow be avoided). But this advantage would be reduced in complex or changing environments because Lamarckism might rapidly lead to the species being locked in to a precarious inferior peak in the fitness surface. Accordingly, there are good theoretical reasons why biological evolution on Planet Lamarck, as on Earth, is largely or entirely non-Lamarckian. Hence, Lamarckism faces severe *theoretical* limits.

The evolutionary biologists made all these theoretical points in their research grant application and then made the case that empirical inquiry into the inheritance mechanisms on Planet Lamarck was essential to ascertain whether such an unlikely outcome of Lamarckian inheritance did, in fact, exist. They left for Planet Lamarck some time ago, and we have yet to receive their research report.

In the meantime, it was noticed by some social scientists that many of the key points in the application for research funding for the expedition of the evolutionary biologists to Planet Lamarck were quite general and applied to all cases of evolution with a population of replicating entities. Accordingly, the key theoretical observations of the evolutionary biologists outlined above also applied to social or cultural evolution on Earth, which several other authors had claimed to be essentially Lamarckian. It is the purpose of the next section to reveal the implications of this wide-ranging observation.

4.3. BACK TO SOCIAL EVOLUTION ON PLANET EARTH

A moral of the fable in the previous section is that the concept of inheritance must be clarified, and, to this end, the distinction between genotype and phenotype (or, more generally, replicator and interactor) is vital. Any specification of a fully fledged evolutionary process, involving a population of developing and replicating entities, must identify the relevant replicators and interactors. This general point applies to social and cultural evolution in human society as well as to biological systems. In particular, any claim that social or cultural evolution is Lamarckian depends on the replicator-interactor distinction for its explication.[13]

Remarkably, however, despite frequent claims of Lamarckism, works in evolutionary economics, organization theory, evolutionary anthropology, and memetics seldom explore the replicators or interactors in their domain.[14] There is much loose discussion of the transmission of ideas, beliefs, knowledge, or memes but relatively little dissection of the processes involved.

We now apply the key insights of the preceding section to evolutionary processes in economies and societies. First, we ask by what criteria a (biological or social) entity qualifies as a replicator. Dawkins (1976) argued that a replicable replicator must have the characteristics of longevity, fecundity, and replicative fidelity. DNA replicates with a high degree of precision and with a low probability of mutation. By contrast, in the social domain,

---

13. Note that Price's (1995) general formulation of the concept of selection does not make use of the replicator-interactor distinction (Knudsen 2004b). The distinction becomes important when the mechanisms of replication and transmission are considered. The significance of the genotype-phenotype distinction was established in Darwinian biology in the twentieth century.

14. Among the exceptions are Winter (1971), McKelvey (1982), Hull (2000), Aunger (2002), and Nelson (2002).

no candidate replicator gets close to DNA by Dawkins's criteria. We must search for other distinguishing criteria.

These criteria must be able to identify social replicators, which, by definition, are not inherited biologically, which act as stores of social dispositions, rules, and knowledge, and which can guide the development of human patterns of behavior and social structures, depending on the overall context. Social replicators are neither genes nor DNA; they are replicated by other means.

Detailed and general definitions of replication have been developed by Kim Sterelny, Kelly Smith, and Michael Dickison (1996), Peter Godfrey-Smith (2000b), Dan Sperber (2000), and Robert Aunger (2002). There are differences between their formulations, but all these definitions agree on the centrality of the following necessary criteria for replication:

1. *Causation*: The source must be causally involved in the production of the copy.
2. *Similarity*: The copy must be like its source in relevant respects.
3. *Information transfer*: During its creation, the copy must obtain the information that makes the copy similar to its source from that same source.[15]

A number of possible social replicators have been suggested, including (*a*) ideas, (*b*) memes, (*c*) habits of thought or behavior, and (*d*) organizational routines. These are not necessarily mutually exclusive, and later in this book we consider additional social replicators such as customs. Notably, organizational routines depend on individual habits as a substrate.

Ideas or Memes as Social Replicators?

Consider ideas and memes as possible replicators. We noted above that there has been some difficulty enforcing a distinction between replicator and interactor in the case of ideas and memes. Are ideas instructions that drive behavior or (phenotypic) rationalizations of preceding actions or attitudes? Are ideas or memes replicators or interactors or both? Without answers to these questions, there is no possibility of adjudicating the question of whether memetic evolution is Lamarckian.

Some meme enthusiasts wish to retain a broad definition of *meme* and

---

15. We refine this broad definition of a replicator in chapter 6 below.

end up treating the meme as a replicator in one context and an interactor in another. This creates havoc with discussions of whether memetic transmission is Lamarckian. Susan Blackmore (1999, 61–62) proposes that whether memetic evolution is Lamarckian depends on whether it is the meme as behavior or the meme as instructions that is being copied. She argues that copying the product brings the possibility of Lamarckian inheritance of acquired modifications to the outcome, whereas copying the instructions does not; any alterations in behavior or outcome will not be passed on because it is the instructions, not the outcomes, that are being replicated.

But, even if we regard the meme as behavior and consider the copying of outcomes, it is still misguided to jump to the conclusion that a Lamarckian possibility exists. In particular, the identity of the replicator behind the meme as behavior is unclear. If this replicator consists of genes, then the analysis switches back to biological mode, where we know that Lamarckian transmission is largely or entirely ruled out by the Weismann barrier. Alternatively, for those who treat the meme as behavior, there must be some *social* replicator that corresponds to that behavioral phenotype. But this remains unidentified. Consequently, within the meme-as-behavior version of memetics, no case for regarding memetic transmission as Lamarckian has been adequately established.

Some prominent proponents of the meme treat it as a replicator, rather than as a phenotypic phenomenon such as behavior (Hull 1982, 2000; Aunger 2002). Hull convincingly argues that memetic transmission—where memes are treated as ideas and genotypes—cannot legitimately be described (literally or metaphorically) as Lamarckian. Hull (see Hull 1982, 311) holds that "memes are analogous to genes, not characteristics." Consequently, they can be modified or acquired, but this is neither the modification nor the acquisition of a characteristic. Memetic transmission is the inheritance of acquired memes, and memes are genotypes, not phenotypic characteristics. Accordingly, social learning and other forms of memetic transmission cannot be instances of the inheritance of acquired characters. For Hull, the replication and spread of memes is more like epidemiological infection or contagion. In conclusion, if we treat the meme as a genotype and a replicator, then any description of memetic transmission as Lamarckian is mistaken.

Habits and Routines as Social Replicators?

Let us now explore the possibility of habits and routines as social replicators (see Hodgson 2001b, 2003c, 2004a, 2006a; Hodgson and Knudsen

2004a, 2004b, 2006a, 2006b). This strategy avoids some of the vagueness and difficulties associated with the meme but creates further problems for the use of the label *Lamarckian* in the social context, as we explain below. We treat habits and routines as dispositions, rather than expressed behavior as such. If we acquire a habit, we do not necessarily use it all the time. It is a *propensity* to behave in a particular way in a particular class of situations.[16]

Similarly, it is preferable to treat routines as propensities (Knudsen 2002b, 2008; Hodgson 2003c, 2008a). As Barbara Levitt and James March (1988, 320) put it: "The generic term 'routines' includes the forms, rules, procedures, conventions, strategies, and technologies around which organizations are constructed and through which they operate." Michael Cohen et al. (1996, 683) also treat a routine as a disposition: "A routine is an executable *capability* for repeated performance in some *context* that [has] been *learned* by an organization in response to *selective pressures*."[17]

In evolutionary, developmental, and functional terms, instinct comes before habit, and habit comes before belief and reason. Instincts provide inherited behavioral cues that guide us initially in our newborn state. Then our actions, resulting from instinct or cultural interaction, lead to the formation of habitual dispositions. In turn, these habits or dispositions form the basis of our conceptualizations and beliefs. Thus, habits are the basis of both reflective and nonreflective behavior (Kilpinen 1999, 2000; Hodgson 2004a, 2006b). They are dispositions that are acquired through repeated mental or physical behaviors in specific social contexts.

16. In everyday English, the word *habit* can refer to regular behavior as well as a propensity. However, the scientific sense of the word as a propensity is clearly prominent in early pragmatist-inspired works by James (1890), Veblen (1914, 1919), Thomas and Znaniecki (1920), Dewey (1922), and others. But, with the rise of behaviorist psychology from the 1920s to the 1960s, behavior became all-important, and underlying dispositions were neglected. Furthermore, neoclassical economists such as Becker and Murphy (1988) and Becker (1992) define *habit* as "serially correlated behavior." By contrast, modern social theorists such as Camic (1986), Margolis (1987, 1994), Murphy (1994), and Kilpinen (1999, 2000) and modern psychologists such as Ouellette and Wood (1998), Wood, Quinn, and Kashy (2002), Wood and Quinn (2004), Wood, Tam, and Witt (2005), Verplanken and Wood (2006), and Ji Song and Wood (2007) have all reinstated the notion of habit as a disposition. See also Hodgson (2004a, 2006a) and Hodgson and Knudsen (2004a).

17. Treating the essence of a phenomenon as its behavior creates the philosophical problem—discussed by Aristotle in his *Metaphysics*—that the entity would cease to exist when the behavior stopped (Hodgson 2008a). By contrast, routines persist as capacities even when a firm closes its gates overnight. Hence, essences reference capacities rather than performances, notwithstanding the causal links between the two (Bhaskar 1975; Harré and Madden 1975; Popper 1990).

Is Habit Replication Lamarckian?

Habits are replicators in the sense that they preserve and transmit social roles, interpretations, attitudes, knowledge, and skills and act as the relatively durable substrate of all beliefs and deliberative reason. To establish this point fully would be to divert us from the main theme of this chapter; our reasons are laid out more extensively in chapter 6 below.

From the biological point of view, habits are part of the biological phenotype or interactor; they are expressions of genetic instructions in interaction with the environment. However, from the social viewpoint, habits become replicators. This is partly because they satisfy the conditions of longevity, fidelity, and fecundity, relative to the shorter timescales and wider margins at the social level. An aspect of the interactor or phenotype at one level becomes a potential replicator at a higher level, but under different standards of longevity and fidelity. The general idea of phenotypic features acting as replicators at a higher level is necessary for a multiple-level selection theory. Habits are both phenotypic features (of individuals with genetic replicators) and replicators (with regard to social evolution).

Essentially, unlike DNA, habits do not replicate directly by making copies of themselves; they replicate indirectly by means of behavioral expressions. People imitate one another, and eventually the copied behavior becomes rooted in the habits of the follower, thus transmitting an imperfect copy of the habit.

But the replication of habits of *thought* is less straightforward. Because they are unobservable, they cannot replicate straightforwardly via imitation. Guided by similar external constraints and similar inborn constraints of brain design, the replication of habits of thought requires the linguistic communication of similar mental models so that two or more individuals can interpret given sense data in a similar way.

Can habit replication be Lamarckian?[18] It may seem so because, with some habits, acquired characters can be inherited because their replication works through characteristics, not through the direct replication of the generative structures. But the question is more complicated. It all depends on how we translate the Lamarckian stages L1 and L2 above from biological to social terms. The transmission of habitual replicators is always indirect. Lamarckism would have to be rendered consistent with indirect transmission, yet the work of Lamarck himself, and much of the relevant subsequent

---

18. The following argument here modifies an earlier suggestion that habit replication could be Lamarckian (Hodgson 2001b, 2003c).

literature, relates to the biological world, where genotypic transmission is always direct. It is an important question (revisited below) whether indirect transmission should, in principle, be admitted within the Lamarckian schema.

Serious problems also arise with stage L2. A Lamarckian process that is defined in these terms would require that the relevant aspect of the interactor or phenotype (an acquired thought or behavior) of the first person was also back-translated into its replicator or genotype (habit). This can occur when repeated (phenotypic) thoughts or behaviors give rise to new or amended (genotypic) habits. But the phenotypic behavior could be occasional or accidental, and not encoded in a habit, yet still imitated by the second person. Strictly, according to the formulation in stage L2, the first case would be Lamarckian, but the second would not.

At first sight, this may seem to resolve the issue: a Lamarckian possibility exists with regard to the replication of habits, as long as the acquired behavior gives rise to an enhanced habit in the first person before the behavior is imitated by a second person. In figure 4.3, behavior B_1 becomes ingrained in habit H_1. Practice and interactions with the environment lead to modified behavior B_1' and modified habits H_1'. The second agent copies this modified behavior, and the process is repeated. A Lamarckian process of habit transmission is shown in figure 4.3 by the downward-pointing arrows l, indicating the effect of the behavioral phenotype on the habitual replicator or genotype.

Comparing figures 4.2 and 4.3, we see an important difference in the role played by the Lamarckian step l. As shown in figure 4.3, this step affects neither the genotype nor the phenotype of the person who imitates the behavior. The modification of habit to H_i', which occurs just prior to the imitation, plays no role in the replication process or its result. The significance of this observation is that the definitionally essential Lamarckian step l plays no causal role in the replication process. It leads into a causal cul-de-sac. What is crucial to the description of Lamarckian replication plays no vital

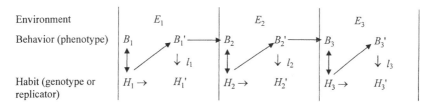

FIGURE 4.3. The replication of corporeal habits.

role in the Lamarckian replication of habits in the social domain! This is because, with the replication of habits, replicator-to-replicator transmission is indirect.

Is Routine Replication Lamarckian?

Let us now consider the possibility of treating routines as organizational-level replicators. While establishing that the replication of habits is a fundamental process in cultural evolution, the literature has, with a few exceptions, downplayed cultural transmission from group to group. The added ingredient is that replication from group to group also involves the transmission of capabilities for action sequences that have been established among members of an organization.

When routines are copied from organization to organization, this may in part involve adoption by the imitator of similar and explicit rules and procedures. Even if routine replication consisted entirely of the "blueprint" copying of codifiable procedures, then a Lamarckian description would still be inappropriate, for reasons similar to Hull's objection to the idea that meme replication is Lamarckian, as discussed above. With blueprint transmission of routines, there is no inheritance of the additionally acquired phenotypic characteristics of the performed routines.

On the basis of extensive research on the nature of routines, we know that much of the know-how inherent in routines is tacit and often uncodifiable (Polanyi 1967; Nelson and Winter 1982; Hannan and Freeman 1989; Cohen and Bacdayan 1994; Cohen et al. 1996). Routines involve interlocked habits of individuals in a team. Hence, habit replication is a part of routine replication. Often, the routine must be observed and practiced because the transfer of blueprint information is not enough to consolidate the routine. As a result, the same problems that emerged with a Lamarckian description of habit replication occur with the replication of routines.

There is an extensive debate within organization science as to how changes in routines in firms occur and whether the evolution of organizations and routines is a Lamarckian process. Near one extreme is the view that rules and routines are difficult to alter within any specific organization and that changes occur principally through the selection and elimination of some organizations, rather than adaptations of routines within the organizations themselves (Hannan and Freeman 1989). A huge case study literature, too massive to begin citing here, testifies to the conservative nature of organizations and the durability of their routines even when more productive or efficient alternatives exist. Our purpose here is not to adjudicate the empirical claims but to consider the applicability of the label *Lamarckian* to significant adaptation and change in the routines in any given organization.

Above all, it is highly misleading to use the label *Lamarckian* to describe the adaptation of routines within any given organization. Adaptation is different from the *inheritance* of characteristics (acquired or otherwise) by one organization from another. The use of *Lamarckian* to categorize a process that does not explicitly involve inheritance is in defiance of most historical uses of the term. It is highly regrettable that valuable empirical investigations into the relative importance of adaptation and selection in the evolution of populations of business firms have been diverted and confused by misleading uses of Lamarckian terminology and a false dichotomy between Lamarckism and Darwinism. Removing this conceptual confusion will help us focus on the facts.

We have explored several options for possible replicators in social evolution. Every one carries problems for the application of the label *Lamarckian* in this domain. If the genotype-phenotype distinction cannot be applied, then the description *Lamarckian* is not meaningful. If it can be applied, then further problems arise. In the case of memes as genotypes, the further problem is that memes can be modified or acquired, but this is neither the modification nor the acquisition of a characteristic. In the case of habits and routines, a crucial and defining Lamarckian step plays no causal role in the replication process.

The conclusion we draw is that Lamarckian concepts do not readily and meaningfully transfer from biological to social evolution. By contrast, we have found no similar barrier to the application of generalized Darwinian principles to the social domain. Darwinian concepts can be generalized more readily, to cover all evolving systems with replicating populations of some kind.

4.4. DARWINISM TRUMPS LAMARCKISM

The label *Lamarckian* has a curious attraction in the social sciences. Despite there being scant evidence and inadequate conceptualization of the actual mechanisms of replication in the social world, many argue that social processes are Lamarckian.

We have noted that enthusiasts of the label *Lamarckian* often emphasize the substantial transmission of knowledge and skill from one generation to another in social evolution and the fact that nothing like this occurs among other species. Our response is that this process does not necessarily involve the *inheritance* of acquired characters, once *inheritance* is defined to exclude virus-like contagion.

Explaining social evolution requires a valid inheritance model that identifies the underlying cause of the information that is transmitted among agents. Otherwise, there is no way of knowing whether observed changes are outcomes of selection processes, drift, diffusion, or something else. Considering these processes, we can see that the inheritance of acquired characters is at most highly limited even in the social sphere.

Of course, the mechanisms of evolution in the social and the biological spheres are very different. But the irony, as we have shown here, is that the essential Lamarckian principles are more closely and exclusively related to the biological sphere than they are to the social, notwithstanding the fact that Lamarckian replication is rare or nonexistent among biological species on Planet Earth. The very concept of Lamarckism depends on relatively direct genotype-to-genotype replication, which is lacking at the social level.

By contrast, the core Darwinian principles of variation, inheritance, and selection have a more general applicability, to social as well as biological evolution. Those who insist that social evolution is Lamarckian often ignore the more accommodating nature of general Darwinian principles.

Against this, some organization theorists propose that volition, deliberation, purpose, planning, and learning cannot be explained by the simple primitives of the general Darwinian principles. For example, Joel Baum and Paul Ingram (1998) argue that organizations capable of adapting during their lifetime are more Lamarckian than Darwinian. Similarly, David Rigby and Jurgen Essletzbichler (1997) view change in firms resulting from profit-induced search, learning, and imitation as Lamarckian. It has also been argued that Lamarckian evolution promotes quick learning (Nelson and Winter 1982; Bruderer and Singh 1996).

These arguments are problematic for a number of reasons. First, as shown above, Lamarckism and Darwinism are not, in principle, mutually exclusive. And learning and imitation are compatible with Darwinism.

Second, in order to speak of Lamarckian evolution, traits that are acquired within a generation must also be inherited through intergenerational processes, a new organization inheriting the genotypic features of others. Acquiring traits through learning and adaptation is a necessary condition of Lamarckism, but it is insufficient. With Lamarckism, the acquired traits must also be encoded in a replicator that is passed on to the next generation.

Third, the traits of an entity develop according to the instructions in its replicator and the influence of environmental conditions. The instructions for a character can be quite open-ended, allowing multiple conditional responses or a gradual fixation through learning. As well as distinguishing between entities on the basis of the range of their behavioral options, we must carefully examine the underlying transmission mechanisms.

Fourth, it is unclear what is meant by the notion that Lamarckism promotes quick learning. Lamarckism promotes a quicker encoding of the properties of the environment, assuming that acquired traits are somehow correctly back-translated into the replicator. But this quicker encoding may have little effect on the pace of learning relative to the rate of replication. To understand quick learning at the population level, we must take a closer look at replication. But quick learning at the individual level does not necessarily involve replication and, thus, has nothing to do with Lamarckism as we define it.

The description *Larmarckian* carries severe problems in the social domain. Whether we regard ideas, memes, habits, or routines as replicators, then their replication is not usefully described as *Lamarckian*. No such a priori problems of transferability apply to the core Darwinian principles.

4.5. THE IMPORTANCE OF THE GENOTYPE-PHENOTYPE AND REPLICATOR-INTERACTOR DISTINCTIONS

Ironically, as noted above, devotees of the Lamarckian idea that acquired characters are inherited are obliged to use the genotype-phenotype (or replicator-interactor) distinction to make this claim and establish a meaningful notion of inheritance. We hold that this distinction is vital in social evolution even if Lamarckian inheritance does not occur. This section underlines its importance.

Darwin did not use the terms *genotype* and *phenotype*, but some such conceptual separation was implicit in his discourse. He assumed that information related to biological characteristics was transmitted from generation to generation through such information-carrying entities as seeds, sperm, ova, pollen, or stigma. Inheritance and preservation of information across many generations was, therefore, central to his theory of evolution by natural selection. As Darwin (1859, 142) put it: "Natural selection can act only by the preservation and accumulation of infinitesimally small inherited modifications, each profitable to the preserved being."

When Darwin (1859, 1868) wrote of "inherited modifications" and "structures" that were preserved in "germ cells" and "instincts," he was referring to the processes of genotypic, not phenotypic, replication.[19] He denied that replication occurred by the immediate or direct copying of characteristics, also suggesting a distinction between genotype and phenotype. This distinction is now central to modern biology.[20]

The literature on the concept of selection establishes the importance of the distinction between the relatively cohesive entities that are actually being selected (the phenotypes or interactors) and the components that replicate differentially as a result of selection (the genotypes or replicators). In later chapters, we propose firms and other cohesive organizations as social interactors. Candidate social replicators include habits, customs, routines, and "folkways" (Keller 1915; Nelson and Winter 1982). The hitherto incomplete task that we attempt below is to develop clear definitions and criteria with which to identify social interactors and replicators.

The application of the replicator-interactor distinction to social evolution is tricky, and some authors have questioned its use or value in the social domain.[21] Some express the fear that the use of this distinction in social evolution implies that, at the social level, there is something very similar to genes or that replicators and interactors are always sharply defined or differentiated. These fears are ungrounded. The replicator and interactor concepts are defined with sufficient abstractness to accommodate their hugely different concrete manifestations in different spheres. And the use of the replicator-interactor distinction in an evolutionary context must consider the very emergence of that distinction and of fuzzy transitional forms.

Furthermore, the use of the replicator-interactor distinction in biology is not simply a matter of genes and organisms. For instance, it has been argued that lengths of RNA, lengths of DNA, chromosomes, and gametes

19. The gene was elusive to Darwin, but he anticipated its function. Throughout *Origin* and other writings, he describes how inherited modifications are preserved in "instincts" and "germ cells." Germ is mentioned in Darwin's Notebooks B and E, and instincts are mentioned in almost all his notebooks. In his theory of "pangenesis," Darwin (1868) conjectured that information is preserved and inherited via "gemmules" given off by cells in the bloodstream.

20. The *genotype-phenotype* terminology was introduced in 1911 by the Danish biologist Wilhelm Johannsen, who also coined the term *gene* in 1909, intending it to serve the same purpose as Darwin's *pangen* (Keller and Lloyd 1992).

21. Nelson and Nelson (2003, 1646) and Nelson (2007a) have expressed doubts regarding the replicator-interactor distinction in the social domain. Previously, by contrast, Nelson and Winter (1982, 134–36, 160–61) described organizational "routines as genes," and Nelson (2002, 140) wrote that "practices and policies embodied in firms are like 'genotypes'" and that firms themselves "are like 'phenotypes.'" This formulation sustains a replicator-interactor distinction but misleadingly associates the replicator with "practices." Practices are not replicators but their expressions. Such imprecision helped engender the doubt.

can function as interactors (Hull 1988, 2001b; Brandon 1998). There is also a case for regarding seeds, pollen, and sperm as interactors while they carry genes as replicators, despite their intimate involvement in the machinery of replication. Dawkins (1982) famously extended the phenotype beyond the organism and its behavior, to include aspects of its environment. Even groups, populations, and species have been considered as possible interactors (Hull 1988, 2001b; Brandon 1998). Furthermore, the boundaries of phenotypes (or interactors) are difficult to determine in many cases, such as with neural and immune systems.

As noted in later chapters, similar definitional and boundary problems exist also in the social or economic domain. It would be a mistake to suggest that, while the replicator-interactor distinction is generally clear and unproblematic in biology, it is not so in social evolution and, hence, that the concepts of replicator and interactor should not be applied to the latter. The premise is false: the replicator-interactor distinction is often tricky in the biological sphere as well.[22]

And some evolutionary processes are possible without the existence of distinct replicators and interactors. Consider our world before the evolution of DNA and RNA. In the primordial soup, it is likely that the first replicating entities in the earliest evolution were both replicators and interactors (Eigen et al. 1981; Darnell and Doolittle 1986; Eigen 1994; Brandon 1998; Joyce 2002; Shapiro 2006). DNA later evolved, with genes fulfilling specialized functions as replicators (Maynard Smith and Szathmáry 1995).

But replicators are important in more complex evolving systems. Without the preservation of valuable information in a replicator, the phenotypes could soak up and transmit any environmental disturbance and cumulate irrelevant and erroneous traits. Replicators provide a degree of baseline stability so that vaguely efficacious selection of interactors (phenotypes) can occur. Such stability, exhibited in substantial information storage and a

22. The problems concerning its biological application are sufficiently severe to lead a minority of philosophers of biology to drop these concepts (Griesemer 1994, 1999; Griffiths and Gray 1994, 1997; Wimsatt 1999). We criticize some of their arguments in chapter 6. Godfrey-Smith (2009) is also skeptical of the replicator concept, which he misleadingly treats as an entity "that makes copies of itself" (p. 5) alongside almost no discussion of the allied concept of the interactor. Instead, in our view, the replicator is an information-retaining and copiable mechanism, hosted by the entity of the interactor. Treating the replicator as an informational mechanism associated with an interactor dispenses with some of the problems identified by Godfrey-Smith. He also rightly points out that not all Darwinian evolution involves replicators. But we add that the evolution of greater complexity depends generally on generative replicators, and that such replicators are important in the social domain (see chapter 6).

high degree of cultural and institutional conservatism, is also characteristic of social evolution. Without faithful social replicators, the accumulation of every panic, craze, fad, and fashion would completely disrupt the transmission and selection of tried and tested social knowledge.

If there are no social replicators, then the principles of generalized Darwinism suggest that there is no mechanism in social evolution by which information concerning adaptations to the environment can be copied with some degree of fidelity through time. This further implies that social evolution is less sophisticated than biological evolution and has a more limited potential for the evolution of more complex phenomena. We see no reason to accept the premise of this argument. It is important to understand mechanisms of inheritance at the social level, and there is at least a prima facie case for identifying interactors and replicators in the social domain.

CHAPTER FIVE

The Principle of Selection and Its Application to Social Evolution

Natural selection will not necessarily produce absolute perfection; nor, as far as we can judge by our limited faculties, can absolute perfection be everywhere found.

CHARLES DARWIN, (1859)

It is . . . only by injecting a wholly illegitimate teleological meaning to the term "fittest" . . . that the expression "survival of the fittest" is made to mean a survival of the socially desirable individuals.

THORSTEIN VEBLEN, (1896)

The central argument in this volume is that Darwinian principles of variation, selection, and replication (or inheritance) apply to social evolution. But this claim depends on sufficiently clear definitions of these core concepts. The purpose of this chapter is to clarify the idea of selection and to consider some of its different forms. Replication is tackled in the next chapter. Variation is discussed in several places in this volume.

Selection operates in nature through the elimination of the relatively unfit members of each species. The gory sight of nature "red in tooth and claw" makes many social scientists recoil from the idea that Darwinian principles might apply to social evolution as well. But, to consider the possibility of their application, we must focus primarily neither on the death agony of the zebra as the lion's teeth rip into its neck, nor on the litany of atrocities committed by humans on numerous species, including our own, but on the abstract definition of *selection* at the core of the Darwinian paradigm. Only then can we carefully consider its possible manifestations in the social realm.

Selection is often presented as a brutal process involving intense competition over limited resources. But even in nature there are examples of selection that depart from this. Processes of selection and evolution where moths change color as a result of changing industrial activity and insects develop immunity to DDT "do not involve there being a common resource in short supply. Competition is a special case, not a defining characteristic, of natural selection" (Sober 1981, 100).[1] Furthermore, Darwin recognized forms of selection—notably sexual selection and artificial selection—that, while having winners and losers, necessarily involve neither pitiless struggle nor painful death. Even in the natural world, selection is not necessarily red in tooth and claw.

Nevertheless, it is important to realize that the definition of *selection* is not a matter of taste or semantics, with one answer being as good as another (Pepper and Knudsen 2001). A tradition of rigorous mathematical description of the selection process in biology provides a foundation for developing a general theory. Formal representations of selection are quite explicit about the possibility of weak selection pressures and suboptimal outcomes.

There is an ongoing dispute over the relative importance of selection in biological evolution. Some evolutionary biologists such as Masahiko Kimura (1983) emphasize drift. But establishing its relative importance in explaining variation is largely a matter of empirical inquiry. But, without some role for selection, evolution would be a random walk—which does not seem to be the case in reality. Darwin's (1859, 6) own position on this question has stood the test of time: "I am convinced that Natural Selection has been the main but not exclusive means of modification." We believe that selection is also important in social evolution, but it is not the only mechanism of change.

A technical definition of *selection* has been developed by George Price (1970, 1995) and is now widely accepted in the biological literature and elsewhere. Using this definition, we describe two forms of selection that commonly occur in both nature and society. These definitions leave aside the explanation of the selection criterion and why entities possess stable traits. Such questions must be tackled in the light of empirical inquiry.

If we define *fitness* as that quality that is selected, then, clearly, selection and fitness are related by definition. To avoid this tautological formulation, *fitness* must be defined in a different way. In biology, there are several ways of doing this (Mills and Beatty 1979; De Jong 1994), but the most promising is to refer to the propensity of a genotype to produce offspring. As George C. Williams (1966, 23) puts it: "[Fitness] is measured by the extent to which [an allele] contributes genes to later generations of the population of which it is a member." Survival of the fittest is no longer a tautology: it is possi-

---

1. Richard Lewontin (1978) also argues that competition for limited resources is unnecessary for natural selection. We agree. And cooperation is an especially important phenomenon, at least in the social world.

bly false. With drift, for example, the composition and characteristics of a population change in a manner unrelated to individual fitness values.

Although fitness plays a central role in Darwinian theory, it is a difficult concept both to define and to measure. Even in biology it is elusive. Few empirical studies measure fitness in terms of a propensity to produce offspring, as this is difficult to ascertain. Use is made instead of proxy measures of fitness. The fitness of male plants is sometimes measured by the rate at which their pollen is removed (Harder 2006). Other fitness proxies include juvenile growth rates (Lampert and Sommer 2007) and the number of offspring produced in a single generation. These examples bluntly allude to reproductive success rather than the fitness value of a particular characteristic or allele. Another approach uses the overall rate of energy acquisition as a proxy for fitness (Mangel 2006).

Measuring fitness in social evolution is arguably even more complicated, partly because of the widespread occurrence of different types of replication processes such as diffusion. *Fitness* in social evolution can usefully refer to a particular property of a replicator and the propensity of replicators with that property to produce copies and increase the frequency of similar replicators in the population. The fitness of an interactor is the propensity of its replicators to replicate, by diffusion to other interactors or by making copies of the interactor. But, again, these are difficult to measure. Evolutionary social scientists have used both survival and profitability rates as proxies for fitness (Klepper 2002a, 2002b; Boschma and Wenting 2007). In section 5.5 below, we elaborate on common principles that relate selection and fitness.

Selection processes both in nature and in human society are relatively complex, operating at multiple levels of organization, and involving multiple interdependent selection criteria. Errors creep in, with the result that the selection process becomes inefficient. Fitness is necessarily context dependent, and this means that no optimum is fixed or absolute. There are often multiple equilibria, and superior fitness peaks can lie undiscovered. Although the fitness of an entity affects its chances of selection, the process does not necessarily lead to optimal or near-optimal outcomes where only the fittest survive. Similar arguments show that the most productive or profitable firms are not necessarily the ones that survive competition (Winter 1964, 1971; Boyd and Richerson 1980; Schaffer 1989; Hodgson 1993).

Consequently, selection does not necessarily lead to overall efficiency or systematic improvement. As Darwin himself explained, it is a haphazard process. Sometimes it can lead to the gradual honing of performance, but it can be diverted in different directions and fail to eliminate inefficiencies or

anomalies. Suboptimal evolutionary processes—producing traits that yield
replication rates or chances of survival that are below the maximum in the
circumstances—are commonplace in both nature and human society.

Both Darwin and his colleague Alfred Russel Wallace worried that use of
the word *selection* might be taken to imply the existence of an agent doing
the selecting and that some could take this agent to be God. Today, social
scientists have a different worry: the use of the term *selection* in the context
of social evolution might undermine the role of human agency and deny
the existence of human intentionality. But, in the social domain, insofar
as selection involves human interaction or deliberation, it always involves
choice and preference in some way: selection excludes neither intentionality nor agency.

In common usage, *selection* is synonymous with *choice*, connoting the act
of selecting, as in the selection of an item from a restaurant menu or a new
manager to fill an open position. In contrast, the scientific usage of *selection*
has a very precise meaning, referring to a change in the composition of a
population leading to a change in its properties (traits), such as the colors
of a population of moths or the size distribution of firms in an industry. But
this scientific meaning does not necessarily exclude choice.

Toward the end of this chapter, we introduce the concept of diffusion
and ask whether it should be treated as a type of selection. Diffusion is
important in the social domain. Although the definition of *selection* adopted
here is very broad, diffusion is established as a separate phenomenon and a
type of inheritance rather than selection.

5.1. *SELECTION* DEFINED

Following a mathematical definition developed by George Price (1995), we
describe the general concept of selection in the following way:

> *Selection* involves an anterior set of entities that is somehow being transformed
> into a posterior set, where all members of the posterior set are sufficiently simi-
> lar to some members of the anterior set, and where the resulting frequencies of
> posterior entities are correlated positively and causally with their fitness in the
> environmental context. The transformation from the anterior to the posterior
> set is caused by the entities' interaction within a particular environment.[2]

2. The technical definition of *selection* is explored at greater length elsewhere (Price 1995;
Frank 1998; Hofbauer and Sigmund 1998; Pepper and Knudsen 2001; Knudsen 2002a, 2004b;
Andersen 2004; Henrich 2004; Okasha 2006) and summarized in the appendix to this chapter.

Price's definition is so general that it would apply to the simple case of the selection of items for purchase in a shop. But such groups of items are not necessarily complex population systems, as described in earlier chapters. Goods in a store do not necessarily struggle to survive or pass on knowledge to others through replication or imitation. Our primary concern here is with complex population systems. Although Price's formulation is more general, we concentrate our discussion of selection on entities that are interactors and embody replicators.

The twin concepts of replicator and interactor lie behind Elliott Sober's (1984) very useful distinction between "selection *of*" and "selection *for*." For example, the selection *of* zebras (owing to predators, disease, and other adversities) leads to changes in the zebra population and its gene pool, involving selection *for* specific genes that may bestow fitness advantages in particular contexts. There is selection *of* interactors (such as organisms or business firms) and selection *for* replicators (such as genes, habits, or routines). The importance of this of/for distinction will be elaborated later, but we must note that it is explicit in neither the Price definition of selection nor the Price equation. The Price formalism does not itself require the replicator-interactor distinction. But *successor selection* (defined below) does refer to replication.

Stephen Gould and Elizabeth Vrba (1986) introduced a distinction between "sorting" and "selection" where sorting is a purely descriptive observation of differential mortality or reproductive success. Sorting includes drift as well as selection. When *sorting* refers to selection, it is selection *of* because *sorting* refers to interactors but not replicators. But sorting and selection *of* are not the same, and, importantly, the selection concept is designed to accommodate causal explanations as well as descriptions.

We regard each anterior set as including and exhausting one universal class of entities, such as a species (a class of organisms) or a population of firms (a class of organizations). This means that elimination from the set can be only through extinction (and not through emigration). New entities can appear in the posterior set, but only in consequence of a replication process (and not through immigration). Particular entities do not reappear after they have gone extinct.

It would be possible to complicate the picture by considering immigration and emigration as well as birth and extinction. The geographic location and boundaries of the anterior and posterior sets would have to be considered. We would have to face the definitional question whether migration entails exit from or entrance into an anterior or a posterior set. If these sets had geographic boundaries, then migration would be a reason for entry or exit. Such redefinitions would make matters much more convoluted without any obvious advantages. At least in the present work, we shall stick to the assumptions outlined in the preceding paragraph.

Through selection, a population of entities will gradually adapt in response to a complex of environmental factors. It is vital to make a distinction between (*a*) changes in a population and its traits that result from selection and (*b*) changes in population traits that result from the adaption or development of individual entities. These processes of adaptation or development can involve growth, experimentation, and the communication of information from entity to entity. Such transmission and innovation effects alter individual entities, even when the population is held constant. In contrast, selection alters the composition of the whole population, even when the properties of individual entities are unchanged.

The general definition of *selection* presented here has a number of advantages. While settling its meaning, it does this in an abstract and general way that makes no reference to any particular empirical domain, be it physical, biological, or social. Furthermore, as shown below, it encompasses two different and important types of selection process (Price 1995; Knudsen 2002a, 2004b).

This general definition does not imply that selection outcomes are necessarily improvements or asymptotic to global optima. All the Price equation implies in this regard is some systematic relation between fitness and survival. It is a frequent misunderstanding that *selection* necessarily means efficiency or improvement.

5.2. SUBSET SELECTION

Two concepts of selection are employed in science. One involves the selection of a subset of elements from a set. Examples include the selection of a subset of chickens that survive an attack by a fox and the selection of a subset of firms that survive an industry shakeout. Price (1995) termed this *subset selection*. Subset selection is very different from the concept of successor selection[3]—which was part of Darwin's great achievement—where offspring are not subsets of parents. Successor selection involves replication, whereas subset selection is a simple elimination process.

---

3. The term *successor selection* is ours. In an earlier work (Hodgson and Knudsen 2006b), we used the term *generative selection*. But this is changed here because below we apply the adjective *generative* (with a different meaning) to the contrasting phenomenon of replication.

Consider the following example from nature (Landa et al. 1999). There is an anterior distribution of speed in a herd of reindeer. A chasing wolverine slays several of the slower beasts. Hence, the distribution of speed in reindeer is transformed in the posterior set, and there is a significant and positive selection for higher average speed. But subset selection would also occur if an avalanche eliminated reindeer at random or perhaps even the fastest reindeer.

A similar argument holds for subset selection as it applies to firms and other institutions. The portrayal of industry dynamics as a selection process is well established in the economics of strategy. For example, subset selection can cause a shift in the industrywide distribution of firm size. Landmark contributions include Lippman and Rumelt (1982), Nelson and Winter (1982), and Klepper (1996). See also box 5.1.

Subset selection is defined as selection through one cycle of environmental interaction and elimination of entities in a population structured in such a way that the environmental interaction causes elimination to be differential. Each cycle of subset selection eliminates some variation. In a formal description, subset selection is a contraction mapping. Each cycle of subset selection contracts the anterior set, yielding a posterior set with fewer elements than are in the anterior set. On its own, subset selection will eventually run dry of variation.

Many natural and social processes involve subset selection. Molecules, cells, plants, moths, reindeer, and tigers are populations of biological interactors whose properties are altered by subset selection. Hard winters, hot summers, and various natural catastrophes commonly eliminate organisms. Similarly, firms and other social organizations are populations of social interactors altered by subset selection, such as through bankruptcy. Through the elimination of some interactors, subset selection also shapes the properties of populations of biological replicators, such as genes, and social replicators, such as habits and routines.

In cases where selection results from physical or natural events, such as earthquakes, subset selection does not generally involve choice and preference. But, when selection operates through deliberative or social processes, human choices and preferences are always involved, even if indirectly. Bankruptcy, for example, can result from inefficient production processes, limited market orientation, actual or perceived dishonesty, or ineffective internal organization (Tushman and Anderson 1986; Aldrich 1999; McMillan 2002). In such cases, choices and preferences are involved in some way because deliberate choices of managers led to failure.

But the overall selection outcome may not itself be a direct reflection of

BOX 5.1 *Industry dynamics and selection*

Empirical studies spanning a large number of industries have established that industry dynamics is a selection process where entry and exit of firms change the industrywide properties of firms, including product technology, efficiency, and size. Here is Steven Klepper and Elizabeth Graddy's (1990, 35) characterization of this selection process:

> The prototypical new industry tends to develop as follows. Initially, little is known about the attributes of the new product desired by demanders. The early entrants into the industry are typically small and have experience in related technologies. Sometimes they are users of the new product, while in other instances they are spinoffs of incumbent firms. They often introduce major product innovations based on information about users' needs and/or the technological means available to satisfy them. Market shares often change rapidly as successful innovators displace less efficient rivals, as was the case in the early history of the auto, aircraft engine, and airframe industries (Klein 1977).
>
> The initial uncertainty that characterizes new industries appears to restrain the growth of incumbent firms. Over time, the uncertainty abates as "dominant designs" emerge for various features of the product. Firms able to produce these designs prosper and grow, while firms that are unable to adapt exit the industry. Innovations in the industry become more incremental and tend to embody a smaller degree of inventiveness (Utterback and Abernathy 1975). The slowdown in major innovations tends to cause market shares to stabilize, as Klein (1977) documents for the automobile and airframe industries and Mansfield (1962) demonstrates for the steel, petroleum, and tire industries.
>
> While new industries tend to follow a prototypical pattern, not all firms in an industry follow the same strategy over time (Hayes and Wheelwright 1979a, 1979b), and not all industries proceed at the same pace (Abernathy 1978; Porter 1983). Two factors appear to have an important effect on the pace of the prototypical evolutionary process: the characteristics of the product's technology and the nature of buyers' preferences. Products characterized by limited opportunities for technological change tend to be subject to less uncertainty and to reach maturity faster. Where products are characterized by considerable diversity in buyers' preferences, it is more difficult for dominant designs to emerge, which tends to lengthen the time it takes to reach maturity.

Industry evolution in a market economy is, thus, a complex process of interaction of firms with buyers, competitors, and suppliers, involving changes

BOX 5.1 (*continued*)

in both technology and market context. It involves processes of subset selection and differential elimination of firms.

Industry entry and exit patterns point to subset selection as a major force in industry evolution. Dunne, Roberts, and Samuelson (1988), Klepper and Graddy (1990), Geroski (1995), and others have provided comprehensive evidence on this. Dunne, Roberts, and Samuelson (1988) examined patterns of firm entry and exit in U.S. manufacturing industries. Their data were based on 387 four-digit U.S. manufacturing industries over the period 1963–82, with each five-year census containing between 300,000 and 350,000 plants. They found that, on average, 38.6 percent of the firms in operation in each industry in each census year were not producing in that industry in the previous census. This massive inflow of new entrants replaced exits, with exit rates varying between 30.8 and 39.0 percent between each pair of census years. These numbers point to selection forces as a major driver of industry evolution.

Selection forces shape industry structures and change the features of populations of firms. For example, Dunne, Roberts, and Samuelson (1988, 500) reported evidence pointing to a fitness advantage of multiplant over single-plant firms. From 1963 to 1982, the total number of multiplant firms increased from 14,691 to 21,632, an increase of 47.2 percent. This change in the composition of features among populations of firms was primarily caused by subset selection in the form of firm entry and exit. It led to dominance of multiplant over single-plant firms. While this example provides striking evidence of the force of subset selection, it should be remembered that the criteria and mechanisms of selection are active at multiple levels of organization and are generally varied and contingent (Katz and Gartner 1988; Aldrich 2004).

Because interactions among buyers, competitors, and suppliers typically lead to changes in the selection environment, the detailed mechanisms and criteria of selection vary through time and location. For example, during the credit crunch of 2007–9, access to credit became the vital selection criterion for many firms. By contrast, during an economic boom, the capacity for adaptive growth may be the most important selection criterion, and, in turn, this may be constrained by the scarcity of skilled management personnel (Penrose 1959).

the discrete decision of a single person or group. When this occurs, it is regarded as artificial selection. Artificial selection can occur as a special case of either subset or successor selection.

It is important to emphasize that the selection environment is not necessarily fixed and that it can be endogenous to the selection process. Powerful (groups of) entities can sometimes change the selection rules. Firms can stimulate consumer demand, lobby governments, or bribe judges. The matter is further complicated because the selection of firms is a process operating at multiple interdependent levels. Even though such complications introduce multiple, recursive, and nested components in the selection criterion (or fitness function)—thus complicating the unique identification of the causes of a change in a population property—they can readily be accommodated in the modern selection formalism derived from Price's formulation.

Environmental feedback effectively selects among firms with stable properties; some survive, while others are eliminated through bankruptcy or closure (McMillan 2002). (The takeover of one firm by another is a more complicated case and discussed in chapter 7 below.) As firms exit the population, the average value of a population property held by these firms can change. Should firms with many hierarchical layers exit, there is a decrease in the average number of hierarchical layers in their population. Change in a population property resulting from the differential elimination of firms is a common case of subset selection in an economy. Similar arguments apply to the selection of nation-states and civilizations.

Subset selection decouples the generation of new variation from the process of selection and leaves unexplained the variation in the anterior set. It assumes a selection criterion that alters the distribution of the variation in a relatively stable population property. According to Winter (1971), Nelson and Winter (1982), Hannan and Freeman (1989), and many others, organizational routines are such stable components.

5.3. SUCCESSOR SELECTION

Successor selection involves replication and is more complex than subset selection. In successor selection, the change in a population property, such as the color of a moth, happens because the interaction of moths with their environment gives rise to differential replication. Moths with better camouflage are less likely to be eaten by predators and, therefore, on average, leave more offspring carrying their genes. In this way, dark moths become more frequent in polluted areas. When smokeless zones are introduced and the bark of trees becomes lighter in hue, the color of the moth population can again become lighter in response (Cook, Mani, and Varley 1986; Cook, Mani, and Wynnes 1985).

Successor selection is defined as selection through one cycle of replication, variation, and environmental interaction so structured that the replication process causes new variation (i.e., novel varieties alter the distribution of population properties) and the environmental interaction causes replication to be differential.[4]

Darwinian evolution involves repeated cycles of successor selection. The generation of novelty is integral to this process. New variation is generated because replication is imperfect or because it involves novel combinations of existing variants.

Consider successor selection among reindeer. There is an anterior distribution of potential speed among these animals. Environmental interaction transforms the anterior distribution into an intermediate set (some reindeer die; some are less attractive mating partners) that is then transformed into a new posterior set by replication. There is replacement of entities because of death and replication. Through genetic inheritance, the faster tend to have the more speedy offspring.[5] The faster have a higher survival rate and, therefore, replicate more, resulting in a significant increase of fast reindeer in the posterior set. There is positive selection *of* faster reindeer and a complementary selection *for* genes bestowing higher speed. But successor selection could also occur because a complex of factors influenced the environmental interaction of reindeer. Attention to unusual environmental factors and care for offspring could influence replication as well as the ability to run at fast pace.

In nature, successor selection often occurs in cycles that correspond to the replacement of one generation by the next. But our definition of *successor selection* does not necessarily imply that any entity in the population expires. It simply requires that there be new variation leading to differential replication. In nature, new genotypic variation is typically created through the procreation of offspring. But, in human society, as we shall elaborate below, there are additional mechanisms through which variety can be enhanced.

Although outcomes of selection processes are seldom designed and often unpredictable, in social evolution human intentions and choices play their part at every stage. They are involved in processes of imitation that lead to replication and in the development of social institutions. Human agency

4. This definition of *successor selection* is based on Hull, Langman, and Glenn (2001). Successor selection is a particularly important member of the set of distinctive selection processes encompassed by Price's (1995) definition, but Price does not use the term.

5. The definitions of *selection*, *replication*, and *interaction* employed here do not in principle exclude the Lamarckian possibility of the inheritance of acquired characters. But see our discussion in chapter 4 above.

is crucial. Successor selection implies neither that humans are passive nor that they are relieved of their powers of reflection or foresight.

Artificial selection often amounts to subset selection followed by successor selection. Choosing pigeons for breeding is subset selection. Breeding them for offspring involves successor selection.

As in the case of subset selection, the definition of *successor selection* leaves aside any explanation of the selection criterion and the existence of a stable population property. The feedback from environmental interaction to replication involves additional specific mechanisms and, likewise, the stability of the population property.

But, unlike subset selection, successor selection encompasses a process by which new variation is created. Through replication error (mutation) and genetic recombination, the offspring of reindeer can acquire properties that differ from those possessed by their parents. More generally, whenever replication processes lead to imperfect copies, successor selection generates new variation.

New variation may or may not result from environmental interaction and fitness. With selection, the outcomes are related to fitness. Replication that does not depend on fitness is defined as drift. In the next two paragraphs, we compare successor selection with the special cases of drift and exaptation.

Drift generates new variation that can fuel subsequent selection processes. Especially with small populations, the effects of drift can be cumulative. This is because random sampling from a small population exhibits longer spells with notable deviations from the average sampling path. In biological and social evolution, innovation and novelty can emerge as a result of drift. This would require that stimuli from the environment led to outcomes unrelated to fitness. But there is evidence of systematic relations between properties of some social organizations and their survival as well of the general impact of the environment.[6] To this extent, selection overshadows drift in social evolution.

Drift would occur only if marginal changes in traits brought little alteration to fitness values. This happens if the fitness surface is relatively flat for a time in a locality. Flatter fitness surfaces sometimes allow evolution

6. On firm properties and survival, see Dunne, Roberts, and Samuelson (1988, 1989), Audretsch (1991), Audretsch and Mahmood (1994, 1995), Suarez and Utterback (1995), Agarwal and Gort (1996), and Klepper (2002b). On environmental stimuli as the dominant drivers of industry evolution, see Rosenberg (1982), Basalla (1989), Vincenti (1990), Lipsey, Carlaw, and Bekar (2005).

to explore possibilities that later prove adaptive, through changes in the fitness landscape. This creates the possibility of *exaptation*, where a trait or feature becomes used for a purpose different from that which it was originally selected by evolution (Gould and Vrba 1982). For example, birds' feathers evolved for insulation but later became used for flight; penguins' wings evolved for flight but are now used for swimming. Vinyl disk players were used to play music but are now revived to create music of a special genre (Faulkner and Runde 2009), words in a language change their meaning, and marriage was originally a religious requirement (partly to establish paternity and to counter illegitimacy) but now has a significantly different function. But such outcomes are always limited by the (possibly changing) fitness landscape and selection pressure. The fact that drift and exaptation are not ubiquitous in social evolution means either that selection is playing a significant role or that other phenomena like lock-in (David 1985; Arthur 1989) are preventing drift.

Environmental changes can introduce new variation by changing the fitness landscape or selection criteria so that the replication process proceeds on a new path (e.g., by altering market or ecological niches).[7] The selection criteria can be captured as components in the fitness function. Environmental changes would set the replication process on a new path if the value of these fitness components were changed.

Successor selection applies to replicating populations in which continuity or similarity result from replication and the transfer of (cultural or genetic) information, whereas subset selection applies to populations in which continuity is secured by the survival of a subset of entities. In successor selection, each instance of replication is capable of creating new variation through imperfect copying or new combinations.

An evolutionary process involving repeated cycles of successor selection can, in principle, continue indefinitely because imperfect replication generates new variation along the way, whereas subset selection removes variation and eventually grinds to a halt. Because of the remarkable endurance of some forms of culture, it is unlikely that they have been sustained principally by subset selection.

It is also possible that successor selection is present at multiple interdependent levels in human society. Identification of a hierarchy of social

7. Environmental changes can also directly alter replicators (e.g., habits modified by institutional adjustments or radioactivity causing genetic mutations). But these are not the most important sources of variation.

BOX 5.2 *Abuse of the Darwinian selection concept*

Consider some examples in which the Darwinian selection concept has been abused, by its critics or by its devotees.

In a widely popularized volume, graced with an adulatory preface by former president Theodore Roosevelt, the American entomologist Vernon L. Kellogg noted conversations with leading echelons of the German academy and military during the First World War. A German professor of biology is reported as saying: "This war is necessary as a test of the German position and claim. If Germany is beaten, it will prove that she has moved along the wrong evolutionary line, and should be beaten. If she wins, it will prove that she is on the right way, and that the rest of the world, at least that part which . . . the Allies represent, is on the wrong way and should, for the sake of the right evolution of the human race, be stopped and put on the right way—or else be destroyed as unfit" (Kellogg 1917, 30). Although Kellogg describes this view as "Neo-Darwinism," meaning "natural selection applied rigorously to human life and society," and his reports helped persuade some social scientists that all links between the social sciences and biology must be severed (Hodgson 2004b, 2006a), no basis for any part of this statement will be found in Darwin's writings. (Notably, Kellogg did not use the term *social Darwinism*. Before the 1940s, this term was very rare [Bannister 1979; Hodgson 2004b].)

There is nothing necessarily right about the survivors of selection, just as the eliminated are not necessarily wrong. *Right* and *wrong* are ambiguous terms, and the German professor covertly shifts their meaning from matters of efficiency to morality. In both nature and human society, there is no general reason why selected entities should be regarded as morally superior.

Furthermore, in general, *selection* does not necessarily mean *efficiency* or *superiority* either (using reasonable definitions of those terms). Failure to be selected does not imply the general inferiority of a whole nation. Military conflict is one among several possible mechanisms of selection, and other forms of competition could lead to different winners. The fact that Genghis Khan invaded much of Asia and established the largest contiguous empire in history can be explained largely in terms of superior Mongol military tactics and numbers. It does not mean that Mongol social organization or culture was more advanced. Market-based competition between nations does not imply that the winners are superior in military, cultural, or moral respects. Both war and markets are of limited effectiveness as tests of either the general fitness or the superiority of a nation. In any case, given the haphazardness of selection as a process, even a long conflict between just two (internally heterogeneous) military blocs is hardly decisive as an experiment.

BOX 5.2 (*continued*)

One cannot conclude from Darwinism that war is either necessary or desirable. The ideology of German opinion leaders at the time was much more nationalist than Darwinian. Yet this war and its bellicose nationalism were factors leading to a widespread rejection of Darwinism among social scientists.

Our second example is the commonplace argument that competitive markets lead to greater efficiency (e.g., Friedman 1953) and that state interference inhibits this process. Writers in this vein sometimes presume that competitive processes similar to natural selection lead to efficient outcomes (Williamson 1975).

But economic theory has demonstrated that markets lead to efficient or optimal outcomes under very special and extreme circumstances only (Stiglitz 1991). The evidence does not confirm that, generally, the most prosperous and efficient economies have minimal states (Kenworthy 1995; Dore 2000; Nelson 2003). The attempt to use biology to justify free market ideology is both undeveloped and unconvincing. It usually emphasizes human selfishness and ignores the biology of human cooperation (Darwin 1871; Field 2001; Hammerstein 2003; Henrich 2004; Bowles and Gintis 2005a, 2005b; Bowles 2006).

In contrast to individualistic or gene-centered conceptions of evolution, economic evolution involves competition at multiple levels, including between individual workers, individual firms, and nation-states. Sometimes the conditions for efficiency improvement at one level conflict with those at another. For example, competition between firms could be more effective if competition and mobility among the workforce were reduced, leading to enhanced teamwork and learning (Campbell 1994).

Competition between firms does not mean that the more efficient or productive will survive (Winter 1964, 1971; Boyd and Richerson 1980; Schaffer 1989; Hodgson 1993). One reason is that the economic environment of selection is highly variable. Firms that do well in one institutional context may do badly in another (Amable 2000, 2003; Aoki 2001; Hall and Soskice 2001; Boyer 2005; Kenworthy 2006; Gagliardi 2009).

As always, fitness is context dependent. And government is unavoidably responsible for that context, including workable institutions of property and contract, on which markets depend. While the Darwinian paradigm points to the limitations of central design and control of highly complex systems, it neither favors or disfavors a predominantly free market ideology nor favors or disfavors the possibility of significant and effective state intervention (Hodgson 1999; Singer 1999; Beinhocker 2006). By contrast, a Darwinian approach entails an adaptive search for a viable mixture of state and market that is sensitive to prevailing circumstances.

organization through which selection processes occur requires that we single out a social interactor at each level (Hull 1988, 2001b; Brandon 1998, 1999). That is, we must provide a definition of a social interactor and its corresponding replicator if we wish to succeed in identifying a possible hierarchy of successor selection processes in the social domain (or rejecting such a claim). These issues are addressed in later chapters.

As in biology, there is no simple and adequate answer to the pressing question of why some entities are selected and others are not. It is necessary to identify those particular characteristics and properties that contribute to fitness in a given environment. In Darwinian theory, fitness is an important placeholder for specific detailed explanations rather than an adequate explanation in itself. Darwinism imposes an explanatory requirement and framework: it does not provide a full and detailed explanation.

This does not mean that the task of detailed explanation is unimportant or avoidable. A developed theory of social evolution requires explanations why some organizations survive and others expire and why some habits and routines proliferate while others decay. Explanations can be different in different contexts. For example, a country with a relatively unregulated banking system can enjoy decades of enhanced prosperity and entrepreneurship but suffer a more serious crisis than its rivals when market confidence is challenged. Specific forms of firm organization seem to work better in some institutional and cultural contexts than others (Whitley 1999; Amable 2000, 2003; Aoki 2001; Hall and Soskice 2001; Boyer 2005; Kenworthy 2006; Barnett 2008; Gagliardi 2009). Nevertheless, there may be properties such as clarity of communication and effective coordination that are widely advantageous for business firms. It is the task of the empirical researcher to uncover the relative importance of these properties as selection criteria (or components in the fitness function).

Because of misunderstanding and ideological abuse (we give examples in box 5.2), many social scientists have eschewed the concept of selection. The precise definition offered here, with acknowledgment of context dependence and careful consideration of the idea of fitness, should demonstrate its analytic utility and avoid such abuses and misunderstandings.

5.4. DIFFUSION, REPLICATION, REPLICATOR MANIPULATION, AND SELECTION

In this section, we compare selection with some other concepts. The discussion of selection offered above did not invoke a spatial dimension. The possibilities of emigration from the anterior set and immigration into the posterior set are excluded. In this section, we consider the particular phenomenon of diffusion, which typically involves space as well as time. In his classic *Diffusion of Innovations*, Everett Rogers (1995) wrote: "Diffusion is a kind of social change, defined as the process by which an innovation is communicated through certain channels over time among the members of a social system. It is a special type of communication, in that the messages are concerned with new ideas." Diffusion is here the successive transmission of a property—involving information and the capacity to use it—from one entity to another, through time and space.

Members of an anterior set possess particular properties. In one increment of diffusion, this anterior set transforms into a posterior set consisting of the same entities only some of which have acquired those properties. Clearly, this is not subset selection because the original set of entities is maintained without any elimination.

Does diffusion amount to successor selection? It does involve replication and an alteration in the distribution of population properties. Novel combinations and new properties are likely outcomes. But *diffusion* refers to processes prior to the test of environmental interaction. Hence, diffusion does not itself amount to selection, although it may help explain the generation of variety on which selection can operate.

Diffusion is here defined in a way that includes the copying of replicators from one entity to another. Infections or epidemics do not amount to diffusion because they do not involve the copying of the replicators that are developmentally crucial for each host. We describe infection as contagion rather than diffusion. Diffusion becomes especially important when there is a culture, meaning that information can be transmitted through imitation, symbols, or other forms of communication. But transmission is not automatic. We must consider how and to what extent the capacities to understand and absorb information are themselves acquired.

Culture greatly complicates the evolutionary process by enhancing the role of diffusion alongside selection. When one firm acquires a new technique by copying another firm, the properties of the firm are altered. Among these properties are the firm's routines and the skills and habits of its workers. The relative importance of diffusion processes in human society has helped sustain the misleading description of social evolution as *Lamarckian*. We argued in the preceding chapter that Lamarckism—defined in terms of the inheritance of acquired characters—requires a sufficiently precise definition of *inheritance*, which can be differentiated from superficial contagion or infection. To establish this, we must distinguish between replicators and interactors. We regard inheritance as the creation or modification of replicators, as a result of the transmission of relevant information from one entity to another. *Inheritance* thus turns out to be synonymous with *replication*.

In human society, all the important examples of diffusion—from technologies to fashions—involve the alteration of human habits and other programmed dispositions as well as the frequent transfer of artifacts. Individuals decide to adopt a new innovation, such as a new corn seed or weed killer, if it has a demonstrable advantage compared to existing alternatives (Rogers and Shoemaker 1971). Diffusion changes social replicators such as habits and routines without necessarily eliminating their individual or organizational hosts. Without the alteration of habits—which are the foundation of skills and organizational routines—the changes would be transitory and of little significance. There is no similar process of replicator modification at the genetic level.

With cultural and technological diffusion, it is not an acquired character that is inherited. Meaningful inheritance is about the copying of replicators, whether phenotypic characteristics change or not. Selection in social evolution typically operates on populations where diffusion helps create new variation, leading to differential replication through further diffusion or the copying of interactors. This generally qualifies as successor selection.

Finally, we consider the case of replicator manipulation and its relation to selection, as found in the famous book by Richard Nelson and Sidney Winter (1982). Firms often change their internal routines, and this typically involves amendments, rather than simply elimination and subset selection. Internal choice of routines is often similar to gene manipulation. With modern technology, the genes of living organisms can also be altered. These are examples of processes that are neither selection *of* (because interactors are not the selected entities) nor selection *for* (because it is not an outcome of interactor selection). They do not represent successor selection because the transformations do not necessarily involve cycles of replication and environmental interaction. Consequently, replicator manipulation is not selection in the technical sense developed here, even if it involves managerial or expert choice.[8]

---

8. But, if they are sufficiently cohesive, additional interactors can, in principle, exist at the level of the team or the division within the firm. In such cases, choice internal to the firm can count as selection. Some corporations with multiple divisions (or plants) may provide examples. If interaction with headquarters leads to differential replication of routines across divisions (e.g., by divesting underperforming divisions), then we have an instance of selection. General Electric under Jack Welch is a possible example of such internal selection (see, e.g., O'Boyle 1998).

5.5. OPERATIONALIZING SELECTION AND FITNESS

Following established practice, we define *fitness* in a nontautological manner, in terms of the propensity of a replicator to produce copies of itself (Williams 1966; Mills and Beatty 1979; De Jong 1994). The fitness of a *replicator* is the propensity to increase its frequency (relative to other replicators). In the social domain, this translates into the propensity of a social replicator (such as a habit or a routine) with a particular feature to produce copies and increase the frequency of similar replicators in the population. The fitness of an *interactor* is the propensity of its replicators to increase their frequency. We would typically be interested in a particular set of replicators or interactors or may even limit the analysis to the study of particular traits of a replicator or an interactor.

Selection can be present when the social environment generates variance in fitness so that there is a systematic change in the frequencies of replicators and interactors between two time steps. This is a necessary condition, but it is not sufficient. The opportunity for selection does not necessarily imply that any particular replicator (or interactor) experiences selection (Wolf, Brodie, and Moore 1999). The additional requirement is that replicators (or interactors) covary with fitness. This can be seen from the Price equation (see this chapter's appendix). According to the Price equation, the fundamental statement about selection of a trait is the existence of covariance between trait values and fitness.

Fitness involves the mapping (De Jong 1994; Nowak 2006)

Genotype $\rightarrow$ Phenotype $\rightarrow$ Fitness,

or, more generally,

Replicator $\rightarrow$ Interactor $\rightarrow$ Fitness.

The first mapping is from genotype (or replicator) to phenotype (or interactor), and the second is from phenotype (or interactor) to fitness. In a biological context, fitness is often the expected number of offspring contributed by a specific class of individuals to the next generation. The phenotype is represented by a numerical trait value, and the genotype references alleles, which are components of genes that produce distinct traits. More generally, the fitness measure is a function of both interactor and replicator fitness attributes, *within a particular environment*. If we wish to include different environmental states, it is necessary either to reproduce a fitness mapping for each environmental state of interest or to include a set of environmental variables.[9]

These mappings are often convoluted for analytic purposes. For example, the so-called fitness landscapes assume a direct mapping from genotype (or replicator) to fitness. This is important because fitness landscapes have become widely used in the analysis of social organizations. Many recent theoretical contributions use the NK model for the analysis of organizational search (starting with Levinthal [1997]). In these models, social replicators are represented by bit strings of length N with K ($0, 1, \ldots, N-1$) interactions among individual bits. Each string of bits maps onto a fitness value, usually a number between zero and one. These models typically subsume social replicators (e.g., routines) in social phenotypes (e.g., firm-specific policies). This is fine for the kind of analysis employed. But an analysis of selection effects would benefit from an elaboration of the causal effects of social replicators (routines) on social interactors (e.g., firm-specific traits). This would, for example, allow researchers to identify developmental effects related to firm growth and increases in scale as opposed to selection effects. In the current formulations, these effects are not parceled out.

The empirical study of selection dynamics in the social world is, perhaps, most advanced in studies of cultural evolution (e.g., Boyd and Richerson 1985; Durham 1991; Richerson and Boyd 2001) and population ecology (Hannan and Freeman 1989). These studies typically identify trait values but evade the problem of identifying social replicators. Another line of empirical studies provides detailed evidence regarding the emergence, stabilization, and disruption of habits and routines in business organizations (Becker 2004). To advance evolutionary studies in the social world, we must combine these streams of empirical work. Then social scientists would be able to formulate detailed, refutable models of selection dynamics.

The investigation would start by identifying relevant fitness components and then consider what the proper fitness model is for the problem under study (De Jong 1994). The fitness model hypothesizes a particular relation between social replicators and interactors—and between social interactors and fitness. This relation is most likely distinct for different classes of social selection processes. We could, for example, consider possible interdependencies among social replicators (for a simple model, see Wolf, Brodie, and Moore [1999]). If present, should they be included in the fitness model? Evidence for the selection of particular social interactors is then compiled and

9. This point emerged from discussions with Sidney G. Winter.

tested in statistical (regression) models that capture the assumptions of the fitness model. While population ecologists, for instance, have documented selection effects in a number of carefully executed empirical studies, their fitness model has excluded any explicit mapping of replicator (genotype) to interactor (phenotype). It is this mapping that we must uncover in social selection processes. G. De Jong (1994), Jay Beder and Richard Gomulkiewicz (1998), and Steven Frank (1998) provide the relevant methods.

5.6. CONCLUSION

In this chapter, we have outlined a rigorous concept of selection that is bereft of any necessary association with blood, gore, or optimization. It is no accident that Darwin's theory of natural selection was inspired by economists such as Adam Smith and Thomas Robert Malthus as we observe selection in the business world when some firms are eliminated through bankruptcy and successful firms are copied by new entrants. But that does not mean that selection must always involve competition or that the fittest always survive.

In establishing a distinction between subset selection and successor selection, we have shown that both concepts apply to the social domain. When some firms expire in an industry or some laws are repealed without substitute, then these are cases of subset selection. When organizations give rise to new copies through demerger, spin-off, or imitation, then that may qualify as successor selection. To consider whether such cases qualify, we must consider the concept of replication as this is integral to the definition of *successor selection*. This is the subject of the next chapter.

APPENDIX: PRICE'S DEFINITION OF SELECTION

According to Price (1995), selection is the act or process of producing a corresponding set. Given a set P containing ω_i amounts of I distinct elements p_i that have the properties x_i, Price (1995, 392) defines a corresponding set as follows: "We will say that a set P' is a corresponding set to a set P if there exists a one-to-one correspondence such that, for each member p_i of P, there is a corresponding member p_i' of P' which (if not empty) is composed partly or wholly of the same material as p_i, or has been derived directly from p_i, or contains one or more replicas of p_i or some part of p_i or has some other special close relation to p_i." Using this definition of a corresponding set, Price (1995, 392) defines selection as follows: "*Selection* on a set P in relation to a property x is the act or process of producing a corresponding set P' in a way such that the amounts ω_i' (or some function of them such as the ratios ω_i'/ω_i) are non-randomly related to the corresponding x_i values."

The terminology introduced by Price yields a useful statistical definition of selection. Let P be a set containing ω_i amounts of I distinct elements that have the properties x_i. A transformation $P \rightarrow P'$ (possibly the identity transformation) results in a second set, P'. The set P' contains ω_i' amounts of I distinct elements with properties x_i'. The transformation $P \rightarrow P'$ is termed a *selection process* that gives rise to the effect $X \rightarrow X'$ in a population property X related to property x of the individual set members. This effect $X \rightarrow X'$ can be calculated as the change in the average value (Price 1995; Frank 1997):

$$(5.1) \quad \Delta X = X' - X = \Sigma\omega_i'x_i' - \Sigma\omega_i x_i \leftrightarrow e\Delta X = \text{Cov}(e_i, x_i) + E(e_i\Delta x_i), \, \omega_i' = \omega_i e_i/e,$$

where e_i is the fitness of element i in the set P, and e is average fitness of the set P. Selection is present whenever $\text{Cov}(e_i, x_i)$ differs significantly from zero.[10] By contrast, a transmission effect is present whenever $E(e_i\Delta x_i)$ differs significantly from zero. In biological populations, the transmission effect can be thought of as changes in traits that are caused by conversion events such as mutations. In social populations, a transmission effect can be considered an individual-level exploration or innovation effect. A selection or a transmission effect references a change in the first moment of the trait distribution; that is, selection is a change in the average trait according to the population in question.

The Price equation provides a useful means of empirical verification of possible selection effects in a population of interest. As the reader can verify, it is straightforward to recursively expand the expression given above to include multiple hierarchical layers of selection (using the expectation term for expansion).[11] It is also possible to use the Price equation on trait frequencies (the fraction of a population with a particular trait), rather than trait values. This would be an obvious way to develop the Price formalism for use in the social sciences.

---

10. Equation (5.1) shows the discrete-time version of Price's equation because this is the most common for empirical analyses. The continuous time version is: $dE(X)/dt = \text{Cov}(e_i, x_i) + E(dx_i/dt)$.

11. A further issue concerns the expansion of the Price equation to encompass selection on higher moments than the first.

Note that the Price equation (eq. [5.1]) has a straightforward and useful relation to regression analysis (Frank 1998):

$$(5.2) \quad e\Delta X = \text{Cov}(e_i, x_i) + E(e_i \Delta x_i) = \beta_{e,x} V_x + E(e_i \Delta x_i),$$

where the covariance, $\text{Cov}(e_i, x_i)$, has been partitioned into the product of the regression coefficient $\beta_{e,x}$ and variance V_x in trait values. This version of the Price equation is useful for empirical purposes. Under the assumption that mean changes in phenotypic traits Z is equal to mean changes in gene traits X, we can write (see Frank 1998):

$$(5.3) \quad e\Delta X = e\Delta Z = \beta_{e,x} V_x + E(e_i \Delta x_i).$$

In genetics, X is the additive genetic value, V_x is the variance attributed to a set of predictors of phenotypic traits, and the β's are total regression coefficients. The standard predictors are alleles (Frank 1998), and traits could, for example, be camouflage color or neck length. As Frank (1998, 17) notes, there is nothing special about genetics as regards the application of this formalism. He mentions that traits Z could be corporate profits with predictors of cash flow and years of experience by management.

The Price formalism also provides a general and rigorous way in which to examine selection effects in social processes. But we are in no position to offer detailed empirical results that use this approach in the social world because the use of rigorous quantitative models for the study of social selection is still in its infancy. Still, we are confident that their application would present a significant advance in studies of selection dynamics in the social world.[12]

12. Wolf, Brodie, and Moore (1999) provide a rare introduction to the study of social selection gradients. This line of work can easily be extended by appropriate definitions of a fitness measure, e.g., number of social replicators or interactors. For formalizations with which to measure fitness, see also De Jong (1994), Beder and Gomulkiewicz (1998), and Frank (1998).

CHAPTER SIX

Information, Complexity, and Generative Replication

It is possible that the complexity revolution, far from revealing the limits of the Darwinian tradition, will serve instead to show the limits only of the background assumptions on which that tradition has hitherto relied.

DAVID J. DEPEW AND BRUCE H. WEBER, (1995)

It is the assumption that nonlinear dynamics testifies solely in favor of Darwinism's historical rivals that we want to call into question. . . . We see no reasons why Darwinism cannot greet the advent of complex systems dynamics as equally as its rivals.

BRUCE H. WEBER AND DAVID J. DEPEW, (1996)

Replication is a key element in Darwinian evolution, often leading to the creation of new entities. It is a recently developed concept that has helped generalize the notion of inheritance beyond the biological domain. Generally, replication involves the transmission of information that can create or modify a replicator. In this chapter, we refine the definition of a replicator and identify some crucial replicators in social evolution.[1]

The aim of this chapter is to salvage the concept of the replicator from some of its critics, to establish a special class of replicators that is important in both social and biological evolution, and to persuade our colleagues in the social sciences of the importance of its relevance and value. Instead of the vague word *meme*, we give specific examples of types of social replicator.

Darwin did not clearly identify the concept *replicator*, and he was ignorant of the precise mechanisms of replication. But the general idea is implicit in his work in terms of continuity by descent. He assumed that

---

1. As mentioned earlier, we treat *replication* and *inheritance* as synonyms. But inheritance is sometimes viewed as any passing of information, while replication is seen as high-fidelity transmission of discrete units of inheritance. Still other writers use a broader definition of *replicator* and others a narrower concept of inheritance: there is a lack of consensus on this issue. While the fidelity of information transmission is important, we do not regard it as the sole criterion, and we do not think that it is useful to distinguish between inheritance and replication in this way.

information was transmitted in reproduction by such information-carrying entities as seeds, sperm, ova, or pollen.

Since it was coined by Richard Dawkins (1976), the concept *replicator* has been clarified by philosophers of biology and others (Hull 1988; Sterelny, Smith, and Dickison 1996; Godfrey-Smith 2000b; Sperber 2000; Aunger 2002; Nanay 2002). We review this work below.

A broad definition of a replicator has emerged, with attributes of causality, similarity, and information transfer. While we accept this general definition, we regard it as too broad for some purposes and requiring further refinement.

We draw inspiration from the literature on "self-reproducing" automata (von Neumann 1966; Sipper 1998; Freitas and Merkle 2004) to strengthen the notion of information transfer in replication processes.[2] To the triple conditions of causality, similarity, and information transfer, we add a fourth condition that defines a generative replicator as including a "conditional generative mechanism" or program that can turn input signals from an environment into developmental instructions. The special case of *generative* replication has the potential to enhance complexity, which, in turn, requires that developmental instructions are part of the information that is transmitted in replication. (We discuss relevant definitions of *complexity* below.) Demonstrating the usefulness of the refined concept in the social domain, we identify social generative replicators that satisfy all four proposed conditions.

This demonstration is significant for several reasons. First, the refined concept of generative replication overcomes objections by "developmental systems" theorists from within the philosophy of biology that the idea of a replicator is too broad to be useful. Second, and contrary to other skeptics, it is shown, not only that replication is a concept relevant to social evolution, but also that the special case of generative replication is important to help understand the evolution of complex social phenomena. Third, the refined definition cuts through the problems associated with the concept *meme* and deals with these by focusing on a more sharply defined set of replicators. Fourth, this argument shows that the project to generalize Darwinian principles to social evolution has a "positive heuristic" (Lakatos 1976) in that it raises new research questions, in particular, the conditions necessary to generate phenomena of greater complexity.

---

2. Gabora (2004) also uses von Neumann's (1966) work to refine the concept of the replicator.

6.1. JUDGMENT DAY FOR THE REPLICATOR

The role of replicators has been touched on in the famous evo-devo dispute concerning the relative roles of development, selection, and genotypic transmission (Gilbert, Opitz, and Raff 1996; Wimsatt 1999; Stadler, Stadler, and Wagner 2001; Baguñà and Garcia-Fernàndez 2003). Our claim is that replication, development, and selection are all essential features of evolution in complex population systems. Consideration of their relative roles is an empirical as well as a theoretical matter, but the outcome would not make any of these features inessential.

Going much further, recent formulations of developmental systems theory try to generalize Darwinian principles in very broad terms that sideline or exclude the replicator (Griesemer 1994, 1999; Griffiths and Gray 1994, 1997; Wimsatt 1999). Theorists emphasizing the developmental side of the evolutionary process point out that inherited information itself cannot provide a complete description of the emerging phenotype and, consequently, that development depends crucially on the particular context. Heredity and development interact in a way that cannot give overwhelming priority to the genotype. James Griesemer (1994) thus roots the concept of inheritance in whole developmental lineages, rather than in genotype-to-genotype transmission.

Partly because of its origination from Dawkins, the replicator idea has been linked with overly gene-centered accounts of the generalized Darwinian evolutionary process. Paul Griffiths and Russell Gray (1997, 473) explain that developmental systems theory "takes to its logical conclusion the slow unraveling of the idea that genes are the sole evolutionary replicators." In particular, some biologists have "drawn attention to the large class of structures which are inherited parallel with the genes and play an essential role in development at the cellular level. . . . These intra cellular elements of the developmental matrix are essential for the replication of DNA and are not themselves constructed on the basis of DNA sequences." As Eva Jablonka and Eörs Szathmáry (1995) argue, these parallel structures constitute an additional "epigenetic inheritance system." Hence, developmental systems theory shifts the focus onto the entire developmental system rather than the replicator and its "interactor" (Hull 1988).

Developmental systems theory has become sufficiently fashionable to receive approval in an important textbook on the philosophy of biology (see Pigliucci and Kaplan 2006). We are unconvinced that its arguments require the abandonment of the replicator-interactor distinction. Some accounts are inconsistent. For example, William Wimsatt (1999) and Massimo Pigliucci and Jonathan Kaplan (2006) reject the replicator-interactor distinction but retain the concepts of genotype and phenotype. This is incoherent if we accept the former distinction as a generalization of the latter (Brandon 1996). Pigliucci and Kaplan (2006, 80) go further and "regard any sharp distinction between replicators and interactors as having outlived its usefulness. Replication itself demands, in general, the organism's ability to interact. Genomes do not 'self-replicate.' . . . There is, therefore, no way to distinguish in general between the things that are replicated, the things that do the replicating, and the things that interact." We agree that replication requires the entity's ability to interact: processes of replication and interaction are causally intermeshed. But they are different facets of evolution. We also agree that neither genomes in particular nor replicators in general self-replicate. Terms such as *self-replication* and phrases such as *making copies of themselves* have been used liberally by modern writers on evolution and memetics, including Richard Dawkins (1976) and Susan Blackmore (1999).[3] But these should not mislead us into believing that replication is an entirely independent and self-driven process. DNA is typically inert. Genetic and other forms of replication require external triggers and specific environmental conditions. Replicators do not literally replicate by themselves.

At most, Pigliucci and Kaplan reveal the misleading use of language, which can wrongly exclude the vital role of external factors or invest the replicator with a purpose or goal. There is nothing new in their valid claim that genomes do not self-replicate. But one cannot jump from this proposition to the conclusion that there is "no way to distinguish in general between the things that are replicated" and "the things that do the replicating." Replicators are not necessarily clearly identifiable things: they are parts or features of the whole that embody replicated information. Against Pigliucci and Kaplan, the distinction can be maintained once we highlight the informational feature of the replicator and the encompassing nature of the interactor.

As elaborated here, prominent recent definitions of a replicator do not literally involve any self-replication that is independent of environmental influences or context. Our sharper concept of generative replication explic-

3. Similar problems arise with the terminology of self-reproducing automata (von Neumann 1966), notwithstanding the value of this literature. Like genes, automata do not reproduce themselves without external inputs.

itly acknowledges the dependence on other structures and environmental inputs.

Much of the literature on cultural and social evolution bypasses the question of the detailed mechanisms of cultural replication or transmission. We aim to explore in more detail the social and psychological mechanisms of sociocultural evolution and, where appropriate, place these in a generalized Darwinian framework. Once we examine the transmission mechanisms involved, we are presented with multiple possible substrates, involving brain patterns, social networks, symbols, and artifacts.

As Stephen Jay Gould (1996), William Wimsatt (1999), Richard Nelson (2006, 2007b), and others elaborate, in the sociocultural domain there are complex patterns of inheritance and few clear boundaries between species. For Gould and Nelson, these are reasons to, respectively, reject or limit the exploration of communalities between biological and sociocultural evolution. For Wimsatt, they mean that evolutionary concepts must be pushed to a high level of generality, after abandoning the distinction between replicator and interactor.

In contrast, we find that the distinction between replicator and interactor is vital. Without it, it is impossible to distinguish between inheritance and contagion. Many cultural selection processes are characterized by the way in which interaction among individuals and organizations causes differential replication of cultural information. To capture adequately such processes in our theories, the distinction between replicator and interactor should be retained in the sociocultural domain. And it should be framed at a sufficiently high level of abstraction to encompass the important differences between social evolution and natural evolution.

Part of our rationale for this devolves from the understanding that Darwinian evolution is essentially about interacting and replicating *populations* of (varied and developing) entities rather than *singular* self-organizing or developing systems. Once this focus on populations is established, we need to understand the sources of both similarity and variation between elements, in the context of the development of individual entities, their informational interaction, and the evolution of entire populations. The concepts *replicator* and *interactor* are essential to this task.

As Sterelny, Smith, and Dickison (1996) argue, developmental systems theory lacks adequate definition of the boundaries of the units in the evolving population. We propose that some such boundaries must exist in an evolutionary system that is capable of retaining relatively successful adaptations and generating increasing complexity. Our definition of the interactor focuses on a relatively cohesive entity with boundaries that hosts replicable information. The loss of vital boundaries is an adverse outcome of abandoning the distinction between replicator and interactor.

Although the argument is at an abstract and conceptual level, it makes some important distinctions that are vital for empirical research into social evolution and establishes some important hypotheses about the origins of social complexity.

The remainder of this chapter is organized as follows. In section 6.2, we scrutinize the widely used definition of *replication* in terms of the triple conditions of causality, similarity, and information transfer. Section 6.3 draws from the literature on self-reproducing automata to strengthen the notion of information transfer in replication processes. Essentially, *generative* replication requires that developmental instructions be part of the information that is transmitted in replication.

Section 6.4 establishes the concept of generative replication. In addition to the triple conditions of causality, similarity, and information transfer, we adopt a new condition that defines a generative replicator as embodying a "conditional generative mechanism," a material structure that embodies mechanisms that can turn input signals from an environment into developmental instructions. By this definition, genes, but not prions, are generative replicators. Section 6.5 examines the conjecture that generative replication has the potential to enhance complexity. Sections 6.6 and 6.7 discuss possible replicators in the social domain. After a critique of the concept of the meme in section 6.6, section 6.7 demonstrates the usefulness of the concept of generative replication in the social domain by identifying habits as generative social replicators that satisfy all four conditions. Section 6.8 considers whether diffusion alone has the capacity to increase complexity. Section 6.9 concludes the chapter.

6.2. REPLICATORS AND REPLICATION

Dawkins (1976) described replicators as having longevity, fecundity, and fidelity. More precisely, Dawkins (1982, 2004) defined *replication* as a process involving genotypic copying fidelity sufficient to limit copying error and to pass on to successive generations the genotypic errors and mutations that actually occur. He identified both genes and memes as replicators.

David Hull (1988, 408) defines a replicator as "an entity that passes on its structure largely intact in successive replications." A key question here is what structures are significant and why. Again, the definition requires refinement. And, if a meme is a replicator, then what structure is passed on?

Sterelny, Smith, and Dickison (1996, 395) offer a more elaborate definition of a replicator. They propose that, if B is a copy of A, and if B is produced through a process of replication, then "A plays a causal role in the production of B," and "B carries information about A in virtue of being relevantly similar to A: This similarity is often functional: B has the same, or similar, functional capacities to A." This definition emphasizes the three key points of causal implication, similarity, and information transfer that are central to most subsequent definitions.

These three elements, taken together, admit a very wide class of entities. Against Dawkins and others, Sterelny, Smith, and Dickison argue that nonorganisms such as birds' nests and animals' burrows qualify as replicators. But the causal role that one nest or burrow plays in the production of another is highly limited. It exists only insofar as the attempt to produce one nest or burrow is crucial, through learning or whatever, in the development of the organism's capacity to produce another. If nests and burrows are to be admitted as replicators, then their causality condition must be interpreted in very weak terms. The causal link is merely that each replicator is a practice model for its successors. We suggest that this is an inadequate account of the causality condition: it must be coupled with stipulations that make the causality more meaningful. The definition we offer below of *generative replicator* excludes nests, burrows, and many human artifacts.

In another refinement of the concept of the replicator, Peter Godfrey-Smith (2002b) also emphasizes that replication involves "two main elements, a *resemblance* between copy and copied, and some suitable *causal* relation linking the copy to the copied" (405). He is also skeptical of versions of cultural evolution based on the meme. For him: "The . . . job of explaining *the heritability of variation*, in the sense relevant to evolution by natural selection, . . . is the proper one for the replicator concept" (413). He then constructs the following definitions: "Y is a *replicate* of X if and only if: (i) X and Y are similar (in some relevant respects), and (ii) X was causally involved in the production of Y in a way responsible for the similarity of Y to X. Replication is any process by which a replicate is produced" (414–15). Notably, this definition requires similarity "in some relevant respects" but does not specify what is "relevant."

Dan Sperber (2000) also argues that replication involves elements of causation, similarity, and information transfer and specifies the "minimal conditions" for replication:

For B to be a replication of A,

    (1) B must be caused by A (together with background conditions),

    (2) B must be similar in relevant respects to A, and

    (3) The process that generates B must obtain the information that makes B similar to A from A. . . . B must inherit from A the properties that make it relevantly similar to A. (169)

He then argues that many cases of so-called memetic replication are not true replication according to this definition, principally because the third condition is violated. Hence, the "grand project of memetics . . . is misguided" (173).

Robert Aunger (2002) refines Sperber's (2000) definition to add a fourth condition: "duplication." By this he means that, during the replication process, one entity gives rise to two (or more). According to Aunger, replication is a special type of inheritance, one in which duplication is involved.

While Aunger's argument is illuminating, we are unconvinced that duplication is necessary to, or useful in, refining the concept of replication. The critical issue in understanding the process of replication is the nature and function of the structure that is passed on, including any information that it might hold. It is not whether the replicator is lucky or unlucky in surviving the process of replication, leading or not to the coexistence of multiple copies. We concentrate on the key issues of structure and information, which are central to replication. The three remaining and aforementioned conditions of causality, similarity, and information transfer are necessary but insufficient for this task.

Why are they insufficient? A problem is that the three conditions of causality, similarity, and information transfer cover a broad class of copying processes. They would also apply to technologies such as photocopying and the copying of data on magnetic media or on compact discs. The similarity condition pertains in these cases. The causality condition is also satisfied because the original is causally implicated in the production of the copy, in the weak sense that, without the original, the copy could not exist. For Sperber (2000), the information-transfer condition is also satisfied because the information in the copy originates from the original.

Although these criteria cover a broad range of copying processes, Sperber points to exceptions, such as the example of contagious laughter spreading through a group. Although one person's laughter may trigger the laughter of another, the laughter itself is "not copied" because the second person does not imitate the laughter of the first. Instead: "There is a biological disposition to laughter that gets activated and fine tuned through encounters with the laughter of others. . . . The motor program for laughing was already fully present in [the second person], and what the laughter of others does is just activate it" (2000, 168). Sperber thus claims that his information-transfer condition is unsatisfied in this case.

If, instead, a second sound recorder were switched on to record the sounds of a first recorder, then, for Sperber, this would be a case of true replication satisfying all three of his conditions. Similar remarks seem to apply to the photocopying of documents. However, while these examples are different from the contagious spread of laughter, the difference is one of degree. The triggering of patterns of laughter may involve a signal that is much simpler than the detailed information copied by a sound recorder or photocopier, but the difference lies in the amount and the kind of information transferred. In no case is the transferred information sufficient in itself to produce the copy. In none of these cases is the copying mechanism itself copied.

What if the intensity and style of the initial laughter trigger mirth of a similar intensity and style in others? Then the initial laughter would be carrying information that was critical in forming the character of the copied laughter. Sperber himself admits the possibility of laughter being "fine tuned" through encounters with others. In this case, the initial laughter becomes more than a mere trigger: it carries significant information that is copied.

Furthermore, Sperber's condition that "B must inherit from A the properties that make it relevantly similar to A" can be interpreted in terms that exclude, not only his example of laughter, but also the examples of copying with sound recorders or photocopiers. It all depends on what we mean by *properties*. In his discussion of laughter, Sperber focuses on the capacity to produce the behavior. The disposition to laugh is not replicated, but neither is the capacity to make copies with a sound recorder or photocopier. These machines already have the capacity to make copies. Hence, if *properties* refers to the capacity to produce a faithful copy, and if this capacity is already there before the response is triggered, then none of these examples satisfy the information-transfer condition because these key properties are not inherited in the copying process.

Although Sperber's information-transfer condition takes us in the right direction, it is insufficiently precise. It depends crucially on what is meant by *information* and what properties must be inherited to constitute true replication. A critical issue pertains to the replication of a copying mechanism or the absence of such processes. Relevant insights appear in our discussion of self-reproducing automata in the next section.

6.3. INSPIRATION FROM
"SELF-REPRODUCING" AUTOMATA

John von Neumann (1966) considered conditions under which automata would be capable of producing copies of themselves and of generating novelty and additional complexity. He did not propose that evolution always increases complexity, but he was interested in the conditions under which further complexity could be generated. He distinguished between the copying of entities that synthesize to produce higher degrees of complexity and the copying of entities that reduced overall complexity: "There is thus this completely decisive property of complexity, that there exists a critical size below which the process of synthesis is degenerative, but above which the phenomenon of synthesis, if properly arranged, can become explosive, in other words, where synthesis of automata can proceed in such a manner that each automaton will produce other automata which are more complex and of higher potentialities than itself" (80).

Following von Neumann, we propose that *generative* replication should be confined to cases with the *potential* to increase complexity. As explained in more detail below, we define *complexity* in terms of (neg)entropy. A replication process increases complexity when the replicators systematically gain more information about an environment (less entropy). This would exclude copying with sound recorders or photocopiers and the copying of nests and burrows. Such copies have no more potential to enhance complexity than their predecessors do. To increase potential complexity, copies must eventually be capable of producing novel additional components or performing novel operations in response to new environmental conditions and input signals.

Von Neumann (1966) examined in detail the properties that a "self-reproducing" automaton must possess to make it capable of producing other automata. These properties include instructions that describe the structure and processes of an automaton, a copying unit that is capable of reading and copying instructions into a new automaton and translating them as directions for a production unit, a production unit that builds a new automaton, and some mechanism of coordination between these elements. His research has influenced robotics and computer science (Sipper 1998; Luksha 2003).

However, biological replicators lack the abstract properties of self-reproducing automata outlined by von Neumann. In particular, as developmental systems theorists emphasize, genes themselves do not carry enough information to describe or generate a new organism. The development of the organism depends additionally, not only on environmental stimuli, but also on cellular structures inherited alongside the genes. Consequently, neither genes nor organisms constitute a complete production unit for new organisms.

The theory of self-reproducing automata points to the potential to enhance complexity. It also sees the developmental instructions as part of the information that is transmitted on replication. These two inspirations lead us to the concept of generative replication. A generative replicator is a material structure that is responsive to environmental stimuli or signals. There is at least one signal that can cause a nondegenerative response from the replicator. Such a response consists of further instructions or signals to the interactor that guide its development. It is nondegenerative in the sense that it leads to outcomes that are conducive to the survival of the replicator and the information it carries.

For example, the DNA code determines the constitution of the protein molecules in the organism. It instructs the processes of cell formation by governing the production of amino acids and proteins, subject to the circumstances and external conditions involved.

6.4. THE GENERATIVE REPLICATOR DEFINED

Dawkins's point about copying fidelity and passing on mutations is important but insufficient for our project. Our concern is to define a special class of replicators with the potential to increase complexity, rather than to define the broader boundaries of replication itself. Furthermore, Dawkins (2004, 391) associates copying fidelity with mutations or errors in *genotypic* information and, by contrast, requires that most "environmentally acquired changes" are *not* passed on. But this important distinction begs the definition of a genotype or a replicator.

On the basis of our discussion of self-reproducing automata, we adopt a fourth condition in the definition of a generative replicator:

4. *Conditional generative mechanisms*: Generative replicators are material structures that embody construction mechanisms (or programs) that can be energized by input signals that contain information about a particular environment. These mechanisms produce further instructions from a generative replicator to their related interactor that guide its development. (External influences that produce outcomes generally unfavorable to the survival of the replicator or interactor are described, not as input signals, but as destructive forces.)

INFORMATION, COMPLEXITY, AND GENERATIVE REPLICATION   123

This fourth proposition adds to the established three definitional features for a replicator, namely, causal implication, similarity, and information transfer. We refine these as follows:

1. *Causal implication*: The source must be causally involved in the production of the copy, at least in the sense that, without the source, the particular copy would not be created.
2. *Similarity*: The replicated entity must be or contain a replicator. The conditional generative mechanisms in the copy must be similar to those in the source. Errors or mutations in these mechanisms must also be copied with some degree of fidelity.
3. *Information transfer*: During its creation, the copy must obtain the conditional generative mechanisms that make the copy similar to its source from that same source.

Note how the causality condition is clarified. The enhanced-similarity condition requires that similarity must apply to the conditional generative mechanisms and takes on board Dawkins's (2004) stipulation. A related refinement appears in the information-transfer condition. These conditions preserve the spirit of Hull's (1988, 408) definition of a replicator as "an entity that passes on its structure." A component that satisfies all four conditions is described as a *generative replicator*.

Both replication in general and generative replication in particular by definition involve the copying of replicators. They may or may not involve the copying of host interactors as well. Diffusion is a special case of replication in which replicators are copied from one existing interactor to another, without the creation of new interactors.

Note that condition 4 above refers to interactors as well as the related generative replicators. Our definition of a generative replicator leads to the following logical condition: *every generative replicator is hosted by at least one interactor*. In the following chapter, we define every interactor as hosting at least one replicator.

One of the problems involved in defining the concept of the replicator is understanding what exactly *information* means. Our specification helps fill this gap. The concept of information here does not necessarily carry interpretations or meanings in the same way as the information communicated by humans does. It is *information* in a cruder sense of a code or a signal, as stored and manipulated by computers and present in DNA. For Claude Shannon and Warren Weaver (1949), a message has "information content" when its receipt causes some action. For us, the information involved consists of signals with the potential to trigger generative mechanisms that guide the production of further replicators or the development of interactors.

We acknowledge that the Shannon-Weaver definition omits key features of information: ideas and knowledge in the human domain, particularly meanings and interpretations. When we discuss social evolution, it is essential to bring these into the picture. But, because our conceptual discussion here is at a high level of generality, spanning both social and biological evolution, information cannot be defined more narrowly (see section 6.6 below).

Our added condition insists on the materiality of the replicator; hence, ideas as such are not replicators. More appropriately, ideas can be regarded as *emergent expressions* of mental habits or dispositions. By contrast, habits qualify as generative replicators, as shown below.

Our concept of a conditional generative mechanism is close to what Ernst Mayr (1974, 1988) describes as a "program." Mayr (1988, 48) regards a program as something that is embodied in a material substrate that gives rise to goal-driven (or "teleonomic") behavior and is, hence, "consistent with a causal explanation."

Nests, burrows, and photocopies are not generative replicators. None of these items is capable of receiving and emitting signals that lead to the development of the interactor. However, given that their survival is dependent on specific environmental conditions, then changes in those conditions can lead to changes in their state. They can be destroyed by (say) water or fire. To exclude such destructive influences, the sentence in parenthesis in condition 4 above establishes that destructive or degenerative environmental factors that lower the survival probability of an entity do not count as signals. They may have important effects, but, definitionally, they are not signals for the purpose of our condition 4. Having made this exclusion, nests, burrows, and photocopies have no conditional mechanisms to guide the development of the interactor.

Dawkins rejects the selfish nest and similar examples on the grounds that they fail to meet the similarity condition—small copying errors in nest and burrow production are not preserved and transmitted to a third generation. Such preservation is essential for cumulative evolution via natural selection, and cumulative evolution is essential for the evolution of complex adapted structure. For Dawkins, replication in conjunction with the right kind of fidelity is the necessary foundation of complexity.

Our analysis complements that of Dawkins, who characterizes the output conditions of inheritance mechanisms if complex systems are to evolve. But we also consider the mechanisms that are required to *generate* complex outputs. We exclude nests and burrows because they do not contain a mechanism that can receive and emit signals that lead to the further development of the interactor. Hence, they cannot compress, transmit, and express the information required in building structures of increasing complexity; they exhibit *limited* heredity in the sense of Maynard Smith and Szathmáry (1995). We identify generative replication as a necessary condition for the evolution of structures that are potentially unbounded in complexity. The emergence of *unlimited* heredity requires generative replication.

Briefly consider some further examples. Widely regarded as replicators, prion proteins are associated with transmissible spongiform encephalopathies (such as BSE, or mad cow disease). They involve the accumulation of an abnormally folded variant of the normal prion protein that spreads by direct contact when the normal form also becomes misfolded and, thus, converted to an abnormal and equally infectious form (Prusiner 1998). The replication of the abnormal form first grows exponentially and then dies out when the pool of normal prion molecules is exhausted. Prion replication does not contain signal-responsive construction mechanisms that hold information about a particular environment. At most, it is a simple form of replication in which no conditional generative mechanisms are passed on. Hence, prions are not *generative* replicators.

Biological viruses are infectious organisms with a nucleic acid genome (DNA or RNA). They spread by genome replication rather than direct contact. The genome of a virus involves a signal-responsive construction mechanism. A newborn genome codes for the protein coat (capsid) within which it is then housed. Thus, viruses are interactors (bounded by the protein coat) that house a replicator (the genome). Biological viruses hold information about special environments and acquire adaptive solutions to particular problems (such as immune response). Their hosts are not their interactors, and, even if biological viruses are destructive for their hosts, their genomes qualify as generative replicators.

Computer viruses also contain signal-responsive construction mechanisms. They also hold information about special environments (e.g., particular types of operating systems), and some even acquire adaptive solutions to particular problems (e.g., to avoid detection). Computer viruses are replicators, and their interactors are, arguably, the computer programs that they infect.[4] This contrasts with biological viruses, whose hosts do not constitute their interactors. Consequently, because computer viruses are generally destructive of the programs they infect, they are not *generative replicators*.[5]

6.5. GENERATIVE REPLICATION AND COMPLEXITY

For two centuries, it has been debated whether evolution generally gives rise to increased complexity (Saunders and Ho 1976, 1981; Gould 1977; Adami, Ofria, and Collier 2000; Adami 2002). Some endorse the proposition, some suggest that the evidence is inconclusive, and others reject the idea.

The disagreement also concerns what definitions and measures of complexity to use when such claims are assessed (Adami, Ofria, and Collier 2000; Adami 2002). Christoph Adami's (2002) useful review of definitions and measures of *complexity* concluded that many have drawbacks. Consistent with mathematical information theory, Adami holds that *the essence of complexity for an evolving entity is the amount of information that it stores about the environment in which it evolves*. He writes:

> The physical complexity of a sequence refers to the amount of information that is stored in that sequence about a particular environment. For a genome, this environment is the one in which it replicates and in which its host lives, a concept roughly equivalent to what we call a niche. Information . . . is always about something. Consequently, a sequence may embody information about one environment (niche) while being essentially random with respect to another. This makes the measure relative, or conditional on the environment, and it is precisely this feature that brings a number of important observations that are incompatible with a universal increase in complexity in line with a law of increasing physical complexity. (1087)

This definition conceptualizes complexity as information relative and conditional on the environment in which the entity evolves. Information is obtained from input signals that are actually recorded in a sequence stored in a replicator (genome), which, in turn, requires a distinction between replicators and interactors. These aspects of complexity are captured by our

4. Note Hull's (1988, 408) definition of an interactor as "an entity that directly interacts as a cohesive whole with its environment in such a way that this interaction *causes* replication to be differential." For a refinement of this definition, see chapter 7 below.

5. Even so-called benign computer viruses can be mildly destructive of the computer systems they infect, by taking up computer memory, causing erratic performance, or triggering system crashes.

proposition that a conditional generative mechanism is a defining feature of a generative replicator in the sense that it is a material entity embodying mechanisms that can be energized by input signals.

Complexity corresponds to the amount of (Shannon-Weaver) information that a replicator stores about a particular environment. The stored information relates the state of a replicator sequence to the actual state of the environment. A replicator sequence whose state perfectly corresponds to the state of the environment has maximal information about the environment in question.

Complexity is measured as (neg)entropy. If the entropy of a replicator population increases, then it contains less information about an environment. That is, fewer replicators pass on useful information to the next generation. There are two major reasons why this can happen. The first is that fewer replicators contain useful information about the environment because they are not able to pick up the relevant selection pressures. The second is that fewer replicators survive and are able to pass their information on to the next generation.

As explained below, we measure complexity as the difference between the theoretical maximum amount of information about an environment and the actual entropy (disorder) present in the relevant replicator population. As this difference increases, the replicator population exhibits less disorder and more complexity and contains more useful information about the environment. By contrast, if there is a diminishing difference between the maximum amount of information and actual entropy (of replicators), then a replicator population looses track of the environment and exhibits less physical complexity.

Before defining *complexity* formally, we briefly consider how our appeal to information relates to the recent controversy about information concepts in biology (Maynard Smith 2000a, 2000b; Sarkar 2000; Sterelny 2000; Griffiths 2001; Godfrey-Smith 2002a; Harms 2004). Griffiths (2001) suggests a distinction between causal and intentional information. Our use of the concept of information falls squarely in the causal category. However, some find that it does not go far enough to characterize the nature and function of the gene because causal concepts of information apply equally to genetic and environmental factors. Thus, Maynard Smith appealed to a stronger symbolic or intentional concept of information to characterize the way genes embody evolved properties that are expressed in particular phenotypic features.

We do not contribute here to this controversy, and our argument does not depend on its outcome. Rather, we use an concept of information that is widely accepted and commonly used across a number of scientific disciplines. This implies that, as defined here, information and complexity apply equally to genetic and nongenetic factors. Genes are just one source of information. Environmental factors also contain important information that influences the developmental history of an organism. The proposition that information (in a broad sense) can be carried by the environment as well as the genes is described by Griffiths and Gray (1994) as the "parity thesis."

Put simply, we do not suggest that genes or replicators are special because they contain a particular kind of information. Instead, we suggest that replicators differ in terms of whether they contain a generative mechanism. Generative replicators have the capacity to increase complexity. Like other generative replicators, genes have this special quality.

Our more detailed definition of the complexity of a replicator population largely follows Adami's (2002) exposition. Consider a specific environment E and the features required of a notional generative replicator to maximize interactor fitness in this environment, captured by a binary string of length L (the number of binary bits used to describe the generative replicator).[6] The theoretical entropy value of these notional fitness maximizers, H_{max}, is simply the sequence length L. Population-level complexity is the difference between H_{max} and the entropy of the actual population of generative replicators operating within this environment, also described in terms of binary strings of length L.

To determine the entropy of the actual population of generative replicators, each bit is addressed in turn. For the population as a whole, the actual frequency of the (binary) fitness-maximizing value at locus i is p_i (where $0 \le p_i \le 1$). The entropy of a population of generative replicators X is denoted by $H(X)$. The measure of physical complexity C of a population of replicating entities is the information that the generative replicator sequences X contain about the environment E:

(6.1) $C = H_{max} - H(X) = L + \Sigma p_i \log p_i$.

Our definition of *generative replication* is based in part on the conjecture that the capacity to increase complexity depends critically on the existence and replication of a conditional generative mechanism. We illustrate this

6. We use a binary string as a useful simplification for expositional reasons.

by considering several different types of error.[7] There is reading error (concerning input signals), developmental error (concerning the development of interactor traits from the generative replicator), and copying error (from a generative replicator to its copies). Retention error—where stored information degrades and loses its fidelity over time—would be a fourth type of error, but, in many practical cases, its effects are similar to copying error. With both copying error and retention error, the source information is corrupted within a finite time period.

A weaker surmise is that copying errors among a population of generative replicators are generally more destructive to complexity than are reading and developmental errors. A stronger proposition is that the capacity to increase complexity depends critically and especially on generative replication with few copying errors.

Consider a process of repeated replication with input signals, the development of interactors, and the copying of generative replicators, as in figure 6.1. We assume that there is no alteration of stored information in any individual generative replicator. In a fixed environment, these generative replicators develop traits clustered around a peak in a fixed fitness landscape. (Changing environments and variable or "dancing" fitness landscapes are excluded for simplicity, not because they would undermine our argument.)

Both reading errors and developmental errors have a similar type of effect: they cause the population to disperse from its original position in the fitness landscape. However, if copying errors are zero and the probabilities of reading and developmental errors remain constant, then the trend of overall dispersion will not increase over time as repeated replication occurs. The effects of reading and developmental errors are *not* cumulative. Information content is preserved through the faithful copying of the generative replicator.

Restart the process, but assume that the probability of a copying error is positive. The population of generative replicators is again clustered around a peak in a fixed fitness landscape. If a generative replicator is close to the fitness peak, then copying error is likely to move it away from that peak. There will be no reliable mechanism to tie it to its previous position. A process of drift will occur, and the overall dispersion in the population will increase unless a sufficiently precise selection process exists to eliminate

7. Prior research on self-replicating automata (Wolfram 1984, 2002; Molofsky 1994) has typically excluded such errors.

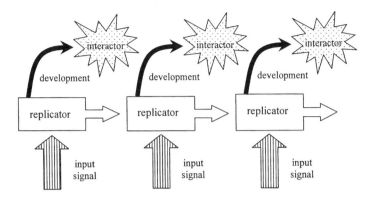

FIGURE 6.1. Generative replication with input signals and interactors.

the outliers. Without such a fortuitous correction via selection, the effects of copying error would be cumulative. The entropy $H(X)$ of the replicator population would increase and overall complexity decline as a result.[8]

This demonstration that copying error can be especially destructive to complexity illustrates the special importance of two of our features of a generative replicator, the existence and the relatively faithful copying of a conditional generative mechanism. It is this mechanism that has the potential to generate structures that are potentially unbounded in complexity (a critical condition in Dawkins's analysis). We acknowledge that the argument presented above depends on restrictive assumptions. Nevertheless, it underlines the importance of copying fidelity and the cumulatively destructive effect on complexity of copying error.

We admit that destructive forces, which reduce the chances of survival of some generative replicators, can undermine complexity in a population. The occurrence of disasters or extinctions may reverse any trend toward greater complexity. Our argument is based on the *potential* to increase complexity and not necessarily its empirical manifestation through time. Furthermore, there are additional sources of complexity other than replication.

Computer simulations that we conducted with simple artificial replicators (see Hodgson and Knudsen 2010) show that even low levels of copy-

---

8. Note that, if it did exist, Lamarckian inheritance could have a similarly negative cumulative effect. Lamarckism holds that the acquired characteristics of the interactor can affect the replicator, leading to the inheritance of these acquired characteristics. This may be an important reason in the biological sphere why Lamarckian mechanisms are rare.

ing error can thwart the enhancement of complexity, which is undermined still further as the level of copying error is increased. However, selection pressure can diminish the destructive effects of copying error by eliminating larger errors. Uppermost, we showed that only if replicators comply adequately with all four of our definitional conditions would complexity increase toward some maximal level. Adami, Ofria, and Collier (2002) reach a result that is consistent with this conclusion.

Our results are redolent of Adami's (2002, 1089) description of evolution as "a process that increases the amount of information a population harbours about its niche." According to Adami, natural selection is the only mechanism necessary to guarantee such an increase in complexity in a constant, unchanging world. Natural selection can be viewed as an instantiation of Maxwell's demon, "a filter, a kind of semipermeable membrane that lets information flow into the genome, but prevents it from flowing out." Our results support and further qualify Adami's claim. Selection, defined as differential replication caused by interaction, leads to an enduring increase in complexity only if replicators are conditional generative mechanisms in addition to satisfying the other three conditions of causality, similarity, and information transfer.

Our argument that generative replication furthers complexity has striking similarities to that of Mark Ridley (2000).[9] Ridley's premise is similar to ours that deleterious mutation must be kept within bounds if evolution is to occur. If the average rate of deleterious mutations is too high, then those mutations will cumulate and quickly swamp the descendant populations.

Like us, Ridley sees a tension between the evolution of complexity and the encoding of information. The evolution of complexity necessarily involves encoding more information about an environment. This requires a larger replicator sequence (L in eq. [6.1]). However, a longer replicator sequence will also more likely hit the critical threshold of one deleterious mutation per copy. The evolution of complexity requires that copying error be kept below a critical threshold.

Ridley focuses on mechanisms that minimize copying error. He convincingly explains how meiosis diminishes the probability that deleterious mutations will swamp a population. By independent assortment and recombination, deleterious mutations are spread thin, and, thus, selection maintains a basis for ridding the population of such mutations.

Ridley's argument translates into the proposition that the maximal level

9. Often confused with Matt Ridley (1996, 1999).

of complexity is determined by the length L (eq. [6.1]) of a replicator sequence and that the length L is determined by the level of copying error. The evolution of mechanisms that decrease copying errors in generative replication will, therefore, enable the evolution of complexity. Known examples include a storage medium that does not degrade its content (e.g., DNA over RNA), the dilution of deleterious mutations through randomized combinatorics (meiosis), error checking and DNA repair, and sexual mating. When such mechanisms evolve, the limit of complexity to be achieved in a population of generative replicators will increase.

6.6. PROBLEMS WITH MEMES

What phenomena qualify as replicators in the social or cultural domain? Dawkins (1976) famously coined the term *meme* to describe the unit of cultural replication and to resonate with *gene*.[10] A danger here is that, in making the social unit of replication seem like that at the biological and genetic level, too much correspondence can be suggested between the mechanisms of genetic and social evolution. The literature on memetics suffers from conceptual confusion and casual descriptions of "information" or "ideas" as the basis of the meme.

The enthusiasm for memes and memetics far outstrips the achieved degree of terminological clarity and consensus. A meme has been variously described as a unit of cultural imitation (Dawkins 1976), a unit of information residing in a brain (Dawkins 1982), a unit of culturally transmitted instructions (Dennett 1995), an influential and replicable unit of information in the mind (Brodie 1996), an actively contagious idea (Lynch 1996), and a behavioral instruction stored in the brain and passed on by imitation (Blackmore 1999).

In the memetics literature, the nature of ideas and the causal mechanisms by which ideas lead to phenotypic behavior are rarely spelled out. As a result, in a very real sense, memetics is insufficiently Darwinian: it does not identify the detailed, causal mechanisms involved. Instead, it relies casually on terminological resonance and the genetic metaphor.

Related reservations are spelled out by John Maynard Smith (1995, 47), who expressed "uneasiness with the notion of memes . . . because we do not know the rules whereby they are transmitted. A science of population

---

10. Although the very similar term *mneme* was coined much earlier. See Semon (1904) and Maeterlink (1927).

genetics is possible because the laws of transmission—Mendel's laws—are known. . . . [N]o comparable science of memetics is as yet possible." The leading evolutionary sociologist, W. Garry Runciman (2001, 236), has expressed a similar concern: "The term 'meme' . . . is perhaps best avoided until there is less disagreement than at present about its precise definition." If the term *meme* is retained at all, as a general term for replicators in the social and cultural domain, then its manifestations and mechanisms must be defined.

However, the problem is not simply the word and its ambiguities but the fact that, once we enter the social domain, we must consider both ideal and material entities. Biologists typically avoid this problem by pointing to the material mechanisms or substrates involved in any genetic or other transmission of information while leaving what they mean by *information* vague. Social scientists cannot legitimately follow such a strategy. In the social sphere, ideas, beliefs, knowledge, and perceptions are central to the story.

A central problem in philosophy since Plato has been the treatment and reconciliation of the ideal and the material worlds. Social scientists must negotiate these issues. In the latter part of the nineteenth century, American pragmatist philosophers such as William James (1890) and John Dewey (1910) recognized the importance of Darwinism for helping overcome the dualisms of ideas and matter, mind and body. They understood that, from an evolutionary and Darwinian perspective, ideas could not be considered as freestanding entities in themselves. There can be no hermetic divide between the ideal and the material. Ideas themselves must be considered expressions of material phenomena, but without reducing them to simple material entities. In modern philosophy, this position is described as "emergentist materialism," according to which ideas are regarded as emergent properties of interacting material and neural entities. Ideas have properties irreducible to those entities themselves. Among the modern expositors of this view is Mario Bunge (1980), who regards Darwin himself as one of the pioneers of this intellectual tradition. There has been a revival of the pragmatist approach in social theory, and Hans Joas (1996, 158) eloquently explains its meaning and significance:

> The alternative to a teleological interpretation of action, with its inherent dependence on Cartesian dualisms, is to conceive of perception and cognition not as preceding action but rather as a phase of action by which action is directed and redirected in its situational contexts. According to this alternative view, goal-setting does not take place by an act of intellect *prior* to the actual action,

but is instead the result of a reflection on aspirations and tendencies that are pre-reflexive and have *already always* been operative. In this act of reflection, we thematize aspirations which are normally at work without our being actively aware of them. But where exactly are these aspirations located? They are located in our bodies. It is the body's capabilities, habits and ways of relating to the environment which form the background to all conscious goal-setting, in other words, to our intentionality. Intentionality itself, then, consists in a self-reflective control which we exercise over our current behavior.

Intentionality is not robbed here of meaning or significance. Intentionality is "self-reflective control." From this position, it is necessary to understand the origins and mechanisms of this control and likewise for the underlying behavioral propensities whose manifestations are being guided (Postrel and Rumelt 1992).

Significantly, this view of intentionality is consistent with experimental research in modern psychology. It is often taken for granted, or by definition, that human action is motivated exclusively by reasons based on beliefs. This proposition has been challenged since the 1970s by experiments that show that conscious sensations are reported about half a second after neural events and that unconscious brain processes are discernible before any conscious decision to act (Libet 1985, 2004; Wegner and Wheatley 1999; Wegner 2002). This evidence suggests that our dispositions are triggered before our actions are rationalized: we contrive reasons for actions already under way.

This undermines explanations of human action wholly in the terms of reasons and beliefs, which is still a commonplace formulation in the social sciences. This "folk psychology" papers over a much more complex neurophysiological reality. It cannot adequately explain the origins of reasons and beliefs. Such "mind-first" explanations of human behavior are unable to explain adequately such phenomena as sleep, memory, learning, mental illness, or the effects of chemicals or drugs on our perceptions or actions (see Bunge 1980; Stich 1983; Churchland 1984, 1989; Churchland 1986; Damasio 1994; Rosenberg 1995, 1998; Kilpinen 1999, 2000).

Humans do act for reasons. But reasons and beliefs themselves are caused and must be explained. From a Darwinian perspective, reasoning itself is based on habits and instincts, and it cannot be sustained without them. Furthermore, consistent with the Darwinian doctrine of continuity, instincts and the capacities to form habits evolved through a process of natural selection that extends far back into our prehuman past.

How does all this affect the concept of the meme? The meme as behavior cannot serve as a replicator because behavior is an outcome rather than a mechanism or a disposition. Furthermore, the concept of meme as idea faces the problem of the identification of its material substrate and of the underlying emotions or dispositions on which the ideas are grounded. The meme as idea points to an untenable dualism of the ideal and the material worlds.

Partly in response to this problem, Robert Aunger (2002) regarded memes, not as ideas or behaviors, but as neurons and electrochemical connections in the brain. For Aunger, a meme is essentially the state of a node in a neuronal network capable of generating a copy of itself in either the same or a different neuronal network, without being destroyed in the process. Acts of communication between people lead to neural nodes replicating their state from one brain to another. Aunger's dramatic reworking of the concept of the meme overcomes the limitations of regarding memes as ideas or behaviors but ends up reducing them to neuronal states.

If an idea is communicated from one person to another, then there is no guarantee that the substructures of neural states relating to the communicated idea in the brains of the receiver and the sender, will be similar. The idea may take hold in the brain of the receiver on the basis of an entirely different substructure of neural states. The idea is communicated, but there is no necessary or likely replication of neural structures. By driving the concept of the meme into the neuron, Aunger moves away from the communication and cultural transmission of identifiable ideas, which memetics originally attempted to address. Any necessary replicative similarity at the level of ideas is abandoned. Aunger's radical refinement of memetics may well procreate viruses of doubt that eventually undermine the whole memetics project.

We propose a different approach. Inspired by Darwinism, the early pragmatist philosophers (James 1890; Dewey 1922) and those inspired by them (Veblen 1914) saw habits as socially transmitted dispositions necessarily underlying thoughts, beliefs, and deliberations. In turn, habits are primed and underlaid by biologically inherited instincts. Both instincts and habits can be the basis of our convictions and emotions. Habits can channel or counter instincts, just as the higher-order habits of reason can restrain or overcome lower-order habits or addictions. The layered ontology of instinct-habit-reason provides the necessary connections between the biological and the social aspects of human agency (Margolis 1987; Murphy 1994; Hodgson 2004a).

Consequently, instead of focusing on the levels of ideas or behaviors—as with the meme—we point to the underlying, materially based replicators at the social level. The material basis of these social replicators is not simply the neural connections in the brain. It also includes the structured, communicative, and causal interactions between individuals. These help create the dispositions and emotions on which ideas emerge and from which they draw their energy. Instincts also play a role, but they are inherited biologically. Above these, the first and most fundamental replicators at the social level are individual habits, to which we turn first.

6.7. HABITS, ROUTINES, AND OTHER SOCIAL GENERATIVE REPLICATORS

Despite his introduction of the concept of the meme as a "new replicator" (Dawkins 1976), generally Dawkins emphasizes genetic replicators because he sees them as an outcome of the law of the "survival of the most stable" (Dawkins 1989, 13). But stability is relative to the evolutionary timescales involved. In genetic evolution, major evolutionary changes take place over millions of years, and timescales of fewer than about ten thousand years are relevant in a minority of cases only. David Hull (1988, 440–68) has pointed out that some evolutionary processes in biology can be very rapid, such as mutations in viruses. But, if we were to travel back ten thousand years, we would be familiar with most of the plants and animal species that we found on Earth, despite significant changes in climate and species distribution. By contrast, technology would be rudimentary and primitive compared to its state today, human institutions would be vastly different, and the language would be incomprehensible. With social and cultural evolution, we are almost entirely confined to timescales of fewer than fifty thousand years, mostly to less than five thousand years, and often to a few hundred years, if not fewer. Relative to such lesser timescales, customs and habits have a sufficient degree of stability to be considered as replicators.

Dawkins (1989, 34–35) says that genes, "like diamonds, are forever" while "individuals and groups are like clouds in the sky or dust storms in the desert." Again, the issue of timescales is relevant. Dawkins denies, not only longevity, but also durable structure to individuals and groups at higher levels. We regard these denials as unwarranted because they ignore the fact that the timescales of biological and social evolution are very different and, consequently, underestimate the structural durability of individuals and groups relative to their evolutionary context.

Habits as Social Generative Replicators

Social replicators are mechanisms that help mold human capacities and that are transmitted, not genetically, but at the social and cultural level. Habits are elemental social replicators in the social world (Hodgson 2003c; Hodgson and Knudsen 2004a, 2004b, 2008b). A habit is a disposition to engage in previously adopted or acquired behavior that is triggered by an appropriate stimulus. Habits are formed through the repetition of behavior or thought. They are influenced by prior activity and are the basis of both reflective and nonreflective behavior. Crucially, we can have habits that lie unused for a long time. Habits are submerged repertoires of potential behavior that can be triggered by an appropriate stimulus or context.

Although all habits involve thoughts or mental activity and thought is a form of behavior, for simplicity we refer to habits expressed visible behavior as *corporeal habits* and to habits that are confined to the mind as *habits of thought*. Unlike DNA or computer viruses, corporeal habits do not directly make copies of themselves. Instead, they replicate indirectly, by means of their behavioral expressions. They can impel behavior that is consciously or unconsciously followed by others, as a result of incentive or imitation. Eventually, the copied behavior becomes rooted in the habits of the follower, thus transmitting from individual to individual an imperfect copy of each habit.

The replication of corporeal habits satisfies all four criteria for generative replication. Both the original habit and its copy embody a *conditional generative mechanism*. The acquired habit both is energized conditionally on the receipt of environmental signals and plays a constructive role in the development of the interactor, that is, the individual with the habit. Furthermore, the habit of behavior in one person *causes* behavior that is copied, at least in the sense that the copy depends on the source, and leads to similar habits being acquired. The acquired habit of behavior is *similar* to the first with respect to the behavior it might promote under specific conditions. Tacit or other *information* is transferred in the process.[11]

Habit-forming behavior can be molded by incentives or constraints. In many cases, such as language or some traffic conventions, we can have powerful incentives to behave like others. In doing so, we too build up hab-

---

11. Similarity in neural connection design, even with similar genes and environment, is very unlikely (Edelman 1989). Underlying neuronal configurations supporting similar habits are likely to differ between individuals.

its associated with these behaviors. The behaviors are reproduced, and the habits giving rise to them are replicated.

Habit replication also often relies on imitation, which need not be fully conscious and can involve some "tacit learning" (Polanyi 1967; Reber 1993; Knudsen 2002b). Imitation can result from an instinctive propensity that has itself evolved for efficacious reasons among social creatures (Boyd and Richerson 1985; Simon 1990; Tomasello 1999a, 1999b). But the evolution of an imitation instinct might require an existing set of common behaviors in the group. Otherwise, an emerging propensity to imitate might not have a selection advantage. If imitation is more than mimicry, then the rules and understandings associated with it must also be transmitted.[12]

By contrast, habits of thought are unobservable and cannot emerge through behavioral imitation. They consist of mental models that enable the conscious deliberation and manipulation of situations. Actors adapt and use their mental models as guides as they proceed through a particular cultural context (Johnson-Laird 1981). As habits, mental models are formed by the repetition of particular associations and patterns of thought. Under specific conditions, when agents experience common external constraints or regularities, they may develop similar mental models that will direct conscious deliberation toward a particular object in a particular class of situations. Different people facing similar environmental regularities will experience similar mental models that may be caused by different patterns of neuronal activity (Kurthen 2001). Hence, similarities in habits of thought and mental models can emerge when enduring similarities in external constraints or conventions exist.

Members of a species are similar in terms of their physical construction, sensory organs, nervous system, and brain function. These similarities provide common constraints that may promote some similarity in mental experiences of the external world; similarities in physical construction become causes as well as evolutionary consequences of similarities in experience. The possibility arises that two human beings will experience similar mental phenomena when confronted with the same external object (Edelman 1989; Kubovy and Epstein 2001).

Cultural circumstances and social institutions vary from society to society, but members of each society must adapt to them. An evolutionary ex-

---

12. The importance of such communication is underlined in recent theoretical and experimental studies of social learning, including Mesoudi and Whiten (2003), Schotter and Sopher (2003), McElreath et al. (2005), and Kirby, Cornish, and Smith (2008). See also box 4.1 above.

planation of the replication of habits of thought or other mental phenomena requires an explanation of the evolution of the social institutions that provide common conventions or constraints. These are a necessary but insufficient requirement for the replication of habits of thought to take place.

However, if two agents in the same context independently produce similar mental models, then no replication has taken place because no mental model is causally implicated in the emergence of the other. Replication of mental models would require that one agent could somehow access the mental model of another. This raises the question of how crucial information in the replication process is communicated.

Language becomes paramount. In psychology and neuroscience, the acquisition of language initially establishes a triadic correspondence of mental models, objects, and behaviors that become mental models common to the members of a society (Tomasello 1999a; Karmiloff and Karmiloff-Smith 2001). The learning of a language involves the development of an elaborate correspondence between mental phenomena and the properties of the physical and social world.

Through a shared language, one person can access the mental model of another. This transmission of mental models is improved by close interaction with error correction. By means of gestures and questions, agents establish joint attention that increases the accuracy of transmission of mental models and establishes mutual understandings. Language is a vital link in this causal chain. Without language, it would be much more difficult to communicate mental models and develop shared understandings at a detailed level.

Habits of thought satisfy all four of our conditions for a generative replicator. They constitute *conditional generative mechanisms* that are essential to a generative replicator. They are energized conditionally on the receipt of external signals and play a role in the development of the individual. Given the existence of a shared common language as well as common extralinguistic points of reference, the habit of thought in one person *causes* a mental model that is transmitted and can lead to a similar habit of thought being acquired. The acquired habit of thought is *similar* to the first with respect to the mental model it might promote under specific conditions. Some kind of *information* regarding a perceived property of the world is transferred in the process.

Genes themselves depend on the biochemical substrate of an organism. Similarly, habits cannot exist apart from the human organisms in which they reside. They are formed and stored in the individual human nervous system. But habits differ from genes in their mechanism of replication, and they do not have anything like the potential durability and copying fidelity of genes. In social evolution, additional mechanisms weed out or alter aberrant habits. Mechanisms of social conformity are particularly important (Henrich and Boyd 2001).

If habits are generative replicators, are there nongenerative replicators at the same level? Possibilities would be acquired capacities to mimic specific behaviors that are retained in short-term memory but not rehearsed enough to become ingrained for the longer term. This amounts to retention error. A person may mimic the accent or body language of another, but the capacity to replicate the behavior in question accurately is quickly lost unless that behavior is stimulated anew. Because they are transient, such short-term capacities have less potential to build up complexity. They replicate but do not endure. By contrast, because habits establish durable regularities, individuals are more able to predict the responses of others and to develop their own capacities accordingly. Understandings, skills, and other capacities that are fixed in habits have more potential to generate more complex interactions and to develop knowledge. Using the example of habit, this argument establishes the importance of generative replication in social evolution, rather than replication in some weaker sense.

Routines as Social Generative Replicators

Having established (observable and unobservable) habits as elemental replicators in the social world, we have the building blocks to understand other social replicators. Consider, for example, routines, in the technical sense employed by evolutionary economists (Nelson and Winter 1982). In this context, the term *routine* is not used in the sense of an individual's regular behavior or schedule. A consensus now exists in this literature that routines relate to groups or organizations, whereas habits relate to individuals (Cohen et al. 1996; Dosi, Nelson, and Winter 2000; Becker 2004). Individuals have habits; groups have routines. Routines are the organizational analogue of habits.

A routine is here defined as a generative structure or capacity within an organization. *Routines are organizational dispositions to energize conditional patterns of behavior within organizations, involving sequential responses to cues that are partly dependent on social positions in the organization.*[13] This qualifies

13. In our earlier definitions of *routine*, this explicit emphasis on social position was omitted. Note also that our definition of an organizational disposition can be broken down into linked

as a conditional generative mechanism and upholds the routine as a social replicator.

A key psychological mechanism in the operation of routines is procedural memory (Tulving and Schacter 1990; Cohen and Bacdayan 1994). This differs from semantic, episodic, or declarative memory. Cognitive memory often operates by building models or representations of the external world. By contrast, procedural memory is triggered by preceding events and stimuli. It typically leads to behavioral responses and has a major tacit component. It is potential action that is energized by social or other cues, often involving physical artifacts. "Procedural knowledge is less subject to decay, less explicitly accessible, and less easy to transfer to novel circumstances" (Cohen and Bacdayan 1994, 557).

Routines depend on a structured group of habituated individuals, among whom many of these habits depend on procedural memory. The behavioral cues exhibited by some members of a structured assembly of habituated individuals trigger specific habits in others. Hence, various individual habits sustain each other in an interlocking structure of reciprocating individual behaviors. Partly because of procedural memory, organizations can have important additional properties and capacities that are not possessed by individuals taken severally. The organization provides the social and physical environment that is necessary to enable specific activities, cue individual habits, and deploy individual memories.

If one person leaves the organization and is replaced by another, then the new recruit may have to learn the habits that are required to maintain specific routines. Just as the human body has a life in addition to its constituent cells, the organization has a life in addition to its members. Generally, the organizational whole is greater than the sum of the properties of its individual members taken severally. The additional properties of the whole stem from the structured relations and causal interactions between the individuals involved.[14]

Just as habits replicate from individual to individual, routines replicate from organization to organization. In large literatures in business studies on technological diffusion, organizations, and strategic management, there is discussion of the diffusion and replication of routines (e.g., DiMaggio and Powell 1983; Hannan and Freeman 1984, 1989; Zucker 1987; Levitt and

---

individual dispositions; i.e., each individual actor has dispositions that are triggered by cues from other individual actors.

14. This is a central proposition in the emergentist tradition of philosophy and social theory (Blitz 1992; Kontopoulos 1993; Weissman 2000; Hodgson 2004a).

March 1988; Stinchcombe 1990; Rogers 1995; Szulanski 1996, 2000; Lazaric and Denis 2001; Aldrich and Martinez 2003; Becker and Lazaric 2003).

The replication of routines is both the replication of organizational dispositions to energize cue-triggered patterns of behavior within organizations and the replication of social positions that define legitimate roles associated with the relevant individual interactions and the performance of the routine.

Prominent mechanisms for the diffusion of routines involve the movement of employees from organization to organization or independent experts or consultants who help transfer knowledge and experience gained in one context to another. Case studies and surveys have examined the transfer of technologies, management procedures, corporate multidivisional structures, accounting conventions, and much else (Zander and Kogut 1995; Szulanski 1996, 2000; Earley 2001; Lapré and Wassenhove 2001; Winter and Szulanski 2001). What is central to these transfers is the replication of organizational positions and practices and relations. What is generally critical is the capacity of the receiving organization to accommodate and utilize these practices and relations in the context of its own ingrained culture of habits and beliefs.

Business organizations are challenged with self-replicating their routines if they wish to increase their scale of operations (Nelson and Winter 1982; Winter and Szulanski 2001). But they also replicate routines that seem to work well elsewhere, such as job systems and administrative innovations (Miner 1990; Venkatraman, Loh, and Koh 1994).[15] As shown in box 6.1, many firms act strategically to minimize copying error when replicating routines.

Another interesting context is the replication of routines from one military unit to another, in particular, if the test bed is engagement in a war zone. A reasonable conjecture is that combat units favor stability and reliability over other aspects of routine performance (Roberts et al. 1994).

The challenge before us is to map out exactly the mechanics of different modes of cultural replication, from individual to individual in differently structured contexts. How does the efficacy of each mode of routine replication vary with context? What are the long-term projections for each mode of routine replication? Some progress has been made (Becker 2004, 2008), but, at the present time, we know fairly little about the evolutionary dynamics of alternative modes of routine replication.

---

15. But, in business organizations, the replication of routines from organization to organization can erode competitive advantage (Kogut and Zander 1992).

BOX 6.1 *Strategic minimization of copy error when replicating routines*

Over one-third of all retail sales in the United States pass through chain organizations, involving a number of similar outlets in different locations that
deliver products or perform services (Winter and Szulanski 2001). Although
firms often experiment in the early stages of process development, most successful chains expand by imposing a single organizational template on all chain
outlets, including those that are franchised (Bradach 1998). Similar replication
strategies are found in firms when they develop new production plants in different locations. All these cases involve the strategic replication of habits and
routines, replicating through a series of business units.

Such replication often tolerates little creative embellishment or modification.
Consider Intel's "Copy Exactly" factory strategy. This gets production facilities
up to speed quickly by copying everything at the development plant—the process flow, the equipment set, suppliers, the plumbing, the manufacturing clean
room, and training methodologies. Everything is selected to meet high-volume
needs, recorded, and then copied exactly to the high-volume plant.

Other prominent examples of firms that try to stimulate growth by reducing copy error include (Knudsen and Winter 2010): McDonald's, Burger King,
Pizza Hut, Kentucky Fried Chicken; Holiday Inn, Novotel, Hilton (various
brands), Marriott (various brands); Bank of America, Wachovia, HSBC; Mer-
rill Lynch, Starbucks, Cosi; Office Depot, Staples; Borders, Barnes and Noble;
Ikea, the Bombay Company; Benetton, Gap.

It seems that replication strategies that minimize copy error have become
widespread through a combination of trial and error and competitive selection
weeding out firms with less successful policies. The concept of generative replication may help explain the otherwise puzzling observation that many firms
base growth strategies on the cloning of existing arrangements as exactly as
possible.

Other social replicators include social customs and rituals. By understanding their preservation and replication in terms of shared similar habits
of thought or behavior, their status as replicators is similarly established.
We discuss customs further in later chapters.

Are Technological Artifacts (Generative) Replicators?

There is a rich and fruitful literature on the evolution of technology (e.g.,
Basalla 1989; Nelson 1994; Arthur 2008). Intermediate stages in the evolution of implements such as the modern hammer from the stones used as

tools by our distant ancestors demonstrate continuity redolent of the evolution of species. But most technological artifacts do not qualify by themselves as replicators, principally because the informtion-transfer condition is violated: the next hammer does not get from its predecessor the information that makes it a hammer. The exceptions are replicating robots or machines. But these are a new and advanced phase in the evolution of technology. Most technological devices are not replicators. They play a catalytic role; they can, instead, be regarded as enzymes of social replication.

Technology is part of a social system, and, if we place it in this social context, we can identify its replicators. Technology involves relations between a group of individuals who share knowledge about the employment and usefulness of particular devices. Much of that knowledge is tacit (Polanyi 1958, 1967).

For much of human history, technology has been maintained and passed on through custom, which engenders particular habits of thought and behavior among the individuals involved. As argued in chapter 8 below, custom is the more general form of a routine. Customs related to technologies are social (generative) replicators for the same reasons that routines are social (generative) replicators.

Of course, the technological device itself is vital, and its interaction with individuals triggers and develops their habits as well as further interactions between individuals. But this does not mean that the device itself is a replicator. Notably, in many other cases, customs and institutions involve material artifacts for various reasons (Searle 1995). In regard to technology and elsewhere, clusters of social relations and human-artifact relations are the relevant replicators.

In chapter 8 below, we consider the transition to a system of institutionalized science and technology that has taken place in advanced societies in the last few hundred years. The creation of organizations that develop and promote technologies, as well as the employment of technology by business organizations, means that routines are established both to use and to develop technologies. Many of these qualify as social (generative) replicators.

6.8. DIFFUSION AND COMPLEXITY

Can diffusion lead to greater complexity? Consider our previous argument concerning generative replicators and their potential to create complexity. We identified four types of error. As diffusion does not necessarily involve much more than the duplication of replicators, then developmental error is irrelevant. We are left with reading error (concerning input signals), copying error (regarding the duplication of replicators from one entity to another), and retention error (the degradation of copied information over time). Our proposition that copying error and retention error are especially destructive to complexity retains its validity.

By this argument, at least the copying of *generative* replicators is required for diffusion to enhance the potential complexity in the system. The existence, and relatively faithful copying, of conditional generative mechanisms such as individual habits or organizational routines is necessary. *Diffusion* must mean more than the spread of tokens, artifacts, or symbols. Consequently, we must compare (*a*) the diffusion of generative replicators with (*b*) fuller replication involving the further copying of interactors.

Note that new interactors are created in case *b* only. This establishes a changed population of interactors on which selection can operate. Selection acts directly on interactors and only indirectly on replicators: it is the properties of the interactor that matter immediately in any struggle for existence. Replicators matter in this context only through their developmental expression in the properties of the interactor.

With caveats concerning its haphazardness, selection may act as a check to weed out disadvantageous variation and promote effective traits. With diffusion, there are less effective mechanisms to verify that new component replicators are capable of creating advantageous development in the interactor. The interactor was already developed when it acquired the new replicators through diffusion. Of course, the newly acquired replicators will affect the further development of the interactor, but, because of the delay, the verification process is inferior.

Furthermore, there is the strong possibility that, while the newly acquired replicators are compatible with the source entity, they may be incompatible with the destination entity and some of its other replicators. The literature on business firms has many examples in which routines have been transplanted from one context to another, only to find that they work much less effectively in the second organizational or cultural location (see box 6.2).

Diffusion bypasses some processes of selection and development and, thereby, can allow for the more rapid transfer of knowledge than through replication alone. But the downside is that the knowledge is not tested as extensively, and even efficacious knowledge can become an impairment when transplanted to an alien context. Diffusion may help enhance complexity, but there is an enhanced risk that it may not do so.

BOX 6.2 *Difficulties in the replication of routines*

The replication of routines would seem to be comparatively easy when it takes place in a common culture with shared knowledge and understandings. A single community of practice would be an obvious example. If there are few demands on performance and minimal managerial interference, *some* habits and routines are likely to emerge. They would serve the purpose of easing task completion for community members even though they would probably not be very efficient. A similar case would be the emergence of habits and routines within organizations lacking clear aims, monitoring, and error-correcting mechanisms. Left to themselves, organization members would be able to satisfice at very low levels of performance. (The concept of satisficing comes, of course, from Herbert Simon [1955, 1979] and refers to decision-making that reaches an aspiration level, reaching "good enough" rather than optimal outcomes.)

While routine formation without error correction is remarkably easy and widespread, the management literature reports great difficulties in replicating routines. This is because routine replication in management is usually constrained by ambitious targets regarding effectiveness and reliability. Routines are typically replicated with the purpose of transplanting superior production processes from one context to another. But this seems to be difficult.

Massive evidence on the slow pace of firm growth is consistent with this point. For example, Dunne, Roberts, and Samuelson (1988) reported that it took entrants more than ten years to increase their output level to match the industry average (evidence from 300,000 and 350,000 plants over the period 1963–82). During this period of self-expansion, firms were particularly exposed to the risk of failure and exit; i.e., small, young firms had much higher failure rates than large, established businesses that had successfully managed to expand their scale of operations. Dunne, Roberts, and Samuelson (1989, 675) summarize relevant evidence from over 200,000 manufacturing plants: "Small plants fail more often than large plants, and young plants fail more often than old plants." Considering multiplant firms — as opposed to single-plant firms — the pattern of declining exposure to the risk of failure is particularly clear. Over a fifteen-year period, survival rates varied from a low of 27.8 percent for a plant that begins with fifteen employees to a high of 67.6 percent for a four-hundred-employee plant (Dunne, Roberts, and Samuelson 1989, 694). By contrast, comparable survival rates for single-plant firms varied between 32.5 and 35.2 percent.

This evidence indicates that the self-replication of routines and other features of a production apparatus are slow and error-prone processes. The litera-

BOX 6.2 (*continued*)

ture on business firms suggests that the transfer of routines from one context to another is particularly challenging (Nelson and Winter 1982; Grant 1996; Szulanski 1996; Szulanski and Winter 2002). Quite often, the recipient will end up with an inferior set of practices when routines are transplanted across firm boundaries and across cultures (Teece 1976; Florida and Kenney 1991; Kogut and Zander 1993; Bonazzi and Botti 1995; Lincoln, Kerbo, and Wittenhagen 1995). This is a remarkable regularity. Even more remarkable are the difficulties of transplanting routines from one context to another within the same company:

> Once a business is doing a good job performing a complex activity— managing a branch bank, say, or selling a new product—the parent organization naturally wants to replicate that initial success. Indeed, one of the main reasons for being a big company rather than a small one is to capture on a grand scale the gains that come with applying smart processes and routines. Yet getting it right the second time is surprisingly difficult. Whole industries are trying to replicate best practices and manage organizational knowledge—but even so, the overwhelming majority of attempts to replicate excellence fail. A slew of studies has confirmed this uncomfortable fact. One found that only 12 percent of senior executives are happy with how their organizations share knowledge internally. Another found that companies invariably have more trouble than they anticipate transferring capabilities between units. (Szulanski and Winter 2002, 62-63)

(Szulanski and Winter cite Ruggles [1998] on knowledge sharing and Galbraith [1990] on transfer capabilities.)

The huge body of empirical work on absorptive capacity initiated by Wesley Cohen and Daniel Levinthal (1990) provides further, massive evidence on impediments to the transfer of routines from one context to another. Put simply, the adoption of a new practice requires routines that are closely related to its operation. Transplanting routines to a new context changes the basis for human interaction and, thereby, disrupts the replication process. The introduction of new technology has a similar disruptive effect even if there is no attempt to transplant routines to a new context (Edmondson, Bohmer, and Pisano 2001).

The literatures on technology transfer and the transfer of best practice have documented severe disruptive effects of transplanting technology and work

(*continued*)

BOX 6.2 (*continued*)

practices to new contexts. Two very different examples can illustrate. First, out of twenty-one cases of technology transfer from Japanese to Indian firms, only one was assessed as very satisfactory by the supplier, while twelve were thought to be less than satisfactory (Ito 1985). Second, in the transfer of electronic solutions, failure rates of 50 percent or more have been reported for software projects (Brown 2003). But the transfer of knowledge even within the same firm can be difficult. Using eighty weekly observations on transfer of learning between night and day shifts in a North American trunk plant, Epple, Argote, and Devadas (1991) were able to show that only 56 percent of the knowledge acquired on one shift is transferred to the other.

Diffusion also meets obstacles at the political level. For example, after independence, nineteenth-century Mexico tried to incorporate elements of the U.S. Constitution, but, without all the necessary habits, customs, and routines to underpin the explicit texts, further upheaval was fueled. Transplanting political and legal structures is often difficult and sometimes disruptive.

Particular circumstances that can lead to the more successful replication in business and politics of habits, customs, and routines are discussed in box 7.1 on page 175.

6.9. CONCLUSIONS

We believe that the concept of the replicator can be rescued from its critics, in both biology and the social sciences. Objections by developmental systems theorists and others are deflated once the concept is defined with care. Crucially, in both social evolution and biological evolution, the concept of the replicator points to the role of information storage and transmission, and the kind of information involved, in the evolutionary process. We go further to identify a class of generative replicators in which this information has the capacity to increase complexity. We establish the importance of these generative replicators in both biological and social evolution.

Inspired by the work of von Neumann on "self-reproducing" automata, we have established the concept of a materially grounded *conditional generative mechanism* (or program) and argued that it plays a key role in the generative replication process. This mechanism is an essential part of the information that is stored in the generative replicator and copied through replication. It also informs and guides the development of the interactor.

We are not saying that generative replication always leads to greater complexity or that complexity results from replication alone. We argue that copying and retention errors are generally more destructive to complexity than other forms of error, particularly in environmental interactions or individual development.[16]

The conditional generative mechanism appears in a four-clause definition of the generative replicator. Genes clearly qualify as generative replicators. Birds' nests, animals' burrows, and photocopiers do not qualify because they lack a conditional generative mechanism and their replication does not have the potential to increase complexity.

Following the work of Eörs Szathmáry (2000) and Szathmáry and John Maynard Smith (1997), we acknowledge different types and degrees of replication. Many processes in evolution do not rely on generative replication. Like Dawkins, we emphasize genotypic copying fidelity, but we associate it with the special class of generative replication, rather than replication per se. Our generative replicators are a subset of Dawkins's replicators because our definition also requires material entities that embody developmental mechanisms (programs) that can be energized by input signals. Entities that replicate such developmental mechanisms can compress, transmit, and express the information required in building structures of increasing complexity.

In social evolution, our concept of generative replication has important implications. As widely acknowledged, the literature on memes suffers from vagueness and ambiguity. If memes are simply ideas, then our materiality condition rules them out as replicators. Instead, we regard ideas as emergent expressions of habits that, in turn, qualify as generative replicators. This overcomes the dualism and separation of the ideal and material worlds by grounding ideas on habits, as in pragmatist philosophy (Joas 1993, 1996; Diggins 1994; Putnam 1995; Hodgson 2004a). We argue that customs and routines also qualify as generative replicators. Consideration of their mechanisms of replication would address the detailed equivalent of the "genetics" of social replicators that has been missing from discussions of memes.

With our definitions, *inheritance* and *replication* are synonyms. Often, replication takes place with the creation of a new entity or interactor. But it

16. With protein synthesis, the work of Lee et al. (2006) supports this conclusion by identifying a catastrophic loss of accuracy associated with accumulation of error.

is also possible for replicators to be copied from one existing interactor to another, without new interactors being created. This is described as *diffusion*, and it is particularly important in social evolution, with commonplace examples such as the copying of habits.

We have underlined the importance of copying fidelity in information transmission from one generative replicator to another. On this, the preservation and potential enhancement of complexity depend. A case can be made in the biological world that the Weismann barrier—limiting any interference by the interactor with the information in the generative replicator—has evolved to deal with this problem (Maynard Smith and Szathmáry 1995). A big question is whether there is an equivalent Weismann barrier in the social domain. Genetic or culturally transmitted mechanisms of conformism may be important in sustaining such a barrier. Mechanisms of conformist transmission (Boyd and Richerson 1985; Henrich and Boyd 1998; Henrich 2004) minimize deviance and standardize individual attitudes. The social culture becomes conservative and unresponsive to change. This would mean that the habits and customs of a population are resistant to social and environmental change—a social Weismann barrier. This is among several research questions prompted by our definition of a generative replicator. It is a matter for future empirical research.

CHAPTER SEVEN

From Group Selection to Organizational Interactors

Bear in mind that natural selection is not concerned essentially with genes at all. Darwin articulated the theory beautifully while remaining utterly ignorant of genetics. So long as there is trait variation, heritability, and trait-dependent differential reproduction, then there is selection. . . . If this selection is guided by purposeful design, it is artificial selection, otherwise it is natural selection. There is nothing in the theory that says that the traits in question must be genetically encoded, or that reproducing entities must be individual organisms.

RICHARD JOYCE, (2006)

If group selection has become respectable again, the reader may well wonder why the news is not generally known.

ELLIOTT SOBER AND DAVID SLOAN WILSON, (1998)

Preceding chapters establish the analytic importance of the replicator-interactor distinction in social as well as biological evolution. Chapter 6 proposed some candidate replicators in the social domain. We now turn to the definition of an interactor and the identification of possible social interactors. This requires discussion of multiple levels of selection and how interactors at different levels relate to their respective replicators.

Such a discussion has emerged from the literature on group selection. An overview of the conditions under which group selection can occur helps us identify factors such as structural coherence that are useful in defining viable entities that function as interactors in evolutionary processes. *Group selection* means selection *for* groups as interactors and the possible selection *of* multiple "component" replicators such as habits and genes, which exist on different levels. This leads to the question of selection on multiple levels.

We establish that social organizations, including business firms, are often interactors. Such organizations are more than simply groups because of the existence of routines and social positions. Accordingly, to understand firms and other organizations, we need more than a dual inheritance theory (Boyd and Richerson 1985; Durham 1991); we must consider the replication of social positions and routines as well. We show how the analytic framework of a generalized Darwinism leads us to pose particular questions, such as those concerning the evolution of business organizations.

The question of group selection is reviewed in the next two sections, underlining the importance of group cohesion as a condition for group selection to occur. The next section takes up the issue of cohesion in defining the interactor. This leads to discussions of organizations in general and business firms in particular as interactors, along with their component replicators. The final section ties the threads together.

7.1. GROUP SELECTION IN BIOLOGY

The idea that natural selection could operate on groups as well as on individual organisms was suggested by Charles Darwin (1871) and famously promoted much later by the biologist Vero C. Wynne-Edwards (1962). As an example, Wynne-Edwards argued that the alarm cry of a bird, telling others in its group of the presence of a predator, would give its group a selection advantage, compared with other groups in which there was a lesser propensity to give such warning alarms.

Critics such as George C. Williams (1966), Richard Dawkins (1976), and others proposed that the arguments in favor of group selection were false.[1] Continuing with the same example of a group of birds, it is possible that a genetic mutation might occur causing some members of the group to lose or diminish their instinctive disposition to give the alarm in the presence of a predator. Birds with this mute mutation would "free ride" in the group, benefiting from the warnings given by others who retained the genetic propensity to cry the alarm. Furthermore, birds with no propensity to give the alarm would be at a selection advantage compared with the others, for any crying bird draws attention to itself and places itself at greater risk from the predator. The critics explained the survival of specific group behaviors in terms of the natural selection of the genes that determined those behaviors, not in terms of the selection of the group as a whole. The critiques of Williams, Dawkins, and others made the idea of group selection unpopular, and it fell out of favor for several years.

---

1. Williams and Dawkins built on the classic work of Hamilton (1964), among others. As noted in chapter 1 above, Dawkins (1983, 422) subsequently modified his view. More dramatically, Williams (1992, 6) later conceded: "It is logically possible for selection to operate at group levels to produce adaptive group organization, and I suggest that certain sorts of group selection are probably important."

But defenders of group selection quickly refined their arguments. A number of attempts were made to give their ideas a more rigorous theoretical grounding and even some experimental support. Prominent in this revival were Niles Eldredge, Richard Lewontin, Elliott Sober, Michael Wade, David Sloan Wilson, William Wimsatt, and several others. Some of their main arguments are briefly summarized below. The possibility of group selection in the biotic world (under restricted conditions) is now quite widely accepted among biologists and is supported by a substantial scientific literature (see, e.g., Boyd and Richerson 1985; Hodgson 1993; Campbell 1994; Sober and Wilson 1998; Bergstrom 2002, 2003; Wilson 2002; Henrich 2004; and Wilson and Wilson 2007).

However, the mechanisms and issues involved in biological group selection are very different from those in the social and cultural context. Hence, it is useful to distinguish between *genetic group selection* and *cultural group selection* (Henrich 2004). Both involve the selection *of* groups; in the former case, the focus is on the changing gene pool that results from group selection; in the latter, the possibility of changing cultural or social entities is considered. This section concerns genetic group selection. Cultural group selection will be addressed later.

In some of the criticisms of genetic group selection, notably those by Dawkins, the emphasis on genes as the sole biotic replicators was used to undermine the idea of the group as a unit of selection. But, even if true, the proposition that the gene is the sole replicator says nothing about the units of selection. As Sober (1981, 113) pointed out: "[The group selectionists] do not deny that the gene is the mechanism by which biological objects pass on their characteristics. . . . [T]his shared assumption about the unit of replication simply cuts no ice. That genes are passed along leaves open the question as to what causes their differential transmission." David Hull (2001b, 61) later observed: "When Dawkins says that genes are the units of selection, he means replication." Dawkins, by false logic, had moved from the proposition that genes are the primary units of replication to the idea that they must also be the main or exclusive units of selection.

A mistake here, as Sober (1984) elaborated, was to muddle two different aspects of the selection process: selection *of* and selection *for*. The selection *of* individual organisms leads to changes in the population and the gene pool, leading, in turn, to selection *for* specific genes that may bestow fitness advantages in particular contexts. More generally, as noted above, there is selection *of* interactors leading to selection *for* replicators.

Both critics and proponents of genetic group selection agree that there is always selection *for* the genes in the population. At the biological level, the group selection controversy is not about group replicators: it concerns the identification of group interactors. Both sides agree that individual organisms are interactors. The proponents of genetic group selection argue that groups are additional interactors, giving rise to a hierarchy of interactors, and with selection operating at multiple levels, including both individuals and groups. Hence, the group selection controversy was about the number of levels of selection, in the sense of selection *of* rather than selection *for*. When selection occurs at a particular level, the object *of* selection must be an interactor at that particular level (Brandon 1996).

Accordingly, the question of whether groups are selected depends partly on whether they are successful candidates for interactors. As discussed in section 7.3 below, Hull (1988) defines an interactor as a cohesive entity that differentially affects replication. A necessary condition for genetic group selection is for the group to constitute itself in this way as an interactor. The viability of genetic group selection thus depends on the cohesiveness of the group with regard to its influence over the selection process and, in particular, the capacity of the cohesive group to influence the selection outcomes at the genetic level.

To understand the differential genetic transmission of genes, we must look to the interactors and how they are structured. Just as individual organisms involve integrated groups of genes that have become functionally organized by natural selection to survive, groups may also sometimes cohere together to the extent that the individuals within them are largely "bound together by a common fate," as Elliott Sober (1981, 107) puts it. As Sober elaborates: "Group selection acts on a set of groups if, and only if, there is a force impinging on those groups which makes it the case that for each group, there is some property of the group which determines one component of the fitness of every member of the group."

The viability of genetic group selection depends in part on the group bestowing fitness advantages on the individual: it depends on the existence of fitness benefits emanating from membership in the group. Hence, the group context is vitally important. A serious underlying error in some arguments against genetic group selection is underestimating that the fitness value of any gene depends on its context. As the leading biologist Ernst Mayr (1963, 296) asserts: "No gene has a fixed selective value; the same gene may confer high fitness on one genetic background and be virtually lethal on another." We shall show below that context matters in the case of cultural group selection as well. A prominent error in the social sciences—particularly in economics, where atomistic and individualistic notions are fashionable—is to downplay the extent to which individual characteristics are molded by their institutional or cultural context.

Some of the arguments against genetic group selection are based on mathematical models of the selection process. Many of these models show that, while group selection is possible, it is highly unlikely (see, e.g., Maynard Smith 1964, 1976; and Williams 1966). Such models suggest that the differential selection *between* groups cannot override the effects of individual selection *within* groups, except for a highly restricted set of parameter values. On these grounds, group selection is considered to be relatively insignificant. However, within such mathematical models of selection, several simplifying assumptions are made. For example, a number of nonlinearities and environmental interdependencies are excluded to obtain a tractable mathematical solution. But the existence of such interdependencies is a crucial factor in determining whether group selection exists.

Michael Wade (1978) noted restrictive assumptions in the basic models of the selection process. In particular, it is typically assumed that the probability of survival of a population can be significantly dependent on the frequency of a single allele. In several models, all populations contribute migrants to a common pool, normally in a number independent of the population size, from which colonists are drawn at random to fill vacant habitats. Variance between populations is assumed to be created primarily by genetic drift between populations, rather than by differential sampling from the migrant pool. Finally, group selection and individual selection are assumed to be operating in opposite directions with respect to the allele in question. Wade (1978) examined the weaknesses of these assumptions in turn. He showed that relaxing them has a significant positive effect on the viability of genetic group selection. He also carried selection experiments with flour beetles (*Tribolium castaneum*) that supported his results (see Wade 1976). His work demonstrated that the mathematical selection models in the literature are based on oversimplifying and restrictive assumptions that reduce the apparent likelihood of group selection and that genetic group selection is more plausible than these models suggest.[2]

In a series of works, Sober and D. S. Wilson also took issue with some of the assumptions in the mathematical selection models (Wilson 1980, 1983, 1999; Wilson and Sober 1994; Sober and Wilson 1998). For instance, they

---

2. For a discussion of the experimental evidence of group selection, see Goodnight and Stevens (1997).

pointed out that all such models assume a spatial homogeneity in the genetic composition of populations and that selection is insensitive to the fitness of the population as a whole. Although these assumptions are mathematically convenient, they are neither necessary nor realistic, and they bias the models against the possibility of genetic group selection.

A real-world experiment illuminates some of the key issues involved (Muir 1995; Sober and Wilson 1998, 121–23). A seemingly obvious way of increasing egg-laying productivity in a chicken farm is to select for breeding the individual chickens that lay the most eggs. But chickens interact in groups. In experiments, selecting the most productive chickens led to lower average egg productivity per chicken, largely because those selected were more aggressive: they attacked other chickens and suppressed their egg production. The experimenters switched to selecting the more productive flocks for breeding purposes, and chicken production dramatically increased. Selection *of* flocks led to different selection outcomes *for* both individuals and their interactions. This experiment shows that one of the key issues involved in group selection is the interaction between the individual and the group and that the most effective groups are not necessarily mere aggregates of the most effective individuals. This lesson clearly applies to human groups as well.

Under specific conditions, selection in nature can occur between groups as well as within groups. A necessary condition of the selection of groups is that membership in the group bestows fitness advantages on individuals. For genetic group selection to occur, these additional fitness advantages must lead to differences among groups. Furthermore, they must be sufficient to ensure that selection between groups, acting indirectly on gene frequencies in the group, overcomes selection forces within each group and, thus, leads to an outcome that is different from the selection of individuals alone.

Genetic group selection is undermined when individual migration between groups and other processes diminish the variation between groups. If migration were unbounded and extensive, then the mixed-up outcome would be much less variation of individual characteristics between groups than within groups themselves, and the variation within groups would approach the variation in the population as a whole. In these circumstances, the groups would have few differentiating features, and group selection would be undermined. By contrast, if migration is constrained, then differences between groups can be maintained. This is a necessary, but not sufficient, condition for group selection to occur.

The Price (1995) equation is useful for clarifying these issues. In chapter 5, we presented the following version of this equation:

$$e\Delta X = \text{Cov}(e_i, x_i) + E(e_i\Delta x_i). \quad (7.1)$$

The term $e\Delta X$ refers to the change of average fitness due to the change through selection in population property X, related to property x of the individual members. The equation shows that this population-level outcome can be regarded as the sum of two distinct effects. The first is the selection effect captured by the covariance of the individual properties (x_i) and their individual fitness values (e_i) showing the extent to which possession of the property bestows fitness on individuals. The second is a transmission effect $E(e_i\Delta x_i)$ whereby properties change in existing individuals leading to a change in their individual fitness. In the social domain, a transmission effect is often expressed in terms of innovative activity.

Following William Hamilton (1975) and others, Joseph Henrich (2004, 14) used an expanded form of the Price equation to examine the conditions under which group selection can occur. This is useful because the analytic separation of within-group and between-group selection forces allows sharp empirical tests of the relative importance of group versus individual selection. From a theoretical viewpoint, we now know when group selection is likely to be present in nature and society (as explained below).

The expanded Price equation is applied to populations of groups where groups (themselves composed of individuals) substitute for the individuals in the preceding case. Where i above refers to individuals, we use g to refer to groups:

$$(7.2) \quad e\Delta X = \text{Cov}(e_g, x_g) + E(e_g\Delta x_g).$$

Then the following is obtained by recursive expansion:

$$(7.3) \quad e\Delta X = \text{Cov}(e_g, x_g) + E(e_g\Delta x_g) = \text{Cov}(e_g, x_g) + E[\text{Cov}(e_{gi}, x_{gi})] + E[E(e_{gi}\Delta x_{gi})].$$

This modified Price equation tells us again that the outcome of the selection process can be partitioned into two effects. The first is the covariance of the range of *group* properties (x_g) and their *group* fitness values (e_g) showing the extent to which possession of a property bestows fitness on *groups*. This term captures selection among groups. The second effect is a transmission effect $E(e_g\Delta x_g)$ where the changing properties of *groups* lead to a change in their *group* fitness. As equation (7.3) shows, this group transmission effect encompasses both intragroup selection effects $E[\mathrm{Cov}(e_{gi}, x_{gi})]$ and intragroup transmission effects. Intragroup selection effects capture those changes in the characteristics of individuals that occur because of selection processes that are specific to that group. Intragroup transmission occurs through processes that are not caused by selection forces decomposed to the level of individuals within groups. Examples include developmental processes, innovation, and other effects that alter the characteristics of individuals within a group. Notably, some of these effects can be attributed to selection processes at lower levels. Formally, this can be achieved by further recursive expansion of equation (7.3), using the term $E(e_{gi}\Delta x_{gi})$ for expansion. That is, innovative activities that are specific to a group can be decomposed into selection among individuals as well as innovative effects attributed to the individual human actor.

Note that this conceptual switch in the Price equation from the individual to the group level neither ignores nor replaces the individuals involved. Individuals and individual properties are still present, through their essential contributions to the properties of groups, including variation within groups. Group selection itself encompasses processes of individual selection. With the selection *of* groups, there is still the selection *of* individuals as well as selection *for* genes.

Crucially, this group-level Price equation (eq. 7.3) tells us that the process of genetic selection (where groups are involved) can be partitioned into the effects of between-group variation and the effects of within-group variation caused by individual migration or other factors that tend to increase variation within groups. Consequently, genetic group selection becomes a stronger force when migration is limited or when other constraints maintain or enhance between-group variation (Jun and Sethi 2007). Knudsen (2002b) provides a detailed analysis of how the effect of migration among competing groups supports or undercuts group selection.

In their enthusiasm to ditch the group selection concept, some gene-centered biologists maintain that, in nature, such conditions are rare. But we should not overlook the fact that, in principle, *any* genetic selection process in a population can be formally partitioned into between-group and within-group components, even in the extreme case where groups have no real substance. In such extreme cases, group effects may be negligible, but that does not undermine the formal result that selection can generally be partitioned in this way. Genetic group selection cannot be ruled out a priori. Determining the degree to which it operates in nature is very much an empirical matter, one that depends on the species involved and its environment.

7.2. CULTURAL GROUP SELECTION

If cultural transmission is regarded as a process by which individuals of a species can learn from one another, then the phenomenon is not confined to humans (Bonner 1980). However, learning is much more profound and extensive among humans than among other species. Learning in other animals is rarely cumulative from generation to generation. Observational learning or high-fidelity detailed imitation is confined to a few species, including apes and possibly some birds. Consequently, we largely confine our attention to cultural phenomena among humans.

To the alarm of some of his individualistic followers, Friedrich Hayek (1979, 1988) promoted the idea of cultural group selection in his later works. The crucial impact of cultural transmission on the issue of group selection was elaborated by the anthropologists Robert Boyd and Peter Richerson (1985, 204-40) and developed by D. S. Wilson (2002), Henrich (2004), and others. The key point is that cultural transmission effects can generate high degrees of conformism within groups, overcoming factors such as individual migration or genetic mutations that tend to increase variation within groups, and that cooperation can then evolve through cultural group selection. For example, cultural factors such as religious allegiance can help reduce cheating and free-riding individuals who would enjoy the benefits of group solidarity without sharing fully in its costs.

Simon (1990) adds the further important possibility that individuals within groups will, on average, benefit from receiving and relying on the information received through social channels.[3] Unless society and its organizations generally cumulate bad information, docile people who enjoy a capacity to be instructed by society and to acquire skills on the basis of this socially transmitted information will experience a fitness advantage over those lacking the capacity. Thus, according to Simon, docile individuals experience a fitness advantage over the nondocile because of their use of socially transmitted skills and their conformity to socially sanctioned behavior. Subsequent work in this area with more sophisticated models has further underlined the adaptiveness of social learning (Boyd and Richerson 1995; Aoki, Wakano, and Feldman 2003; Kameda and Nakanishi 2003).

---

3. For an elaboration and qualification of Simon's (1990) argument, see Knudsen (2003).

One of the most important processes involved is conformist transmission (Henrich and Boyd 1998), namely, a psychological propensity to imitate behaviors that are common in the immediate social group. Conformism is widely established in social psychology, including by the famous experiments of Solomon Asch (1952) showing that subjects often agree with the opinions of others even when the majority are secretly instructed to make claims that are manifestly false. Evidence suggests that people increase their probability of imitating others when uncertainty, difficulty, or incentives are greater (Baron, Vandello, and Brunsman 1996).

A second process is prestige-based transmission, involving a propensity to copy successful individuals who are sufficiently similar to themselves (Henrich and Gil-White 2001). Like conformist transmission, this process can create clusters of individuals adopting similar behaviors. It means that actions that promoted the success of prestigious individuals may spread more rapidly than other, less effective behaviors, thus, like conformism, shortcutting the haphazard processes of trial-and-error learning for many individuals.

Although most social cultures teach people to conform to others and to emulate prestigious individuals, there are strong reasons to believe that these conformist and prestige-oriented propensities are also inherited as instincts. Their universality among human cultures supports this view, as does the observation that other social animal species have similar dispositions (de Waal 1982; Goodall 1986; Brown 1991; Schwartz 1994). In any social species, there are reasons why these hardwired propensities would be selected over time as they often bestow survival advantages for the group, even if the behavior generated is not necessarily optimal for the individual. Among humans, these genetically inherited propensities are massively reinforced by our exceptional learning capacities in groups.

But, in changing environments, conformism must not be so strong that obsolete information is endlessly replicated: there must be some space for cultural modification and individual innovation. Hence, selection pressure— both genetic and cultural—in favor of conformist and prestige-based transmission has its limits. And the instinctive foundations of conformist and prestige-based transmission allow for considerable modification through individual and cultural variations.

Even if the instinctive component is large, these mechanisms do not mean that cultural differences between groups will disappear. On the contrary, conformist and prestige-based transmission involve positive feedback effects that can lead to clusters of behaviors that are very different from group to group. Among humans, the learning effects and positive feedbacks are so strong that accidental factors and minor differences in the environment can lead to huge, path-dependent differences from group to group and especially from culture to culture. In different cultures, people cooperate in different ways over very different tasks. Customs and religious beliefs vary to an enormous degree.

Consequently, conformist and prestige-based transmission reduces diversity within groups but can accompany greater variation between groups. This enhances the conditions for strong cultural group selection. In contrast to the skepticism that greeted group selection in the 1970s, the reality of human cultural group selection is now firmly established in the literature and has widening approval.

The debate over group selection establishes that the selection of groups occurs when interaction effects between individuals are so strong that the fates of individuals are tied up with the survival of groups. The group must embody internal structural relations that are sufficiently meaningful to facilitate causal interactions between individuals that enhance their survival as a group.

However, there has been relatively little discussion of how this outcome marries with the conceptual framework involving replicators, interactors, and units of selection. Clearly, with the selection *of* groups, the group is established as a possible interactor.

An obvious question arises: When there is cultural selection *of* groups (as interactors), what replicators are selected (*for*)? Obviously, with genetic group selection, the appropriate replicator (selected *for*) is the gene. But the corresponding cultural replicators are much less clearly defined. Despite the enormous recent success of evolutionary cultural anthropologists in highlighting and modeling key evolutionary processes, this issue has been neglected.

It is now possible to make some progress toward understanding the detailed mechanisms and placing these processes in a generalized evolutionary framework. What would amount to an "internal genetics of culture"? In chapters 4 and 6 above, we establish that habits are elemental replicators in human society, and we point to the possibility of social replicators at even higher social levels.

Where do habit replicators fit in the picture? Table 7.1 compares both interactors and replicators in both genetic and cultural selection where group selection occurs. The selection *of* interactors leads to selection *for* any component replicators because, as a result, the composition of the replicator pool is altered and that is the crucial marker of phylogenetic evolution. But the selection *of* interactors may also involve—as part and parcel of the

TABLE 7.1. Cultural and Genetic Selection of Groups: Interactors and Replicators on Two Levels

Levels	Interactors	Replicators
Genetic selection:		
Higher	Groups	. . .
Lower	Individuals	Genes
Cultural selection:		
Higher	Groups	. . .
Lower	Individuals	Habits

same process — the selection *of* any component interactors. This happens in nature with the elimination of parasites after the demise of their host. With genetic group selection, the selection *of* groups means also the selection *of* individuals (as component interactors) and selection *for* genes (as replicators). Between groups, cultural group selection involves the selection *of* groups and selection *for* both individuals and individual habits. Simultaneously, cultural group selection involves a degree of selection *of* individuals leading to selection *for* genes.

Note that table 7.1 defines two levels of interaction and two levels of replication. The lower-level biological replicators (genes) relate to both individual human organisms and groups as possible interactors. The lower-level cultural replicators (habits of individuals) relate to both individuals and groups as interactors. Consequently, both individuals and groups are carriers for (at least) two kinds of replicator, namely, genes and habits.

When cultural group selection and genetic group selection are combined, the result is that there are interactors on two levels (individuals and groups) and replicators on two levels (habits and genes). This establishes a picture of selection on multiple levels, as widely acknowledged in the literature on group selection and elsewhere (see, e.g., Lewontin 1970; Hull 1980, 1981; Brandon and Burian 1984; Boyd and Richerson 1985; Eldredge 1985; Buss 1987; Durham 1991; Goertzel 1992; Depew and Weber 1995; Maynard Smith and Szathmáry 1995, 1999; Brandon 1996; Sober and Wilson 1998; Keller 1999; and Kerr and Godfrey-Smith 2002a). We add to this insight a more precise identification of the replicators and interactors involved.

Our relatively simple schema shows that replicators (such as genes) may correspond to multiple interactors (namely, individuals and groups) at different levels. Obversely, it shows that some interactors (such as groups) may embody multiple types of replicator (namely, habits and genes).

Our argument leads to a conclusion that differs from that of some other authors. For example, Laurent Keller and H. K. Reeve (1999) admit multiple levels of interactor but consider genes as the only replicators. Accordingly, as well as the aforementioned resistance to the idea of the selection of groups, there is also some enduring resistance to the idea of other replicators above the level of the gene. But the recent development of a precise definition of a replicator (see chapter 6 above) shows that the concept applies to additional entities, including those at the social level.

In work on group selection so far, there has been relatively little discussion of the detailed mechanisms and structures that make the group a sustainable and coherent unit, other than the important reference to the evolution of conformist and cooperative traits among individuals. While group selection depends critically on structured interaction effects, the structures themselves are relatively neglected. The group is treated as an agglomeration of interacting individuals, with relatively little further consideration of its structural and binding features.

Social structure refers to a set of significant social rules, social relations, or social positions involving a multiplicity of individuals, with properties that are not properties of individuals taken alone. The properties of a social structure are additional to the sum of the properties of the individuals involved.

Even when group selection depends on a propensity to conformism, implicitly it involves such a notion of structure. It involves more than an individual propensity. Roger Myerson, Gregory Pollack, and Joroen Swinkels (1991), Theodore Bergstrom (2002), Thorbjørn Knudsen (2002b), and others have shown how the evolution of cooperation can be affected by the spatial clustering of structured populations. A social structure is implicated because relevant conformist behavior relates to behaviors and conventions that have become prominent in the group. Without such a social structure, conformist pressures would be less significant.

Typically, such structures bear the marks of the group's own unique history. As Henrich (2004) points out, different groups can develop different patterns of behavior. It is to these historically determined group patterns of behavior that individuals may conform. The past emergence of prominent group patterns is a matter of path dependence. Once it is established, then others must subsequently conform. Group selection is maintained by some sort of structured cohesion in the group and is undermined as the effects of these structures on individuals are lessened.

The issue of structure bears on the question of the nature of culture and cultural transmission. Individualistic conceptions are widespread. Boyd and Richerson (1985, 33) define *culture* as "information capable of affecting individuals." They approvingly quote Ward Goodenough (1981, 54), who writes: "People learn as individuals. Therefore, if culture is learned, its ultimate locus must be in individuals rather than in groups." The first sentence is valid: people *do* learn as individuals, and there is no supraindividual brain in which knowledge is stored. But the conclusion in the second sentence is invalid and does not logically follow. Groups are not simply individuals; they consist of individuals plus interactive relations between individuals. In particular, group selection depends on the existence of beneficial interactive relations. Furthermore, and more generally, what individuals learn depends on their environment; this includes the other individuals with whom they interact and is affected by the relations between all the individuals involved. Hence, there can be no "ultimate locus" of analysis in individuals *alone* without *additional* consideration of crucial *relations between individuals*.

For this reason, social and group entities are, in general, more than mere aggregates of individuals: they also involve relations between individuals (Arrow 1994; Bunge 2000; Hodgson 2007b, 2007c). Consideration of such relations is unavoidable and omnipresent in social science, and it contradicts rhetorical claims that social phenomena are reducible to individuals alone. Just as culture is about relations between individuals as well as individuals themselves, knowledge in groups and organizations also depends on individual interactions. As Sidney Winter (1982, 72) puts it: "What requires emphasis is that . . . the learning experience is a shared experience of organization members. . . . Thus, even if the contents of the organizational memory are stored only in the form of memory traces in the memories of individual members, it is still an organizational knowledge in the sense that the fragment stored by each individual member is not fully meaningful or effective except in the context provided by the fragments stored by other members." Winter argues that, although tacit or other knowledge must reside in the nerve or brain cells of a set of human beings, its enactment depends crucially on the existence of a structured context in which individuals interact with each other. More broadly, much of the information that is used and transmitted in a culture is embedded in social structures and organizations, in the sense that its existence and transmission depend on them. The information held by single individuals is, typically, context dependent; knowledge and structure are mutually intertwined (Langlois 2001).

We elaborate on this significance of structure at various stages. Having established groups as possible interactors, the next step is to refine the definition of an interactor in the light of the issues involved.

7.3. DEFINING THE INTERACTOR

Hull (1980, 1981, 1988) criticized Dawkins's concept of a vehicle because it downplayed the important causal role of the organism. Dawkins suggested that vehicles were simply convenient repositories for genetic replicators, which were regarded as doing most of the evolutionary work. Hull argued, successfully, that replication is only part of the evolutionary process and that interaction between the organism and its environment also plays a major part in determining the outcome. Hence, he substituted the concept of an interactor, defined as "an entity that directly interacts as a cohesive whole with its environment in such a way that this interaction *causes* replication to be differential" (1988, 408). This stresses not only the cohesive nature of the replicator-carrying unit but also the evolutionary importance of its interaction with its environment. These interactions cause differential replication of the replicators and the evolution of the population as a whole. To identify interactors, we must look at processes of successor selection and mechanisms of differential replication among such populations.

As established above, for group selection to occur, the members of the group must depend to some degree on one another and on the group as a whole. Structured interactions in the group must promote conformism, limit migration, or both. Similarly, Hull's term *cohesive whole* indicates that its components mostly stick together and remain united. This suggests that the components depend critically on the survival of the whole and that, to some degree, the components depend on the survival of each other.

Note that our definition of *generative replication* in the preceding chapter also referred to the respective interactor of each replicator. We proposed the general principle that every generative replicator is hosted by (at least) one interactor. In this chapter, we propose an inverse principle: *that every interactor hosts at least one replicator*. With these points in mind, we can attempt a more formal definition of an interactor.

This definition depends on the identification of an equivalent set of component replicators. This equivalent component set is defined as the set of replicators at the highest ontological level that are hosted by the interactor in question. For example, individuals host both habits and genes as replicators. Why are habits described as being at the higher level? Generally, entities at higher levels are grounded on those below but involve novel and qualitative emergent properties resulting from particular interactions of lower-level elements. Habits depend on genes, but genes do not necessarily depend on habits: the evolution of habits can affect the gene pool, but this is not universal for all habits or, indeed, for all species. Consequently, habit replication is at a higher level than genetic replication.

We define $p_{i,j}$ as the probability, with respect to a given environment E, that entity i will (more or less immediately) expire as a functioning unit (losing much of its preceding integrity or cohesion) if entity j expires. By E, we refer to one environmental state or a set of possible environmental states that are similar in relevant respects. These environmental conditions also include other interactors. For each interactor, there is a corresponding nonempty equivalent component set of replicators R. In cases where an interactor hosts replicators at multiple ontological levels, the R refers exclusively to replicators that are at the highest possible ontological level within the interactor.

The component status of R does not rule out the possibility of an interactor changing several of its component replicators, just as firms may change their routines (Nelson and Winter 1982). But it is reasonable to suggest that the relative expected longevities of interactors and their component replicators is a crucial factor in determining the nature of the evolutionary process and its capacity to produce complex adaptations. If interactors were short-lived by comparison with their equivalent replicators, then selection processes would be less likely to favor replicators that reflected the lifetime adaptive experiences of their interactor hosts.

We assume a world of multiple, competing interactors and of other replicators that are not members of R. If an entity w is an interactor, then it must satisfy all the following minimal conditions:[4]

1. *Integrity*: An interactor is a relatively cohesive entity with effective boundaries between itself and its surrounding environment, including other entities. This means that the internal relations among its component parts are generally more substantial and dense than the relations between the entity and elements in its external environment.
2. *Sustained integrity despite environmental variation*: Given shifting environmental states E_j, where j is a positive index over possible states of the

---

4. Note that we have amended and refined these conditions significantly in comparison with our previous attempt (Hodgson and Knudsen 2004b). Such refinements were prompted by extended reflection on possible real-world cases, in both the social world and the natural.

environment, the interactor has sustained integrity owing to the nature of the components of the interactor and the internal relations between them.

3. *Shared dependence of component replicators on the interactor*: Given E, for every member r of R, $1 - p_{r,w} < \varepsilon$, where ε is a small and nonnegative number.

4. *Inclusion and shared organization of components*: Every member r of R must be a component part of w, in the further sense that every r is within the boundary and part of the structure of w.

5. *Replication dependent on the properties of the interactor and its environment*: Every w has a set of properties C_w that, in the interaction of w with the given environment E, is a major factor in determining the (possibly different) set R' of successors of R.

The first of these conditions establishes the interactor as an integrated, cohesive, and bounded entity. The second condition establishes the durability of this entity over a number of environmental states. In systems theory, these tricky but essential concepts of cohesion, boundary, and durability are further refined (Bertalanffy 1971; Miller 1978; Bunge 1979; Emery 1981). The third condition means that, if the cohesive whole perishes, then all the component replicators are also likely to perish. This implies some degree of cohesion, and (given that some members of this replicator population are not members of R) it creates the possibility of differential replication among a whole population of similar types of replicator. The fourth condition elaborates the status of members of R as components of w. The first four conditions define an interactor as a cohesive whole. The fifth condition defines an interactor as an entity that causes differential replication within this environment.[5]

Note how the fifth condition relates to our earlier discussion of group selection, where we identified the crucial issue of the covariance of group properties (x_g) with group fitness values (e_g), showing the extent to which possession of such properties bestows fitness on groups. The identification of the group as a possible unit *of* selection and an interactor depends on this issue, and the fourth condition generalizes this to apply to all possible in-

5. Terms such as *relatively cohesive* and *a major factor* introduce some imprecision in our definition of an interactor. Likewise, our preceding definition of *replication* was dependent on features such as similarity. At least for the present, we require identifiable points of navigation more than exact definitional boundaries, and it is an open philosophical and semantic question of how precise definitions can be.

teractors. Crucially, the existence of group selection depends on properties that simultaneously qualify the group as an interactor. As Robert Brandon (1996, 135) puts it: "When selection occurs at a given level, the entities at that level must be interactors." Accordingly, if groups are proper objects *of* selection, then that implies that they are interactors as well.[6]

Our definition of an interactor is not confined to groups. It applies to all forms of interactor, in both nature and society, including organisms and human individuals. In the following sections, we establish that business firms and other social organizations are also interactors.

Are human individuals interactors by our definition? The first condition applies as individuals are bounded and relatively cohesive entities. Their component replicators are their genes and instincts at the biological level and their habits at the social or cultural level. Clearly, the second condition is satisfied as these particular genes and habits will expire if the individual expires. Note that this does not rule out the possibility that similar or identical genes or habits continue to survive among other members of the population: it is simply the individual's genes or habits that are relevant in this condition. The third condition is also satisfied: genes are part of the molecular structure of the individual, habits are encoded in the individual's neurons, and both sets of replicators interact with the outside world through the individual. The fourth condition applies because the individual interacts with the environment, including other individuals, and creates the possibility of either genetic (sexual) replication or habit replication through imitation. Overall, individuals qualify as interactors, with respect to both component genes and component habits.

How does group selection relate to our definition of an interactor? With regard to the first condition, we have argued above that, insofar as groups are meaningful entities in group selection and other terms, they must have a degree of cohesion and boundaries of limited permeability. With genetic group selection, the replicators are genes, and the process can be formally partitioned into between-group and within-group components. The first component matters here. Between-group selection depends on the covariance of the genetic properties of different groups and their group fitness values, showing the extent to which possession of a property bestows fit-

---

6. Brandon (1996, 137) considers interdemic group selection, where groups are more or less reproductively isolated. In this case, group selection results from processes of differential group extinction and propagation. He questionably concludes that "the replicators are the groups themselves" as well as the gene replicators. However, Brandon's words were originally written in 1988, before the recent definitional refinement of the concept of replication.

ness on groups. Genetic group selection thus involves a widely shared genetic characteristic of individuals in a group that gives a fitness advantage to
the group that is not found to nearly the same extent in the genes of other
groups. Given this group-related distribution of genes, the survival of the
particular genes bestowing the fitness advantage depends crucially on the
survival of the related group. The second condition for a group to be an interactor thus applies, as long as a genetic group selection is significant.

Given this proviso, then the third condition is also satisfied. Genes are
part of the physical structure of individuals, and individuals are, in turn,
structured into groups. Hence, genes are part of the structure of groups.
The fourth condition applies by definition since genes are carried by group
members. The fifth condition means in this context that the interaction
of the group with its environment partly determines the genes within the
group that are replicated. Clearly, this is part of the meaning of *genetic group
selection*, as formalized by the Price equation.

Likewise, the four conditions also apply to groups involving cultural
group selection, where habits are the replicators. The first condition for
a group to be an interactor is clearly valid. Given a group-related distribution of habits, the survival of a particular habit bestowing a fitness advantage on a group depends crucially on the survival of that group. The
second condition thus applies. The third and fourth conditions are also
satisfied because habits are encoded in the physical structure of individuals and individuals are, in turn, structured into groups. The fifth condition means in this context that the interaction of the group with its environment partly determines which habits within the group are replicated.
If cultural group selection is significant, then groups likewise qualify as
interactors.

Note that whether groups qualify as interactors depends critically on
whether (genetic or cultural) group selection is significant. Ephemeral or
arbitrarily demarcated groups do not qualify as interactors. With less cohesive groups, relations between individuals in the same group are of little or
no more significance than relations between individuals in different groups.
Consequently, in such cases, the replication of genes or habits depends little, if at all, on the properties of the group.

However, as argued above, for group selection to occur, groups must
be structured in some significant and cohesive manner so as to prevent
group selection being undermined by cheating, free riding, mutation, or
migration. Significant (genetic or cultural) group selection depends on social structures that promote cohesion and limit migration. Only when such

conditions are present will group selection be significant, and it is only with such structural features that groups can qualify as interactors.

Consequently, organized groups such as tribes can be interactors. In such circumstances, while habit transmission is always from individual to individual, the behaviors that express these habits depend crucially on structured relations with others in the group.[7] This leads us to consider more closely the conditions under which organizations become interactors and the nature of their constituent replicators.

7.4. ORGANIZATIONS AS INTERACTORS AND THEIR COMPONENT REPLICATORS

As noted above, groups vary enormously in terms of their structure and bonding, and only the more cohesively structured groups can qualify as interactors. This leads us to reflect on whether organizations in general and business firms in particular can qualify as interactors.

Before we do this, consider the companion term *institution*. There is now quite a wide consensus that this term refers broadly to systems of rules that structure social interactions (North 1990; Knight 1992; Hodgson 2006c). These rules include norms of behavior and social conventions as well as legal or formal rules. Accordingly, systems of language, money, law, weights and measures, traffic conventions, table manners, and all organizations are institutions.[8] But not all institutions are organizations.

Examples of organizations are tribes, families, states, business firms, universities, and trade unions. We define an organization as a special type of institution involving (*a*) criteria to establish its boundaries and to distinguish its members from nonmembers, (*b*) principles of sovereignty concerning who is in charge, and (*c*) a chain of command delineating responsibilities within the organization.[9] These conditions imply the existence of

---

7. This point was missed when we previously dismissed the possibility of groups *in general* as being interactors (Hodgson and Knudsen 2004b). Our position is modified here to admit more openly the possibility of group interactors, as long as the groups have structures that create strong conditions for group selection.

8. On the untenable claim that organizations are not institutions, see n. 28, chapter 1, above. This claim results from a misreading of Douglass North's work and is denied by North himself.

9. This is a broader definition than some others. For example, for Aldrich (1999, 2) "organizations are goal-directed, boundary maintaining, and socially constructed systems of human activity." Aldrich then excludes "families and friendship circles" from the set of organizations. The problem here is precisely what is meant by *goal-directed*. Many firms act routinely, without explicit goals. If a family or friendship circle met together and declared a common objective,

social roles or positions that have properties irreducible to those of their incumbents. Social positions carry significant powers and obligations that do not emanate from the characteristics of the individuals in those positions (Runciman 2001, 2002).

A social position is a specified social relation with other individuals or social positions (such as priest, prime minister, production manager, or sales representative) that might, in principle, be occupied by alternative individuals. When individuals occupy social positions, they not only bring their own qualities or powers but also acquire additional qualities or powers associated with the position.

The introduction of social positions brings us to a still higher ontological level. Although the maintenance and replication of an organization and its social positions depend critically on habits of thought or behavior that sustain and buttress this social structure, more is involved than these individual habits. The organizational relations between individuals, including the relevant social positions, must be sustained and possibly replicated as well.

To determine whether organizations are interactors, we must first identify the equivalent component replicators at this higher level. Following the seminal work of Richard Nelson and Sidney Winter (1982), we identify routines as component replicators of organizations. As noted in the preceding chapter, we adopt the now-consensus position that routines relate to groups or organizations, whereas habits relate to individuals (Cohen et al. 1996; Becker 2004; Dosi, Nelson, and Winter 2000). But routines are not simply habits that are shared by many individuals in an organization or a group. If this were the case, there would be no need for the additional concept of a routine. Routines are not reducible to habits alone: they are organizational metahabits, existing in a substrate of habituated individuals in a social structure. Routines are one ontological layer above habits themselves.

This does not mean that routines exist independently of individuals or that individuals take a subsidiary place in the analysis. Without individuals, there would be neither organizations nor routines. Routines exist because structured interactions of individuals give rise to emergent properties that (by definition) are not properties of individuals taken severally.

---

would it then become an organization? Because of the difficulty of defining goal-directed behavior in crucial boundary cases, it is suggested here that a better criterion is the existence of principles of sovereignty concerning who is in charge. This sovereignty makes possible the declaration of organizational goals, even if they are not made explicit. Organizations as here defined have the capacity for goal-directed behavior, irrespective of whether goals are actually declared. In this sense, an organization has the capacity to be a "collective actor" (Knight 1992, 3).

Now consider whether organizations are interactors, with respect to a set R of routines as their equivalent component replicators. Note that the habits or genes of individual members of the firm are also component replicators, but are not members of R because they are at a lower ontological level than are routines, which are the highest-level replicators hosted by the organization. The protocol established above requires us to consider only those component replicators at the highest level.

The features of membership and internal power relations help make organizations bounded and cohesive entities, thus potentially satisfying the first condition of an interactor. Crucially, routines that are members of R are likely to expire if the organization ceases to exist. If so, the second condition in the definition of an interactor given above is satisfied. Routines are also components of the organization in the sense of the third and fourth conditions. The fifth condition requires that the properties of the organization determine the expected number of its particular routines within a given environment. Depending on the organization's ability to interact with its environment, its routines will become either rarer or more common. Consider modern business organizations: firms sometimes copy the routines of their more profitable competitors, and more profitable firms may expand by internally replicating their own routines. Many organizations thus qualify as interactors, at least by these minimal and preliminary conditions.

Consequently, organizations such as nation-states, tribes, families, business firms, universities, charities, and churches may qualify as interactors. However, in many cases, the definitional issues of boundaries, cohesion, and expiration are problematic. Some of these difficulties are explored in the next section, with particular reference to business firms and other related structures.

Nevertheless, we are now in a position to expand the previous picture by considering the multiple levels of selection illustrated in table 7.2. The highest tier—involving social positions and routines—is the *organizational level*. The next tier is the *group level*, which is meaningful only for groups that do not qualify as organizations but are sufficiently cohesive for group selection to occur. The third level refers to individual-to-individual learning or cultural transmission, which can occur with minimal social organization: this is described as the *individual level*.[10]

---

10. Runciman (2001, 2002, 2005) refers to the organizational and individual levels as the *social* and *cultural* levels, respectively. This terminology is slightly misleading as all cultures and individual interactions could be regarded as social.

TABLE 7.2. The Selection of Organizations: Interactors on Three Levels and Their Replicators

Levels	Interactors	Replicators
Organizational	Organizations	Routines, habits, genes
Group	Groups	Habits, genes
Individual	Individuals	Habits, genes

When we consider the selection *of* organizations or individuals as interactors, the selection process also involves selection *for* all the component replicators at the equivalent and lower levels, plus the selection *of* any component interactors of a different type below. Hence, the selection *of* organizations may involve the selection *of* groups and individuals, plus selection *for* habits and genes. The cultural selection *of* groups or individuals involves selection *for* habits and genes. The genetic selection *of* individuals involves selection *for* genes.

7.5. BUSINESS FIRMS AND OTHER POSSIBLE INTERACTORS

The firm is more than a set of individuals. It has a corporate culture and structured environment consisting of behavioral norms and routinized practices that can augment individual skills and output per person (Argyris and Schön 1996; Hodgson 1998). In this way, it can sometimes be a more efficient means of organizing production than the market. The importance of structured relations within the firm, the effects of corporate norms and culture, and the consequential firm-specific capabilities and learning effects mean that the firm often has the necessary cohesion to qualify as an interactor (Hodgson and Knudsen 2004b, 2007).

Furthermore, the routines within the firm largely and normally share the common fate of the firm itself. If the survival of the firm is jeopardized, then skilled individuals and much physical capital can be moved elsewhere. But the firm is not simply an aggregate of individuals, physical capital, and codifiable knowledge. It also consists of idiosyncratic structures, relations, and routines that typically are not readily tradable and are specific to the firm itself (Winter 1988; Langlois and Robertson 1995). These routines are important repositories of knowledge that is not readily codified or sold. This means that most or all of the firm's routines share the fate of the firm in which they reside.

The competitive selection of cohesive groups such as firms is due to their differential properties in a common environment. In turn, these differential properties of firms partly emanate from the organized structure of the firms as a whole and are not due merely to the aggregate properties of the individuals in the firm, taken severally. Structured and cohesive interactions between individuals within the firm give rise to, and are properly regarded as, properties of the firm. These are a cause of differential profitability and, thus, differential replication of the firm's routines resulting from competitive selection. In economics and the social sciences more generally, the definition of the firm has been a matter of some neglect, and a consensus is lacking (Hodgson 2002b; Gindis 2009). A firm has been variously regarded as a collection of resources, a nexus of contracts, a locus of strategic control, and much else. Below we suggest that the legal nature of the firm must be taken into account. From our perspective, what is important about the firm is its integrity, cohesion, and relative durability in the face of changing market conditions. The qualities that constitute a firm are illustrative of the more general qualities of an interactor.

The special focus on the business firm is useful because it illustrates some of the problems involved in defining and identifying interactors in the social and economic domains. For example, what about parts of the business firm, such as teams? Do these qualify as interactors?

The key conditions that come into play here are the first (concerning cohesion, durability, and boundaries) and the fifth (concerning property-dependent replication) elements in the definition of an interactor given above. With regard to the first condition, only in exceptional cases would the internal relations between individuals within the team remain for long periods as more dense and strong than their relations with the firm as such. When these conditions occur, the firm is vulnerable to fragmentation, which is a relatively common outcome in these circumstances.[11] Generally, the individuals in the team remain members of the firm and are under the control of its management.

With regard to the fifth condition, we must consider interactions between the team and its environment that might cause the replication of the routines involved to be differential. Such replication could occur if the management of the firm decides to build another plant and build up a second and similar production team. Another possible mode of replication is the

---

11. The fragments may expire or lead to spin-offs, where a team of employees breaks away from a parent firm and creates a new and separate firm of its own. This is a replication process that creates a new interactor, and it is discussed in box 7.1.

BOX 7.1 *When organizations create offspring*

Just as there are many mergers and takeovers in business, there are also numerous cases where groups break away from a parent firm (Dahlstrand 1998; Bünstorf 2007). Sometimes these spin-off firms are very successful and become household names. Steven Klepper (2008) shows that spin-offs are often triggered by the parent firm's reluctance to pursue employee ideas for new products or processes. Evidence from the U.S. automobile (Klepper, 2002a), laser (Klepper and Sleeper 2005), and disc drive (Christensen 1993) industries likewise indicates that frustrated attempts to pursue innovative opportunities by teams within the parent firm are a major impetus behind spin-offs. Adverse developments with the parent firm are another major cause (Eriksson and Kuhn 2006; Dahl and Reichstein 2007). As evidenced by household names such as Ford, Intel, and Adobe (Chesbrough 2003), the spin-off process sometimes leads to major firms that change the character and trajectory of their industries.

Some spin-offs result from one or a few entrepreneurs breaking away from the parent company. But the evidence in the literature suggests that many more successful spin-offs involve the breaking away of teams of workers or managers with different and complementary skills. This means that, not only individual knowledge and habits, but also knowledge enabled by routines and social relations is replicated or transferred.

Although much social replication is via diffusion, where no new interactors are created, spin-offs are an important case in which replication is tied up with the creation of new organizational interactors. Both individual-level replication and organization-level replication take place during the creation of the new firm.

New interactors are created when replication occurs in the political sphere, as with the secession of states or the achievement of independence by colonies. The newly formed nations often adopt the legal systems and other features of their parent nations.

In nature, the creation of offspring is the principal means of replication. This is not the case in socioeconomic evolution, but it is significant nevertheless in this domain.

copying of the team type and its routines by another firm. What is notable in these examples is that the firm, as well as the team itself, plays a crucial causal role in team replication. This does not disqualify routines within teams from being replicators, but it does not make the team an interactor. Compared with the definition of a replicator, the definition of an interactor entails the additional criterion that the entity must interact with its environment as a cohesive unit, thus causing differential replication. In the case of the team, the firm generally plays a more important role in this regard. Just as genes require very strong connections with organisms in order to bring about differential replication, so too do routines and teams require strong connections with the firm for differential replication to occur. For these reasons, we do not generally consider teams within firms to be interactors.

Consider cases when one firm merges with, or is taken over by, another one. This absorption of one entity into another may keep many of the features of the original entity intact. Component teams can survive the merger or acquisition of their host firm. In the natural world, the consumption of one organism by another means the dissolution of one of these organisms.[12] In the social or economic world, much of the cohesion of an original firm can sometimes be retained when it is merged with or acquired by another firm; absorption does not necessarily mean dissolution.

Does a merger or a takeover amount to the expiration of the original firm? If the absorbed firm does not expire, then does it remain an interactor? The constitution, boundaries, or title of the firm can change radically with a merger or an acquisition. But, on the other hand, many of its components, rules, routines, and structures and much of its property may remain intact. Some employees and customer goodwill may survive the metamorphosis. Clearly, merger or acquisition is not the same as bankruptcy or dissolution.

We have a case that is atypical of organisms in the natural world. When a cat eats a mouse, the consumed interactor expires. But, when the whale consumed the biblical Jonah, he remained an interactor and lived to tell the tale. With the takeover of one firm by another, the legal identity of one firm may expire, but some of its teams and their routines may live on, like Jonah, in the belly of the predator. In these Jonah-like cases, we need to develop further criteria to decide whether the original firm has expired. Expiration means the loss of preceding coherence, integrity, and structure. Although mergers and acquisitions often lead to major structural changes, this is not always the case, and sometimes the acquired firm can function much as before. In other significant cases, its preceding integrity and coherence are lost.[13]

---

12. However, there are some cases of symbiotic and close structural integration of separate organisms, as with lichen and the Portuguese Man O'War quasi jellyfish. A degree of symbiotic integration occurs in some ecosystems, including some forests where vast networks of fungi redistribute nutrients among trees and plants.

13. While we fully acknowledge real-world cases of acquisitions or mergers resulting in little change, the literature on mergers and acquisitions suggests that the survival of acquired teams or routines within the acquiring or merged firm is relatively rare. With mergers, managers have often found it very difficult to fully integrate the component parts of merged firms. Acquisitions tend to work out better when the unit acquired is relatively small and the acquiring firm breaks

Although they are far from the entire story, legal factors are important in defining the boundaries of the firm (Blair 1999, 2003; Soderquist 2000; Hodgson 2002b; Hansmann, Kraakman, and Squire 2006; Gindis 2007, 2009). The firm is a legal entity, and its legal status is an important element, alongside others, in its capacity to protect its assets and remain a cohesive whole. Even if the firm has multiple plants or divisions, it still has a degree of cohesion resulting from its unitary legal status as a single "legal person." The criterion of legal personhood is helpful in identifying the relevant boundaries between the firm and its environment and, thereby, identifying the relevant interactor. The legal status of the firm is crucial in cohering its interactions with a market environment and its competition or cooperation with other firms. In a legal and meaningful sense, it is firms, not teams or divisions, that contract with customers or suppliers. However, important exceptions do exist, especially where multiple legal entities in practice function as unitary integrated wholes, particularly as a result of concentrated ownership by a group of shareholders or a single shareholder.

If a firm is broken into parts, or becomes bankrupt, or dissolves, then generally it ceases to exist, both as a legal entity and as a specific interactor. Of course, there are examples of firms that appear to have more lives than a cat; often for dubious reasons they go bust, only to be reopened the next day with unaltered structures and personnel but new legal identities. At first glance, this may lead us to disregard legal issues and treat the cat-like firm as a single, enduring entity. On closer inspection, the legal issues are vital to understanding what is going on. Such firms use the legal devices of dissolution or bankruptcy to escape from their former debts and obligations to customers. Such cases are akin to cloning: a new interactor emerges, but it is using the DNA (i.e., the component replicators such as routines and habit-based skills) and structures of its predecessor.

It must be recognized that there are other relevant structures, such as conglomerates, business units, joint ventures, and so on, that involve multiple firms in close and relatively durable relations with one another. Many of these qualify as interactors according to the criteria laid down here. Just as both groups and individuals are interactors, it is possible to have a nested hierarchy of different types of organization where the members of one organization are themselves organizations.[14] As noted above, similar nested

up and replaces the prevailing culture of the acquired firm (Kusewitt 1985; Datta 1991; Walter 1991).

14. As suggested in chapter 5 above, it is possible that, in the corporate world, a product division in a multidivision corporation can function as an interactor, as long as the division is sufficiently cohesive to satisfy our criteria.

hierarchies of objects of selection have been considered in biology. Similarly, there are multiple levels of social interactors.

However, the existence of evolutionary selection on multiple levels does not necessarily involve replicators at different levels. There need not be a one-to-one correspondence between a hierarchy of replicators and a hierarchy of interactors (Brandon 1998). Rigorous accounts of multiple levels of selection establish a hierarchy of interactors, without necessarily establishing a corresponding hierarchy of replicators as well. Consider, for example, the "genetic selection" rows in table 7.1 above. These show two levels of interactor (individuals and groups) but replicators (genes) at one level only.

There is a hierarchy of interactors, including firms at one level and individuals at another. There is also a hierarchy of replicators, namely, routines, habits, and genes. How do these two hierarchies relate? Just as the selection *of* individual organisms in genetic evolution results in selection *for* the corresponding genes, selection *of* firms in a competitive environment results in selection *for* some of the replicators associated with the firms, such as their constituent routines. That is, the current properties of the firm determine whether its routines, and the habits of its individual members, will be more common or rarer in the next time period.[15]

Further descending the hierarchy, the selection *of* firms can also have a slight effect in selection *for* human genes, given that employment opportunities in the firm can have an effect on the survival opportunities of human individuals. The selection *of* firms has effects that cascade down to the selection *of* individuals and, in turn, to selection *for* genes. But selection *for* these lower-level, biological replicators can often be ignored for purposes of analyzing economic evolution. It is too slight to be of significance, given the much slower pace of genetic evolution.

7.6. CONCLUSION

This chapter has demonstrated the connection between the analysis of group selection and the definition of an interactor. The possibility of group selection depends on the existence of structures and mechanisms in the group that limit migration or promote conformism. When group selection occurs, the group functions as an interactor. Our analysis establishes that social organizations, including business firms, are, generally, interactors.

---

15. Including product divisions or multiple plants as an additional layer of selection does not alter the logic. We omit this detail to increase clarity of exposition.

Our proposal that the firm can be considered to be an interactor is consistent with the general line of argument in Nelson and Winter's (1982) work, which considered firms as units of selection in a competitive process and "routines as genes" or replicators. We have endorsed and refined that perspective here, using insights from modern evolutionary theory and the philosophy of biology.

Many of these insights have been gained from the development of a framework of generalized Darwinism. The application of Darwinism to social or economic evolution depends simply on the existence of meaningful variation, inheritance, and selection in that sphere. Understanding this, in turn, depends on adequately precise definitions of those Darwinian concepts. Within evolutionary economics, over a quarter of a century after the appearance of Nelson and Winter's (1982) classic work, these issues are only beginning to be explored.

As noted above, detailed exploration of the processes of replication and selection in any context requires the identification of the interactors and the levels of interaction. The contribution of this chapter is, first, to establish in general and formal terms some of the essential characteristics of the interactor, characteristics that apply to any evolutionary context. Second, on this basis, we have established the status of the firm as an interactor in social or economic evolution.

This opens the door to the wholesale application of Darwinian principles to industry dynamics. Of course, this means, not the reckless adoption of biological analogies, but the use of a Darwinian framework to organize middle-range theories that are applicable to the specific mechanisms involved. Some progress has been made in this direction through the work in "organizational ecology" of Michael Hannan and John Freeman (1989) and others. But the Darwinian framework of these researchers is incomplete. They emphasize selection on extant variation but pay relatively little attention to inheritance or replication. While stressing the importance of organizational diversity, they give an inadequate explanation of its causes (Reydon and Scholz 2009). Replication of routines receives more analysis in the work of Richard Nelson and Sidney Winter (1982) and the whole tradition that they have inspired, but there is relatively little discussion there of the overarching Darwinian framework. The hope is that a more complete and explicit Darwinian approach will give a further boost to these research programs and help develop a more dynamic picture of industry evolution, one that establishes its superiority over equilibrium-oriented mainstream approaches.

CHAPTER EIGHT

Major Information Transitions in Social Evolution

Living organisms are highly complex, and . . . some lineages have become more complex in the course of time. . . . Our thesis is that the increase has depended on a small number of major transitions in the way in which genetic information is transmitted.

MAYNARD SMITH AND EÖRS SZATHMÁRY, (1995)

Once we see that other levels of selection are theoretically possible, we should not adopt a methodology that blinds us to their existence.

ROBERT N. BRANDON, (1996)

In this chapter, we sketch how social evolution has led to greater complexity. There are many important features of this story. Among these are a number of major transitions in the way information (above the genetic level) is transmitted, stored, and utilized. Each information transition has produced a major new class of replicator that can transmit, store, and utilize more complex social information. A few major information transitions in social evolution have transformed social life. They account for the evolution of prelinguistic culture, human language, tribal customs, writing and records, judicial laws, and the institutionalization of science and technology. We consider each of these transitions chronologically, from early humans to modern times.

The title of this chapter is a tribute to the famous 1995 work by John Maynard Smith and Eörs Szathmáry, who considered several biological transitions, from replicating molecules, through RNA and DNA, to animal societies. Their final chapter is on the origins of language.

It is important to appreciate that, although their book is entitled *The Major Transitions in Evolution*, they omit a number of evolutionary innovations of major significance, including the evolution of complex brains, lungs, backbones, eyes, flight, warm-blooded circulation, and mammary glands. The evolution of the eye, for example, is believed to have facilitated an explosion of different types of species. No one doubts the significance of these innovations. Yet they are excluded from the account by Maynard Smith and Szathmáry because their focus is on *information* transitions — on the evolution of new forms of information retention, use, and replication.

We share this focus on information in this chapter (while we extend it beyond the gene). Consequently, we omit several important milestones in social evolution. Like Maynard Smith and Szathmáry, our focus is on the evolution of systems of information replication. While it is vital thread in the story, it is neither a complete account nor an adequate periodization of the development of human society. We omit very important other transitions such as the development of agriculture, money, wage labor, and markets.

Information transitions in social evolution create new ways of retaining, correcting, and copying conditional response mechanisms, each built on novel forms of habit and social structure and embodying information directly or indirectly relevant to the organization of the production or the distribution of means of human survival or development. Our choice of six major transitions is illustrative and not necessarily exhaustive.

We do not argue that information transitions are the sole drivers of change. Instead, we are led to focus on this aspect because our Darwinian framework establishes information replication as a key part of the broader process. And these core mechanisms of social evolution have been relatively neglected.

Our narrative differs from that of Maynard Smith and Szathmáry in terms of time frame and degree of abstraction. First, we begin with the development of culture and language and end with some of the more sophisticated social institutions of modern society. Second, their work concentrates very much on explanations at the detailed level, whereas our concern is the development of a general scheme to account for information transitions in social evolution, leaving many of the in-depth explanations for later. We skip over many details, and we do not attempt a full causal account of how every new transition occurs. Where possible, we build on scientific evidence. But, in the spirit of Darwin, some aspects of our account are speculative.

The preceding chapter established the possibility of evolution on multiple levels. We pointed out that more complex, multiple-level evolution involves social as well as genetic replicators in addition to both individual and social interactors. We considered the evolution of modern organizations and used the business firm as an example. Business firms are interactors that enroll a number of human individuals. Their component replicators are routines that orchestrate social interaction in work groups, that is, who does what, when, and with whom.

Tribes also qualify as organizations. What are the component replicators in tribes? The term *routine* has been developed in the more specific context of business firms and military organizations. We therefore use the more general and inclusive *custom* to refer to replicators within cohesive social groups, including tribes.[1]

We define customs as dispositions in cohesive groups to energize patterns of behavior and interaction, involving conditional and sequential responses to behavioral cues that are partly dependent on social positions in the group.[2] Rituals, ceremonies, and work routines are examples of customs. The set of customs in a group defines its culture. Broadly, cultural evolution takes place in all societies in which custom plays an important role in providing group cohesion and transmitting information.

There are many definitions of *culture* and enduring difficulties in obtaining a consensus formulation (Kroeber and Kluckhohn 1963; Keesing 1974). Our conception is close to some earlier views. For example, Edward Tylor (1871, 1) regarded culture as "that complex whole which includes knowledge, belief, art, morals, law, custom, and any other capabilities and habits acquired by man as a member of society." Thorstein Veblen (1919, 39) saw the "cultural scheme of any community" as "a complex of the habits of life and thought prevalent among the members of the community." Malcolm Willey (1929, 207) saw culture as "common and interrelated habits that constitute the mode of life of the people."

Culture refers to shared habits of thought and behavior prevalent in a group, community, or society. Habits are seen as capabilities or dispositions, placing this definition in an older tradition that includes Tylor, Veblen, and Willey. While our definition of *culture* can be rendered compatible with recent work in cultural anthropology (Boyd and Richerson 1985; Durham 1991), many newer definitions are problematic because they fail to give culture an adequate psychological foundation. This reflects an unwarranted abandonment of the psychological concept of habit by social scientists since the 1920s (Camic 1986; Hodgson 2004a).

What is the difference between culture and institutions? Members of a group or society are not necessarily involved in all its institutions, but they

---

1. An alternative to the word *custom* would be *folkway* (Sumner 1906; Keller 1915; Fischer 1989). We see no overall advantage in this alternative.

2. Like *routine* and *habit*, *custom* suffers from some ambiguity in general parlance, referring both to observed behaviors and to the dispositions that give rise to such behaviors. If custom were behavior, then the characteristic would logically disappear when the behavior ceased. Yet, just as we retain habits and organizations retain routines, groups retain customs, even when they are not exercised: they do not have to be re-created anew after every period of inactivity.

are affected by its culture. Institutions are specific systems of rules. Institutional boundaries do not necessarily coincide with those of the group or society as a whole. By contrast, *culture* refers to general attributes of a distinctive group or society.

Having defined some key terms, we can begin to discuss six major information transitions in social evolution. The first is the emergence of culture. The second is the transition from prelinguistic to linguistic culture. The third is that from cultural groups to tribes. The fourth involves the establishment of exosomatic means for the storage and transmission of information. The fifth involves the emergence of judicial legal systems within many civilizations.[3] The sixth concerns the institutionalization of science and technology. We emphasize that our discussion is schematic and incomplete. It omits several intermediate transitions of importance to focus on the six that we think are the most significant in terms of information transmission. It is intended to illustrate and develop our theoretical framework, rather than to illuminate all the causal mechanisms involved.

It will be shown that the six major information transitions in social evolution generate greater complexity by nesting prior social adaptations in more complex structures. While these transitions involve the recent emergence of new social structures or entities, they build on a human psychology that has evolved over the millions of years that humans and our ape-like ancestors have lived in social groups. Over this period, we have developed the capacity to form habits. We have also evolved conditional instincts to conform to others, to punish others who do not conform, to recognize prestigious individuals and imitate them, to obey those in perceived authority, to communicate with gestures, and to acquire the elements of language. On this genetically inherited foundation, new forms and levels of information transmission have emerged, associated with the major information transitions toward more complex social formations. In recent millennia, humans have built a multilevel edifice well above these primeval foundations.

8.1. THE EMERGENCE OF CULTURE

The first major information transition is the emergence of prelinguistic human culture. It has been a matter of dispute whether humans alone have what could properly be described as a culture (Holloway 1969; Bonner

---

3. Although there is no unanimously accepted definition of *civilization* (Daniel 1968), several prominent definitions involve the existence of cities, states, internal trade, and property. The term *civilization* is used here to refer to sedentary societies with developed state bureaucracies.

1980). If *culture* is defined to require linguistic mediation (Bloch 1991), then it must be confined to humans and postdate the origin of relatively sophisticated language, which some scholars date as recently as fifty thousand years ago. We choose to define *culture* more broadly. But we also fully acknowledge that the adoption of language was a crucial step in human social evolution: this is discussed later.

The first major information transition in social evolution is characterized by the emergence of sophisticated habits—new generative replicators that enabled rapid learning and adaptation within social groups. This transition was especially gradual and started among our ape-like ancestors. Habits store, transmit, and translate information gained through learning about particular situations in particular contexts. In contrast, instincts are unlearned, inherited response mechanisms.

From a prior state of instinct-driven behavior, habits made it possible to form and transmit dispositions to engage in useful behaviors in response to particular situations. The evolution of habits facilitated the coding and transmission of experiential learning relating to essential tasks such as hunting and gathering. The medium was learning by imitation in human populations, and the advantage was that it became possible to change behavioral repertoires on timescales much shorter than those accounting for the genetic evolution of instincts. Cultural evolution involves a replication machinery through which we spread our habits of action and thought rather than our genes.

Are other animals capable of learning by imitation? Some birds apparently learned from others to drink milk by piercing the foil tops of full bottles delivered to the front doors of British homes (Fisher and Hinde 1949). But it has been claimed that this was not genuinely imitative behavior, that the birds were, instead, each learning independently to access the milk. Macaque monkeys are said to learn and imitate techniques such as washing potatoes in saltwater and using water to separate grain from sand. It is also noted that chimpanzees learn to use sticks to extract and eat termites from a mound (Degler 1991, 344–46). Even in these primate cases, it has been disputed whether such techniques have been learned by imitation (Galef 1992).[4]

But there is some evidence of sophisticated communication among apes.

4. The further literature on imitation and social learning among animals and its implications for understanding humans is too vast to be reviewed here. See, e.g., Zental and Galef (1988), Laland, Richerson, and Boyd (1996), and Tomasello (1999a, 1999b).

Frans de Waal (1996, 2006) argues that primates can read or even transmit emotional states such as approval, empathy, and fear through sounds, body language, facial expressions, and pheromonal excretions. This is known as *emotional contagion* (Hatfield, Cacioppo, and Rapson 1993). De Waal further argues that the communication of emotional states is at the core of the capacity for empathy: apes can understand and even share the joys or sufferings of others.

The possibility of reading emotions in others and even replicating emotional states is a crucial mechanism, both for transmitting useful information and for enhancing social cohesion. For example, the transmission of fear in the group can lead to collective flight from a predator. Hence, these dispositions are likely to have a long evolutionary history and be partly inherited as instincts.

Sounds, body language, and facial expressions are information signals. They can trigger responses in their recipients through genetically inherited mechanisms. The behavioral cascade results from information triggers, not from the acquisition of new propensities. It is only when new mechanisms and propensities are acquired that some form of genuine inheritance takes place.

Emotional transmission and other information signals would not have any survival function unless they triggered some kind of behavior. Hence, the triggering mechanism must already have been acquired before the signals are received. Many of these mechanisms will be inherited genetically. Such mechanisms are ubiquitous in nature, even among nonsocial species. Most organisms will be genetically programmed to respond to signals that are relevant for their survival.

Among the repertoires of response is the imitation of the behavior of others. In the preceding chapter, we noted that there are at least two types of imitation. The first is conformist transmission (Boyd and Richerson 1985). It has been shown that genes disposing individuals to such conformism would be selected in some contexts (Henrich and Boyd 1998). A second psychological mechanism is prestige-based imitation (Henrich and Gil-White 2001; Henrich 2004), through which people learn advantageously from the more successful. Clearly, this second mechanism must involve capabilities to recognize social hierarchy and prestige. In any social species, such instinctive propensities are likely to be selected over time; they would bestow survival advantages when there are substantial group selection effects.

There is also evidence for learned or inherited dispositions to punish those who break the rules or fail to enforce them (Boyd and Richerson 1992;

Andreoni 1995; de Waal 1996; Fehr and Gächter 2000a, 2000b, 2002; Gintis 2000; Field 2001; Price, Cosmide, and Tooby 2002; Boyd et al. 2003; Gintis et al. 2005; Henrich et al. 2006; Fehr and Gintis 2007; Guzmán, Rodriguez-Sicken, and Rowthorn 2007). The relevant inherited dispositions have evolved in our social species over millions of years. Some such punishment involves "strong reciprocity" (Gintis 2000), where there is a propensity, not only to punish cheats, free riders, rule breakers, and self-aggrandizers, but also those who fail to punish the offenders. Especially within small groups, these propensities are driven by strong emotional feelings of anger. There is also evidence of such dispositions among primates (de Waal 1996).

In a complex culture, emotionally empowered rules can help enhance notions of justice and morality (Darwin 1871; de Waal 2006; Robinson, Kurzban, and Jones 2007), which, after later information transitions, may become codified. If these emotions were present in our ape-like ancestors, it is possible that morality has a genetic as well as a cultural foundation.

Propensities to conform, emulate, or punish are likely to be genetically guided. But, when they lead to the acquisition of new conditional behavioral mechanisms, a new level of transmission is established. A key step in the emergence of culture is the development of the capacity to acquire new response mechanisms through imitation and social interaction rather than genetic inheritance. A culture is an outcome of specific circumstances and history. Notwithstanding important "human universals" in all cultures (Brown 1991; Schwartz 1994), significant cultural variation is apparent. Culture depends on the development within individuals of nongenetic response mechanisms that reflect specific circumstances and interactions. We call these mechanisms *habits*.

Culture requires the capacity to form habits as additional and contingent mechanisms. The social insects show little evidence of such a capacity, although bees can signal to one another important contingent information such as the location of distant pollen. Although the information itself may be novel, such communication seems to rely on genetically acquired rather than learned mechanisms. By contrast, the acquisition of habits involves new conditional mechanisms that enable new responses to new types of information input, rather than merely new information inputs to existing mechanisms. The capacity to acquire habits is found in most mammals, some birds, and possibly some fish. When many of these habits are acquired through social interaction among members of the same species, we have the existence of at least a protoculture.

As Derek Freeman (1983) argues, higher animals exhibit "behavioral flexibility." Instead of a reflex response to a stimulus, they sometimes deliberate and weigh up their options. More complex stimuli and enhanced neural information-processing capacities sometimes throw up multiple potential responses. With the evolution of a more developed brain and neural system, the cultural adaptations of the human species arose. Culture is both a biological and a social phenomenon, and human evolution is "a long existent and deep symbiosis between the genetic and the cultural" (Freeman 1983, 300). The capacity to produce culture arose via natural selection because it enhanced reproductive success.

But what is to stop natural selection from eventually creating sophisticatedly programmed instincts that are sufficiently flexible to deal with most circumstances? Why do instincts to provide the complete apparatus of cognition and action not evolve? If this happened, then no major role would be left for habits as instincts would be sufficient for survival.

Habits and instincts differ in their speed of emergence. Instincts take a long time to evolve in a population. For this reason, they cannot readily take small, transient changes into account. Instincts entail response mechanisms that react to broad categories of enduringly frequent stimuli. If the stimuli were infrequent or variable, then the instinct could not evolve through genetic selection among a population.

By contrast, habits can be acquired by individuals in weeks. Consequently, they can embody more nuanced responses to episodic circumstances. Instincts remain vital even among intelligent organisms dealing with complex conditions, but the modificatory power of habits becomes relatively more important. The social and natural environment is too inconstant to allow the natural selection of sufficiently complex and refined instincts to take place. In contrast, habit is a relatively flexible means of adapting to complexity, disturbance, and unpredictable change. The capacity to form new habits, aided by both instincts and reason, has helped enhance the fitness of the human species in the process of selection.

But all mechanisms and adaptations emerge at a cost. The capacity to form habits depends on a well-developed brain and neural system. The human brain is a very expensive organ in terms of energy consumption. While it accounts for less than 2 percent of our weight, it consumes up to 20 percent of our caloric intake (Drubach 2000). Bigger brains mean that we have to consume more calories, and our ancestors had to spend more time hunting and gathering.

Given these costs, there must be compensating advantages. According to the "social brain hypothesis," the human brain has become larger and more complex in tandem with the evolution of adaptive social groups of around 150 people (Dunbar 1993, 1998; Mesoudi, Whiten, and Dunbar 2006).

There must have been frequent changes in the environment to provide a sufficient evolutionary payback for habit-based cultural adaptations. Several authors have proposed that capacities for sophisticated habit formation and cultural growth emerged among humans to deal with a rapidly changing climate and natural environment. Environmental change, particularly climate change, is now emerging as a major explanation of the evolution of both intelligence and culture among humans (Potts 1996; Richerson, Boyd, and Bettinger 2001; Calvin 2002). When more sophisticated social structures emerged among early hominoids, they developed a greater capacity to form sophisticated and adaptable habits than was found in other species.[5]

Once a habit-based culture begins to develop in a social species, interactions become more complex, and novel situations emerge. This, in turn, can give a selection advantage to individuals who develop new habits to deal with new circumstances: culture feeds on itself. Over a much longer period, the genetic mechanisms that enable adaptation through the development of new habits are also given a selection advantage. Some enduring cultural features may slowly, by selection, affect the genes in the whole population (Durham 1991). Through different mechanisms, and at different rates, there is feedback in both directions.

In sum, human culture became established on the basis of capacities to form habits that enabled rapid learning and adaptation within social groups and involved conditional generative mechanisms. Without these mechanisms, there would be no programmed responses to input signals. At most, imitation of others would be immediate, and programmed responses would not be learned and stored in the neural system. Nongenerative replicators that trigger immediate imitation are likely to have preceded the evolution of capacities to form habits. Such crude capacities for immediate imitation may have some survival value in some contexts, but they do not store much enduring information.

The capacity to form habits evolved over millions of years. The major information transition that laid down the habitual foundations of culture involved the development of a new type of *generative* replicator. The development of new forms of generative replicator accompanies every major information transition in social evolution.

---

5. The evolutionary and functional difference between culturally acquired habits and genetically inherited instincts was appreciated by Thorstein Veblen (1914) and has reemerged in modern theories of cultural evolution (Richerson and Boyd 2001, 2004; Richerson, Boyd, and Bettinger 2001).

Before we discuss the next major information transition, we turn to an important methodological issue. We hold that the emergence of culture involves both genetic changes enhancing the capacity to form habits and the development of social structures and interactions to enable the transmission of useful information within groups.

To a significant extent, science proceeds by explaining wholes in terms of component parts and their interactions. But great advances in genetics and other disciplines have promoted the illusion that wholes can be explained *entirely* in terms of their parts. Hence, in their work on the emergence of culture, Richard Klein and Blake Edgar (2002, 279) propose a "bold new theory" that the origin of human culture was the result of "a fortuitous [genetic] mutation that promoted the fully modern brain." But the notion of a lucky genetic leap toward a fully modern brain is insufficient to explain the evolution of culture.

True enough, there must have been fortuitous genetic mutations enabling the development of a greater capacity to form habits. But the context is crucial. Habits are efficacious in social groups because they enable the transmission of information that is useful for survival. They perform this function in social species only. The "fortuitous" development of relevant social structures and interactions is also necessary for the selection of the genes that underlie habits. The evolutionary process must work simultaneously on multiple levels.

What came first? The answer to this chicken-and-egg problem is that genetic mutations promoting habit formation may have occurred from time to time but would have spread among the population only when the relevant social structures also began to emerge. Such mutations came first *among individuals* but did not become *population* characteristics until later. And new social structures were required to render any individual mutations fortuitous.

Generally, the goal of explaining wholes *entirely* in terms of their parts is a mirage. We cannot entirely explain the properties of water in terms of those of hydrogen and oxygen, taken separately. Any explanation must take into account the structured relations between the atoms in the molecule. Similarly, we cannot ever explain social phenomena in terms of the properties of individuals alone; we also must take account of the structured causal interactions between them (Arrow 1994; Bunge 2000; Hodgson 2007c). The same goes for genes. The major information transitions in social evolution involve the creation of new social structures and interactions that create new contexts for genetic selection. Genetic changes are necessary in some cases but generally insufficient.

The second major information transition in social evolution involves the emergence of linguistic habits, a new kind of generative replicator that enabled sophisticated communication and, thereby, gave an enormous boost to technological evolution. Linguistic habits are a new kind of generative replicator because they store, transmit, and translate information about a particular individual's mental model. They facilitate access to another person's mental model and build up complex intersubjective understandings (Searle 1995; Gifford 1999). In contrast, simpler habits merely involve the imitation of behavior.

From a prior state of habit-driven behavior, linguistic habits made it possible to form and transmit dispositions to engage in useful mental activity in response to particular situations. The evolution of linguistic habits facilitated the coding and transmission of solutions to complicated tasks such as the production of tools and buildings. The medium was the evolution of language, and the advantage was that it became possible to engage in the systematic accumulation of knowledge.

The evolution of language has been called the biggest invention of the last 600 million years (Nowak 2006). It is of such enormous significance that it has been compared to major evolutionary events like the origin of life, the first bacteria, the first higher cells, and the evolution of multicellularity. The continuing linguistic selection processes can easily be observed as they shape grammar, vocabulary, and phonetics.

The timing of the evolution of human language is a matter of ongoing controversy. Some authors propose a "great leap forward" as recently as fifty thousand years ago (Diamond 1991), and others suggest a more gradual accumulation of knowledge, skills, and culture occurring over hundreds of thousands of years (Oppenheimer 2004). To some degree, the resolution of this dispute hinges on what precisely is meant by *language*. There are an infinite number of gradations between utterances or speech, such as the cries of animals, and language proper. Human language involves shared symbolic references, vocabulary, syntax, tenses, and auxiliary verbs. It is capable of expressing unfulfilled desires, future intentions, conditional states, and abstract beliefs.

Carliss Baldwin and Kim Clark (2000, 97) infer that, about sixty thousand years ago, in the transition from the Middle to the Upper Paleolithic, "tools used by humans improved dramatically, becoming more specialized and complex in the process. Components were made out of different materials, and were assembled into composite wholes—like a spear with a serrated point and a detachable foreshaft." Although some simple technologies can be replicated by observation, language vastly facilitates the process, especially as it becomes more complex. These technologies were probably associated with a specialized division of labor, which would involve a degree of social organization and cooperation that is unlikely without language.

As we are here principally concerned with the nature of this transition, we do not need yet to take a stand on its timing. We are persuaded by the recent evidence of early cultural and decorative artifacts (see below), but we leave the experts in the area to resolve the issue. For similar reasons, it is not necessary here to take a position on the unresolved question of the origins of language, about which several theories have been proposed (Dunbar 1996; Deacon 1997; Christiansen and Kirby 2003).

Darwin (1871, 1:106) referred to the "half-art and half-instinct of language." Because it would be impossible for an infant to learn all the rules of a complex language solely by reinforcement learning and cultural transmission, we accept the resurgent view (eclipsed by behaviorist psychology for much of the twentieth century) that some very basic linguistic capacities must be inherited as instincts. But the nature and extent of this instinctive legacy is a matter of current dispute among psychologists (Pinker 1994; Deacon 1997; Evans and Levinson 2009). And, of course, most language acquisition depends on interaction with others in specific cultural contexts.

Language enables the communication of abstract ideas, including mental models about the world. As argued in chapter 6 above, it involves elaborate correspondences between mental phenomena and properties of the physical and social world. The acquisition of language initially establishes triadic correspondences of objects, behaviors, and mental models where the latter are shared among the members of a society (Tomasello 1999a; Karmiloff and Karmiloff-Smith 2001). Mental models enable conscious deliberation and manipulation of situations (Johnson-Laird 1981). As habits, they are formed by the repetition of particular associations and patterns of thought. When agents experience common external constraints or regularities, they may develop similar mental models that will direct conscious deliberation toward a particular object in a particular class of situations.

Crucially, through a shared language, one person can access the mental model of another. This transmission of mental models is improved by close interaction. With gestures or questions, communication is enhanced, errors are corrected, and mutual understandings are established. Habits of thought involving concepts and mental models are the relevant replicators. And their replication depends on communication through language. Essentially, a linguistic culture involves the development of an interpersonal complex of shared habits of thought.

Like other habits, habits of thought are generative replicators. They also involve conditional generative mechanisms. Habits of thought are hosted by individuals as interactors. Furthermore, just as the emergence of all habits as generative replicators depends on preexisting genes, the emergence of habits of thought also depends on other preexisting habits. Without these other habits, there would be no basis for the regular gestures and vocalizations that were involved in the evolution of language.

The coevolution of language and culture led to more highly developed notions of self and identity. Humans developed a "theory of mind" in the sense of an ability to picture what someone else is thinking or intending (Tomasello 1999a). By accessing the thoughts of others, they developed an enhanced sense of their own individuality. They could get an idea of the intentions of others and compare them with their own. Prefigurative judgments about appropriate or justifiable behavior became possible. Intersubjective communication became the grounding not only of behavioral expectations but also of behavioral norms.

Although there is evidence that primates also have a sense of self and an ability to recognize the identity of others belonging to the same species (conspecific identities), their normative and moral sense is much less well developed (Goodall 1986; de Waal 1996, 2006). A major reason for this is their lack of a developed language. Richard Joyce (2006) argues that language is a prerequisite for the evolution of morality, which is essential for the recognition and enforcement of ethical social rules.

A linguistic culture permits the transmission of both technical rules, concerning how to perform or produce something, and moral rules, concerning what should be done to conform to some adopted ethical standards. These rules, as conditional dispositions, are transmitted through the replication of specific habits of thought. Institutions are systems of rules, and language itself is an institution. Building on language, humans began to develop other sophisticated social institutions.

Whatever its more detailed causal explanation, the evolution of language and a linguistic culture involved not only the bipedal gait and the vocal organs but also structures of social interaction in which linguistic communication was efficacious. Like other major transitions in evolution (Maynard Smith and Szathmáry 1995), it was a complex emergent process rather than unidirectional upward causation. Language, culture, and the human brain coevolved (Edelman 1992; Deacon 1997; Thibault 2000).[6]

Hence, it is a big mistake to explain the emergence of language as a monocausal result of a fortuitous genetic mutation. This error is made by the evolutionary anthropologists Richard Klein (1999, 18) and Spencer Wells (2002). Some writers refer to a "language" gene, known as FOXP2, whose appearance seems to date to the Late Pleistocene (Enard et al. 2002). Wells (2002, 85) describes an imaginary scenario: one infant acquires such a gene through a fortuitous mutation, learns to speak earlier than others, breeds more, and leaves more descendants. This is an exclusively bottom-up explanation, ignoring the interactions between genes, language, and culture and the fact that language and culture amplify niches for new individual capabilities. Without such niches, the evolution of language would be unable to take off. The fortuitous genetic mutation would have no selection advantage. Some new genes did evolve with the development of language, but they required the partial emergence of social structures and interactions before they could prosper. Social and genetic changes were both necessary and interdependent. It was a coevolutionary process, involving interactions between genetic, physiological, and social levels.

8.3. FROM CULTURED GROUPS TO TRIBAL CUSTOMS

The third major information transition in social evolution is the emergence of interpersonal replicators pertaining to rank and social position. The new generative replicator enabled the transfer of social position and, thereby, promoted hierarchy and the division of labor in primitive societies. Customs are a new kind of generative replicator because they store, transmit, and translate information about abstract roles and interpersonal relations from generation to generation.

From prior habits, tribal customs made it possible to form and stabilize social hierarchies. The evolution of tribal customs thereby facilitated the coding and transmission of solutions to tasks involving a larger group of people. With the evolution of tribal customs, ranks and social positions became more rigid. Rights of access to resources became more differentiated

---

6. Regrettably, we do not have the space here to tackle the rapidly expanding literature in evolutionary linguistics. But we note briefly that the evolution of language fits into a Darwinian framework and, in particular, that the replicator-interactor distinction remains relevant. Habits of thought that embody rules of association between words and grammatical rules are linguistic replicators. Interactors include individuals (or even groups) with linguistic aptitudes.

(Woodburn 1982). Rituals also became much more significant in human interaction and, typically, involved a division of roles (Etkin 1954), thus helping reinforce the social hierarchy. Interpersonal replicators would, thus, stimulate the advance of hierarchy and specialization.

Hierarchical societies with differentiated social positions probably outcompeted their less complex rivals for several reasons. The more complex division of labor led to enhanced skill formation and greater productivity in the provision of food and other basic needs. It also led to more effective warrior groups. Rivals could be defeated as long as these advantages were not negated by the disadvantages of a more ossified social structure. Some degree of hierarchy provided advantages in terms of coordination and cohesion.

Current primate evidence suggests that hierarchy existed among our ape-like ancestors. Individual primates recognize their place in the social hierarchy and sometimes strive for higher social positions (de Waal 1982; Goodall 1986). Male gorillas often fight until one emerges triumphant. The victorious gorilla attracts a harem of females and drives away other adult males. Among chimpanzees, the dominant male displays his strength and forces others into submissive postures. He enjoys exclusive access to several females. Occasionally, some males join forces to overthrow the dominant ape. They then share the sexual and other rewards. Social primates compete for power and resources within a social hierarchy.

Defined rituals are unique to the human species. Language probably emerged in a context of ritual, gesture, and other symbolic communication (Deacon 1997). Primitive rituals such as dance and ceremony coevolved with the linguistic means of their improved replication. As in other cases, elements of the next major information transition were there at the time of the preceding evolutionary stage of linguistic evolution. The transitions to both linguistic culture and tribal customs were probably very slow, taking tens of thousands of years.

Beads used as jewelry from between 70,000 and 120,000 years ago have been found in various places throughout Africa and in the Levant (see "Beads Confirm Ancient Jewellry Making" 2007; "Ancient Jewellry Points to Early Origins of Language" 2006; and Mayell 2004). Such decorative and symbolic artifacts confirm the existence of a symbolic culture and a social structure. They could not exist without tools and, arguably, some form of language, which, in turn, were supported by the prior emergence of habits of thought and behavior.

Archaeological evidence of ritual is fragmentary and requires careful interpretation (Fogelin 2007). One way of determining the existence of ritual is through burials. The Neanderthals buried some of their dead, more than

200,000 years ago. Grave offerings among Homo sapiens appear much later, about 92,000 years ago in the Levant. About 30,000 years ago, burials with grave goods became more common in Europe.

Whenever and however they emerged, prehistoric social cultures with hierarchy, social positions, rituals, and a division of labor can be imagined. Language would serve to codify and reinforce these social formations, which we describe as *tribes*.

In part, interactions between individuals would be framed in terms of customs or rituals and depend on specific social positions. These customs would serve all sorts of functions, from reinforcing social hierarchies to orchestrating productive activity. Customs become a form of organizational knowledge, allowing individuals to understand many details, including the roles they must perform, but no one individual might fully understand the function of the custom itself.

Customs depend on a structured group of individuals, each with habits of a particular kind, many of which triggered through procedural memory (Cohen and Bacdayan 1994). Behavioral cues offered by some trigger specific habits in others. Many of these conditional behaviors relate to social positions. Various individual habits sustain each other in an interlocking structure of reciprocating individual behaviors. Together, these behaviors take on collective qualities associated with groups.

The tribe provides a structured social and physical environment for each individual, including rules and norms of behavior. This environment is made up of the other individuals, the relations between them, and the technological and physical artifacts that they may use in their interactions. This social and physical environment enables, stimulates, and channels individual activities, which, in turn, can help trigger the behavior of others, produce or modify some artifacts, and help change or replicate parts of this social and physical environment. Partly because of procedural memory, tribes can have important additional properties and capacities that are not possessed by individuals, taken severally.

Customs are not behavior; they are stored behavioral capacities or capabilities. These capacities involve knowledge and memory. They entail organizational structures, social positions, and individual habits that, when triggered, lead to sequential behaviors. Customs generally rely on tacit as well as explicit knowledge, and this fact is clearly relevant for understanding their replication.

In chapter 6, we argued that routines are generative replicators. *Custom* is a more inclusive term, and similar arguments establish customs as generative replicators. Customs satisfy all four conditions for a generative replicator. They involve *conditional generative mechanisms* that are energized conditionally on the receipt of external signals and play a role in the development of the tribe. When a custom is copied within or between tribes, the copy is *similar* to the original with respect to the social structures and individual habits involved. Some kind of *information* is transferred in the process.

The host interactor for a custom could be any relevant organization, including a family or a tribe. Given that a family is itself an organization but also part of the bigger organization of the tribe, there is the possibility that customs as replicators relate to interactors at multiple levels.

As with previous major information transitions in social evolution, the new replicators depend on lower-level replicators to function. Customs require a host of genetically primed capabilities, including language acquisition, habit acquisition, and procedural memory. They also depend on habits of body and thought. Each new level of replication builds and functions on lower levels.

Custom remains enormously significant and can be extraordinarily persistent, even in modern societies. Like language, it survives and prospers after later transitions. Some studies have revealed the striking transmission through the generations of virtually unchanging role structures and behavioral dispositions. Emmanuel Todd (1985, 1987) shows that different, largely unwritten family structures and property inheritance patterns persist in different parts of the world. David Hackett Fischer (1989) argues that U.S. regional differences in family structure, gender relations, community attitudes, and propensities to violence emanate from different phases of migration from the seventeenth century to the nineteenth from contrasting cultures in different regions of Britain. In line with this, Richard E. Nisbett and Dov Cohen (1996) provide remarkable experimental evidence of the survival of a "culture of honor" in the U.S. South. Sonya Salamon and Jack Temple Kirby (1992) show that very different cultural patterns of farm management, land tenure, and inheritance survive among Illinois farming communities, depending whether they are of German or British Protestant descent. Differential cultural transmission can persist for centuries and remain highly significant even after globalization and mass media.

8.4. THE EMERGENCE OF EXOSOMATIC AND SYMBOLIC SYSTEMS

After the emergence of more complex social structures and a finer division of labor, it becomes possible to develop systems of information storage that survive individual memories. The fourth major information transition in social evolution is the emergence of symbolic systems. The most important technological innovation in this context is writing, which is a form of *exosomatic* memory, to use Alfred Lotka's (1945) term.

New technologies play a role in social evolution that can be likened to that of enzymes. They are catalysts of social replication, but they are not replicators in their own right. For example, the written record is not itself a replicator. It is the actual social mechanisms stimulated by writing systems that qualify as new generative replicators. These new replicators transcend custom and culture because they allow reliable storage of much more complex information about social interaction. This paved the way for the replication of social structures that were much more complex than customs.

Exosomatic and symbolic systems are a tremendous leap forward because they mean that information can be stored and transmitted beyond the life of an individual. Previously, all information transmission required the presence of a person who knew the information. The replication of information depended precariously on direct and immediate contact with knowledgeable individuals. By contrast, exosomatic and symbolic systems provide access to information without the originator being present or even alive.

The first exosomatic systems involved tools and artifacts. Following the creation of tools from bone or stone, other humans might come across these objects in the absence of their creators and infer from their context the purpose and manner of their use. In part, knowledge would be transmitted exosomatically. Accordingly, the first limited exosomatic information system emerged tens of thousands of years ago with the development of commonplace tools. It has also been argued that cave paintings and stone monuments are also important means of storing important functional information concerning hunting, agriculture, and the seasons.

But there are limits to these early exosomatic systems. Cave paintings are often difficult to interpret. Duplication of a tool or artifact requires tacit skills that are acquired by imitation over long periods of time. The purpose and correct use of any tool are infrequently obvious without practical demonstration.

Exosomatic replication could not take off until there was some symbolic representation of key bits of information. Consequently, the largest exosomatic leap is the emergence of symbols and writing, which mostly depend on the existence of a language. Even then, much technology remains difficult to learn and copy without face-to-face interaction. Writing found its early uses in recordkeeping and the codification of laws.

Writing was invented independently in Mesopotamia, China, and Mesoamerica. Some scholars argue that it was also invented in Egypt and the Indus independently of Mesopotamia (Senner 1991). Because of the need for codified records and laws, writing often appears when societies are in their early stages of civilization. But this outcome is not automatic. Andean civilizations such as the Incan did not have conventional systems of writing, but they did use tallies and symbols. By contrast, runic and oghamic scripts were used in parts of Northern Europe many centuries before the local development of bureaucratic states.

Writing as an exosomatic and symbolic system provided a new means of storing and replicating information. But the information in writing cannot be extracted and used without a trained reader. Writing systems are not purely exosomatic because they also depend on the minds of individuals. Instead, they are extensions of human minds, explicable in terms of the "situated" cognition emphasized by modern psychology. Instead of assuming that individuals proceed largely by building representative models of their world in their brains, psychologists now argue that human cognition depends on its social and material environment and the cues provided by structured interactions with individuals and artifacts. Human cognitive capacities are, thus, irreducible to individuals alone; they also depend on social structures and material cues (see Blumer 1969; Rogoff and Lave 1984; Suchman 1987; Lave 1988; Brown and Duguid 1991; Donald 1991; Lave and Wenger 1991; Hutchins 1995; Hendriks-Jansen 1996; Clark 1997a, 1997b; Wenger 1998; Nooteboom 2000; Keijzer 2001; Lorenz 2001; Nelson and Nelson 2002).

Writing is a major leap beyond forms of replication confined to imitation or spoken language. The extended nature of this new replicator is an expression of a fundamental feature of all human cognition. The written record is not itself a replicator: it is an exosomatic feature of a social and cognitive system involving habits and rules. This system is different from mere custom and culture because of the emergence of the exosomatic and symbolic element.

The actual social mechanisms stimulated by writing systems qualify as generative replicators. Their hosting interactors are the social organizations (tribes or states) that use them. Writing systems involve conditional generative mechanisms that are energized according to habits or rules as individuals use or augment the written record. When habits or rules are promulgated by means of writing, then the copied habit or rule is similar to the original.

The extended reliance on exosomatic cues and symbolic representations constitutes a major information transition in social evolution. But we have noted that this transition has a long, gradual, and partial takeoff with the development of exosomatic artifacts prior to writing. The full force of this transition arrives with the development of written records. Historically, its consummation has been associated with the development of civilizations. These ancient states also provide the context for the fifth major information transition—the emergence of judicial law—for which writing is generally a major precondition.

8.5. THE EMERGENCE OF JUDICIAL LAW

The fifth major information transition in social evolution is the emergence of a new kind of generative replicator that is extended to entail, not only mental habits and written records, but also the organized legal system and the written codification of much law. Prior transitions in social evolution produced instincts, habits, and customs that dispose us to acquiesce to what we perceive as legitimate legal authority. The threat of punishment is also important, but our ingrained dispositions to obey authority, as well as our acquired and enhanced feelings of morality and justice (Darwin 1871; de Waal 2006; Robinson, Kurzban, and Jones 2007), are vital in effective legal systems.

Obedience to developed legal authority leads us to follow recorded rules that are not necessarily ingrained in our habits. The fourth transition requires the written record as a medium and storage system for effective social rules. This enabled an enormous increase in reliable storage and transfer of information pertaining to social interaction.

But law is more than codified custom. A key feature of law as distinct from custom is an institutionalized judiciary. This degree of role specialization required the emergence of large, sedentary social formations with a complex division of labor. Sedentism is regarded as a precondition for the emergence of states. Circumstances must have emerged that not only permitted a sedentary population but also imposed disincentives or constraints on renewed mobility.

About fourteen thousand years ago, the Natufians established in the Levant the first ever permanent settlements with a stratified social order, even before the introduction of agriculture (Bar-Yosef 1998, 2001). Later civilizations in Egypt, Sumer, and elsewhere relied heavily on agricultural production. But the precise dating and detailed analysis of the origins of states in antiquity need not concern us here (Carneiro 1970; Runciman 1982, 2001, 2005; Yoffee 2005). Once sedentism was established, the division of labor helped the further accumulation of wealth in one location and bolstered a greatly enhanced stratification of society. Trained armies became possible, and emergent states could resist or subdue less-developed tribal adversaries (Diamond 1997). With the emergence of the state came the transition from tribal custom to complex social hierarchies with specialized roles as well as written records.[7]

In proposing the change from tribal custom to legal systems as a major information transition in social evolution, our argument differs sharply from prior views that see law as reducible to custom.[8] Our view is that legal systems have properties exceeding encoded behavioral conventions. We acknowledge that written law in some cases encodes conventions that arise as robust Nash equilibria to coordination games. With some rules or laws, we have strong incentives to follow reigning conventions, whatever our marginal preferences. We willingly drive on the same side of the road as others and follow shared rules of linguistic communication. But these "coordination games" or "self-enforcing" institutions do not represent all cases (Vanberg 1994b; Schultz 2001; Hodgson 2003a), and we must explain enforcement in the many other instances where incentives for conformism are less apparent.

To help understand why people follow rules, we must delve into psychology (Engel 2008). The mere codification, legislation, or proclamation of a rule is insufficient. It might simply be ignored, just as drivers today break speed limits on roads. Clearly, the psychological mechanisms of conformism or imitation discussed above account for much rule enforcement. But, in a complex society, imitation is insufficient to establish general compliance with the law. Once a legal system emerges with a minimal degree of complexity, then neither imitation, habit, nor instinct can be relied on to explain fully the enforcement of laws. Law cannot be reduced to custom

7. Ancient civilizations differed in their degrees of hierarchy and centralization. Among the least centralized was the Harappan civilization (2600–1900 BCE) of the Indus Valley (Maisels 1999).

8. Writers in this tradition include David Hume, Edmund Burke, Friedrich C. von Savigny, Henry S. Maine, James C. Carter, Friedrich A. Hayek, and Robert Sugden. Carter (1907, 173)— a resolute defender of common law and a president of the American Bar Association—wrote: "Law . . . *is* custom, and like custom, self-existing and irrepealable." Hayek (1973, 72) insisted that law "is older than legislation" and that "in the sense of enforced rules of conduct [it] is undoubtedly coeval with society." For Robert Sugden (1986, 5), legal codes "merely formalize . . . conventions of behavior."

because it is a complex system of written law with sophisticated juridical institutions.

In a complex legal system, it would be absurd to suggest that most people follow a particular law principally because they have a habit or other disposition to conform to that law. The number of laws becomes too great for a population to ground most of them on habit. Many laws are unknown, obscure, or difficult to understand. While imitating others can help explain conformity to some laws, it cannot explain adherence to a law when the relevant behavior of others is unobserved. Laws cannot generally become translated into habitual dispositions. Some other reason must be found to explain why laws are enforced. Habit and imitation are insufficient to carry the burdens of legislation and enforcement.

We have discussed the evidence for inherited dispositions to punish those who break the rules or fail to enforce them. When culture developed, it enhanced, refined, or diverted these emotionally charged instincts through the learning and imitation of habits of censoriousness or disapproval (Boyd and Richerson 1992; Runciman 2005). Expressions of inherited instincts for the punishment of social transgressors are molded by culture.

But reliance on punishment instincts would mean people taking the law into their own hands and some defiance of judicial authorities. A problem concerning the evolution of law is to explain how culture could suppress the emotions and behaviors triggered by these instincts to the extent that the punishment of rule breakers is regulated by the institutionalized enforcement of abstract legal principles rather than freelance outpourings of visceral emotions. Specific cultural mechanisms of control must evolve to contain such punishment instincts and also bestow some survival value for the group.

A system of law removes the right to punish from unauthorized individuals; it makes punishment a legitimized monopoly of the judiciary. This implies the establishment of judicial institutions and strong mechanisms to suppress dispositions to punish among the ordinary population. Law is not a system of reciprocal individual punishment. The qualitative change from custom to law entails a more complex and stratified society with developed judicial institutions.

Unlike dispositions to punish those who break social rules, instincts to obey authority—which have likewise evolved over millions of years—do not have to be restrained for modern political and legal systems to function. Instead, they must be channeled and energized by cultural cues.

Complexity and stratification are linked with the transition from groups and tribes to larger-scale societies with a greater division of labor. In societies where interaction is on a small and personal level, customs and norms may suffice to maintain order and cooperation. Larger, more complex and stratified societies make interaction more impersonal and enhance the possibilities of internal conflict (Ostrom 1990; North 2005). Particular institutions are required to deal with this problem.

Developed juridical and other institutions contain social positions that might in principle be occupied by alternative individuals (Runciman 2001). A judge, lawyer, clerk, or jailor occupying such a social position within a juridical system acquires additional powers associated with that role. Such sophisticated institutions involve "information encoded in rules governing the reciprocal behavior of interacting pairs of institutional role incumbents independently of their personal beliefs or values" (Runciman 2005, 138).

This is not to undermine the role of custom in the evolution and maintenance of any system of law. Instead, it is to expose serious weaknesses in the identification of law with custom and to emphasize the crucial transition from customary adjudication to a complex legal system with institutional roles embedded in the state.

A precondition for this transition was the use of a sophisticated language involving abstract referents and complex conditional formulations. Furthermore, behavioral imitation and verbal communication could not cope with this complex transition, and the use of some form or writing or record became necessary, rather than merely convenient. Disputes had to be judged and proportional punishments administered with procedures involving codifiable, abstract rules. Legal processes involve the description and identification of abstract social positions or roles independently of the personal characteristics of their occupants.

Emotionally charged punishment instincts go back millions of years to our ape-like ancestors. By contrast, states and civilizations involving judicial systems have been in existence for no more than ten thousand years. Culture had a lot of work to do in a short time to suppress and divert all rudimentary punitive emotions into legal channels. This achievement required strong institutional enforcements and supports.

An additional psychological mechanism that has also evolved over millions of years acquired an enhanced role in the context of states and laws. This mechanism has instinctive and cultural components: it is the propensity to defer to authority. In the famous experiments on obedience conducted by Stanley Milgram (1974), members of the public were recruited to help in a laboratory experiment ostensibly about learning. To punish wrong answers to questions, a "scientist" asked the recruits to administer electric

shocks to a subject. Milgram found that a majority of adults would administer shocks that were apparently painful, dangerous, or even fatal if ordered
to do so by the person in authority. In fact, there were no shocks, and the
subject was an actor, feigning agony or even death. This experiment shows
that people can willingly accept the orders of perceived authority figures
even when their own moral feelings are violated. Particular institutional
contexts, procedures, and surroundings can engender an "agentic state" in
which people obey the commands of what they perceive to be legitimate
authority.

Milgram (1974, 124–25, 131) argues that our capacities to behave in this
way emanate from the evolutionary survival advantages of cohesive social
groups. He proposes that the human species has evolved an inherited, instinctive propensity for obedience that is framed and triggered by specific
social circumstances. Conditional dispositions to accept authority, notwithstanding challenges and rebellions to the contrary, have evolved in order to
enhance the chances of survival of both the individual and the group.[9]

Such inherited propensities are overlaid by culturally acquired proclivi-
ties. From the moment of our birth, we learn to accept the authority of our
parents. Instinctive triggers are likely to be relatively primitive, and deference to authority will rely heavily on nuanced habits of recognition and
obeisance largely acquired during childhood.

These habits involve dispositions to interpret specific aspects of bodily
deportment, interpersonal interaction, ceremony, clothing, decoration,
symbolism, and so on as markers of social authority and power, depending
on the cultural context. Once such authority is recognized and accepted as
appropriate in the context, then additional habits trigger obeisance. Habits
of obeisance are general, rule-like dispositions to accept and follow regula-
tions imposed by those in authority. They have a second-order character;
they are rules to recognize and follow other (possibly unknown) existing or
future rules.

Habits of obeisance may come into conflict with other norms and dispositions, such as moral sentiments for fairness or equity. As the Milgram
experiments illustrate, the powers of authority and obeisance may lead us
to do things that we would otherwise regard as wrong.

The existence and functioning of complex state machines depend on the

---

9. Perhaps because of the challenge in Milgram's work to conventional ideas of the autonomous individual, these striking experiments have had less impact on the social sciences than one
might expect. Relatively rare exceptions include Akerlof (1991), who emphasizes their challenge
to mainstream assumptions in economics.

creation of these habits of obeisance. In specific institutional and cultural circumstances, often involving the symbols and uniforms of state or legal power, we are disposed to accept and obey authority. The emergence of policing and military institutions reinforced tendencies to obey powers of authority and, thus, served to legitimize law. Religious beliefs and institutions have also played a major part in the legitimation of law. This was recognized by leading nineteenth-century authors (Maine 1861; Fustel De Coulanges 1980), but they confused the legitimation of law with its origins.[10] Mixtures of nationalism and democratic involvement also help legitimate modern legal systems.[11]

Effective systems of authority do not require that habits of obeisance are uniform or universal. Their prevalence among a critical mass of individuals of intermediate or higher social status is necessary. Then habits of conformism and emulation can ensure more widespread deference and consent to authority. Conformism, while culturally transmitted, may also rely on an inherited instinctive grounding (Veblen 1899; Boyd and Richerson 1985; Henrich and Boyd 2001; Richerson and Boyd 2004). But note that conformist habits are different from habits of obeisance because the latter means the acceptance of authority rather than the imitation of others. Furthermore, conformist habits emerge in the early stages of cultural transmission, long before the evolution of states and other complex organizations. By contrast, habits of obeisance begin to play a greatly enhanced and critical auxiliary role with the emergence of states, including complex and highly stratified systems of power and authority.[12]

Crucially, the creation of a legal system means that there is an overarching system of rule enforcement that guides the operation of other institutions or systems or rules and interacts with custom. States with legal institutions provide a framework within which customs and other organizations operate. The state and the judiciary are higher-level interactors, containing

10. However, unlike Western law, Islamic law retains a strong textual and institutional foundation in religion. Its replicator dynamics follow a different pattern.

11. Tyler's (1990) evidence suggests that, the more people regard themselves as part of the process of law formation, the more likely they are to accept legal rulings, even if they disagree in particular cases.

12. None of this suggests that the power of authority is absolute. Systems of power rely on a ramshackle ensemble of different habits and instincts tangled among many varied individuals. Variation is essential to the Darwinian evolutionary approach on which this argument depends. Some respect authority more than others. Furthermore, habits of obeisance and conformism can work among dissident groups or organizations, potentially undermining popular support for the existing regime. No social power is invincible.

further nested organizational interactors and social replicators on multiple levels. Selection operates on interactors below the state itself through competition for resources or power or the decisions of the courts (Commons 1924). Selection operates on states through military or economic competition with other states.

States and legal systems are new interactors at a higher level than tribal organization. To understand the new replicators involved, we must consider the structure of habits of obeisance. Simple habits are of the form "with sensory input X we are disposed to give response Y." Habits of obeisance are more complex, involving the recognition of an authoritative individual or institution W. We follow a codified legal rule—"if X, then Y"—not necessarily because of any ingrained disposition to do so but often because of a disposition to obey authority. Obedience to authority leads us to follow rules that lie in some venerated written record, rather than our habits. These rules require habits of thought for their implementation, but they are not necessarily habits of thought themselves.[13] Rather than simply "if X, then we are disposed to Y," the pattern is "if recognition of W, then (if X, then Y)," where "if X, then Y" is on the written record. This is the structure of the replicators of legal power. The replicator is extended to entail, not only habits, but also the legal system and the written codification of law.

These extensions entail institutionalized mechanisms to guide and refine the law along channels prescribed by the legislature and deal with misapplications and misunderstandings. Some fidelity of legal replication is maintained by these mechanisms of codification, scrutiny, and clarification.

Laws are replicated when they are copied from one state to another, either by agreement or by coercion. Both the original law and its copy embody a *conditional generative mechanism*. Each law is energized conditionally on the receipt of environmental signals and plays a constructive role in the development of the interactor, that is, the organization of the state. Furthermore, the law in one national state *causes* similar behavioral capacities in the other, at least in the sense that the copy depends on the source and leads to similar codifications being acquired. The acquired law is *similar* to the first with respect to the behavior it might promote under specific conditions.

Several social scientists and historians attest to the difference between law and custom and the crucial transformation involved in the emergence of judicial systems. For example, the institutional economist John R. Com-

---

13. This point was overlooked by Veblen (1919) in his frequent claim that institutions amount to habits of thought. Previously, we have made the same mistake ourselves.

mons (1925, 687) was clear that, even though common law relies on custom, it is more than custom and develops through dispute:

> It is out of these customs that the common law arises. But we do not reach the need of a common law until disputes arise which must be decided promptly in order to keep the association, or community, or nation, in a peaceable frame of coöperation. In this sense, there is a common law that arises in all private associations without any intervention of the State. . . . The peculiar common law of the State comes in only when a decision is made by a court which directs the use or the collective physical violence of the community.

The influential anthropologist Arthur Radcliffe-Brown (1933, 205) made an important distinction between the existence of an "organized system of justice"—as found in many tribal societies—and a system of law. The former may lack a "juridical authority," which is a necessary condition for the latter: "An important step is taken toward the formation of a legal system where there are recognized arbitrators or judges who hear evidence, decide upon responsibility and assess damages; only the existence of some authority with power to enforce the judgments delivered by the judges is then lacking." Also running against the identification of law with custom, some neglected legal historians stress that the essence of law resides in its *transcendence of custom*, particularly at a stage when breaches of customary conventions arise (Diamond 1935; Seagle 1941; Redfield 1950, 1957). According to the evidence, disputes over *violations of custom* in large part gave rise to protolegal actions and institutions. Far from being reduced to custom, the emergence of law also involves the emergence of the state and a legal apparatus. Seagle (1941, 35) writes: "It is in the process of retaliation that custom is shaped into law. Breach is the mother of law as necessity is the mother of invention. . . . [L]aw deals with the abnormal rather than the normal. . . . Only confusion can result from treating law and custom as interchangeable phenomena. If custom is in the truest sense of the terms spontaneous and automatic, law is the product of organized force."

According to Seagle (1941, 62): "The origin of the state was bound up with some form of social stratification. . . . The chief point of dispute is really whether social stratification resulted from external causes such as conquest . . . or from internal causes [such as] the division of labour, the accumulation of agricultural surpluses, or the exploitation of superior ability as well as superstition." Law requires the existence of a state, and the state itself arises when society becomes complex, divided and hierarchical. In emphasizing the state, the role of custom is not denied. Customary social rules were often transformed into laws by the state apparatus. As Seagle (1941, 69) explains: "The custom had to be declared to be law by a judgement in order to receive the necessary étatistic stamp. . . . It is in this sense that there is no law until there are courts." Later, Robert Redfield (1950, 581) similarly argued that custom differs from law: "Custom is understood to exist whenever the members of a primitive group expect one another to follow one line of conduct rather than another in circumstances that more or less repeat themselves, and when on the whole they do follow that line." By contrast, law is associated with the potential use of force purportedly "on behalf of the whole group." The "beginning of law and the beginnings of the state are thus closely associated."

E. Allan Farnsworth (1969) dissects in detail the requirements of a system of contract wherein an agreement between two parties becomes enforceable in law. Today, we take this for granted, but, on reflection, the automatic investment of pledges with legal enforceability is an extraordinary outcome, unlikely to evolve spontaneously from custom. Farnsworth argues that the legal basis of contract emerged in ancient Rome: "The notion that a promise itself gives rise to a duty was an achievement of Roman law. It came, however, through the development of a series of exceptions rather than through the establishment of a general principle of the enforceability of promises" (588). Again, this undermines the view that law is a simple extension of custom and points to the role of disputes in the evolution of rules of contract and to the judicial functions of the state.

The distinction between common law and civil law is important in the modern context but does not undermine the historical case. Common law evolves by the accumulation and modification of the decisions of judges. Nevertheless, the existence of a judiciary implies the existence of discernible and robust legal institutions that transcend arrangements based on popular custom. Indeed, systems of common and civil law both rely heavily on elements—including contract law—derived from the legal system of ancient Rome. As Seagle (1941, 153–60) argues, the distinction between the two systems is not as severe as some enthusiasts propose. Common law also depends on the machinery of the state.[14]

Crucially, the creation of a legal system means that there is an overarching

---

14. Commons, Diamond, Seagle, Redfield, and Radcliffe-Brown implied that societies without states did not have systems of law proper. This proposition was regarded by many as an ethnocentric prejudice, and it is a possible reason why their views of became unpopular after the 1950s. Cultural relativism became fashionable, no society being regarded as superior to another.

system of rule enforcement that guides the operation of other institutions or systems or rules and interacts with custom. States became huge social interactors whose properties are, in crucial aspects, defined by their component replicators: the legal system and the written codification of law.

The sixth major information transition in social evolution came with the institutionalization of science and technology. Here, a new kind of generative replicator emerged. Its rule structure is similar to the extended replicator encoded in legal systems. But its rules are grounded on causal relations in the physical or social world. Even the most well-established judicial laws are arbitrary, and their verification can change with circumstance. By contrast, institutionalized science and technology involve guided interactions with nature that result in discoveries of underlying, nonarbitrary, causal principles.

Note that we are not referring to the emergence of technology as such. We observed above that quite sophisticated technology has been around for tens of thousands of years (Baldwin and Clark 2000, 97). The sixth—and much later—major information transition considered here is the emergence of an institutionalized social system that embodies habits and routines of scientific inquiry and technological innovation and not merely the ritualistic replication of existing ideas and techniques.

The modern scientific and technological revolution followed the establishment of science and technology within organized bodies of systematic and codified knowledge. As expressions of this process, the Royal Society of London for the Improvement of Natural Knowledge was formed in 1662, and the Académie de science was formed in 1666 in France. By the twentieth century, the institutions of science and technology had become extensive and complex, entwining universities, corporations, and states on a global scale (Lundvall 1992; Nelson 1993). These became "epistemic communities" and "machineries of knowing," to use the phrases of Peter M. Haas (1992) and Karin Knorr-Cetina (1981, 5). There is an enormous additional literature on the institutionalization and professionalization of science and technology, and we cannot go into details (Hull 1988; Mokyr 1990a, 2003; Huff 1993; Kitcher 1993; Bowler and Morus 2005; Lipsey, Carlaw, and Bekar 2005).

Critiques of the alleged verificatory, progressive, and cumulative nature of science have become fashionable after the downfall of positivism in the latter part of the twentieth century and our entry into the era of so-called postmodernism. We recognize that attempts by philosophers to elucidate the method of science in terms of clear rules for the forming and testing of hypotheses have failed. There is no consensus on what *the scientific method* is. But, whatever its procedures, the achievements of the modern scientific and technological revolution are manifest. Consider the following facts:

- Between 1800 and 2000, life expectancy at birth rose from about thirty years to a global average of sixty-seven years and to more than seventy-five years in several developed countries (Lancaster 1990; Riley 2001; Fogel 2004). In part, this dramatic change in longevity followed the development of cures for several major diseases. It meant a huge (albeit very uneven) revolution in health and well-being.
- In 1620, the *Mayflower* took sixty-six days to cross the Atlantic. By 1833, with the development of steamships, the Atlantic crossing had been reduced to twenty-two days (Geels 2002). This was then the minimum time for any form of transatlantic communication. Today, a scheduled aircraft flies from London to New York in under eight hours.
- The laying of the first intercontinental telegraphic cable in 1866 meant that transatlantic messages took seconds rather than weeks. By 1907, the development of radio made intercontinental communication nearly instantaneous.
- In the nineteenth century, it would take one person several days to calculate a typical ballistic trajectory. Hand calculators developed in the early twentieth century reduced this time to twenty hours. In 1927, the Bush Differential Analyzer at the Massachusetts Institute of Technology took fifteen minutes. In 1946, the ENIAC computer at the University of Pennsylvania accomplished this task in thirty seconds. Today, electronic computers take a fraction of a second.
- In 1800, artillery would take several hours to reduce a large stone building to rubble. In 1945, the cities of Hiroshima and Nagasaki were almost completely destroyed in seconds by two atomic bombs.

For good or ill, these revolutionary developments are due to the evolution of an institutionalized system of science and technology. Given these tangible achievements, any attempt to reduce the stature of modern science to that of myth or witchcraft must be rejected (Parsons 2003).

Institutionalized science/technology becomes a new generative replicator in part because experimental results—determined by natural laws and other regularities—can be checked by the professional scientific community.[15] With the advance of science, the laws of nature became common reference points across time and social context. In adding the impersonal scientific experiment, the sixth major information transition built on prior advances in social evolution. This led to an enormous gain in reliable storage and transfer of information pertaining to social interaction.

It may be objected that experimental verification falls foul of the problem that all observation is theory laden and, therefore, that no theory-free empirical foundation is possible. Philip Kitcher (1993) circumvents such arguments by emphasizing that science is a process involving a trained community of diverse and interacting investigators. The institutionalization of science and technology created organizational machines of discovery and application, notwithstanding the theory-bound nature of observation. Against postmodernist fashion, Kitcher (1993) offers a powerful defense of the notion that science does indeed, in a progressive and cumulative manner, discover significant truths about nature and that this ongoing practical process is embodied in an organized social system of skilled scientists. Scientific inquiry is not a solitary encounter with nature: it involves critical and ongoing conversations with peers. Thus, the relevant epistemology for modern science is social rather than individual. Groups of individuals, operating according to various rules for modifying their individual procedures of inquiry, succeed through their critical interactions in generating a progressive sequence of consensus practices.

Economic and other historians working in this area generally agree that the institutionalization of science and technology depended on other specific institutional developments. Property rights had to be sufficiently well established to provide sufficient incentives for the necessary investment of time and resources. The political system had to be sufficiently polycentric to allow freedom of scientific inquiry without destructive interference by political or religious authorities. Providing incentives for research and innovation, Western countries developed patent laws. Relatively autonomous institutions such as universities and business corporations permitted independent inquiry and investment. Obversely, some authors have argued that

---

15. See, e.g., Johnson's (2008) fascinating account of ten of the most influential scientific experiments, beginning with Galileo's demonstration that light objects fall as fast as heavier objects. The institutionalization of procedures of replication and verification has led some leading authors to describe the scientific system as "self-correcting" (Kaufmann 1941; Schutz 1954; Bunge 1961).

the absence of such institutional autonomy was a crucial reason for the failure of Islamic and imperial Chinese science to become a powerhouse of economic growth (Huff 1993; Lipsey, Carlaw, and Bekar 2005). It was the explosive combination of a capitalist economy, a relatively pluralist polity, and institutionalized science and technology that led to the economic take-off of the West from the eighteenth century.

Scientific knowledge is partly built up in a codified form; it is open to development, scrutiny, and criticism. Scientists and engineers access this knowledge when inclined or required, and it would be impossible for any individual to have an acquaintance with anything more than a small part of this codified material. As with law, it is impossible for an individual to know or understand everything. The system is institutionalized so that the synergetic cooperation of different specialists is possible.

For science and technology to be institutionalized, habits of rational inquiry had to be adopted by a community of scientists and engineers. Scientific and technological institutions embody habits and routines. Particular habits of thought had to be inculcated. These included beliefs in the aim of science to investigate and understand the real world as well as particular procedures of inquiry, scrutiny, and debate. Instead of religious dogma, much more weight had to be given to evidence and experiment.

Habits and routines are generative replicators associated with earlier transitions, so in what sense does the institutionalization of scientific or technological knowledge mean the emergence of *new* replicators? Such knowledge does not exist in discrete elements. It is embodied in individual habits, in habits to access and understand codified knowledge, in tacit intuitions, and in relations between individuals that enable common understandings. It has individual, social, tacit, and codified dimensions. Scientific and technological cognitions are again situated or embodied, but in a particular context that enables testing, experiment, and critical scrutiny.

Where law is partly enforced by widespread dispositions to acknowledge and obey authority, science and technology proceed by instilling particular cultural norms concerning scientific and technological endeavor among a subset of the population. Through habituation and the use of codified material, the institutionalization of science and technology impels inquiry and creativity.

We noted that judicial law was built on the structure "if recognition of W, then (if X, then Y)," where W is a legitimate authoritative individual or institution and "if X, then Y" is a legal rule. The structure of scientific or technological replicators is similar, but, in this case, W typically represents

an accredited scientific or technological source for our authority. And the "if
X, then Y" represents knowledge of (or knowledge how to obtain) a particular scientific principle or piece of technological know-how. The scientific or
technological "if X, then Y" principles are very different from judicial laws,
although, interestingly, the word *law* is used in common parlance to refer
to them both. The rule structure is similar, but the content and the means of
accreditation or legitimation are very different. Judicial laws are arbitrary
and malleable, but we cannot tamper with the laws of nature.

Occasionally, the W will represent, not an established consensual source
or authority, but a novel result generated by an individual or group that
is backed by accredited evidence or methods. It is on such risky occasions
that innovation and advance depend. But some such presumptions do not
survive protracted scrutiny. A Darwinian process of selection is involved
(Hull 1988).

Crucially, the scientific and technological community institutionalizes
procedures through which new results can be established and errors can be
corrected. Although science depends on more than fact, the role of evidence
and experiment is crucial.[16] A habit of thought common to a modern scientific community is the acknowledgment of the authority of accredited evidence. The mechanisms of accreditation are themselves institutionalized.

While the rules of law emanate from political and legal authority, the
principles of modern science and technology are obliged to pay homage to
the facts. While science feeds on facts for its growth and development, law is
sustained by authority and acknowledges facts in its implementation. While
both systems entail good measures of hierarchy and deference, the bases of
their claims of legitimacy are fundamentally different. Furthermore, while
law existed for millennia in totalitarian regimes, the processes of scientific
and technological invention and correction require substantial freedom of
speech, openness of inquiry, and robust systems of scrutiny.

Scientific and technological knowledge replicates much as habits and
routines do. The distinctive feature of this knowledge replication is that
it is embodied jointly in individual habits, codified material, and a structured scientific and technological community. In this sense, institutionalized scientific and technological knowledge involves generative replicators.

16. Contrary to Comtean positivism, science is not *entirely* a matter of fact. Modern philosophers of science widely acknowledge that some ontological presuppositions are necessary to all
scientific inquiry (Veblen 1919; Quine 1953; Bunge 1974, 1977; Bhaskar 1975; Chalmers 1985).
The facts do not speak for themselves, but their presence is essential.

It is not simply ideas that are replicators. The knowledge is necessarily embodied in the habits of groups of organized individuals. This knowledge is replicated when it is transmitted from one group, community, or nation to another. There may be knowledge diffusion or the additional copying of the organizational interactors. Both the original and its copy embody a *conditional generative mechanism*. Each is energized conditionally on the receipt of environmental signals and plays a constructive role in the development of the interactor, that is, the scientific and technological institutions. Furthermore, the original knowledge *causes* similar behavioral capacities in the other context, at least in the sense that the copy depends on the source and leads to similar codifications being acquired. The acquired knowledge is *similar* to the original with respect to the behavior it might promote under specific conditions.

With modern technology, we are in sight of another transition, with the creation of robots or other automata that can themselves replicate without human intervention. These possible developments have become the stuff of science fiction. But it is important to understand that replicating automata are not the next major transition in *human* social evolution. Instead, it would be the creation of new species.

8.7. OVERVIEW OF THE MAJOR INFORMATION TRANSITIONS

Table 8.1 portrays the transitions in social evolution discussed above, along with the emerging replicators and interactors on multiple levels. We now make some general points about these transitions.

In the context of major biological transitions, James Griesemer (2000) notes that it is important not to take the levels of the hierarchy for granted. Instead of merely presuming the appearance of a new level, its emergence from preceding elements must be explained. Samir Okasha (2005, 2006) and Griesemer raise a problem with the deployment of the replicator-interactor framework that must be dealt with here.

Replicators entail relatively high copying fidelity, and interactors must be relatively cohesive (Godfrey-Smith 2006). But new replicators and interactors must have evolved from elements with lower copying fidelity or cohesion. Higher levels of evolution, with refined replicators and interactors, could not suddenly appear. In the biological world, the very first protoreplicators must have had relatively poor copying fidelity (Maynard Smith and Szathmáry 1995), and the earliest multicellular organisms would have been

TABLE 8.1. Genetic, Cultural, and Organizational Evolution: Interactors and Replicators on Multiple Levels

Level	Genetic Evolution	Prelinguistic Cultural Evolution	Linguistic Cultural Evolution	Customary Organizational Evolution	Symbolic Evolution	Legal and Customary Evolution	Scientific and Technological Revolution
Interactors:							
Scientific and technological organizations	...						Scientific institutions
National	...	...	...	...	...	States	States
Organizational	Groups (under restrictive conditions)	Groups	Groups	Tribes and Families	Families, tribes and other organizations	Families, tribes and other organizations	Firms and other organizations
Individual	Individuals	Individuals	Individuals	Individuals	Individuals	Individuals	Individuals
Replicators:							
Scientific and technological	...	...	...	...	...	...	Scientific and technological knowledge
Legal	...	...	...	...	...	Laws	Laws
Symbolic	...	...	...	...	Writing systems	Writing systems	Writing systems
Organizational	...	...	Customs	Customs	Customs	Customs	Customs
Individual	...	...	Linguistic habits	Linguistic habits	Linguistic habits	Linguistic habits	Linguistic habits
Individual	...	Corporeal habits	Corporeal habits	Corporeal habits	Corporeal habits	Corporeal habits	Corporeal habits
Genetic	Genes	Genes	Genes	Genes	Genes	Genes	Genes

less cohesive because of competition between their constituent cell lineages (Buss 1987; Michod 1999). Corresponding remarks apply to the emergent levels in the major information transitions of social evolution.

Accordingly, the cohesion of groups would have developed gradually, until those groups qualified as new interactors. The copying fidelity of corporeal habits would have been improved over millions of years and been greatly enhanced by emerging error-correcting mechanisms such as punishment and a protolanguage. Customs similarly would have taken a long time to evolve and become relatively accurate replicators. Language and writing would have facilitated both the accuracy of replication and the cohesion of higher-level social interactors. New higher levels could then emerge more rapidly.[17]

In addressing this problem, Okasha (2005, 2006) builds on an earlier dissection of contrasting formulations of multilevel selection by John Damuth and Lorraine Heisler (1988). These authors point to different conceptions of group and multilevel selection. Much of the group selection literature focuses on the evolution of an individual trait such as altruism and sees the fitness of the group as the average fitness of the individuals in the group. The fitter groups are those that produce more individual offspring than others. By contrast, the macroevolutionary literature on species selection focuses on the changing frequency of different types of species, not individuals. This is a different formulation of multilevel selection, one in which a collective's fitness is defined as the expected number of offspring collectives (rather than individual offspring) contributed to the next generation. This gives us two very different meanings of *collective fitness*. Okasha suggests that the transition from average individual fitness in collectives to fitness in terms of the procreation of collectives is crucial in the establishment of higher levels of selection. When collectives acquire the capacity to multiply through their hosted replicators, they become fully fledged interactors, and their fitness diverges from that of their members taken severally.

We can apply these arguments to the transitions and levels exhibited in table 8.1. Note in particular that, in the row displaying organizational interactors (from groups to families to other organizations), these interactors become more defined and cohesive through time. It is only the more cohesive organizational interactors that have the capacity to produce cohesive organizational offspring, through division or generational succession.

---

17. This Darwinian focus on processes of emergence is a further reason for retaining a degree of imprecision in the definitions of *replicator* and *interactor*.

Consider some of the general observations made by Maynard Smith and Szathmáry (1995) in their discussion of the major transitions in biological evolution. They pointed out that smaller entities have often come together to form higher-level entities, that entities often become differentiated as part of a larger entity, and that smaller entities are often unable to replicate in the absence of the larger entity. These observations are also valid in several major information transitions of social evolution. Individuals come together to form groups, and tribes come together to form states. Maynard Smith and Szathmáry also observed that smaller entities are often unable to replicate in the absence of larger entities and that smaller entities can sometimes disrupt the development of the larger entities. Equivalently, human replication depends on social structures of support such as families. Individuals can disrupt groups, and organizations can conflict with even higher-level entities.

Maynard Smith and Szathmáry emphasize that major transitions in evolution have been associated with new ways of transmitting information. We have considered the emergence of gestural communication, then linguistic communication, then the replication of organizational structures, then the establishment of codified laws, and, finally, the transmission of scientific and technological knowledge.

Maynard Smith and Szathmáry also suggest that the existence of higher-level interactors depends on the stability of lower-level replicators. This is reminiscent of the evolutionary laws developed by Karl Ernst von Baer, which influenced Darwin and retain a following today (Gould 1977). Von Baer argued that characters of specialist use are developed from those of more general function, thus increasing the degrees of both complexity and specialization in the organism. Arthur Reber (1993, 85) formulated this law as follows: "Once successful forms are established, they tend to become fixed and serve as foundations for emerging forms." In addition: "Earlier appearing, successful, and well-maintained forms and structures will tend towards stability, showing fewer successful variations than later appearing forms." In other words, the more basic structures, once established, stabilize and become less changeable than the layers that are built on them. Also, it seems that, in social evolution, higher-level forms depend on the stability of lower elements. Every emergent social level depends on the stability and security of constituent parts: organizations depend on the durability and copying fidelity of habits, laws depend on the durability of customs, and so on.

On what basis does selection at higher levels operate? Given the primary survival need to provide for the material prerequisites of human life, it follows that organizations and routines devoted to such provisioning also have some survival value in the ongoing processes of selection. Unless such organizations and routines endure and are effective, society will collapse. Accordingly, organizations with such routines and propensities will have a higher survival value.

Some social formations will give greater priority than others to the organizations and customs that are important for the production, acquisition, and protection of the requisites of human life. When there is competition between different groups, the processes of selection work at the organizational level. Organizations promoting the production of necessities, their pillage from elsewhere, and their protection from outside plunderers will have some survival value for the community. The evolutionary fitness of each social formation will relate to some degree to the efficiency and viability of its organizations concerned with production, acquisition, and military capability.

Other institutions or customs—such as those of ceremony or leisure—are less crucial to the reproduction and survival of the society. If such customs stand apart from institutions connected with production, acquisition, and defense, then they may become extinct through an extended process of group competition and selection.

But, in many societies, the routines of production and acquisition are also infused with traditional customs of ceremony and may themselves rely on ritual for their social reproduction and survival (Bush 1986). Ceremony sometimes encapsulates technological knowledge or sustains productive activity. In that case, such ceremony will not readily disappear through institutional selection. Furthermore, structured learning typically involves the acceptance of authority. As Michael Polanyi (1958, 58) puts it: "To learn by example is to submit to authority. . . . A society which wants to preserve a fund of personal knowledge must submit to tradition." Some measure of hierarchical deference is necessary for knowledge to replicate. Progress may rely to some extent on conservative institutions. Nevertheless, despite these complications, provisioning organizations may still have some haphazard but ultimate selective advantage in the evolutionary process.

A key factor here is the overall level of productivity of vital goods and services. Although there are exceptions to this rule, a society of greater productive efficiency, in terms of the requisites of human life, will have the greater capacity to expand, whether by further productive investment or by conquest. Historical studies, at least of the postmedieval period, give broad confirmation of the close parallel between levels of productivity and the capacity for politicoeconomic expansion (Kennedy 1988; Maddison 1991).

Social formations in which the routines of production, distribution, and acquisition have greater cultural weight and durability will be the stronger. Customs that help sustain industriousness and acquisition tend to assume some cultural prominence. But the particular customs and routines involved can vary enormously, depending on history and other cultural attributes, and leading to a wide range of possible behaviors. Often the possession rather than the production of wealth is associated with higher status. Sometimes higher status is accorded the hunter and the warrior. The general principle discussed here is consistent with a wide range of cultural outcomes.

The selection of relatively productive societies was particularly effective in the earlier periods of human history, prior to the rise of civilization, when people lived in competing tribal groups, all close to the brink of extinction. The relative advantage of a provisioning culture would be all the more apparent. But, as civilizations grew and production provided more than the immediate requisites of human life, the mechanisms of cultural selection could have given less immediate priority to provisioning institutions. Nevertheless, the dependence of each community on the means of human life remained, and a haphazard process of selection of these institutions continued. A cultural outcome, in the modern period, has been the evolution of societies in which production and acquisition have overtaken religion as a font of human beliefs and aspirations.

The general impulse to produce and acquire in all human societies is a cultural propensity, itself a product of cultural evolution and backed by provisioning instincts within individuals. Rather than a universal actuality, it is a propensity not always realized in outcomes. Other factors may interfere. Nevertheless, it is an evolutionary principle of some importance, applying to all human societies.

Furthermore, it seems that each major information transition has enabled some societies to gain an advantage over their laggard neighbors. Each transition has enhanced the possibilities for production, protection, and predation. The transitions themselves are the outcomes of a Darwinian evolutionary process.

8.8. FINAL REMARKS: MULTILEVEL AND NONOPTIMAL SOCIAL EVOLUTION

We have established several levels of replication and selection in human societies above the genetic. It must be emphasized that social evolution is very different from the evolution of genes. As noted before, social replicators differ from genes in having much lower durability and copying fidelity. Furthermore, the context of the selection of social replicators has also changed dramatically, at least in the last few thousand years. By contrast, genetic evolution takes place over a much longer period of time and reflects the enduring aspects of the environment. The process of selecting and honing genes has time to lead to efficacious adaptations. Evolution is never an optimizer, but biological evolution has produced many remarkable adaptations for fitness and survival. Because of shorter timescales and more variable contexts of selection, social evolution is much less effective in this regard (Van Parijs 1981).

Our discussion of the major information transitions of social evolution indicates that each transition has been associated with the emergence of a new type of generative replicator. With the particular transitions associated with language, culture, legal systems, and the institutionalization of science and technology, we noted that there were mechanisms to correct errors and maintain the robustness and copying fidelity of the generative replicators. These mechanisms have the fortuitous outcome of preserving some useful knowledge from the past. But, because the processes of selection are more haphazard and less protracted than those in the natural sphere, this fidelity is less often rewarded by the evolution of highly efficient outcomes.

In the social sphere, at neither the cultural nor the individual level does the selection process hone the socioeconomic system to its highest productive efficiency. Mechanisms of selection are erratic and imperfect, particularly in the cultural sphere. Inefficient or destructive institutions can tenaciously survive (Edgerton 1992). Furthermore, as noted above, aspects of ceremony and productive efficiency sometimes buttress one another. There is always the possibility, as Veblen (1914, 25) recognized, of "instances of the triumph of imbecile institutions over life and culture."

There are several reasons why social evolution is far from being an optimizer, including path dependence, frequency dependence, and the role of institutional complementarities (North 1990; Hodgson 1993; Amable 2000, 2003; Aoki 2001; Hall and Soskice 2001; Boyer 2005; Kenworthy 2006; Gagliardi 2009). What concerns us here is the suboptimality that results from the way in which each major information transition builds on an earlier evolutionary architecture.

Social evolution builds on sufficiently successful but imperfect survivals from the past. Any complex system is a linked structure of imperfect but rigid modular adaptations that were sufficiently successful in a given environment. Even if a modular component was highly efficient in the past, it is unlikely to be as efficient in the changed circumstances of the present. Yet, if any imperfect component retains a functional role in the system, then it can be preserved through selection. If the more basic structures of the system are less changeable than others, then selection cannot always readily and incrementally improve each organ or module within the structure.

Evolution is unable to rebuild everything to a near-optimal arrangement. It is not an expert redesigner, somehow understanding the complex interconnections between each part of the system. Such a degree of detailed, complicated, and fortuitous reengineering is unlikely to happen in the haphazard turmoil of nature. Evolution is forced to use vestigial modules from the past. Hence, it rarely, if ever, produces an optimal outcome. Complex systems carry the baggage of their own history. Hence, to understand the nature of an organism, we must know something about its evolutionary past.

The practice of building on former, successful innovations is also found in the evolution of complex technologies. For example, contemporary Microsoft Windows software carries at its basis some elements of the former MS-DOS software architecture of the 1980s. Software redesign is complex and expensive, so it was expedient to rely on tested and successful modules from former systems.

One of the insights of complexity science has been to suggest that a degree of irreversibility will be inherent in hierarchical organizations such as firms. As Brian Loasby (1998) elaborates, a firm may build on its established core capabilities in ways that rely on past accumulations of experience and are themselves difficult to reverse.

These insights are also of major importance in socioeconomic systems. Because of the complex, interlocking relation between substructures, the processes of adaptation are typically confined to incremental and partial adjustments within an existing structural configuration. Competitive forces alone cannot always achieve radical, overall redesign.

For example, Ugo Pagano (1991, 2001) has considered the relation between specific technologies and different systems of property rights and labor relations. Each is linked to the other, and each adapts taking the other as given. He argues that the existing technology is a result of preceding social relations and that the scope of adjustment is, thus, confined. Furthermore, existing social relations limit the possibilities of technological change. Because they do not change together, systems of property rights and labor relations do not necessarily adjust toward a configuration that is optimal for them both. Such an outcome might require adjustments that are not selected because they are initially suboptimal. Evolutionary pressures are unable radically to redesign the whole. If more efficient configurations of technology and property relations exist, then social evolution will typically be unable to find them.

Given these points, we should emphasize that the Darwinian character of social evolution is no ground for a Panglossian view that the outcomes of competitive evolution are necessarily optimal. Just as suboptimality is prevalent in the natural world (Gould 1980, 2002), it is commonplace in the social context as well.

Market competition can have the benefit of showing which firms are more able to innovate and make profits, but economic theory and experience teach us that markets have limitations as well as advantages (Nelson 1981, 2003). It is also important to emphasize that markets are themselves institutions and that their emergence depends on legal structures associated with the fifth major information transition (Hodgson 1988, 2008b). Hence, earlier phases of evolution cannot take part in a market environment. Furthermore, when markets are established, organizational selection cannot entirely be a matter for markets. Competition between legal systems, for example, does not amount to the supply and purchase of legal services, despite some rhetoric to the contrary. Even if it did, it would have to take place within another, overarching legal system to legitimate the trade. In reality, systems of law are typically established through invasion or imitation. Finally, limits to the commodification of scientific and technological knowledge are well established (Nelson 1959; Arrow 1962; Mirowski and Sent 2002). In sum, Darwinian social evolution neither establishes perfection nor shows that the market can become a universal forum of competition and selection.

CHAPTER NINE

Conclusions and Agenda for Future Research

All scientific theories are conjectures, even those that have successfully passed many and varied tests. . . . [T]he doctrine of natural selection . . . raises detailed problems in many fields, and it tells us what we would expect of an acceptable solution of these problems. I still believe that natural selection works this way as a research programme.

KARL POPPER, (1978)

The development of the Darwinian conceptual framework is a major unfulfilled promise for the social sciences. This book explains how Darwinian principles also apply to social evolution and why prominent objections to their use are unwarranted. We clarify common misunderstandings relating to the nature of social and economic evolution and outline a constructive path for the realization of Darwin's conjecture that his core principles had a wider application than biology alone and that they helped explain the evolution of social phenomena. This path promises to reap huge benefits from a systematic application of Darwinian principles to an explanation of the evolution of social and economic organization.

Our overall aim has been to resolve pressing problems, nail the misconceptions, and reinvigorate this project to generalize Darwinism on clearer and well-defined conceptual foundations. We elucidate the analytic power of general Darwinian principles and show their application to the socioeconomic domain. After clarifying the key Darwinian concepts and processes, we have shown how they can be generalized to social and economic evolution.

9.1. OVERCOMING RESISTANCE

The resistance to Darwinian ideas has been especially strong in sociology and some branches of cultural anthropology. Darwinian ideas have made their way into economics, but often in a crude form, for example, by stressing the ideas of individualism and competition and neglecting Darwin's substantial compensating discussion of group selection, mutual aid, sympathy, and cooperation (Becker 1976; Hirshleifer 1977, 1978). Ironically, furthermore, the new generation of evolutionary economists that has arisen within economics since the 1980s has neglected the question of generalizing Darwinism until recently. When the question has surfaced, it has been met with several misconceptions and misreadings of what actually is proposed.

The idea of extending Darwinian principles is found in Darwin's work and was also mooted by several authors who followed in his footsteps. Resistance to this idea has resulted from a misplaced concern that the generalization of Darwinism to cover the social domain might imply the adoption of individualist, uncritically promarket, or other simplistic ideological notions that have sometimes been gathered under the misleading label *social Darwinism*. In fact, much that is ritually taught about the history of social Darwinism is mythological (Bannister 1979; Jones 1980; Bellomy 1984; Hodgson 2004b, 2006a).

This concern is also misplaced because any evaluation of whether the generalization of Darwinian principles helps explain social phenomena is a matter for science, not ideology. Ideology cannot adjudicate over scientific principles. Of course, all scientists are human and have their ideological prejudices. Ideology often interferes with science, and, in the social sciences, this is especially—and, perhaps, unavoidably—the case, but the goal should be to expose and isolate this influence, rather than to give it scientific legitimacy. The generalization of Darwinian principles should be judged on scientific rather than ideological grounds.

Although Darwin did not endorse all cooperative endeavors—in particular, he was critical of trade unions (Weikart 1995), and, unlike his codiscoverer, Alfred Russel Wallace, he was not a socialist—his analysis of human evolution found sympathy, cooperation, and morality to be vital for the survival of human groups in their competition with others (Darwin 1871). Like all scientists, Darwin had his ideological views, but, when he examined the processes of human evolution in detail, he depicted the complex interplay of competitive forces and cooperative dispositions.

The argument that the core Darwinian principles of variation, inheritance, and selection apply to social as well as biological phenomena has stood the test of time. Darwinism in biology has made major breakthroughs. But an adequate refinement of *general* Darwinian concepts such as selection, replication, and inheritance—in terms that could be applied to social or economic evolution without forcing it into a biological mold—has been lacking, at least until the final years of the twentieth century. Our work aims to bring all the threads together and help fill this gap in evolutionary theory. We pinpoint the general features of a Darwinian process and show how they can be related to the evolution of organizations and cultures in the social domain.

To guide the research effort in a more constructive direction, we had to show that this central argument can resist a number of common objections and misunderstandings. For instance, some authors point to the theory of self-organization and suggest that it is an alternative to Darwinian selection. Others point to human intentionality and claim that it is inconsistent with the allegedly blind processes of Darwinism. Others regard Lamarckism and Darwinism as rivals, seeing social evolution as an exemplification of the former rather than the latter. We have argued that all these objections are mistaken. Processes of self-organization are important in nature and society. Human intentionality and choice are distinctive and should not be ignored. Some Lamarckian inheritance of acquired characters may occur in social evolution. But none of these propositions rules out Darwinism. On the contrary, all accounts *require* Darwinian principles to complete their explanations.

It is a common misunderstanding that generalizing Darwinism assumes that the detailed mechanisms of social and biological evolution are similar. This amazing misconception contradicts the very notion of explanatory unification in the face of complex and varied phenomena, which is central to all scientific explanation (Kitcher 1989). Scientific explanations always involve generalities because they abstract from specific detail relating to the expression of particular phenomena. When metal airplanes and feathered birds fly, some similar principles are at work. But the detailed mechanisms are very different. It is obvious that social evolution and biological evolution are different. And evolutionary mechanisms are expressed in very different ways *within* the biological (or the social) domain. Instead of detailed similarity, the idea of generalizing Darwinism depends on a degree of ontological communality at a high level of abstraction. This communality is captured by the broad idea of a complex population system and the formulation of general concepts of selection and replication.

Proposals for a generalized Darwinism are also unaffected by the valid claim that Darwinism, or the principles of selection, inheritance, and variation, is inadequate to explain social evolution. It is also insufficient to explain detailed outcomes in the biological sphere. In both cases, auxiliary principles are required. But none of this undermines the validity of generalization at an abstract level. Insufficiency does not amount to invalidity.

Furthermore, given the existence of complex population systems in both nature and society, a generalized Darwinism is the only overarching framework we have for placing detailed specific mechanisms.

9.2. "WITHOUT THE MAKING OF THEORIES . . ."

As Darwin put it: "Without the making of theories . . . there would be no observation" (Darwin 1887, 2:315). But he was neither a mathematical model builder nor an armchair theorist. The development and application of his theory took place in the context of rich and extensive empirical inquiry. He conducted numerous experiments of his own.

But, although Darwinism points to the need for empirical inquiry, its greatest achievement is in terms of an overarching and unifying framework of principles, rather than meticulous explanations at every level. Darwin himself accepted that he had not provided detailed evidence of evolutionary processes. He wrote to F. W. Hutton on 20 April 1861: "I am actually weary of telling people that I do not pretend to adduce direct evidence of one species changing into another, but that I believe that this view in the main is correct because so many phenomena can be thus grouped together and explained" (Darwin and Seward 1903, 1:183–84). Several of his detailed explanations turned out to be wrong. It was not until the development of genetics in the twentieth century that biology began to piece together detailed causal explanations of evolutionary processes. In this respect, and despite his use of extensive empirical research, Darwin's achievement was more conceptual than empirical.[1]

The analysis of social evolution is, likewise, in need of detailed empirical evidence. But factual inquiry does not bring theories as cows eating grass yield milk. It must be related to an improved understanding of general evolutionary principles. How exactly are these general mechanisms expressed as firms, industries, institutions, and economies evolve? There has been a great deal of empirical work of evolutionary spirit in the social sciences, but, at least until recently, a unified framework has been lacking, and the theoretical side of evolutionary social science has been mired in controversy. We believe, not only that Darwinism offers a way out of these theoretical difficulties, but also that it is the unique and unavoidable solution.

1. Kitcher (1993) notes that "conceptual progress" is as vital to science as "explanatory progress," where the former provides more adequate specifications of referents and points to new zones of inquiry.

Our work on the Darwinian evolution of human social institutions is very much at the stage of preliminary general explanation that follows the classification and grouping together of phenomena. We have provided clarifications and explained how the general Darwinian principles apply to social evolution. Instead of starting from the vague and fruitlessly contested word *evolution*, we commenced from the general types of phenomena involved. We started from the observation that the Darwinian framework applies to a broad class of systems, involving populations of entities and all feasible manifestations of development and change. We then showed, under some minimal conditions, that ongoing change in such systems is inevitably Darwinian in the sense that it must involve Darwin's central principles of variation, inheritance, and selection. But this demonstration depends on adequate and sufficiently precise definitions of these and other central concepts.

9.3. SOME OF THE CONCEPTUAL ADVANCES PRESENTED IN THIS VOLUME

We took special care in defining the notion of selection. Advances over the last decades have led to a refined understanding of the concept. The scientific usage of *selection* has a very precise meaning, referring to a change in the distribution of a population property, such as the capabilities of firms in an industry. But this is not to downplay the role of choice in these and other processes in the social sphere.

While much work on evolution in economics and the social sciences more generally has benefited from the application of a loose notion of selection, we believe that it is time to adopt a more sophisticated concept of selection. We believe that this will stimulate much progress in studies of economic and social evolution. In our discussion of social evolution, we treat successor selection and generative replication as two-level processes that couple knowledge conditions with human actions in the evolution of customs, language, and more.

Inspired by the work of von Neumann (1966) on self-reproducing automata, we further strengthened the notion of information transfer in replication processes. To the triple conditions required for the characterization of general replication processes (causality, similarity, and information transfer), we add a fourth condition that defines a generative replicator. A generative replicator is a *conditional generative mechanism* that can turn input signals from an environment into developmental instructions. In contrast to other replication processes, the special case of *generative* replication has the potential to enhance complexity. Demonstrating the usefulness of the concept of the generative replicator in the social domain, we identified social habits and routines as generative social replicators.

A further problem with the forensic generalization of Darwinian principles to social evolution has been the simplistic treatment and faddish reception of the concept of the meme, which continues to be ill defined, has yielded relatively little insight, and has been met by a measure of both right-headed as well as wrongheaded skepticism.

While the introduction of the meme by Dawkins (1976) helped revive the important principle that Darwinian principles also apply to evolving entities outside the biological world, in some ways the idea of the meme has stultified rather than stimulated research. It is too easy to jump to the conclusion that memes (as ideas) are replicators in the social domain. A problem is that, while genes are material entities, the ontological status of ideas has baffled philosophers for centuries. The sloppy identification of memes as social replicators falls into a swamp from which causal or explanatory principles are extremely difficult to recover. After some advance, memetics has done much to entangle the generalization of Darwinian principles in the social domain.

Instead, we have turned to a pragmatist approach — originally developed in the late nineteenth century but enjoying a revived popularity among philosophers today — in which ideas do not float in a world of their own but are emergent expressions of mental programs and dispositions (Joas 1993, 1996; Putnam 1995). Classic pragmatism fully acknowledges human intentionality but places it within an evolutionary framework and avoids the dualism of material and mental worlds. It is a form of emergentist materialism that takes minds and ideas as real and distinct entities but sees them as emerging from a material foundation (Bunge 1980). It offers a means of explaining purposes, beliefs, and preferences in material and causal terms, rather than simply taking them as given. Ideas, emotions, and mental dispositions are grounded on habits, which, in turn, are prompted by instincts (James 1890; Dewey 1910, 1922; Veblen 1914; Plotkin 1994).

While instincts are grounded on genes, habits are acquired by each individual in a cultural context. Habits are elemental social replicators and form a basis for other social replicators at higher, organizational levels. We thus overcome the vagueness of the idea of the meme and point to specific psychological and social entities and processes that can be objects of detailed empirical investigation.

Far from undermining or neglecting human agency, Darwinism offers a means to overcome the widespread dualism within the social sciences, where human intentionality and purposefulness are simply assumed or regarded as first or "uncaused" causes within a material and natural world. Such dualism is incompatible with the facts that life evolved from matter and humans from other organisms. Darwinism is invaluable in this regard because it helps explain the evolution of intention and purpose without simply taking them as given. Indeed, we would go so far as to suggest that the Darwinian evolutionary framework accommodates a resolution of the thorny problem of individual agency and social structure that has confounded the social sciences since their inception (Hodgson 2004a, 2006a, 2007b, 2007c; Hodgson and Knudsen 2004a).

We adopt the distinction between a replicator and an interactor as pioneered by David Hull (1988). We show that a clear understanding of these concepts is essential and particularly vital if we are to avoid further confusion over such concepts as the units of selection. We refine the definition of each concept, and we point to an important subclass of generative replicators that have the potential to enhance complexity in evolving systems.

Having sharpened these definitions, we give a broad outline of empirical domain where socioeconomic replicators or interactors can be observed. Paying particular attention to generative replicators, we have discussed the conditions under which socioeconomic evolution can advance the overall level of complexity in the system.

We have argued that social evolution works unavoidably on multiple levels. We have developed an argument for identifying the most basic of these levels and outlined a hierarchy with multiple tiers of social interaction, replication, and selection. Our sketch of six major information transitions in social evolution highlights the emergence of new types of generative replicator and new levels and types of information transmission. Each information transition has produced a major new class of replicator that can transmit, store, and utilize more complex social information. New generative replicators are involved at each stage in the evolution of prelinguistic culture, human language, tribal customs, writing and records, states and laws, and the institutionalization of science and technology. A next development in this particular research program would be a systematic accumulation of evidence about the micromechanics that generated these major information transitions in social evolution.

The establishment of these multiple levels underlines the fact that societies are not merely collections of individuals. Individuals necessarily interact with one another, and our analysis points to multiple modes of interaction of evolving complexity.

9.4. A DOUBLE GESTALT SHIFT IN THE SOCIAL SCIENCES

In chapter 2 above, we outlined the basic ontology of complex population systems. The first gestalt shift involves an understanding that Darwinian principles apply to all such systems, including human society and its organizations. The second results from an appreciation of the information and algorithmic processes with the potential to create greater complexity that are found in both nature and human society.

Information here is defined in the Shannon-Weaver sense of an input signal that results in a change of state or behavior. The information mechanisms involved in complex evolutionary processes are conditional, rule-like structures. Hence, the ontology of complex population systems is enhanced by this second shift: we address evolving systems of entities carrying and processing information through algorithms or rules.

This enhanced ontology differs from preceding conceptions in the social sciences. Much of economics, at least from the 1950s until the rise of game theory in the 1990s, was built on a conception of interdependent, interconnected, continuous variables (Mirowski 1989; Potts 2000). Within sociology, the prevailing concepts were (and remain) structures, positions, and roles. Rules have been less prominent in both disciplines, in terms of both the general relations of social interaction and the constitutive drivers of individual agency.[2]

An ontology where rules are seen as constitutive of social reality contrasts with the former emphasis in mainstream economics on incremental change and equilibria in systems in which every individual impinges on everyone else. The ontological fundamentals of the emerging paradigm involve institutional structures and algorithmic learning processes involving program-like habits and rules (see, e.g., Arthur 2006; Dopfer 2004; Dopfer, Foster, and Potts 2004; Hodgson 1997, 2004a, 2007a; Hodgson and Knudsen 2004a; Ostrom 2005; Parra 2005; Potts 2000; Vanberg 2002, 2004). As Kurt Dopfer, John Foster, and Jason Potts (2004, 263) put it: "The central

2. An important exception is Hayek (1967, 1973, 1988), who emphasized rule-following behavior.

insight is that an economic system is a population of rules, a structure of rules, and a process of rules."[3]

Society is not merely a collection of individuals (Bunge 2000; Weissman 2000); it also unavoidably involves systems of (both constitutive and procedural) rules through which individuals communicate and interact. This would be as true of the anarchist utopia as it is of the market-dominated economy proposed by some libertarians. Even voluntary anarchist cooperation requires some rules concerning individual rights and interpersonal communication. And, as Friedrich Hayek (1960) accepts, the market itself requires rules in order to operate, just as some kinds of institutions are required to protect private property and enforce contracts.

The emerging vision is of limited interconnectedness within social systems, essentially composed of structures and algorithmic processes of rules. Game theory provides a partial glimpse of this rule-structured world, with its evocation of payoff rules and strategies, but the new, emerging paradigm is by no means restricted to this particular mathematical approach. Much mainstream game theory still evokes agents with unrealistically powerful and rapid rational capacities (Kirman 1993, 2005; Bicchieri 1994; Hargreaves Heap and Varoufakis 1995). Instead of powerful rational minds, the new paradigm stresses highly bounded rationality and the use of rough-and-ready rules of thumb (Gigerenzer et al. 1999; Gigerenzer and Selten 2001). More generally, what is involved is an ontology of structured algorithms and rule-like dispositions interacting and evolving at the microlevel to create complex and often unpredictable macro-outcomes.

From such an ontological standpoint, the very idea of individual interaction of any kind without rules or institutions is untenable. Instead, the policy agenda becomes to improve on some existing institutions and to replace others where possible and desirable.

The principles of generalized Darwinism focus on the development, retention, and selection of information concerning adaptive solutions to survival problems faced by organisms or other relevant entities in their environment. The storage and replication of such information are general

3. While we agree with this ontological stress on information and rules, we do not agree that "all existences are matter-energy actualizations of ideas" (Dopfer and Potts 2008, 3). This ontological idealism reverses our emergentist materialism (Bunge 1980) into its opposite: matter-energy somehow emerges from ideas. The Dopfer and Potts ontology omits any existences before the evolution of ideas. Another defect of Dopfer and Potts's (2008) work, as with that of Lawson (2003) and Martins (2009), is an inexplicable failure to address the literature on generalized Darwinism.

features of complex population systems. When we apply this framework to particular cases, questions naturally arise concerning the nature, mechanisms, and material substrate of these adaptive solutions.

As noted earlier in this volume, the biologist and philosopher Ernst Mayr (1988) developed the related concept of program-based behavior involving sets of conditional, rule-like dispositions linked together into what he termed *programs*.[4] Instincts and biological genotypes involve programs. The rule-like dispositions that make up institutions also have program-like qualities. A generalized Darwinism highlights their importance in evolutionary processes. In sum, the emerging ontology of social reality as consisting of systems of rule-like dispositions—described as *institutions*—fits perfectly into a generalized Darwinian framework. The links between institutional and Darwinian ontologies are established.

Shortly after the hundredth anniversary of *The Origin of Species*, Mayr (1964, xviii) wrote: "It has taken 100 years to appreciate fully that Darwin's conceptual framework is, indeed, a new philosophical system." And, 150 years after the *Origin*, several features of the underlying ontology and methodological approach are clearer. In particular, the potential impact on the social sciences is much more apparent.

9.5. THE POSITIVE HEURISTIC OF GENERALIZED DARWINISM

We are aware of many limits to our achievement in this book. Our argument remains at a relatively high level of abstraction, and, while citing a large number of empirical studies, we have considered more closely only a few empirical examples. We have developed no new mathematical models of the evolutionary process. Much of the discussion here is in terms of definition and conceptual clarification, rather than empirical testing or inquiry. We have done relatively little to show how various kinds of auxiliary theory would fit into the metatheoretical framework provided by generalized Darwinism. There is relatively little "middle range theory" (Merton 1949) here that would focus on more specific phenomena and yield more precise explanations or predictions. Acknowledging these omissions, we believe that generalized Darwinian principles in the social sciences should show their worth by linking up with auxiliary theories at lower levels of abstraction.

---

4. In important respects, the idea of program-based behavior was foreshadowed by Simon (1957) in his famous work on bounded rationality (March and Simon 1958; Vanberg, 2002).

Nevertheless, while our argument has been at a relatively high level of abstraction, it illuminates a "positive heuristic" (Lakatos 1976) that points to multiple and important detailed questions and future areas of inquiry.[5]

Our first claim in this regard is that our discussion and refinement of the concept of a replicator—inspired by the work of John von Neumann (1966)—led to a consideration of the conditions under which the potential for complexity in an evolving system may be increased. This is manifestly an important question for evolutionary biology as well as evolution in the socioeconomic domain. By all accounts, the complexity of the social world has increased enormously in the last five thousand years or so. The identification of generative replicators at the core of this process is a key step in the understanding of socioeconomic evolution. Our work needs now to be further illuminated by empirical material.

Continuing further in this direction, our identification of six major information transitions in social evolution is an additional component of the positive heuristic. Our conceptual framework pointed to the importance of information transitions, and we focused on the evolution of prelinguistic culture, human language, tribal customs, writing and records, judicial laws, and the institutionalization of science and technology. The development of new social modes of storing and replicating information is central to this account.

Our Darwinian conceptual framework places the generation and inheritance of information (broadly defined in the Shannon-Weaver sense), and the selection of entities that carry information, central to the analysis. It thus confirms and extends Daniel Dennett's (1995) observation that Darwinism is essentially algorithmic in nature. It is algorithmic not only in the sense that it obliges us to focus on detailed, sequential, causal processes. We have also pointed to the algorithmic mechanisms central to an evolutionary process capable of creating greater complexity, which involve sets of conditional, rule-like structures that retain and process such information.

This focus on mechanisms of information retention, selection, and replication leads us to address the nature and consequences of major information transitions in social evolution and even speculate on future transitions. The examination of the detailed mechanisms of information transmission in social evolution is pushed up the theoretical and empirical research agenda.

---

5. We are neither proposing that the content of the positive heuristic is an adequate criterion to assess a theory nor suggesting that Lakatos's philosophy of science is without problems (Nooteboom 1993). But we do believe that the existence of a rich positive heuristic is a promising trait for a scientific approach.

Our analysis affects existing research programs in a number of ways. Consider two examples. The literature on dual inheritance or gene-culture coevolution (Boyd and Richerson 1985; Durham 1991; Richerson and Boyd 2004) lacks an adequate definition of *culture* and has given inadequate attention to the detailed psychological and social mechanisms of information transmission. It is true that it postulates several psychological dispositions, such as conformism, but it does not consider specific psychological mechanisms (such as habit) that help explain how these dispositions are acquired, retained, and transmitted. Our analysis not only identifies these omissions but also shows that two levels are insufficient to appreciate human social evolution, at least after the acquisition of language. When applied to modern societies, dual inheritance models must be expanded to at least six levels of inheritance, involving particular social structures. Once there are multiple levels in addition to genetic inheritance, we must examine how evolutionary processes on different tiers interact with one another. Dual inheritance is not the final theory but an indicative — albeit powerful — simplification.

We do not wish to underestimate the major achievements of these dual inheritance theorists. Since the classic work of Robert Boyd and Peter Richerson (1985), a huge research program has developed, leading to some powerful models and results. Boyd and Richerson's focus is on how genes and culture coevolve. They demonstrated the power of Darwinian theory, but they bypassed the more philosophical and definitional elucidation of the core Darwinian principles. We attempt to fill this gap. Furthermore, we consider the multilevel ramifications of social evolution that pertain even if genetic evolution is negligible in the time span involved.

For example, our examination of major information transitions in social evolution is centered on the rise of novel generative replicators. The more recent of these developments do not necessarily require genetic changes. They are principally outcomes of interactions within and between social systems and their environment. Importantly in our account, the institutionalized system of scientific and technological knowledge emerges as a recent major information transition. This means that our understanding of social evolution cannot simply be confined to changes in social relations or relations of production as in the work of Marx and others. Accounts that center on culture (in evolutionary anthropology) or *Geist* (as in the German historical school) are also insufficient. They all miss the importance of the institutionalization of science and technology from the seventeenth century. While this too depended on prior institutions and political conditions, it was itself a major information transition. Thus, generally, we cannot periodize socioeconomic evolution simply in terms of changes of culture, systems of property rights, or modes of production. Historical periodization must also encompass new systems for the transmission of information and the generation of knowledge.

The discussion presented above shows that the project of generalizing Darwinian principles involves much more than establishing definitions and refining concepts. It enhances our understanding of the processes of socio-economic evolution and empowers an ongoing theoretical and empirical research agenda. Nevertheless, as we have taken pains to emphasize, Darwinian principles cannot give the whole story, and—as in biology—they must always be supplemented by auxiliary theories and informed by specific data. Much of this detailed labor is left to future publications. It is hoped that this volume will help stimulate this work.

9.6. DEVELOPING AN AGENDA FOR FUTURE RESEARCH

In this chapter, and throughout this work, we have pointed to questions requiring further research. There are many. Let us underline a few more here, particularly those of an empirical nature.

Our account of the major information transitions in social evolution needs to be scrutinized and expanded by the use of empirical material. Does a detailed examination of the evidence support our theory? We need a more finely grained account of these major information transitions, one that focuses on the mechanisms that led to their occurrence. No doubt, this account will be complex. In regard to later transitions, specific questions arise such as the role of religion and military institutions. It is also important to gauge the relative influence of adaptation and selection in different contexts and in different phases of organizational maturity and the degree to which external impulses provoked change, in addition to change from within. Human culture and institutions are often remarkably conservative and difficult to alter, so how did these remarkable transitions occur?

A major part of this enterprise involves uncovering the detailed mechanisms of information transmission in social evolution. We must understand more fully both the psychological and the social mechanisms involved. How does new knowledge from brain and neuroscience help? What are the constraints and evolutionary pathways? In the modern era, what is the role and effect of new communication media?

In the second half of the twentieth century, transport and telecommunications developed to the point at which huge amounts of information could be rapidly transmitted around the world, lowering transaction costs, and vastly increasing the scale and scope of financial and other markets. The scale and complexity of the modern capitalist system has, in part, been impelled by these developments in the communication of information. But we need to look more closely at the processes involved, and it is hoped that the Darwinian theoretical framework will help guide this enquiry.

To address these major challenges, the Darwinian program needs to study the micromechanics of replication. This requires empirical studies that cover both the temporal and the spatial dimension. We need to understand how stable habits and routines are recombined to produce increasingly complex social organizations, how habits and routines become stable in the first place, and how consistency and stability are maintained and, sometimes, break down across multiple levels of analysis, including individual human actors, organizations, and institutions.

We have a huge amount of empirical studies that (explicitly or implicitly) document the general Darwinian principles at work, including elaborate empirical case studies spanning the emergence, growth, and demise of entire cultures and their institutions. But we have only a small number of studies that document how replication processes actually happen in the social domain—how behavior and knowledge are stabilized and recombined in the generation of social outcomes. One of the most important items on our agenda is, therefore, to stimulate large-scale, longitudinal studies of social replication processes.

We need to look, not only at the conditions under which the potential to generate greater complexity can be enhanced, but also at the vulnerability of evolving social systems to internal and external shocks. Severe financial crises show that—as in nature—complexity can bring, not only adaptive benefits, but also new vulnerabilities. Furthermore—as in nature—often we cannot rely on some process of competitive selection to leave us with the best or fitter outcomes. Notwithstanding the fact that political intervention in the social and economic world is always treacherous and uncertain, and sometimes counterproductive, Darwinism does not mean that we simply sit on our hands.

Analyzing the viability of alternative organizations and social systems is high on the agenda of the evolutionary program. The fulfillment of this aim will require new analytic tools that complement the well-understood mathematical equations of evolution. Of particular interest is developing our understanding of evolutionary dynamics in heterogeneous populations. This is because interaction among agents in human societies is directed by the social structures in which agents are situated. The mathematical study of evolutionary dynamics in heterogeneous populations is of obvious importance, yet it is largely unexplored territory (Nowak 2006)

Further understanding will be stimulated as the Darwinian program unfolds. This program offers a common understanding of evolutionary processes that greatly helps the accumulation of knowledge across scientific disciplines and empirical domains. It thereby stimulates invaluable insights about the nature of the coupled dynamic processes that characterize economic and social evolution.

Glossary

adaptation. *Adaptation* has two meanings, each referring to a process. It more widely refers to the development of traits with a *fitness* advantage in a population. A second meaning of *adaptation* is the phenotypic development of the characteristics of an individual entity in a given environment. This latter use is common in economics and organization theory but not in biology. (Contrast with *adaptedness* and *exaptation*.)

adaptedness. Adaptedness is a quality of an entity, rather than a process. It refers to the *fitness* of a trait (or trait complex) in a specific environment.

complex population systems. Complex population systems contain multiple (intentional or nonintentional), varied entities that interact with the environment and each other. They face immediately *scarce* resources and struggle to survive, whether through conflict or cooperation. They *adapt* and can pass on information to others, through replication or imitation. Complex population systems are found in both the natural and the social domains. An economic example is an industry involving cohesive organizational entities such as business firms.

complexity. Following Christoph Adami (2002, 1087), we relate complexity in an evolving entity to the amount of information that entity stores about the environment in which it evolves: "The physical complexity of a sequence refers to the amount of information that is stored in that sequence about a particular environment." This measure is relative and conditional on the environment.

contagion. In biology, contagion occurs when one phenotype influences or infects a second phenotype without corresponding changes in the second genotype. More generally, contagion occurs when one entity (interactor) affects a second without significant changes in the replicators hosted by the second entity. When such changes do occur, this is described as *diffusion*.

continuity, doctrine of. Thomas Henry Huxley (1894, 1:236–37) defined the doctrine of continuity as the principle that no "complex natural phenomenon comes into existence suddenly, and without being preceded by simpler modifications." This applies in particular to both the individual development and the species evolution of human consciousness. (Compare with *continuity hypothesis*.)

continuity hypothesis. Following Ulrich Witt (2004, 131–32), the continuity hypothesis is the idea that natural evolution has "shaped the ground, and still defines the constraints, for man-made, or cultural, evolution . . . not withstanding that the mechanisms and regularities of cultural evolution differ from those of natural evolution. The historical process of economic evolution can be conceived as emerging from, and being embedded in, the constraints shaped by evolution in nature." We regard this hypothesis as an undeniable fact. It is entirely compatible with Darwinian principles.

culture. Edward Tylor (1871, 1) regarded culture as "that complex whole which includes knowledge, belief, art, morals, law, custom, and any other capabilities and habits acquired by man as a member of society." Thorstein Veblen (1919, 39) saw the "cultural scheme of any community" as "a complex of the habits of life and thought prevalent among the members of the community." Malcolm Willey (1929, 207) saw culture as "common and interrelated habits that constitute the mode of life of the people." Our definition is similar to these early statements. *Culture* refers to shared habits of thought and behavior that are prevalent in an entire group, community, or society. *Habits* are seen as capabilities or dispositions. Members of a group or society are not necessarily involved in all its institutions, but they are affected by its culture. Institutions are specific systems of rules. Institutional boundaries do not necessarily coincide with those of the group or society as a whole. By contrast, *culture* refers to general attributes of a group or society.

customs. Customs are dispositions in cohesive groups to energize patterns of behavior and interaction, involving conditional and sequential responses to cues that are partly dependent on social positions in the group. Rituals, ceremonies, and work routines are examples of customs. Customs typically qualify as *generative replicators*. (See also *routines*.)

Darwinism. Darwinism is a general theoretical framework for understanding evolution in *complex population systems*, involving the inheritance of *replicator* instructions by individual units, a variation of replicators and *interactors*, and a process of selection of the consequent interactors in a population.

diffusion. Diffusion is a type of inheritance that involves the copying of *replicators*, but not of *interactors*. Diffusion is common in the social domain, particularly in regard to ideas and technologies. In these cases, associated habits and routines are copied from one interactor to another. (See also *contagion*.)

drift. Drift is the alteration, through replication, interactor birth or death, or some other process, of the properties or membership of a population of entities and, in particular, the frequencies of particular *replicators*, where frequency outcomes are unrelated, in the long run, to *fitness*. As with *selection*, there is an anterior set of entities that is transformed into a posterior set, but (unlike selection) the resulting frequencies of posterior entities are uncorrelated with their fitness in the environmental context.

evolution. The word *evolution* has been, and continues to be, used in such a variety of ways that it is pointless trying to give it a sharper or more specific meaning. It broadly refers to change, including qualitative change, in a single entity or population of entities.

exaptation. Exaptation occurs when a trait or feature evolves for a purpose different from that which it originally was selected by evolution. Exaptation would not occur if the feature was selected out once it made no positive marginal contribution to fitness. Consequently, it requires a relatively flat fitness landscape where there is relatively weak selection pressure on traits so that they can survive in the transitional phase, before their novel use and contribution to fitness on another fitness hill. By contrast, *adaptation* involves climbing a pronounced fitness peak.

fitness. In biology, fitness is most usefully defined as the propensity of a genotype to produce offspring (De Jong 1994). Survival of the fittest is no longer a tautology: it is possibly false. The fitness of a *replicator* is the propensity to increase its frequency (relative to other replicators). In the social domain, this definition of *fitness* translates into the propensity of a social replicator (such as a *habit* or a *routine*) with a particular feature to produce copies and increase the frequency of similar replicators in the population. The fitness of an *interactor* is the propensity of its replicators to increase their frequency.

genotype. The genotype is the genetic constitution of an organism. It is a biological example of the more general class of replicators, which includes genotypes and replicators at the social and other levels. (See *replicator.*)

habits. A habit is a disposition to engage in previously adopted or acquired behavior (including patterns of thought) that is triggered by an appropriate stimulus or context. Habits are influenced by prior activity and have durable, self-sustaining qualities. Although formed through repetition of action or thought, habits themselves are not behaviors. If we acquire a habit, we do not necessarily use it all the time. Habits are the basis of both reflective and nonreflective behaviors. They are elemental social *replicators* in social evolution. They also qualify as *generative replicators.*

habits of thought, linguistic and corporeal habits. Habits of thought include linguistic habits and culturally acquired emotional habits. Linguistic habits constitute a special class of habits of thought that depend on language for their replication. By contrast, corporeal habits replicate through behavioral imitation, without the necessity of linguistic or gestural communication.

information. *Information* is defined here in the broad and basic sense of some conditional dispositions or coding that can be transmitted to other entities and cause a response. This definition omits key features of information, ideas and knowledge in the human domain, particularly meanings and interpretations. When we consider social evolution, it is essential to bring these into the picture. Because our concept is at a high level of generality, spanning both social and biological evolution, information cannot be defined more narrowly.

information transition. An information transition in social evolution creates a new way of retaining, correcting, and copying conditional response mechanisms, each built on novel forms of habits and social structure that embody information directly or indirectly relevant to the production and distribution of means of human survival or development. As in biological evolution (Maynard Smith and Szathmáry 1995), each major information transition in social evolution involves the creation of a new type of generative replicator.

inheritance. *Inheritance* refers to the passing of information concerning adaptive solutions from one entity to another. By our definitions, it turns out to be synonymous with *replication.*

inheritance, principle of. The *principle of inheritance* in *complex population systems* refers to a broad class of mechanisms, including diffusion and other forms of replication, by which information concerning adaptations is passed on or copied through time. These mechanisms require explanation.

institutions. Institutions are systems of established and prevalent social rules that structure social interactions. In short, they are social rule systems. The term *rule* is broadly understood as an injunction or disposition to do Y in circumstances X. A rule can be constitutive or procedural, and include norms of behavior and social conventions as well as legal or formal rules. By their nature, institutions must involve some shared conceptions in order to make rules operative. Systems of language, money, law, weights and measures, traffic conventions, table manners, and firms (and all other organizations) are all institutions. *Organizations* are an important subclass of institutions.

interactors. Terms such as *phenotype* and *vehicle* have been applied to biological entities. Following David Hull (1988) and others, we use the term *interactor* to describe the general form of such entities, to be found in complex population systems in nature and human society. Hull (1988, 408) defines an interactor as "an entity that directly interacts as a cohesive whole with its environment in such a way that this interaction *causes* replication to be differential." To refine this definition of an interactor, we use the following symbols:

w, an interactor;

E, one environmental state or a set of possible environmental states that are similar in relevant respects (environmental conditions that, also include other interactors);

$p_{i,j}$, the probability, with respect to a given environment E, that entity i will (more or less immediately) expire as a functioning unit (losing much of its preceding integrity or cohesion) if entity j expires.

For each interactor, there is a corresponding nonempty equivalent component set of replicators R. In cases in which an interactor hosts replicators at multiple ontological levels, the R refers exclusively to replicators that are at the highest possible ontological level within the interactor. The component status of R implies that the replicators are relatively durable in comparison with their host interactor. We assume a world of multiple, competing interactors and of other replicators that are not members of R. If an entity w is an interactor, then it must at least satisfy all the following minimal conditions:

1. *Integrity*: An interactor is a relatively cohesive entity with effective boundaries between itself and its surrounding environment, including other entities. This means that the internal relations among its component parts are generally more substantial and dense than the relations between the entity and elements in its external environment.
2. *Sustained integrity despite environmental variation*: Given shifting environmental states E_j, where j is a positive index over possible states of the environment, the interactor has sustained integrity owing to the nature of the components of the interactor and the internal relations between them.
3. *Shared dependence of component replicators on the interactor*: Given E, for every member r of R, $1 - p_{r,w} < \varepsilon$, where ε is a small and nonnegative number.
4. *Inclusion and shared organization of components*: Every member r of R must be a component part of w in the further sense that every r is within the boundary and part of the structure of w.
5. *Replication dependent on the properties of the interactor and its environment*: Every w has a set of properties C_w that, in the interaction of w with the given environment E, is a major factor in determining the (possibly different) set R' of successors of R.

Lamarckism. Lamarckism is a doctrine upholding the possibility of the (genotypic/replicator-to-replicator) inheritance of acquired (phenotypic/interactor) characters by individual organisms or entities in evolutionary processes. Lamarckism is logically compatible with *Darwinism* (broadly defined). And, even if Lamarckian inheritance did occur, Darwinian principles would still be required to provide a complete causal explanation of the evolutionary process. Most descriptions of social evolution as Lamarckian turn out to be misleading because there is no straightforward inheritance of acquired characters.

ontogeny. Ontogeny is the process of development of an individual entity, typically including interactions with its environment and other entities.

organizations. An organization is a special type of *institution* involving (*a*) criteria to establish its boundaries and to distinguish its members from its nonmembers, (*b*) principles of sovereignty concerning who is in charge, and (*c*) a structure of command and responsibility delineating roles within the organization. These conditions imply the existence of social roles or positions that have properties irreducible to those who occupy them. These social positions carry some rights, powers, and duties that are independent of characteristics or preferences of their incumbents.

phenotype. The phenotype is the ensemble of traits or characteristics of an organism. It is typically applied to the biological domain. The more general term is *interactor*, which applies to social as well as biological entities. (See *interactor*.)

phylogeny. Phylogeny is the process of evolution of a population of entities, including changes in the composition of a population, its attributes, and its stored information.

replication and replicators. Replication is a process whereby replicators are copied under the following conditions:

1. *Causal implication*: The source must be causally involved in the production of the copy, at least in the sense that, without the source, the particular copy would not be created.
2. *Similarity*: The copy must be like its source in relevant respects. In particular, the replicated entity must also be or contain a replicator.
3. *Information transfer*: During its creation, the copy must obtain the information that makes the copy similar to its source from that same source.

A replicator is a material structure hosted by the entity that is causally involved in the replication process and carries the information in condition 3 above. *Replication* is synonymous with *inheritance*. *Diffusion* is a special case of replication that does not also involve the copying of interactors. Replication is more general than *generative replication* because it does not necessarily involve conditional generative mechanisms.

Replication, generative, and generative replicators. Generative replicators are a special type of *replicator*, arguably with the enhanced potential to augment complexity in evolving systems. Generative replication is a process whereby interactors and component generative replicators are copied under the following conditions:

1. *Causal implication*: The source must be causally involved in the production of the copy, at least in the sense that, without the source, the particular copy would not be created.
2. *Similarity*: The replicated entity must also be or contain a replicator. The conditional generative mechanisms in the copy must be similar to those in the source. Errors or mutations in these mechanisms must also be copied with some degree of fidelity.
3. *Information transfer*: During its creation, the copy must obtain the conditional generative mechanisms (see below) that make the copy similar to its source from that same source.

A generative replicator is a material structure with the capacity for generative replication. A necessary feature of a generative replicator is a conditional generative mechanism:

4. *Conditional generative mechanisms*: Generative replicators are material structures that embody construction mechanisms (or programs) that can be energized by input signals that contain information about a particular environment. These mechanisms produce further instructions from a generative replicator to their related interactor, to guide its development. (External influences that produce outcomes generally unfavorable to the survival of the replicator or interactor are described, not as *input signals*, but as *destructive forces*.)

Note that, compared with replication, generative replication involves stricter conditions 2 and 3 plus the additional condition 4. Generative replication is, thus, a special case of *replication* that is, in turn, equivalent to *inheritance*.

routines. Routines are organizational dispositions to energize conditional patterns of behavior and interaction within *organizations*, involving sequential responses to cues that are partly dependent on social positions in the organization. The term *routine* is typically applied to business and military organizations, whereas *custom* is a term applied more broadly to other organizations, and *ritual* and *ceremony* apply to specific organizational contexts. Routines, customs, rituals, and ceremonies often qualify as *generative replicators*. (See *custom*.)

scarcity. Scarcity has several meanings, but one particular sense is relevant here. *Scarcity* in a local and immediate sense applies to all mortal and degradable entities, which must consume materials and energy in order to survive or minimize degradation. Local and immediate scarcity exists because these entities do not have instant access to all environmental resources and must expend time, materials, or energy in order to obtain specific inputs.

selection. Selection in a *complex population system* involves an anterior set of entities that is somehow being transformed into a posterior set, where all members of the posterior set are sufficiently similar to some members of the anterior set, and where the resulting frequencies of posterior entities are correlated positively and causally with their fitness in the environmental context. The transformation from the anterior to the posterior set is caused by the entities' interaction within a particular environment.

selection, principle of. The principle of selection is the idea that, in any given context, some entities in a *complex population system* are more adapted than others, some survive longer than others, and some are more successful in producing offspring or copies of themselves than others, and this differential process requires explanation.

selection, subset. Subset selection is defined as selection through one cycle of environmental interaction and elimination of entities in a population, structured so that the environmental interaction causes elimination to be differential, and where survival outcomes are correlated positively and causally with fitness in that environment.

selection, successor. Successor selection is defined as selection through one cycle of replication, variation, and environmental interaction, which leads to differential replication, novel entities, and a changed distribution of population properties that correlates positively and causally with the fitness of entities in that environment.

struggle for existence. The struggle for existence is the effort of an entity to survive and minimize degradation in the context of scarcity.

variation, principle of. The principle of variation holds that, when there is variation in a population of evolving entities, there must be some explanation of how such variety is generated and replenished.

Weismannism. After August Weismann (1893), Weismannism is a doctrine denying the possibility of the (genotypic/replicator-to-replicator) inheritance of acquired (phenotypic/interactor) characters by individual organisms or entities in evolutionary processes. It establishes a special case of Darwinian evolution.

References

Abernathy, William J. 1978. *The Productivity Dilemma: Road Block to Innovation in the Automobile Industry*. Baltimore: Johns Hopkins University Press.

Adami, Christoph. 2002. "What Is Complexity?" *BioEssays* 24, no. 12:1085–94.

Adami, Christoph, Charles Ofria, and Travis C. Collier. 2000. "Evolution of Biological Complexity." *Proceedings of the National Academy of Sciences (USA)* 97, no. 9:4463–68.

Agarwal, Rajshree, and Michael Gort. 1996. "The Evolution of Markets and Entry, Exit and Survival of Firms." *Review of Economics and Statistics* 78, no. 3 (August): 489–98.

Akerlof, George A. 1991. "Procrastination and Obedience." *American Economic Review (Papers and Proceedings)* 81, no. 2 (May): 1–19.

Alchian, Armen A. 1950. "Uncertainty, Evolution, and Economic Theory." *Journal of Political Economy* 58, no. 2 (June): 211–22.

Aldrich, Howard E. 1999. *Organizations Evolving*. 1st ed. London: Sage.

———. 2004. "Entrepreneurship." In *Handbook of Economic Sociology*, ed. Neil Smelser and Richard Swedberg, 451–77. Princeton, NJ: Princeton University Press.

Aldrich, Howard E., Geoffrey M. Hodgson, David L. Hull, Thorbjørn Knudsen, Joel Mokyr, and Viktor J. Vanberg. 2008. "In Defence of Generalized Darwinism." *Journal of Evolutionary Economics* 18, no. 5 (October): 577–96.

Aldrich, Howard E., and Martha Martinez. 2003. "Entrepreneurship as Social Construction: A Multi-Level Evolutionary Approach." In *Handbook of Entrepreneurial Research*, ed. Z. C. Acs and David B. Audretsch, 359–99. Boston: Kluwer.

Aldrich, Howard E., and Martin Ruef. 2006. *Organizations Evolving*. 2nd ed. London: Sage.

Alexander, Samuel. 1892. "Natural Selection in Morals." *International Journal of Ethics* 2, no. 4:409–39.

Allen, E., et al. 1976. "Sociobiology—Another Biological Determinism." *Bioscience* 26, no. 3:182–86.

Allen, Garland. 1968. "Thomas H. Morgan and the Problem of Natural Selection." *Journal of the History of Biology* 1:113–39.

Allen, Peter M., and J. M. McGlade. 1987a. "Evolutionary Drive: The Effects of Microscopic Diversity, Error-Making and Noise." *Foundations of Physics* 17, no. 7:723–38.

———. 1987b. "Modelling Complex Human Systems: A Fisheries Example." *European Journal of Operational Research* 30, no. 2:147–67.

Amable, Bruno. 2000. "Institutional Complementarity and Diversity of Social Systems of Innovation and Production." *Review of International Political Economy* 7, no. 4 (Winter): 645–87.

———. 2003. *The Diversity of Modern Capitalism.* Oxford: Oxford University Press.

Ammon, Otto. *Die Gesellschaftsordnung und ihre natürlichen Grundlagen.* Jena: Fischer, 1895.

"Ancient Jewellry Points to Early Origins of Language." 2006. *New Scientist,* 1 July. Available at http://www.newscientist.com/article/mg19125585.000-ancient-jewellery-points-to-early-origins-of-language.html.

Andersen, Esben Sloth. 2004. "Population Thinking, Price's Equation and the Analysis of Economic Evolution." *Evolutionary and Institutional Economics Review* 1, no. 1 (November): 127–48.

Anderson, Carl. 2002. "Self-Organization in Relation to Several Similar Concepts: Are the Boundaries to Self-Organization Indistinct?" *Biological Bulletin* 202, no. 3:247–55.

Andersson, Claes. 2008. "Sophisticated Selectionism as a General Theory of Knowledge." *Biology and Philosophy* 23:229–42.

Andreoni, James. 1995. "Cooperation in Public Goods Experiments: Kindness or Confusion?" *American Economic Review* 85, no. 4 (December): 891–904.

Aoki, Kenichi, Joe Yuichiro Wakano, and Marcus W. Feldman. 2003. "The Emergence of Social Learning in a Temporally Changing Environment: A Theoretical Model." *Current Anthropology* 46, no. 2 (April): 334–44.

Aoki, Masahiko. 2001. *Toward a Comparative Institutional Analysis.* Cambridge, MA: MIT Press.

Archer, Margaret S. *Realist Social Theory: The Morphogenetic Approach.* Cambridge: Cambridge University Press, 1995.

Argyris, Chris, and Donald A. Schön. 1996. *Organizational Learning II: Theory, Method, and Practice.* Reading, MA: Addison-Wesley.

Arkin, Ronald C. 1998. *Behavior-Based Robotics.* Cambridge, MA: MIT Press.

Arrow, Kenneth J. 1962. "Economic Welfare and the Allocation of Resources to Invention." In *The Rate and Direction of Inventive Activity: Economic and Social Factors,* ed. Richard R. Nelson, 609–25. Princeton, NJ: Princeton University Press.

———. 1994. "Methodological Individualism and Social Knowledge." *American Economic Review (Papers and Proceedings)* 84, no. 2 (May): 1–9.

Arrow, Kenneth J., and Gerard Debreu. 1954. "Existence of an Equilibrium for a Competitive Economy." *Econometrica* 22, no. 3:265–90.

Arthur, W. Brian. 1989. "Competing Technologies, Increasing Returns, and Lock-in by Historical Events." *Economic Journal* 99, no. 1 (March): 116–31.

———. 2006. "Out-of-Equilibrium Economics and Agent-Based Modeling." In *Handbook of Computational Economics,* vol. 2, *Agent-Based Computational Economics,* ed. Kenneth L. Judd, Leigh Tesfatsion, Michael D. Intrigilator, and Kenneth J. Arrow, 1551–64. Amsterdam: North-Holland.

———. 2008. *The Nature of Technology: What It Is and How It Evolves.* New York: Free Press.

Asch, Solomon E. 1952. *Social Psychology.* New York: Prentice-Hall.

Audretsch, David B. 1991. "New-Firm Survival and the Technological Regime." *Review of Economics and Statistics* 73, no. 3 (August): 441–50.

Audretsch, David B., and Talat Mahmood. 1994. "Firm Selection and Industry Evolution: The Post-Entry Performance of New Firms." *Journal of Evolutionary Economics* 4, no. 3:243–60.

———. 1995. "New Firm Survival: New Results Using a Hazard Function." *Review of Economics and Statistics* 77, no. 1 (February): 97–103.

Aunger, Robert. 2002. *The Electric Meme: A New Theory of How We Think.* New York: Free Press.

Ayres, Clarence E. 1932. *Huxley.* New York: Norton.

Bagehot, Walter. 1872. *Physics and Politics; or, Thoughts on the Application of the Principles of "Natural Selection" and "Inheritance" to Political Society.* London: Henry King.

Baguñà, Jaume, and Jordi Garcia-Fernàndez. 2003. "Evo-Devo: The Long and Winding Road." *International Journal of Developmental Biology* 47:705–13.

Baldwin, Carliss Y., and Kim B. Clark. 2000. *The Power of Modularity*. Vol. 1 of *Design Rules*. Cambridge, MA: MIT Press.

Baldwin, James Mark. 1909. *Darwin and the Humanities*. 1st ed. Baltimore: Review Publishing.

Bannister, Robert C. 1973. "William Graham Sumner's Social Darwinism: A Reconsideration." *History of Political Economy* 5, no. 1 (Spring): 89–108.

———. 1979. *Social Darwinism: Science and Myth in Anglo-American Social Thought*. Philadelphia: Temple University Press.

Barnett, William P. 2008. *The Red Queen among Organizations: How Competitiveness Evolves*. Princeton, NJ: Princeton University Press.

Baron, Robert S., Joseph A. Vandello, and Bethany Brunsman. 1996. "The Forgotten Variable in Conformity Research: Impact of Task Importance on Social Influence." *Journal of Personality and Social Psychology* 7, no. 5:915–27.

Barr, Nicholas. 1988. "The Phillips Machine." *LSE Quarterly* 2, no. 4:305–37.

Bar-Yosef, Ofer. 1998. "The Natufian Culture in the Levant: Threshold to the Origins of Agriculture." *Evolutionary Anthropology* 6, no. 5:159–77.

———. 2001. "From Sedentary Foragers to Village Hierarchies: The Emergence of Social Institutions." In *The Origin of Human Social Institutions*, ed. Walter Garry Runciman, 1–38. Oxford: Oxford University Press.

Basalla, George. 1989. *The Evolution of Technology*. Cambridge: Cambridge University Press.

Baum, Joel A. C., and Paul Ingram. 1998. "Survival Enhancing Learning in the Manhattan Hotel Industry, 1898–1980." *Management Science* 44, no. 7:996–1016.

"Beads Confirm Ancient Jewellry Making." 2007. *Natural History Museum News*, 5 June. Available at http://www.nhm.ac.uk/about-us/news/2007/june/news_11808.html.

Becker, Gary S. 1976. "Altruism, Egoism, and Genetic Fitness: Economics and Sociobiology." *Journal of Economic Literature* 14, no. 2 (December): 817–26.

———. 1992. "Habits, Addictions and Traditions." *Kyklos* 45, no. 3:327–46.

Becker, Gary S., and Kevin M. Murphy. 1988. "A Theory of Rational Addiction." *Journal of Political Economy* 96, no. 4:675–700.

Becker, Markus C. 2004. "Organizational Routines: A Review of the Literature." *Industrial and Corporate Change* 13, no. 4:643–77.

———, ed. 2008. *Handbook of Organizational Routines*. Cheltenham: Edward Elgar.

Becker, Markus C., and Nathalie Lazaric. 2003. "The Influence of Knowledge in the Replication of Routines." *Économie appliquée* 56, no. 3 (September): 65–94.

Beder, Jay H., and Richard Gomulkiewicz. 1998. "Computing the Selection Gradient and Evolutionary Response of an Infinite-Dimensional Trait." *Journal of Mathematical Biology* 36, no. 3:299–319.

Beinhocker, Erik D. 2006. *The Origins of Wealth: Evolution, Complexity, and the Radical Remaking of Economics*. New York: Random House.

Bellomy, Donald C. 1984. "'Social Darwinism' Revisited." *Perspectives in American History*, n.s., 1:1–129.

Bennett, A. W. 1870. "The Theory of Selection from a Mathematical Point of View." *Nature* 3:30–31.

Bergstrom, Theodore C. 2002. "Evolution of Social Behavior: Individual and Group Selection." *Journal of Economic Perspectives* 16, no. 2 (Spring): 67–88.

———. 2003. "The Algebra of Assortative Encounters and the Evolution of Cooperation." *International Game Theory Review* 5, no. 3 (September): 211–28.

Berle, Adolf A. 1950. *Natural Selection of Political Forces*. Lawrence: University of Kansas Press.

Berle, Adolf A., and Gardiner C. Means. 1932. *The Modern Corporation and Private Property*. New York: Macmillan.

Bertalanffy, Ludwig von. 1971. *General Systems Theory: Foundation, Development, Applications*. London: Allen Lane.

Bhaskar, Roy. 1975. *A Realist Theory of Science*. Leeds: Leeds Books.

Bicchieri, Cristina. 1994. *Rationality and Coordination*. Cambridge: Cambridge University Press.

Blackmore, Susan. 1999. *The Meme Machine*. Oxford: Oxford University Press.

Blair, Margaret M. 1999. "Firm-Specific Human Capital and Theories of the Firm." In *Employees and Corporate Governance*, ed. Margaret M. Blair and Mark Roe, 58–89. Washington, DC: Brookings.

———. 2003. "Locking in Capital: What Corporate Law Achieved for Business Organizers in the Nineteenth Century." *UCLA Law Review* 51, no. 2:387–455.

Blitz, David. 1992. *Emergent Evolution: Qualitative Novelty and the Levels of Reality*. Dordrecht: Kluwer.

Bloch, Maurice. 1991. "Language, Anthropology and Cognitive Science." *Man* 26:183–98.

Blumer, Herbert. 1969. *Symbolic Interactionism: Perspective and Method*. Chicago: University of Chicago Press.

Blute, M. 1997. "History versus Science: The Evolutionary Solution." *Canadian Journal of Sociology* 22:345–64.

Boesiger, Ernest. 1974. "Evolutionary Theories after Lamarck and Darwin." In *Studies in the Philosophy of Biology*, ed. Francisco J. Ayala and Theodosius Dobzhansky, 21–44. London: Macmillan; Berkeley and Los Angeles: University of California Press.

Bogdan, Radu. 2000. *Minding Minds: Evolving a Reflexive Mind in Interpreting Others*. Cambridge, MA: MIT Press.

Bonazzi, Giuseppe, and Hope Finney Botti. 1995. "Asymmetric Expectations: Cross-National Coalitions in a Japanese Transplant in Italy." *International Executive* 37, no. 4:395–414.

Bonner, John T. 1980. *Evolution of Culture in Animals*. Princeton, NJ: Princeton University Press.

Boschma, Ron A., and Rik Wenting. 2007. "Spatial Evolution of the British Automobile Industry: Does Location Matter?" *Industrial and Corporate Change* 16, no. 2:213–38.

Boulding, Kenneth E. 1981. *Evolutionary Economics*. Beverly Hills, CA: Sage.

Bowler, Peter J. 1983. *The Eclipse of Darwinism: Anti-Darwinian Evolution Theories in the Decades around 1900*. Baltimore: Johns Hopkins University Press.

———. 1988. *The Non-Darwinian Revolution: Reinterpreting a Historical Myth*. Baltimore: Johns Hopkins University Press.

Bowler, Peter J., and Iwan Rhys Morus. 2005. *Making Modern Science: A Historical Survey*. Chicago: University of Chicago Press.

Bowles, Samuel. 2006. "Group Competition, Reproductive Leveling, and the Evolution of Human Altruism." *Science* 314, no. 5805 (8 December): 1569–72.

Bowles, Samuel, and Herbert Gintis. 2005a. "Can Self-Interest Explain Cooperation?" *Evolutionary and Institutional Economics Review* 2, no. 1 (October): 21–41.

———, eds. 2005b. *Moral Sentiments and Material Interests: The Foundations of Cooperation in Economic Life*. Cambridge, MA: MIT Press.

Boyd, Robert, Herbert Gintis, Samuel Bowles, and Peter J. Richerson. 2003. "Evolution of Altruistic Punishment." *Proceedings of the National Academy of Sciences (USA)* 100, no. 6:3531–35.

Boyd, Robert, and Peter J. Richerson. 1980. "Sociobiology, Culture and Economic Theory." *Journal of Economic Behavior and Organization* 1, no. 1 (March): 97–121.

———. 1985. *Culture and the Evolutionary Process*. Chicago: University of Chicago Press.

———. 1992. "Punishment Allows the Evolution of Cooperation (or Anything Else) in Sizable Groups." *Ethology and Sociobiology* 13, no. 3:171–95.

———. 1995. "Why Does Culture Increase Human Adaptability?" *Ethology and Sociobiology* 16, no. 2 (March): 125–43.

Boyer, Robert. 2005. "Coherence, Diversity, and the Evolution of Capitalisms—the Institutional Complementarity Hypothesis." *Evolutionary and Institutional Economics Review* 2, no. 1 (October): 43–80.

Bradach, Jeffrey L. 1998. *Franchise Organizations*. Boston: Harvard Business School Press.

Brandon, Robert N. 1996. *Concepts and Methods in Evolutionary Biology*. Cambridge: Cambridge University Press.

———. 1998. "The Levels of Selection: A Hierarchy of Interactors." In *The Philosophy of Biology*, ed. D. L. Hull and M. Ruse, 176–97. Oxford: Oxford University Press.

———. 1999. "The Units of Selection Revisited: The Modules of Selection." *Biology and Philosophy* 14:167–80.

Brandon, Robert N., and Richard M. Burian, eds. 1984. *Genes, Organisms, Populations: Controversies over the Units of Selection*. Cambridge, MA: MIT Press.

Brodie, Richard. 1996. *Virus of the Mind: The New Science of the Meme*. Seattle: Integral.

Brown, Donald E. 1991. *Human Universals*. New York: McGraw-Hill.

Brown, John Seely, and Paul Duguid. 1991. "Organizational Learning and Communities of Practice: Toward a Unified View of Working, Learning and Innovation." *Organizational Science* 2, no. 1:40–57.

Brown, Mary M. 2003. "Technology Diffusion and the 'Knowledge Barrier': The Dilemma of Stakeholder Participation." *Public Performance and Management Review* 26, no. 4:345–59.

Bruderer, Erhard, and Jitendra V. Singh. 1996. "Organizational Evolution, Learning, and Selection: A Genetic-Algorithm-Based Model." *Academy of Management Journal* 39, no. 5:1322–49.

Bunge, Mario. 1961. "The Weight of Simplicity in the Construction and Assaying of Scientific Theories." *Philosophy of Science* 28, no. 2 (April): 120–49.

———. 1974. *Interpretation and Truth*. Vol. 2 of *Treatise on Basic Philosophy*. Dordrecht: Reidel.

———. 1977. *Ontology I: The Furniture of the World*. Vol. 3 of *Treatise on Basic Philosophy*. Dordrecht: Reidel.

———. 1979. *Ontology II: A World of Systems*. Vol. 4 of *Treatise on Basic Philosophy*. Dordrecht: Reidel.

———. 1980. *The Mind-Body Problem: A Psychobiological Approach*. Oxford: Pergamon.

———. 2000. "Ten Modes of Individualism—None of Which Works—and Their Alternatives." *Philosophy of the Social Sciences* 30, no. 3 (September): 384–406.

Bünstorf, Guido. 2007. "Opportunity Spin-Offs and Necessity Spin-Offs." Working Paper no. 0718. Jena: Max Planck Institute of Economics.

Burkhardt, Richard W., Jr. 1977. *The Spirit of System: Lamarck and Evolutionary Biology*. Cambridge, MA: Harvard University Press.

———. 1984. "The 'Zoological Philosophy' of J. B. Lamarck." In *Zoological Philosophy: An Exposition with Regard to the Natural History of Animals*, by J. B. de Lamarck, trans. Hugh Elliot, xv–xxxix. Chicago: University of Chicago Press.

Bush, Paul Dale. 1986. "On the Concept of Ceremonial Encapsulation." *Review of Institutional Thought* 3 (December): 25–45.

Buss, Leo W. 1987. *The Evolution of Individuality*. Princeton, NJ: Gordon & Breach.

Butler, Samuel. 1878. *Life and Habit*. London: Trübner.

Calvin, William H. 2002. *A Brain for All Seasons: Human Evolution and Abrupt Climate Change*. Chicago: University of Chicago Press.

Camazine, Scott, Jean-Luis Deneubourg, Nigel R. Franks, James Sneyd, Guy Theraulaz, and Eric Bonabeau. 2001. *Self-Organization in Biological Systems*. Princeton, NJ: Princeton University Press.

Camic, Charles. 1986. "The Matter of Habit." *American Journal of Sociology* 91, no. 5 (March): 1039–87.

Campbell, Donald T. 1965. "Variation, Selection and Retention in Sociocultural Evolution." In *Social Change in Developing Areas: A Reinterpretation of Evolutionary Theory*, ed. H. R. Barringer, G. I. Blanksten, and R. W. Mack, 19–49. Cambridge, MA: Schenkman. Reprinted in *General Systems* 14 (1969): 69–85.

——. 1974. "Evolutionary Epistemology." In *The Philosophy of Karl Popper*, ed. P. A. Schlipp, 313–463. La Salle, IL: Open Court.

——. 1975. "On the Conflicts between Biological and Social Evolution and between Psychology and Moral Tradition." *American Psychologist* 30, no. 12 (December): 1103–26.

——. 1987. "Blind Variation and Selective Retention as in Other Knowledge Processes." In *Evolutionary Epistemology, Theory of Rationality, and the Sociology of Knowledge*, ed. Gerard Radnitzky and William W. Bartley III, 91–114. La Salle, IL: Open Court.

——. 1994. "How Individual and Face-to-Face Group Selection Undermine Firm Selection in Organizational Evolution." In *Evolutionary Dynamics of Organizations*, ed. Joel A. C. Baum and Jitendra V. Singh, 23–38. New York: Oxford University Press.

Carneiro, Robert L. 1970. "A Theory of the Origin of the State." *Science* 169, no. 3947 (21 August): 733–38.

Carter, James Coolidge. 1907. *Law: Its Origin, Growth and Function*. New York: Putnam's.

Chalmers, Alan F. 1985. *What Is This Thing Called Science?* Milton Keynes: Open University Press.

Chapin, F. Stuart. *Introduction to the Study of Social Evolution—the Prehistoric Period*. New York: Century, 1913.

Chesbrough, Henry. 2003. "The Governance and Performance of Xerox's Technology Spin-Off Companies." *Research Policy* 32, no. 3 (March): 403–21.

Childe, V. Gordon. 1951. *Social Evolution*. London: Watts.

Christensen, Clayton M. 1993. "The Rigid Disk Drive Industry: A History of Commercial and Technological Turbulence." *Business History Review* 67, no. 4:531–88.

Christiansen, Morten H., and Simon Kirby. 2003. "Language Evolution: Consensus and Controversies." *Trends in Cognitive Sciences* 7, no. 7 (July): 300–307.

Churchland, Patricia S. 1986. *Neurophilosophy: Toward a Unified Science of the Mind-Brain*. Cambridge, MA: MIT Press.

Churchland, Paul M. 1984. *Matter and Consciousness*. Cambridge, MA: MIT Press.

——. 1989. *A Neurocomputational Perspective: The Nature of Mind and the Structure of Science*. Cambridge, MA: MIT Press.

Clark, Andy. 1997a. *Being There: Putting the Brain, Body and World Together Again*. Cambridge, MA: MIT Press.

——. 1997b. "Economic Reason: The Interplay of Individual Learning and External Structure." In *The Frontiers of the New Institutional Economics*, ed. John N. Drobak and John V. Nye, 269–90. San Diego: Academic.

Closson, Carlos C. 1896a. "Dissociation by Displacement: A Phase of Social Selection." *Quarterly Journal of Economics* 10, no. 2:156–86.

——. 1896b. "Social Selection." *Journal of Political Economy* 4, no. 4:449–66.

Cohen, Michael D., and Paul Bacdayan. 1994. "Organizational Routines Are Stored as Procedural Memory—Evidence from a Laboratory Study." *Organization Science* 5, no. 4 (November): 554–68.

Cohen, Michael D., Roger Burkhart, Giovanni Dosi, Massimo Egidi, Luigi Marengo, Massimo Warglien, and Sidney Winter. 1996. "Routines and Other Recurring Action Patterns of Organizations: Contemporary Research Issues." *Industrial and Corporate Change* 5, no. 3:653–98.

Cohen, Wesley M., and Daniel A. Levinthal. 1990. "Absorptive Capacity: A New Perspective on Learning and Innovation." *Administrative Science Quarterly* 35, no. 1:128–52.

Collins, Randall. 1988. *Theoretical Sociology*. San Diego: Harcourt, Brace, Jovanovich.

Colp, Ralph. 1974. "The Contacts between Karl Marx and Charles Darwin." *Journal of the History of Ideas* 35, no. 2 (April–June): 329–38.

——. 1982. "The Myth of the Marx-Darwin Letter." *History of Political Economy* 14, no. 4 (Winter): 416–82.

Commons, John R. 1897. "Natural Selection, Social Selection, and Heredity." *Arena* 18 (July): 90–97.

———. 1924. *Legal Foundations of Capitalism*. New York: Macmillan.

———. 1925. "Marx To-Day: Capitalism and Socialism." *Atlantic Monthly*, November, 682–93.

———. 1934. *Institutional Economics—Its Place in Political Economy*. New York: Macmillan.

Comte, Auguste. 1853. *The Positive Philosophy of Auguste Comte*. Translated by Harriet Martineau from the 1830–42 French ed. 2 vols. London: Chapman.

Conn, Herbert William. 1914. *Social Heredity and Social Evolution: The Other Side of Eugenics*. New York: Abingdon.

Cook, L. M., G. S. Mani, and M. E. Varley. 1986. "Postindustrial Melanism in the Peppered Moth." *Science* 231, no. 4738 (7 February): 611–13.

Cook, L. M., G. S. Mani, and G. Wynnes. 1985. "Evolution in Reverse: Clean Air and the Peppered Moth." *Biological Journal of the Linnaean Society* 13:179–98.

Copeland, Morris A. 1936. "Commons's Institutionalism in Relation to the Problem of Social Evolution and Economic Planning." *Quarterly Journal of Economics* 50, no. 2 (February): 333–46.

Cordes, Christian. 2006. "Darwinism in Economics: From Analogy to Continuity." *Journal of Evolutionary Economics* 16, no. 5 (December): 529–41.

Corning, Peter A. 1983. *The Synergism Hypothesis: A Theory of Progressive Evolution*. New York: McGraw-Hill.

Cziko, Gary. 1995. *Without Miracles: Universal Selection Theory and the Second Darwinian Revolution*. Cambridge, MA: MIT Press.

———. 2001. "Heeding Darwin but Ignoring Bernard: External Behaviors Are Not Selected." *Behavioral and Brain Sciences* 24, no. 3 (June): 534–35.

Dahl, Michael S., and Toke Reichstein. 2007. "Are You Experienced? Prior Experience and the Survival of New Organizations." *Industry and Innovation* 14:497–511.

Dahlstrand, Åsa Lindholm. 1998. "Growth and Inventiveness in Technology-Based Spin-Off Firms." *Research Policy* 26, no. 3 (October): 331–44.

Damasio, Antonio R. 1994. *Descartes' Error: Emotion, Reason, and the Human Brain*. New York: Putnam.

Damuth, John, and I. Lorraine Heisler. 1988. "Alternative Formulations of Multi-Level Selection." *Biology and Philosophy* 3, no. 4 (October): 407–30.

Daniel, Glyn. 1968. *The First Civilizations: The Archaeology of Their Origins*. London: Thames & Hudson.

Darden, Lindley, and Joseph A. Cain. 1989. "Selection Type Theories." *Philosophy of Science* 56:106–29.

Darnell, J. E., and W. F. Doolittle. 1986. "Speculations on the Early Course of Evolution." *Proceedings of the National Academy of Sciences (USA)* 83, no. 5:1271–75.

Darwin, Charles R. 1859. *On the Origin of Species by Means of Natural Selection; or, The Preservation of Favoured Races in the Struggle for Life*. London: Murray.

———. 1868. *The Variation of Animals and Plants under Domestication*. 2 vols. 1st ed. London: Murray; New York: Orange Judd.

———. 1871. *The Descent of Man, and Selection in Relation to Sex*. 2 vols. 1st ed. London: Murray; New York: Hill.

———. 1974. *Metaphysics, Materialism, and the Evolution of Mind: Early Writings of Charles Darwin*. Transcribed and annotated by Paul H. Barrett, with commentary by Howard E. Gruber. Chicago: University of Chicago Press.

Darwin, Francis, ed. 1887. *Life and Letters of Charles Darwin*. 3 vols. London: John Murray.

Darwin, Francis, and Albert C. Seward, eds. 1903. *More Letters of Charles Darwin*. 2 vols. London: John Murray.

Datta, Deepak K. 1991. "Organizational Fit and Acquisition Performance." *Strategic Management Journal* 12, no. 4: 281–97.

David, Paul A. 1985. "Clio and the Economics of QWERTY." *American Economic Review (Papers and Proceedings)* 75, no. 2 (May): 332–37.

Dawkins, Richard. 1976. *The Selfish Gene*. Oxford: Oxford University Press.

———. 1982. *The Extended Phenotype: The Gene as the Unit of Selection*. Oxford: Oxford University Press.

———. 1983. "Universal Darwinism." In *Evolution from Molecules to Man*, ed. D. S. Bendall, 403–25. Cambridge: Cambridge University Press.

———. 1986. *The Blind Watchmaker*. Harlow: Longman.

———. 1989. *The Selfish Gene*. 2nd ed. Oxford: Oxford University Press.

———. 2004. "Extended Phenotype—but Not *Too* Extended: A Reply to Laland, Turner and Jablonka." *Biology and Philosophy* 19, no. 3 (June): 377–96.

Deacon, Terrence W. 1997. *The Symbolic Species: The Co-Evolution of Language and the Brain*. New York: Norton.

Degler, Carl N. 1991. *In Search of Human Nature: The Decline and Revival of Darwinism in American Social Thought*. Oxford: Oxford University Press.

De Jong, G. 1994. "The Fitness of Fitness Concepts and the Description of Natural Selection." *Quarterly Review of Biology* 69, no. 1 (March): 3–29.

Dennett, Daniel C. 1995. *Darwin's Dangerous Idea: Evolution and the Meanings of Life*. London: Allen Lane; New York: Simon & Schuster.

Depew, David J., and Bruce H. Weber. 1995. *Darwinism Evolving: Systems Dynamics and the Genealogy of Natural Selection*. Cambridge, MA: MIT Press.

De Vries, Hugo. 1909. *The Mutation Theory: Experiments and Observations on the Origin of Species in the Vegetable Kingdom*. Translated by J. B. Farmer and A. D. Darbishire from the German ed. of 1901. 2 vols. Chicago: Open Court.

de Waal, Frans B. M. 1982. *Chimpanzee Politics: Power and Sex among Apes*. New York: Harper & Row; London: Jonathan Cape.

———. 1989. *Peacemaking among Primates*. Cambridge, MA: Harvard University Press.

———. 1996. *Good Natured: The Origin of Right and Wrong in Humans and Other Animals*. Cambridge, MA: Harvard University Press.

———. 2006. *Primates and Philosophers: How Morality Evolved*. Princeton, NJ: Princeton University Press.

Dewey, John. 1910. *The Influence of Darwin on Philosophy and Other Essays in Contemporary Philosophy*. New York: Holt.

———. 1922. *Human Nature and Conduct: An Introduction to Social Psychology*. 1st ed. New York: Holt.

Diamond, A. S. 1935. *Primitive Law*. London: Watts.

Diamond, Jared. 1991. *The Rise and Fall of the Third Chimpanzee*. London: Vintage.

———. 1997. *Guns, Germs and Steel: The Fates of Human Societies*. New York: Norton.

Diggins, John Patrick. 1994. *The Promise of Pragmatism: Modernism and the Crisis of Knowledge and Authority*. Chicago: University of Chicago Press.

DiMaggio, Paul J., and Walter W. Powell. 1983. "The Iron Cage Revisited: Institutional Isomorphism and Collective Rationality in Organizational Fields." *American Sociological Review* 48, no. 2 (April): 147–60.

Dobzhansky, Theodosius. 1962. *Mankind Evolving: The Evolution of the Human Species*. New Haven, CT: Yale University Press.

Donald, Merlin. 1991. *Origins of the Modern Mind: Three Stages in the Evolution of Culture and Cognition*. Cambridge, MA: Harvard University Press.

Dopfer, Kurt. 2004. "The Economic Agent as Rule Maker and Rule User: *Homo sapiens oeconomicus*." *Journal of Evolutionary Economics* 14, no. 2 (May): 177–95.

Dopfer, Kurt, John Foster, and Jason Potts. 2004. "Micro-Meso-Macro." *Journal of Evolutionary Economics* 14, no. 3 (July): 263–79.

Dopfer, Kurt, and Jason Potts. 2008. *The General Theory of Economic Evolution.* London: Routledge.

Dore, Ronald. 2000. *Stock Market Capitalism: Welfare Capitalism: Japan and Germany versus the Anglo Saxons.* Oxford: Oxford University Press.

Dorfman, Joseph. 1934. *Thorstein Veblen and His America.* New York: Viking.

Dosi, Giovanni, Richard R. Nelson, and Sidney G. Winter. 2000. "Introduction: The Nature and Dynamics of Organizational Capabilities." In *The Nature and Dynamics of Organizational Capabilities,* ed. Giovanni Dosi, Richard R. Nelson, and Sidney G. Winter, 1–22. Oxford: Oxford University Press.

Drubach, Daniel. 2000. *The Brain Explained.* Englewood Cliffs, NJ: Prentice-Hall.

Drummond, Henry. 1894. *The Ascent of Man.* London: Hodder & Stoughton.

Dunbar, Robin I. M. 1993. "Coevolution of Neocortical Size, Group Size, and Language." *Behavioral and Brain Sciences* 16:681–94.

———. 1996. *Grooming, Gossip and the Evolution of Language.* London: Faber & Faber.

———. 1998. "The Social Brain Hypothesis." *Evolutionary Anthropology* 6:178–90.

Dunbar, Robin, Chris Knight, and Camilla Power. 1999. *The Evolution of Culture.* New Brunswick, NJ: Rutgers University Press.

Dunne, Timothy, Mark J. Roberts, and Larry Samuelson. 1988. "Patterns of Firm Entry and Exit in U.S. Manufacturing Industries." *RAND Journal of Economics* 19, no. 4:495–515.

———. 1989. "The Growth and Failure of U.S. Manufacturing Plants." *Quarterly Journal of Economics* 104, no. 4:671–98.

Durham, William H. 1991. *Coevolution: Genes, Culture, and Human Diversity.* Stanford, CA: Stanford University Press.

Earley, Christine E. 2001. "Knowledge Acquisition in Auditing: Training Novice Auditors to Recognize Cue Relationships in Real Estate Valuation." *Accounting Review* 76, no. 1:81–97.

Edelman, Gerald M. 1987. *Neural Darwinism: The Theory of Neuronal Group Selection.* New York: Basic.

———. 1989. *The Remembered Present: A Biological Theory of Consciousness.* New York: Basic.

———. 1992. *Bright Air, Brilliant Fire: On the Matter of the Mind.* Harmondsworth: Penguin; New York: Basic.

Edgerton, Robert B. 1992. *Sick Societies: Challenging the Myth of Primitive Harmony.* New York: Free Press.

Edmondson, Amy C., Richard M. Bohmer, and Gary P. Pisano. 2001. "Disrupted Routines: Team Learning and New Technology Implementation in Hospitals." *Administrative Science Quarterly* 46, no. 4:685–716.

Ehrlich, Paul R. 2000. *Human Natures: Genes, Cultures and the Human Prospect.* Washington, DC: Island.

Eigen, Manfred. 1994. "The Origin of Genetic Information." *Origins of Life and Evolution of Biospheres* 24, nos. 2–4 (June): 241–62.

Eigen, Manfred, William C. Gardiner, Peter Schuster, and Ruthild Winkler-Oswatitsch. 1981. "The Origin of Genetic Information." *Scientific American* 244, no. 4:78–94.

Eigen, Manfred, and Peter Schuster. 1979. *The Hypercycle: A Principle of Natural Self-Organization.* New York: Springer.

Eldredge, Niles. 1985. *Unfinished Synthesis: Biological Hierarchies and Modern Evolutionary Thought.* Oxford: Oxford University Press.

Eldredge, Niles, and Stephen Jay Gould. 1977. "Punctuated Equilibria: The Tempo and Mode of Evolution Reconsidered." *Paleobiology* 3:115–51.

Emery, Fred E., ed. 1981. *Systems Thinking.* 2 vols. Harmondsworth: Penguin.

Enard, W., M. Przeworski, S. E. Fisher, C. S. L. Lai, V. Wiebe, T. Kitano, A. P. Monaco, and

S. Pääbo. 2002. "Molecular Evolution of *FOXP2*, a Gene Involved in Speech and Language." *Nature* 418 (22 August): 869–72.

Engel, Christoph. 2008. "Learning the Law." *Journal of Institutional Economics* 4, no. 3 (December): 275–97.

Epple, Dennis, Linda Argote, and Rukmini Devadas. 1991. "Organizational Learning Curves: A Method for Investigating Intra-Plant Transfer of Knowledge Acquired through Learning by Doing." *Organization Science* 2, no. 1:58–70.

Eriksson, Tor, and Johan Moritz Kuhn. 2006. "Firm Spin-Offs in Denmark, 1981–2000—Patterns of Entry and Exit." *International Journal of Industrial Organization* 24:1021–40.

Etkin, William. 1954. "Social Behavior and the Evolution of Man's Mental Faculties." *American Naturalist* 88, no. 840:129–42.

Evans, Nicholas, and Stephen C. Levinson. 2009. "The Myth of Language Universals: Language Diversity and Its Importance for Cognitive Science." *Behavioral and Brain Sciences* 32, no. 5:429–92.

Farnsworth, E. Allan. 1969. "The Past of Promise: An Historical Introduction to Contract." *Columbia Law Review* 69, no. 4 (April): 576–607.

Faulkner, Philip, and Jochen Runde. 2009. "On the Identity of Technological Objects and User Innovations in Function." *Academy of Management Review* 34, no. 3 (July): 442–62.

Fay, Margaret A. 1978. "Did Marx Offer to Dedicate *Capital* to Darwin?" *Journal of the History of Ideas* 39, no. 1 (January–March): 133–46.

Fehr, Ernst, and Simon Gächter. 2000a. "Cooperation and Punishment in Public Goods Experiments." *American Economic Review* 90, no. 4 (December): 980–95.

———. 2000b. "Fairness and Retaliation: The Economics of Reciprocity." *Journal of Economic Perspectives* 14, no. 3 (Summer): 159–81.

———. 2002. "Altruistic Punishment in Humans." *Nature* 415 (10 January): 137–40.

Fehr, Ernst, and Herbert Gintis. 2007. "Human Motivation and Social Cooperation: Experimental and Analytical Foundations." *Annual Review of Sociology* 33:43–64.

Feuer, Lewis S. 1975. "Is the Darwin-Marx Correspondence Authentic?" *Annals of Science* 32:11–12.

Field, Alexander J. 2001. *Altruistically Inclined? The Behavioral Sciences, Evolutionary Theory, and the Origins of Reciprocity*. Ann Arbor: University of Michigan Press.

Fischer, David Hackett. 1989. *Albion's Seed: Four British Folkways in America*. Oxford: Oxford University Press.

Fisher, J., and R. A. Hinde. 1949. "The Opening of Milk Bottles by Birds." *British Birds* 42: 347–57.

Fisher, Ronald A. 1930. *The Genetical Theory of Natural Selection*. Oxford: Clarendon.

Florida, Richard, and Martin Kenney. 1991. "Organisation vs. Culture: Japanese Automotive Transplants in the US." *Industrial Relations Journal* 22, no. 3:181–96.

Fogel, Robert William. 2004. *The Escape from Hunger and Premature Death, 1700–2100: Europe, America, and the Third World*. Cambridge: Cambridge University Press.

Fogelin, Lars. 2007. "The Archaeology of Religious Ritual." *Annual Review of Anthropology* 36:55–71.

Foster, John. 1997. "The Analytical Foundations of Evolutionary Economics: From Biological Analogy to Economic Self-Organisation." *Structural Change and Economic Dynamics* 8, no. 4 (October): 427–51.

Foster, John, and J. Stanley Metcalfe, eds. 2001. *Frontiers of Evolutionary Economics*. Cheltenham: Edward Elgar.

Fracchia, Joseph, and Richard C. Lewontin. 1999. "Does Culture Evolve?" *History and Theory* 38, no. 4:52–78.

Frank, Steven A. 1997. "The Design of Adaptive Systems: Optimal Parameters for Variation and Selection in Learning and Development." *Journal of Theoretical Biology* 184:31–39.

———. 1998. *Foundations of Social Evolution*. Princeton, NJ: Princeton University Press.

Freeman, Derek. 1983. *Margaret Mead and Samoa: The Making and Unmaking of an Anthropological Myth*. Cambridge, MA: Harvard University Press.

Freitas, Robert A., and Ralph C. Merkle. 2004. *Kinematic Self-Replicating Machines*. Georgetown, TX: Landes Bioscience.

Friedman, Milton. 1953. "The Methodology of Positive Economics." In *Essays in Positive Economics*, 3-43. Chicago: University of Chicago Press.

Fustel De Coulanges, Numa Denis. 1980. *The Ancient City: A Study of the Religion, Laws, and Institutions of Greece and Rome*. Translated from the French edition of 1864. Baltimore: Johns Hopkins University Press.

Gabora, Liane. 2004. "Ideas Are Not Replicators but Minds Are." *Biology and Philosophy* 19, no. 1 (January): 127-43.

Gagliardi, Francesca. 2009. "Financial Development and the Growth of Cooperative Firms." *Small Business Economics* 32, no. 4 (April): 439-64.

Galbraith, Craig S. 1990. "Transferring Core Manufacturing Technologies in High-Technology Firms." *California Management Review* 32, no. 4:56-70.

Galef, Bennett G. 1992. "The Question of Animal Culture." *Human Nature* 3, no. 2 (June): 157-78.

Geels, Frank W. 2002. "Technological Transitions as Evolutionary Reconfiguration Processes: A Multi-Level Perspective and a Case-Study." *Research Policy* 31, nos. 8-9 (December): 1257-74.

Geroski, Paul A. 1995. "Innovative Activity over the Business Cycle." *Economic Journal* 105, no. 3 (July): 916-28.

Gersick, Connie J. G. 1991. "Revolutionary Change Theories: A Multilevel Exploration of the Punctuated Equilibrium Paradigm." *Academy of Management Review* 16, no. 1 (January): 10-36.

Gifford, Adam. 1999. "Being and Time: On the Nature and Evolution of Institutions." *Journal of Bioeconomics* 1, no. 2 (November): 127-49.

Gigerenzer, Gerd, and Reinhard Selten, eds. 2001. *Bounded Rationality: The Adaptive Toolbox*. Cambridge, MA: MIT Press.

Gigerenzer, Gerd, Peter M. Todd, et al. 1999. *Simple Heuristics That Make Us Smart*. Oxford: Oxford University Press.

Gilbert, Scott F., John M. Opitz, and Rudolf A. Raff. 1996. "Resynthesizing Evolutionary and Developmental Biology." *Developmental Biology* 173, no. 2 (February): 357-72.

Gindis, David. 2007. "Some Building Blocks for a Theory of the Firm as a Real Entity." In *The Firm as an Entity: Implications for Economics, Accounting and Law*, ed. Yuri Biondi, Arnaldo Canziani, and Thierry Kirat, 266-91. London: Routledge.

———. 2009. "From Fictions and Aggregates to Real Entities in the Theory of the Firm." *Journal of Institutional Economics* 5, no. 1 (April): 25-46.

Gintis, Herbert. 2000. "Strong Reciprocity and Human Sociality." *Journal of Theoretical Biology* 206:169-79.

———. 2007. "A Framework for the Integration of the Behavioral Sciences." *Behavioral and Brain Sciences* 30, no. 1 (February): 1-16.

Gintis, Herbert, Samuel Bowles, Robert Boyd, and Ernst Fehr, eds. 2005. *Moral Sentiments and Material Interests: The Foundations of Cooperation in Economic Life*. Cambridge, MA: MIT Press.

Godfrey-Smith, Peter. 2000a. "Information, Arbitrariness, and Selection: Comments on Maynard Smith." *Philosophy of Science* 67, no. 2:202-7.

———. 2000b. "The Replicator in Retrospect." *Biology and Philosophy* 15:403-23.

———. 2006. "Local Interaction, Multilevel Selection, and Evolutionary Transitions." *Biological Theory* 1, no. 4 (Fall): 372-80.

———. 2009. *Darwinian Populations and Natural Selection*. Oxford: Oxford University Press.

Goertzel, Ben. 1992. "What Is Hierarchical Selection?" *Biology and Philosophy* 7, no. 1 (January): 27-33.

Goodall, Jane. 1986. *The Chimpanzees of Gombe*. Cambridge, MA: Harvard University Press.

Goodenough, Ward H. 1981. *Culture, Language and Society*. Menlo Park, CA: Benjamin/ Cummings.

Goodnight, C., and L. Stevens. 1997. "Experimental Studies of Group Selection: What Do They Tell Us about Group Selection in Nature?" *American Naturalist* 150:S59–S79.

Gottlieb, Gilbert. 2001. *Individual Development and Evolution: The Genesis of Novel Behavior*. Hillsdale, NJ: Erlbaum.

Gould, Stephen Jay. 1977. *Ontogeny and Phylogeny*. Cambridge, MA: Harvard University Press.

———. 1980. *The Panda's Thumb: More Reflections in Natural History*. New York: Norton.

———. 1996. *Life's Grandeur: The Spread of Excellence from Plato to Darwin*. London: Cape.

———. 2002. *The Structure of Evolutionary Theory*. Cambridge, MA: Harvard University Press.

Gould, Stephen Jay, and Elizabeth S. Vrba. 1982. "Exaptation—a Missing Term in the Science of Form." *Paleobiology* 8, no. 1 (Winter): 4–15.

———. 1986. "The Hierarchical Expansion of Sorting and Selection: Sorting and Selection Cannot Be Equated." *Paleobiology* 12:217–28.

Gowdy, John M. 1993. "The Implications of Punctuated Equilibria for Economic Theory and Policy." *Methodus* 5, no. 1 (June): 111–13.

Grant, Robert M. 1996. "Toward a Knowledge-Based Theory of the Firm." *Strategic Management Journal* 17:109–22.

Griesemer, James R. 1994. "Tools for Talking: Human Nature, Weismannism and the Interpretation of Genetic Information." In *Are Genes Us? The Social Consequences of the New Genetics*, ed. Carl Cranor, 69–88. New Brunswick, NJ: Rutgers University Press.

———. 1999. "Materials for the Study of Evolutionary Transition." *Biology and Philosophy* 14:127–42.

———. 2000. "The Units of Evolutionary Transition." *Selection* 1, nos. 1–3: 67–80.

Griffiths, Paul E. 2001. "Genetic Information: A Metaphor in Search of a Theory." *Philosophy of Science* 68, no. 3 (September): 394–412.

Griffiths, Paul E., and Russell D. Gray. 1994. "Developmental Systems and Evolutionary Explanation." *Journal of Philosophy* 91, no. 6 (June): 277–304.

———. 1997. "Replicator II—Judgment Day." *Biology and Philosophy* 12:471–90.

Gruber, Howard E. 1974. *Darwin on Man: A Psychological Study of Scientific Creativity, together with Darwin's Early and Unpublished Notebooks*. Transcribed and annotated by P. H. Barret. New York: Dutton.

Guzmán, Ricardo Andrés, Carlos Rodriguez-Sicken, and Robert Rowthorn. 2007. "When in Rome, Do as the Romans Do: The Coevolution of Altruistic Punishment, Conformist Learning, and Cooperation." *Evolution and Human Behavior* 28:112–17.

Haas, Peter M. 1992. "Introduction: Epistemic Communities and International Policy Coordination." *International Organization* 46, no. 1:1–35.

Hall, Peter A., and David Soskice. 2001. *Varieties of Capitalism: The Institutional Foundations of Comparative Advantage*. Oxford: Oxford University Press.

Hamilton, William D. 1964. "The Genetical Evolution of Social Behavior, I and II." *Journal of Theoretical Biology* 7, no. 1 (July): 1–32.

———. 1975. "Innate Social Aptitudes of Man: An Approach from Evolutionary Genetics." In *Biosocial Anthropology*, ed. R. Fox, 133–55. New York: Wiley.

Hammerstein, Peter, ed. 2003. *Genetic and Cultural Evolution of Cooperation*. Cambridge, MA: MIT Press.

Hannan, Michael T., and John Freeman. 1984. "Structural Inertia and Organizational Change." *American Sociological Review* 49, no. 2 (April): 149–64.

———. 1989. *Organizational Ecology*. Cambridge, MA: Harvard University Press.

Hansmann, Henry, Reinier Kraakman, and Richard Squire. 2006. "Law and the Rise of the Firm." *Harvard Law Review* 119, no. 5 (March): 1333–1403.

Harder, Lawrence D. 2006. *Ecology and Evolution of Flowers*. Oxford: Oxford University Press.

Hargreaves Heap, P. Shaun, and Yanis Varoufakis. 1995. *Game Theory: A Critical Introduction*. London: Routledge.

Harms, William F. 2004. *Information and Meaning in Evolutionary Processes*. Cambridge: Cambridge University Press.

Harré, Rom, and Edward H. Madden. 1975. *Causal Powers: A Theory of Natural Necessity*. Oxford: Blackwell.

Hatfield, Elaine, John T. Cacioppo, and Richard L. Rapson. 1993. "Emotional Contagion." *Current Directions in Psychological Science* 2, no. 3 (June): 96–99.

Hayek, Friedrich A. 1960. *The Constitution of Liberty*. London: Routledge & Kegan Paul; Chicago: University of Chicago Press.

———. 1967. *Studies in Philosophy, Politics and Economics*. London: Routledge & Kegan Paul.

———. 1973. *Rules and Order*. Vol. 1 of *Law, Legislation and Liberty*. London: Routledge & Kegan Paul.

———. 1979. *The Political Order of a Free People*. Vol. 3 of *Law, Legislation and Liberty*. London: Routledge & Kegan Paul.

———. 1988. *The Fatal Conceit: The Errors of Socialism*. Edited by William W. Bartley III. Vol. 1 of *The Collected Works of Friedrich August Hayek*. London: Routledge.

Hayes, Robert H., and Steven C. Wheelwright. 1979a. "The Dynamics of Process-Product Life Cycles." *Harvard Business Review* 57, no. 2:127–36.

———. 1979b. "Link Manufacturing Process and Product Life Cycles." *Harvard Business Review* 57, no. 1:133–40.

Hedlund, Gunnar. 1994. "A Model of Knowledge Management and the N-Form Corporation." *Strategic Management Journal* 15:73–90.

Helfat, Constance E. 1994. "Evolutionary Trajectories in Petroleum Firm R&D." *Management Science* 40, no. 12 (December): 1720–47.

Hendriks-Jansen, Horst. 1996. *Catching Ourselves in the Act: Situated Activity, Interaction, Emergence, Evolution and Human Thought*. Cambridge, MA: MIT Press.

———. 1997. *Catching Ourselves in the Act: Situated Activity, Interactive Emergence, Evolution and Human Thought*. Cambridge, MA: MIT Press.

Henrich, Joseph. 2004. "Cultural Group Selection, Coevolutionary Processes and Large-Scale Cooperation." *Journal of Economic Behavior and Organization* 53, no. 1 (February): 3–35.

Henrich, Joseph, and Robert Boyd. 1998. "The Evolution of Conformist Transmission and the Emergence of between Group Differences." *Evolution and Human Behavior* 19:215–42.

———. 2001. "Why People Punish Defectors: Why Conformist Transmission Can Stabilize Costly Enforcement of Norms in Cooperative Dilemmas." *Journal of Theoretical Biology* 208, no. 1:79–89.

Henrich, Joseph, and Francisco J. Gil-White. 2001. "The Evolution of Prestige: Freely Conferred Deference as a Mechanism for Enhancing the Benefits of Cultural Transmission." *Evolution and Human Behavior* 22, no. 3:165–96.

Henrich, Joseph, Richard McElreath, Abigail Barr, Jean Ensminger, Clark Barrett, Alaexander Bolyanatz, Juan Camilo Cardenas, Michael Gurven, Edwins Gwako, Natalie Henrich, Carolyn Lesorogol, Frank Marlowe, David Tracer, and John Ziker. 2006. "Costly Punishment across Human Societies." *Science* 312, no. 5781 (23 June): 1767–70.

Herrmann-Pillath, Carsten. 1991. "A Darwinian Framework for the Economic Analysis of Institutional Change in History." *Journal of Social and Biological Structures* 14, no. 2:127–48.

Himmelfarb, Gertrude. 1959. *Darwin and the Darwinian Revolution*. London: Chatto & Windus.

Hirshleifer, Jack. 1977. "Economics from a Biological Viewpoint." *Journal of Law and Economics* 20, no. 1 (April): 1–52.

———. 1978. "Competition, Cooperation, and Conflict in Economics and Biology." *American Economic Review* 68:238–43.

———. 1982. "Evolutionary Models in Economics and Law: Cooperation versus Conflict Strategies." *Research in Law and Economics* 4:1–60.

Ho, Mae-Wan, and Peter T. Saunders, eds. 1984. *Beyond Neo-Darwinism: An Introduction to the New Evolutionary Paradigm*. London: Academic.

Hodgson, Geoffrey M. 1988. *Economics and Institutions: A Manifesto for a Modern Institutional Economics*. Cambridge: Polity Press; Philadelphia: University of Pennsylvania Press.

———. 1993. *Economics and Evolution: Bringing Life Back into Economics*. Cambridge: Polity; Ann Arbor: University of Michigan Press.

———. 1997. "The Ubiquity of Habits and Rules." *Cambridge Journal of Economics* 21, no. 6 (November): 663–84.

———. 1998. "Competence and Contract in the Theory of the Firm." *Journal of Economic Behavior and Organization* 35, no. 2 (April): 179–201.

———. 1999. *Economics and Utopia: Why the Learning Economy Is Not the End of History*. London: Routledge.

———. 2001a. *How Economics Forgot History: The Problem of Historical Specificity in Social Science*. London: Routledge.

———. 2001b. "Is Social Evolution Lamarckian or Darwinian?" In *Darwinism and Evolutionary Economics*, ed. John Laurent and John Nightingale, 87–118. Cheltenham: Edward Elgar.

———. 2002a. "Darwinism in Economics: From Analogy to Ontology." *Journal of Evolutionary Economics* 12, no. 2 (June): 259–81.

———. 2002b. "The Legal Nature of the Firm and the Myth of the Firm-Market Hybrid." *International Journal of the Economics of Business* 9, no. 1 (February): 37–60.

———. 2003a. "The Enforcement of Contracts and Property Rights: Constitutive versus Epiphenomenal Conceptions of Law." *International Review of Sociology* 13, no. 2 (July): 373–89.

———. 2003b. "John R. Commons and the Foundations of Institutional Economics." *Journal of Economic Issues* 37, no. 3:547–76.

———. 2003c. "The Mystery of the Routine: The Darwinian Destiny of *An Evolutionary Theory of Economic Change*." *Revue économique* 54, no. 2:355–84.

———. 2004a. *The Evolution of Institutional Economics: Agency, Structure and Darwinism in American Institutionalism*. London: Routledge.

———. 2004b. "Social Darwinism in Anglophone Academic Journals: A Contribution to the History of the Term." *Journal of Historical Sociology* 14, no. 4:428–63.

———. 2005. "Generalizing Darwinism to Social Evolution: Some Early Attempts." *Journal of Economic Issues* 39, no. 4 (December): 899–914.

———. 2006a. *Economics in the Shadows of Darwin and Marx: Essays on Institutional and Evolutionary Themes*. Cheltenham: Edward Elgar.

———. 2006b. "Instinct and Habit Before Reason: Comparing the Views of John Dewey, Friedrich Hayek and Thorstein Veblen." *Advances in Austrian Economics* 9:109–43.

———. 2006c. "What Are Institutions?" *Journal of Economic Issues* 40, no. 1 (March): 1–25.

———. 2007a. "Evolutionary and Institutional Economics as the New Mainstream?" *Evolutionary and Institutional Economics Review* 4, no. 1 (September 2007): 7–25.

———. 2007b. "Institutions and Individuals: Interaction and Evolution." *Organization Studies* 28, no. 1 (January): 95–116.

———. 2007c. "Meanings of Methodological Individualism." *Journal of Economic Methodology* 14, no. 2 (June): 211–26.

———. 2008a. "The Concept of a Routine." In *Handbook of Organizational Routines*, ed. Markus C. Becker, 3–14. Cheltenham: Edward Elgar.

———. 2008b. "Markets." In *New Palgrave Dictionary of Economics* (2nd ed.). Basingstoke: Macmillan.

———. 2009. "On the Institutional Foundations of Law: The Insufficiency of Custom and Private Ordering." *Journal of Economic Issues* 43, no. 1 (March): 143–66.

Hodgson, Geoffrey M., and Thorbjørn Knudsen. 2004a. "The Complex Evolution of a Simple Traffic Convention: The Functions and Implications of Habit." *Journal of Economic Behavior and Organization* 54, no. 1:19–47.

———. 2004b. "The Firm as an Interactor: Firms as Vehicles for Habits and Routines." *Journal of Evolutionary Economics* 14, no. 3 (July): 281–307.

———. 2006a. "Dismantling Lamarckism: Why Descriptions of Socio-Economic Evolution as Lamarckian Are Misleading." *Journal of Evolutionary Economics* 16, no. 4 (October): 343–66.

———. 2006b. "The Nature and Units of Social Selection." *Journal of Evolutionary Economics* 16, no. 5 (December): 477–89.

———. 2006c. "Why We Need a Generalized Darwinism, and Why a Generalized Darwinism Is Not Enough." *Journal of Economic Behavior and Organization* 61, no. 1 (September): 1–19.

———. 2007. "Firm-Specific Learning and the Nature of the Firm: Why Transaction Costs May Provide an Incomplete Explanation." *Revue économique* 58, no. 2 (March): 331–50.

———. 2008a. "In Search of General Evolutionary Principles: Why Darwinism Is Too Important to Be Left to the Biologists." *Journal of Bioeconomics* 10, no. 1 (April): 51–69.

———. 2008b. "Information, Complexity and Generative Replication." *Biology and Philosophy* 43, no. 1:47–65.

———. 2010. "Generative Replication and the Evolution of Complexity." *Journal of Economic Behavior and Organization* 75, no. 1:12–24.

Hofbauer, Josef, and Karl Sigmund. 1998. *Evolutionary Games and Population Dynamics*. Cambridge: Cambridge University Press.

Hofstadter, Richard. 1944. *Social Darwinism in American Thought, 1860–1915*. Philadelphia: University of Pennsylvania Press.

Holland, John H. 1995. *Hidden Order: How Adaptation Builds Complexity*. Reading: Helix.

Holloway, Ralph L., Jr. 1969. "Culture: A *Human* Domain." *Current Anthropology* 10, no. 4, pt. 2 (October): 395–412.

Huff, Toby. 1993. *The Rise of Early Modern Science: Islam, China and the West*. Cambridge: Cambridge University Press.

Hull, David L. 1973. *Darwin and His Critics: The Reception of Darwin's Theory of Evolution by the Scientific Community*. Cambridge, MA: Harvard University Press.

———. 1976. "Are Species Really Individuals?" *Systematic Zoology* 25, no. 2:174–91.

———. 1978. "A Matter of Individuality." *Philosophy of Science* 45:335–60.

———. 1980. "Individuality and Selection." *Annual Review of Ecology and Systematics* 11:311–32.

———. 1981. "Units of Evolution: A Metaphysical Essay." In *The Philosophy of Evolution*, ed. U. L. Jensen and Rom Harré, 23–44. Brighton: Harvester.

———. 1982. "The Naked Meme." In *Learning, Development and Culture: Essays in Evolutionary Epistemology*, ed. Henry C. Plotkin, 273–327. New York: Wiley.

———. 1985. "Darwinism as a Historical Entity: A Historiographic Proposal." In *The Darwinian Heritage*, ed. David Kohn, 773–812. Princeton, NJ: Princeton University Press.

———. 1988. *Science as a Process: An Evolutionary Account of the Social and Conceptual Development of Science*. Chicago: University of Chicago Press.

———. 2000. "Taking Memetics Seriously: Memetics Will Be What We Make It." In *Darwinizing Culture: The Status of Memetics as a Science*, ed. Robert Aunger, 43–68. Oxford: Oxford University Press.

———. 2001a. "In Search of Epistemological Warrant." In *Selection Theory and Social Construction: The Evolutionary Naturalistic Epistemology of Donald T. Campbell*, ed. Celia C. Heyes and David L. Hull, 155–68. Albany: State University of New York Press.

———. 2001b. *Science and Selection: Essays on Biological Evolution and the Philosophy of Science*. Cambridge: Cambridge University Press.

Hull, David L., Rodney E. Langman, and Sigrid S. Glenn. 2001. "A General Account of Selection: Biology, Immunology and Behavior." *Behavioral and Brain Sciences* 24, no. 3 (June): 511–73.

Hutchins, Edwin. 1995. *Cognition in the Wild*. Cambridge, MA: MIT Press.

Huxley, Thomas Henry. 1894. *Collected Essays*. 9 vols. London: Macmillan.

Ito, Shoji. 1985. "Technology Transfer from Japanese to Indian Firms." *Economic and Political Weekly* 20, nos. 45/47:2031–42.

Jablonka, Eva, M. Lachmann, and M. J. Lamb. 1992. "Evidence, Mechanisms and Models for the Inheritance of Acquired Characters." *Journal of Theoretical Biology* 158:245–68.

Jablonka, Eva, and Eörs Szathmáry. 1995. "The Evolution of Information Storage and Heredity." *Trends in Ecology and Evolution* 10:206–11.

James, William. 1880. "Great Men, Great Thoughts, and the Environment." *Atlantic Monthly* 46:441–59. Reprinted in *The Will to Believe and Other Essays in Popular Philosophy* (New York: Longmans Green, 1897), 216–54.

———. 1890. *The Principles of Psychology*. 2 vols. 1st ed. New York: Holt; London: Macmillan.

Jenkin, Fleeming. 1867. "The Origin of Species." *North British Review* 46:149–71.

Ji Song, Mindy F., and Wendy Wood. 2007. "Purchase and Consumption Habits: Not Necessarily What You Intend." *Journal of Consumer Psychology* 17, no. 4:261–76.

Joas, Hans. 1993. *Pragmatism and Social Theory*. Chicago: University of Chicago Press.

———. 1996. *The Creativity of Action*. Chicago: University of Chicago Press.

John, Peter. 1999. "Ideas and Interests; Agendas and Implementation: An Evolutionary Explanation of Policy Change in British Local Government Finance." *British Journal of Politics and International Relations* 1, no. 1 (April): 39–62.

Johnson, George. 2008. *The Ten Most Beautiful Experiments*. New York: Knopf.

Johnson-Laird, Philip N. 1981. "Comprehension as the Construction of Mental Models." *Philosophical Transactions of the Royal Society of London*, ser. B, *Biological Sciences* 295, no. 1077 (2 October): 353–74.

Jones, Greta. 1980. *Social Darwinism and English Thought*. Brighton: Harvester; Atlantic Highlands, NJ: Humanities.

Jones, Lamar B. 1995. "C. E. Ayres's Reliance on T. H. Huxley: Did Darwin's Bulldog Bite?" *American Journal of Economics and Sociology* 54, no. 4 (October): 413–20.

Joyce, Gerald F. 2002. "The Antiquity of RNA-Based Evolution." *Nature* 418 (11 July): 214–21.

Joyce, Richard. 2006. *The Evolution of Morality*. Cambridge, MA: MIT Press.

Jun, Tackseung, and Rajiv Sethi. 2007. "Neighborhood Structure and the Evolution of Cooperation." *Journal of Evolutionary Economics* 17, no. 5 (October): 623–46.

Kameda, Tatsuya, and Daisuke Nakanishi. 2003. "Does Social/Cultural Learning Increase Human Adaptability? Rogers's Question Revisited." *Evolution and Human Behavior* 24, no. 4:242–60.

Karmiloff, Kyra, and Annette Karmiloff-Smith. 2001. *Pathways to Language: From Fetus to Adolescent*. Cambridge, MA: Harvard University Press.

Katz, Jerome A., and William B. Gartner. 1988. "Properties of Emerging Organizations." *Academy of Management Review* 13:429–41.

Kauffman, Stuart A. 1993. *The Origins of Order: Self-Organization and Selection in Evolution*. Oxford: Oxford University Press.

———. 1995. *At Home in the Universe: The Search for Laws of Self-Organization and Complexity*. Oxford: Oxford University Press.

———. 2000. *Investigations*. Oxford: Oxford University Press.

Kaufmann, Felix. 1941. "The Structure of Science." *Journal of Philosophy* 38, no. 11 (22 May): 281–93.

Keesing, Roger. 1974. "Theories of Culture." *Annual Review of Anthropology* 3:73-97.

Keijzer, Fred. 2001. *Representation and Behavior*. Cambridge, MA: MIT Press.

Keller, Albert Galloway. 1915. *Societal Evolution: A Study of the Evolutionary Basis of the Science of Society*. New York: Macmillan.

——. 1923. "Societal Evolution." In *The Evolution of Man*, ed. George Alfred Baitsell, 126-51. New Haven, CT: Yale University Press.

Keller, Evelyn Fox. 2002. *Making Sense of Life: Explaining Biological Development with Models, Metaphors, and Machines*. Cambridge, MA: Harvard University Press.

Keller, Evelyn Fox, and Elizabeth Lloyd, eds. 1992. *Keywords in Evolutionary Discourse*. Cambridge, MA: Harvard University Press.

Keller, Laurent, ed. 1999. *Levels of Selection in Evolution*. Monographs in Behavior and Ecology. Princeton, NJ: Princeton University Press.

Keller, Laurent, and H. K. Reeve. 1999. "Levels of Selection: Burying the Units-of-Selection Debate and Unearthing the Crucial New Issues." In *Levels of Selection in Evolution* (Monographs in Behavior and Ecology), ed. Laurent Keller, 3-14. Princeton, NJ: Princeton University Press.

Kellogg, Vernon L. 1917. *Headquarters Nights: A Record of Conversations and Experiences at the Headquarters of the German Army in France and Belgium*. Boston: Atlantic Monthly Press.

Kennedy, Paul. 1988. *The Rise and Fall of the Great Powers: Economic Change and Military Conflict from 1500 to 2000*. London: Unwin Hyman.

Kenworthy, Lane. 1995. *In Search of National Economic Success: Balancing Competition and Cooperation*. Thousand Oaks, CA: Sage.

——. 2006. "Institutional Coherence and Macroeconomic Performance." *Socio-Economic Review* 4, no. 1 (January): 69-91.

Kerr, Benjamin, and Peter Godfrey-Smith. 2002a. "Individualist and Multi-Level Perspectives in Structured Populations." *Biology and Philosophy* 17, no. 4 (September): 477-517.

——. 2002b. "On Price's Equation and Average Fitness." *Biology and Philosophy* 17, no. 4 (September): 551-65.

Kidd, Benjamin. *Social Evolution*. London: Macmillan, 1894.

Kilpinen, Erkki. 1999. "What Is Rationality? A New Reading of Veblen's Critique of Utilitarian Hedonism." *International Journal of Politics, Culture and Society* 13, no. 2:187-206.

——. 2000. *The Enormous Fly-Wheel of Society: Pragmatism's Habitual Conception of Action and Social Theory*. Helsinki: University of Helsinki.

Kimura, Masahiko. 1983. *The Neutral Theory of Molecular Evolution*. Cambridge: Cambridge University Press.

Kirby, Simon, Hannah Cornish, and Kenny Smith. 2008. "Cumulative Cultural Evolution in the Laboratory: An Experimental Approach to the Origins of Structure in Human Language." *Proceedings of the National Academy of Sciences (USA)* 105, no. 31:10681-86.

Kirman, Alan P. 1993. "Ants, Rationality and Recruitment." *Quarterly Journal of Economics* 108, no. 1 (February): 137-55.

——. 2005. "Individual and Aggregate Behaviour: Of Ants and Men." In *Complexity and the Economy: Implications for Economic Policy*, ed. John Finch and Magali Orillard, 33-53. Cheltenham: Edward Elgar.

Kitcher, Philip. 1989. "Explanatory Unification and the Causal Structure of the World." *Minnesota Studies in the Philosophy of Science* 13:410-505.

——. 1993. *The Advancement of Science: Science without Legend, Objectivity without Illusions*. Oxford: Oxford University Press.

Klein, Burton H. 1977. *Dynamic Economics*. Cambridge, MA: Harvard University Press.

Klein, Richard G. 1999. *The Human Career: Human Biological and Cultural Origins*. Chicago: University of Chicago Press.

Klein, Richard G., and Blake Edgar. 2002. *The Dawn of Human Culture*. New York: Wiley.

Klepper, Steven. 1996. "Entry, Exit, Growth, and Innovation over the Product Life Cycle." *American Economic Review* 86, no. 3 (June): 562–83.

———. 1997. "Industry Life Cycles." *Industrial and Corporate Change* 6, no. 1:145–82.

———. 2002a. "The Capabilities of New Firms and the Evolution of the US Automobile Industry." *Industrial and Corporate Change* 11, no. 4:645–66.

———. 2002b. "Firm Survival and the Evolution of Oligopoly." *RAND Journal of Economics* 33, no. 1 (Spring): 37–61.

———. 2008. "Silicon Valley—a Chip Off the Old Detroit Bloc." In *Entrepreneurship, Growth, and Public Policy,* ed. David B. Audretsch and Robert Strom, 79–118. Cambridge: Cambridge University Press.

Klepper, Steven, and Elizabeth Graddy. 1990. "The Evolution of New Industries and the Determinants of Market Structure." *RAND Journal of Economics* 21, no. 1:27–44.

Klepper, Steven, and Sally D. Sleeper. 2005. "Entry by Spinoffs." *Management Science* 51, no. 8 (August): 1291–1306.

Knight, Jack. 1992. *Institutions and Social Conflict.* Cambridge: Cambridge University Press.

Knorr-Cetina, Karin D. 1981. *The Manufacture of Knowledge: An Essay on the Constructivist and Contextual Nature of Science.* Oxford: Pergamon.

Knudsen, Thorbjørn. 2001. "Nesting Lamarckism within Darwinian Explanations: Necessity in Economics and Possibility in Biology?" In *Darwinism and Evolutionary Economics,* ed. John Laurent and John Nightingale, 121–59. Cheltenham: Edward Elgar.

———. 2002a. "Economic Selection Theory." *Journal of Evolutionary Economics* 12, no. 4 (October): 443–70.

———. 2002b. "The Significance of Tacit Knowledge in the Evolution of Human Language." *Selection* 3, no. 1:93–112.

———. 2003. "Simon's Selection Theory: Why Docility Evolves to Breed Successful Altruism." *Journal of Economic Psychology* 24, no. 2 (April): 229–44.

———. 2004a. "Economic Evolution without Variation, Selection and Retention?" *Erwägen, Wissen, Ethik* 15:75–78.

———. 2004b. "General Selection Theory and Economic Evolution: The Price Equation and the Replicator/Interactor Distinction." *Journal of Economic Methodology* 11, no. 2 (June): 147–73.

———. 2008. "Organizational Routines in Evolutionary Theory." In *The Handbook of Organizational Routines,* ed. Markus Becker, 125–51. Cheltenham: Edward Elgar.

Knudsen, Thorbjørn, and Sidney G. Winter. 2010. "An Evolutionary Model of Spatial Competition." Typescript.

Kogut, Bruce, and Udo Zander. 1992. "Knowledge of the Firm, Combinative Capabilities, and the Replication of Technology." *Organization Science* 3:383–97.

———. 1993. "Knowledge of the Firm and the Evolutionary Theory of the Multinational Corporation." *Journal of International Business Studies* 24, no. 4:625–45.

Kohn, David ed. 1985. *The Darwinian Heritage.* Princeton, NJ: Princeton University Press.

Kontopoulos, Kyriakos M. 1993. *The Logics of Social Structure.* Cambridge: Cambridge University Press.

Kottler, Malcolm Jay. 1985. "Charles Darwin and Alfred Russel Wallace: Two Decades of Debate over Natural Selection." In *The Darwinian Heritage,* ed. David Kohn, 367–432. Princeton, NJ: Princeton University Press.

Krasner, Stephen. 1988. "Sovereignty." *Comparative Political Studies* 21:64–94.

Kroeber, Alfred L. 1948. *Anthropology.* New York: Harcourt Brace Jovanovich.

Kroeber, Alfred L., and Clyde Kluckhohn. 1963. *Culture: A Critical Review of Concepts and Definitions.* New York: Random House.

Kronfeldner, Maria N. 2007. "Is Cultural Evolution Lamarckian?" *Biology and Philosophy* 22, no. 4 (September): 493–512.

Kropotkin, Petr A. 1902. *Mutual Aid: A Factor of Evolution*. London: Heinemann.

Kubovy, Michael, and William Epstein. 2001. "Internalization: A Metaphor We Can Live Without." *Behavioral and Brain Sciences* 24, no. 4:618–25.

Kurthen, Martin. 2001. "The Archeology of Internalism." *Behavioral and Brain Sciences* 24, no. 4:682–83.

Kusewitt, J. B. 1985. "An Exploratory Study of Strategic Acquisition Factors Relating to Performance." *Strategic Management Journal* 6, no. 2:151–69.

Kutschera, Ulrich, and Karl J. Niklas. 2004. "The Modern Theory of Biological Evolution: An Expanded Synthesis." *Naturwissenschaften* 91:255–76.

Lakatos, Imre. 1976. *Proofs and Refutations*. Cambridge: Cambridge University Press.

Laland, Kevin N., Peter J. Richerson, and Robert Boyd. 1996. "Developing a Theory of Animal Social Learning." In *Social Learning in Animals: The Roots of Culture*, ed. Cecilia M. Heyes and Bennett G. Galef, 129–54. San Diego: Academic.

Lamarck, Jean Baptiste de. 1984. *Zoological Philosophy: An Exposition with Regard to the Natural History of Animals*. Translated by Hugh Elliot from the 1st French ed. of 1809, with introductory essays by David L. Hull and Richard W. Burkhardt. Chicago: University of Chicago Press.

Lampert, Winfried, and Ulrich Sommer. 2007. *Limnoecology*. Oxford: Oxford University Press.

Lancaster, Henry Oliver. 1990. *Expectations of Life: A Study in the Demography, Statistics, and History of World Mortality*. Berlin: Springer.

Landa, A., K. Gudvangen, J. E. Swenson, and E. Røskaft. 1999. "Factors Associated with Wolverine *Gulo gulo* Predation on Domestic Sheep." *Journal of Applied Ecology* 36, no. 6 (December): 963–73.

Langlois, Richard N. 2001. "Knowledge, Consumption, and Endogenous Growth." *Journal of Evolutionary Economics* 11, no. 1:77–93.

Langlois, Richard N., and Paul L. Robertson. 1995. *Firms, Markets and Economic Change: A Dynamic Theory of Business Institutions*. London: Routledge.

Lapouge, Georges Vacher de. 1896. *Les sélections socials*. Paris: Fontemoing.

———. 1897. "The Fundamental Laws of Anthropo-Sociology." Translated from the French by Carlos C. Closson. *Journal of Political Economy* 6, no. 1 (December): 54–92.

Lapré, Michael A., and Luk N. van Wassenhove. 2001. "Creating and Transferring Knowledge for Productivity Improvement in Factories." *Management Science* 47, no. 10:1311–25.

Lave, Jean. 1988. *Cognition in Practice: Mind, Mathematics, and Culture in Everyday Life*. Cambridge: Cambridge University Press.

Lave, Jean, and Etienne Wenger. 1991. *Situated Learning: Legitimate Peripheral Participation*. Cambridge: Cambridge University Press.

Lawson, Tony. 2003. *Reorienting Economics*. London: Routledge.

Lazaric, Nathalie. 2000. "The Role of Routines, Rules and Habits in Collective Learning: Some Epistemological and Ontological Considerations." *European Journal of Economic and Social Systems* 14, no. 2:157–71.

Lazaric, Nathalie, and Blandine Denis. 2001. "How and Why Routines Change: Some Lessons from the Articulation of Knowledge with ISO 9002 Implementation in the Food Industry." *Économies et sociétés: Dynamique technologique et organisation* 6, no. 4:585–611.

Lee, Jeong Woong, Kirk Beebe, Leslie A. Nangle, Jaeseon Jang, Chantal M. Longo-Guess, Susan A. Cook, Muriel T. Davisson, John P. Sundberg, Paul Schimmel, and Susan L. Ackerman. 2006. "Editing-Defective tRNA Synthetase Causes Protein Misfolding and Neurodegeneration." *Nature* 443:50–55.

Lemos, John. 2009. "In Defense of Organizational Evolution: A Reply to Reydon and Sholz." *Philosophy of the Social Sciences* 39, no. 3 (September): 463–74.

Levinthal, Daniel A. 1997. "Adaptation on Rugged Landscapes." *Management Science* 43, no. 7:934–50.

Levitt, Barbara, and James G. March. 1988. "Organizational Learning." *Annual Review of Sociology* 14:319–40.

Lewes, George Henry. 1879. *Problems of Life and Mind: Third Series.* Vol. 1. London: Trübner.

Lewontin, Richard C. 1970. "The Units of Selection." *Annual Review of Ecology and Systematics* 1:1–18.

———. 1978. "Adaptation." *Scientific American,* no. 239:212–30.

Libet, Benjamin. 1985. "Unconscious Cerebral Initiative and the Role of Conscious Will in Voluntary Action." *Behavioral and Brain Sciences* 8:529–66.

———. 2004. *Mind Time: The Temporal Factor in Consciousness.* Cambridge, MA: Harvard University Press.

Lincoln, James R., Harold R. Kerbo, and Elke Wittenhagen. 1995. "Japanese Companies in Germany: A Case Study in Cross-Cultural Management." *Industrial Relations* 34, no. 2: 417–40.

Lippman, Steven A., and Richard P. Rumelt. 1982. "Uncertain Imitability: An Analysis of Interfirm Differences in Efficiency under Competition." *Bell Journal of Economics* 13:418–38.

Lipsey, Richard G., Kenneth I. Carlaw, and Clifford T. Bekar. 2005. *Economic Transformations: General Purpose Technologies and Long Term Economic Growth.* Oxford: Oxford University Press.

Loasby, Brian J. 1998. "The Organisation of Capabilities." *Journal of Economic Behavior and Organization* 35, no. 2 (April): 139–60.

Lorenz, Edward H. 2001. "Models of Cognition, the Development of Knowledge and Organisational Theory." *Journal of Management and Governance* 5:307–30.

Lotka, Alfred James. 1945. "The Law of Evolution as a Maximal Principle." *Human Biology* 17:167–94.

Luksha, Pavel O. 2003. "Formal Definition of Self-Reproductive Systems." In *Artificial Life VIII: Proceedings of the Eighth International Conference on Artificial Life,* ed. Russell K. Standish, Mark A. Bedau, and Hussein A. Abbass, 414–17. Cambridge, MA: MIT Press.

Lundvall, Bengt-Åke, ed. 1992. *National Systems of Innovation: Towards a Theory of Innovation and Interactive Learning.* London: Pinter.

Lyell, Charles. 1863. *The Geological Evidences of the Antiquity of Man, with Remarks on Theories of the Origin of Species by Variation.* London: John Murray.

Lynch, Aaron. 1996. *Thought Contagion: How Beliefs Spread through Society.* New York: Basic.

Maddison, Angus. 1991. *Dynamic Forces in Capitalist Development: A Long-Run Comparative View.* Oxford: Oxford University Press.

Maeterlink, Maurice. 1927. *The Life of the White Ant.* London: George Allen & Unwin.

Maine, Henry Sumner. 1861. *Ancient Law, Its Connection with the Early History of Society, and Its Relation to Modern Ideas.* London: Murray.

Maisels, Charles Keith. 1999. *Early Civilizations of the Old World.* London: Routledge.

Mangel, Marc. 2006. *The Theoretical Biologist's Toolbox: Quantitative Methods for Ecology and Evolutionary Biology.* Cambridge: Cambridge University Press.

Mansfield, Edwin. 1962. "Entry, Gibrat's Law, Innovation, and the Growth of Firms." *American Economic Review* 52, no. 5:1023–51.

March, James G., and Herbert A. Simon. 1958. *Organizations.* New York: Wiley.

Margolis, Howard. 1987. *Patterns, Thinking and Cognition: A Theory of Judgment.* Chicago: University of Chicago Press.

———. 1994. *Paradigms and Barriers: How Habits of Mind Govern Scientific Beliefs.* Chicago: University of Chicago Press.

Margulis, Lynn, and Dorion Sagan. 2001. "Marvellous Microbes." *Resurgence* 206:10–12.

Marshall, Alfred. 1923. *Money Credit and Commerce*. London: Macmillan.

Martins, Nuno. 2009. "A Transformational Concept of Evolutionary Processes." *Evolutionary and Institutional Economics Review* 6, no. 1:71–102.

Marx, Karl. 1976. *Capital*. Translated by Ben Fowkes from the 4th German ed. of 1890. Vol. 1. Harmondsworth: Pelican.

Mayell, Hillary. 2004. "Oldest Jewelry? 'Beads' Discovered in African Cave." *National Geographic News*, 15 April. Available at http://news.nationalgeographic.com/news/2004/04/0415_040415_oldestjewelry.html.

Maynard Smith, John. 1964. "Group Selection and Kin Selection." *Nature* 201:1145–47.

——. "Group Selection." *Quarterly Review of Biology* 51:277–83.

——. 1988. *Did Darwin Get It Right? Essays on Games, Sex and Evolution*. New York: Chapman & Hall.

——. 1995. "Genes, Memes, and Minds." *New York Review of Books* 42, no. 19:46–48.

——. 2000a. "The Concept of Information in Biology." *Philosophy of Science* 67, no. 2 (June): 177–94.

——. 2000b. "Reply to Commentaries." *Philosophy of Science* 67, no. 2 (June): 214–18.

Maynard Smith, John, and Eörs Szathmáry. 1995. *The Major Transitions in Evolution*. Oxford: W. H. Freeman.

——. 1999. *The Origins of Life: From the Birth of Life to the Origin of Language*. Oxford: Oxford University Press.

Mayr, Ernst. 1960. "The Emergence of Evolutionary Novelties." *Evolution after Darwin* (3 vols.), ed. Sol Tax, 1:349–80. Chicago: University of Chicago Press.

——. 1963. *Animal Species and Evolution*. Cambridge, MA: Harvard University Press.

——. 1964. Introduction to *On the Origin of Species by Means of Natural Selection; or, The Preservation of Favoured Races in the Struggle for Life* (facsimile of the 1st [1859] ed.), by Charles R. Darwin, vii–xxvii. Cambridge, MA: Harvard University Press.

——. 1974. "Behavior Programs and Evolutionary Strategies." *American Scientist* 62, no. 6:650–59.

——. 1976. *Evolution and the Diversity of Life*. Cambridge, MA: Harvard University Press.

——. 1982. *The Growth of Biological Thought: Diversity, Evolution, and Inheritance*. Cambridge, MA: Harvard University Press.

——. 1985. "How Biology Differs from the Physical Sciences." In *Evolution at a Crossroads: The New Biology and the New Philosophy of Science*, ed. David J. Depew and Bruce H. Weber, 43–63. Cambridge, MA: MIT Press.

——. 1988. *Toward a New Philosophy of Biology: Observations of an Evolutionist*. Cambridge, MA: Harvard University Press.

——. 1991. *One Long Argument: Charles Darwin and the Genesis of Modern Evolutionary Thought*. Cambridge, MA: Harvard University Press; London: Allen Lane.

McClearn, G. E., B. Johansson, S. Berg, N. L. Pedersen, F. Ahern, S. A. Petrill, et al. 1997. "Substantial Genetic Influence on Cognitive Abilities in Twins 80 or More Years Old." *Science* 276, no. 5318 (6 June): 1560–63.

McElreath, Richard, Mark Lubell, Peter J. Richerson, Timothy M. Waring, William Baum, E. Edsten, Charles Efferson, and Brian Paciotti. 2005. "Applying Evolutionary Models to the Laboratory Study of Social Learning." *Evolution and Human Behavior* 26:483–508.

McKelvey, William. 1982. *Organizational Systematics: Taxonomy, Evolution, Classification*. Berkeley and Los Angeles: University of California Press.

McMillan, John. 2002. *Reinventing the Bazaar: A Natural History of Markets*. New York: Norton.

Merton, Robert K. 1949. *Social Theory and Social Structure*. 1st ed. Glencoe, Il: Free Press.

Mesoudi, Alex, and Andrew Whiten. 2003. "The Hierarchical Transformation of Event Knowledge in Human Cultural Transmission." *Journal of Cognition and Culture* 4, no. 1:1–23.

Mesoudi, Alex, Andrew Whiten, and Robin Dunbar. 2006. "A Bias for Social Information in Human Cultural Transmission." *British Journal of Psychology* 97:405–23.

Mesoudi, Alex, Andrew Whiten, and Kevin N. Laland. 2004. "Perspective: Is Human Cultural Evolution Darwinian? Evidence Reviewed from the Perspective of *The Origin of Species*." *Evolution* 58, no. 1:1–11.

Metcalfe, J. Stanley. 1988. "Evolution and Economic Change." In *Technology and Economic Progress*, ed. Aubrey Silberston, 54–85. Basingstoke: Macmillan.

———. 1994. "Evolutionary Economics and Technology Policy." *Economic Journal* 104, no. 4 (July): 931–44.

———. 1998. *Evolutionary Economics and Creative Destruction*. London: Routledge.

Michod, Richard E. 1999. *Darwinian Dynamics: Evolutionary Transitions in Fitness and Individuality*. Princeton, NJ: Princeton University Press.

Milgram, Stanley. 1974. *Obedience to Authority: An Experimental View*. New York: Harper & Row; London: Tavistock.

Miller, Danny. 1994. "What Happens After Success: The Perils of Excellence." *Journal of Management Studies* 31, no. 3:325–58.

Miller, Danny, and Peter H. Friesen. 1980. "Momentum and Revolution in Organizational Adaptation." *Academy of Management Journal* 23:591–614.

Miller, James G. 1978. *Living Systems*. New York: McGraw-Hill.

Mills, Susan, and John Beatty. 1979. "The Propensity Interpretation of Fitness." *Philosophy of Science* 46, no. 2:263–86.

Miner, Anne S. 1990. "Structural Evolution through Idiosyncratic Jobs: The Potential for Unplanned Learning." *Organization Science* 1, no. 2:195–210.

———. 1994. "Seeking Adaptive Advantage: Evolutionary Theory and Managerial Action." In *Evolutionary Dynamics of Organizations*, ed. Joel A. C. Baum and Jitendra V. Singh, 76–89. New York: Oxford University Press.

Mirowski, Philip. 1989. *More Heat Than Light: Economics as Social Physics, Physics as Nature's Economics*. Cambridge: Cambridge University Press.

Mirowski, Philip, and Esther-Mirjam Sent, eds. 2002. *Science Bought and Sold: Essays on the Economics of Science*. Chicago: Chicago University Press.

Misteli, Tom. 2001. "The Concept of Self-Organization in Cellular Architecture." *Journal of Cell Biology* 155, no. 2:181–85.

Mitchell, Wesley C., ed. 1936. *What Veblen Taught*. New York: Viking.

Mokyr, Joel. 1990a. *The Lever of Riches: Technological Creativity and Economic Progress*. Oxford: Oxford University Press.

———. 1990b. "Punctuated Equilibria and Technological Progress." *American Economic Review (Papers and Proceedings)* 80, no. 2 (May): 350–54.

———. 1996. "Evolution and Technological Change: A New Metaphor for Economic History?" In *Technological Change*, ed. Robert Fox, 63–83. London: Harwood.

———. 2003. *The Gifts of Athena: Historical Origins of the Knowledge Economy*. Princeton, NJ: Princeton University Press.

———. 2006. "Useful Knowledge as an Evolving System: The View from Economic History." In *The Economy as an Evolving Complex System III: Current Perspectives and Future Directions*, ed. Lawrence E. Blume and Steven N. Durlauf, 307–37. Oxford: Oxford University Press.

Molofsky, Jane. 1994. "Population Dynamics and Pattern Formation in Theoretical Populations." *Ecology* 1:30–39.

Morgan, Conwy Lloyd. 1896. *Habit and Instinct*. London: Edward Arnold.

———. 1923. *Emergent Evolution*. London: Williams & Norgate.

Muir, W. M. 1995. "Group Selection for Adaptation to Multiple-Hen Cages: Selection Program and Direct Responses." *Poultry Science* 75:447–58.

Murphy, James Bernard. 1994. "The Kinds of Order in Society." In *Natural Images in Economic Thought: Markets Read in Tooth and Claw*, ed. Philip Mirowski, 536-82. Cambridge: Cambridge University Press.

Myerson, Roger B., Gregory B. Pollack, and Joroen M. Swinkels. 1991. "Viscous Population Equilibrium." *Games and Economic Behavior* 3, no. 1 (February): 101-9.

Nagel, Ernest. 1961. *The Structure of Science*. London: Routledge; Indianapolis: Hackett.

Nanay, Bence. 2002. "The Return of the Replicator: What Is Philosophically Significant in a General Account of Replication and Selection." *Biology and Philosophy* 17, no. 1 (January): 109-21.

Nelson, Katherine, and Richard R. Nelson. 2003. "The Cumulative Advance of Human Know-How." *Philosophical Transactions of the Royal Society of London*, ser. A, *Mathematical, Physical and Engineering Sciences* 361, no. 1809 (15 August): 1635-53.

Nelson, Richard R. 1959. "The Simple Economics of Basic Scientific Research." *Journal of Political Economy* 67, no. 3 (June): 297-306.

———. 1981. "Assessing Private Enterprise: An Exegesis of Tangled Doctrine." *Bell Journal of Economics* 12, no. 1:93-111.

———. 1991. "Why Do Firms Differ, and How Does It Matter?" *Strategic Management Journal* 12 (Winter): 61-74.

———, ed. 1993. *National Innovation Systems: A Comparative Analysis*. Oxford: Oxford University Press.

———. 1994. "The Co-Evolution of Technology, Industrial Structure, and Supporting Institutions." *Industrial and Corporate Change* 3, no. 1:47-63.

———. 1995. "Recent Evolutionary Theorizing about Economic Change." *Journal of Economic Literature* 33, no. 1 (March): 48-90.

———. 2002. "Evolutionary Theorising in Economics." In *The Evolution of Cultural Entities*, ed. Michael Wheeler, John Ziman, and Margaret A. Boden, 135-43. Oxford: Oxford University Press.

———. 2003. "On the Complexities and Limits of Market Organization." *Review of International Political Economy* 10, no. 4 (November): 697-710.

———. 2006. "Evolutionary Social Science and Universal Darwinism." *Journal of Evolutionary Economics* 16, no. 5 (December): 491-510.

———. 2007a. "Comment on 'Dismantling Lamarckism: Why Descriptions of Socio-Economic Evolution as Lamarckian Are Misleading,' by Hodgson and Knudsen." *Journal of Evolutionary Economics* 17, no. 3 (June): 349-52.

———. 2007b. "Universal Darwinism and Evolutionary Social Science." *Biology and Philosophy* 22, no. 1 (January): 73-94.

Nelson, Richard R., and Katherine Nelson. 2002. "On the Nature and Evolution of Human Know-How." *Research Policy* 31, no. 5 (July): 719-33.

Nelson, Richard R., and Sidney G. Winter. 1982. *An Evolutionary Theory of Economic Change*. Cambridge, MA: Harvard University Press.

———. 2002. "Evolutionary Theorizing in Economics." *Journal of Economic Perspectives* 16, no. 2 (Spring): 23-46.

Nisbett, Richard E., and Dov Cohen. 1996. *Culture of Honor: The Psychology of Violence in the South*. Boulder, CO: Westview.

Nooteboom, Bart. 1993. "The Conservatism of Programme Continuity: Criticism of Lakatosian Methodology in Economics." *Methodus* 5, no. 1 (June): 31-46.

———. 2000. *Learning and Innovation in Organizations and Economies*. Oxford: Oxford University Press.

North, Douglass C. 1990. *Institutions, Institutional Change and Economic Performance*. Cambridge: Cambridge University Press.

———. 2005. *Understanding the Process of Economic Change*. Princeton, NJ: Princeton University Press.

Nowak, Martin A. 2006. *Evolutionary Dynamics: Exploring the Equations of Life*. Cambridge, MA: Harvard University Press.

Nowak, Martin A., and Karl Sigmund. 2004. *Evolutionary Dynamics: Exploring the Equations of Life*. Cambridge, MA: Harvard University Press.

O'Boyle, Thomas E. 1998. *At Any Cost: Jack Welch, General Electric, and the Pursuit of Profit*. New York: Knopf.

Okasha, Samir. 2005. "Multilevel Selection and the Major Transitions in Evolution." *Philosophy of Science* 72 (December 2005): 1013–25.

———. 2006. *Evolution and the Levels of Selection*. Oxford: Oxford University Press.

Oppenheimer, Stephen. 2004. *The Real Eve*. New York: Carroll & Graf. Published in the United Kingdom as *Out of Eden* (London: Constable & Robinson).

O'Reilly, Randall C., and Yuko Munakata. 2000. *Computational Explorations in Cognitive Neuroscience*. Cambridge, MA: MIT Press.

Ostrom, Elinor. 1990. *Governing the Commons: The Evolution of Institutions for Collective Action*. Cambridge: Cambridge University Press.

———. 2005. *Understanding Institutional Diversity*. Princeton, NJ: Princeton University Press.

Ouellette, Judith A., and Wendy Wood. 1998. "Habit and Intention in Everyday Life: The Multiple Processes by Which Past Behavior Predicts Future Behavior." *Psychological Bulletin* 124:54–74.

Pagano, Ugo. 1991. "Property Rights, Asset Specificity, and the Division of Labour under Alternative Capitalist Relations." *Cambridge Journal of Economics* 15, no. 3 (September): 315–42.

———. 2001. "The Origin of Organisational Species." In *The Evolution of Economic Diversity*, ed. Antonio Nicita and Ugo Pagano, 21–48. London Routledge.

Page, Karen Mary, and Martin A. Nowak. 2002. "Unifying Evolutionary Dynamics." *Journal of Theoretical Biology* 219, no. 1:93–98.

Parra, Carlos M. 2005. "Rules and Knowledge." *Evolutionary and Institutional Economics Review* 2, no. 1 (October): 81–111.

Parsons, Keith, ed. 2003. *The Science Wars: Debating Scientific Knowledge and Technology*. Amherst, NY: Prometheus.

Parsons, Talcott. 1932. "Economics and Sociology: Marshall in Relation to the Thought of His Time." *Quarterly Journal of Economics* 46, no. 2 (February): 316–47.

———. 1934. "Some Reflections on 'The Nature and Significance of Economics.'" *Quarterly Journal of Economics* 48, no. 3 (May): 511–45.

Peirce, Charles Sanders. 1878. "How to Make Our Ideas Clear." *Popular Science Monthly* 12 (January): 286–302.

———. 1992. *Reasoning and the Logic of Things: The Cambridge Conferences Lectures of 1898*. Edited by Kenneth Ketner. Cambridge, MA: Harvard University Press.

Pennisi, Elizabeth. 2008. "Modernizing the Modern Synthesis." *Science* 321, no. 5886 (11 July): 196–97.

Penrose, Edith T. 1952. "Biological Analogies in the Theory of the Firm." *American Economic Review* 42, no. 4 (December): 804–19.

———. 1959. *The Theory of the Growth of the Firm*. Oxford: Basil Blackwell.

Pepper, John W., and Thorbjørn Knudsen. 2001. "Selection without Multiple Replicators?" *Behavioral and Brain Sciences* 24, no. 3:550.

Perry, Ralph Barton. 1918. *The Present Conflict of Ideals: A Study of the Philosophical Background of the World War*. New York: Longmans Green.

Pfeifer, Edward J. 1965. "The Genesis of American Neo-Lamarckism." *Isis* 56, no. 2 (Summer): 156–67.

Pigliucci, Massimo, and Jonathan Kaplan. 2006. *Making Sense of Evolution: The Conceptual Foundations of Evolutionary Biology*. Chicago: University of Chicago Press.

Pinker, Steven. 1994. *The Language Instinct: The New Science of Language and Mind*. London: Allen Lane; New York: Morrow.

Plotkin, Henry C. 1994. *Darwin Machines and the Nature of Knowledge: Concerning Adaptations, Instinct and the Evolution of Intelligence*. Harmondsworth: Penguin.

Polanyi, Michael. 1958. *Personal Knowledge: Towards a Post-Critical Philosophy*. London: Routledge & Kegan Paul.

———. 1967. *The Tacit Dimension*. London: Routledge & Kegan Paul.

Popper, Karl R. 1972. *Objective Knowledge: An Evolutionary Approach*. Oxford: Oxford University Press.

———. 1978. "Natural Selection and the Emergence of Mind." *Dialectica* 32, nos. 3–4:339–55.

———. 1990. *A World of Propensities*. Bristol: Thoemmes.

Porter, Michael E. 1983. "The Technological Dimension of Competitive Strategy." In *Research on Technological Innovation, Management, and Policy* (vol. 1), ed. Richard S. Rosenbloom, 1–33. Greenwich, CT: JAI.

Postrel, Steven, and Richard P. Rumelt. 1992. "Incentives, Routines, and Self-Command." *Industrial and Corporate Change* 1, no. 3:397–425.

Potts, Jason. 2000. *The New Evolutionary Microeconomics: Complexity, Competence and Adaptive Behaviour*. Cheltenham: Edward Elgar.

Potts, Richard. 1996. *Humanity's Descent: The Consequences of Ecological Instability*. New York: William Morrow.

Price, George R. 1970. "Selection and Covariance." *Nature* 227:520–21.

———. 1972. "Extensions of Covariance Selection Mathematics." *Annals of Human Genetics* 35:485–90.

———. 1995. "The Nature of Selection." *Journal of Theoretical Biology* 175, no. 3:389–96.

Price, Michael E., Leda Cosmides, and John Tooby. 2002. "Punitive Sentiment as an Anti-Free-Rider Device." *Evolution and Human Behavior* 23:203–31.

Prusiner, Stanley B. 1998. "Prions." *Proceedings of the National Academy of Sciences (USA)* 95, no. 23:13363–83.

Putnam, Hilary. 1995. *Pragmatism*. Oxford: Blackwell.

Quine, Willard van Orman. 1953. *From a Logical Point of View*. Cambridge, MA: Harvard University Press.

Radcliffe-Brown, Arthur R. 1933. "Law: Primitive." *Encyclopaedia of the Social Sciences* (15 vols.), 9:202–6. New York: Macmillan.

Reber, Arthur S. 1993. *Implicit Learning and Tacit Knowledge: An Essay on the Cognitive Unconscious*. Oxford: Oxford University Press.

Redfield, Robert. 1950. "Maine's *Ancient Law* in the Light of Primitive Societies." *Western Political Quarterly* 3, no. 4 (December): 574–89.

———. 1957. *The Primitive World and Its Transformations*. Ithaca, NY: Cornell University Press.

Reeke, George N., Jr., and Olaf Sporns. 1993. "Behaviorally Based Modeling and Computational Approaches to Neuroscience." *Annual Review of Neuroscience* 16 (March): 597–623.

Reydon, Thomas A. C., and Markus Scholz. 2009. "Why Organizational Ecology Is Not a Darwinian Research Program." *Philosophy of the Social Sciences* 39, no. 3 (September): 408–39.

Richards, Robert J. 1987. *Darwin and the Emergence of Evolutionary Theories of Mind and Behavior*. Chicago: University of Chicago Press.

———. 1992. *The Meaning of Evolution: The Morphological Construction and Ideological Reconstruction of Darwin's Theory*. Chicago: University of Chicago Press.

Richardson, R. Alan, and Thomas C. Kane. 1988. "Orthogenesis and Evolution in the Nineteenth Century: The Idea of Progress in American Neo-Lamarckism." In *Evolutionary Progress*, ed. Matthew H. Nitecki, 149–67. Chicago: University of Chicago Press.

Richerson, Peter J., and Robert Boyd. 2001. "Built for Speed, Not for Comfort: Darwinian Theory and Human Culture." *History and Philosophy of the Life Sciences* 23, nos. 3/4:423–63.

——. 2004. *Not by Genes Alone: How Culture Transformed Human Evolution*. Chicago: University of Chicago Press.

Richerson, Peter J., Robert Boyd, and Robert L. Bettinger. 2001. "Was Agriculture Impossible during the Pleistocene but Mandatory during the Holocene? A Climate Change Hypothesis." *American Antiquity* 66:387–411.

Ridley, Mark. 2000. *Mendel's Demon: Gene Justice and the Complexity of Life*. London: Weidenfeld & Nicolson.

Ridley, Matt. 1996. *The Origins of Virtue: Human Instincts and the Origins of Cooperation*. Harmondsworth: Penguin.

——. 1999. *Genome*. London: Fourth Estate.

Rigby, David L., and Jurgen Essletzbichler. 1997. "Evolution, Process Variety, and Regional Trajectories of Technological Change in U.S. Manufacturing." *Economic Geography* 73, no. 3:269–84.

Riley, James C. 2001. *Rising Life Expectancy: A Global History*. Cambridge: Cambridge University Press.

Ritchie, David G. 1896. "Social Evolution." *International Journal of Ethics* 6, no. 2:165–81.

——. 1889. *Darwinism and Politics*. 1st ed. London: Swan Sonnenschein.

——. 1891. *Darwinism and Politics*. 2nd ed. London: Swan Sonnenschein.

Robbins, Lionel. 1932. *An Essay on the Nature and Significance of Economic Science*. London: Macmillan.

Roberts, Karlene H., Suzanne K. Stout, and Jennifer J. Halpern. 1994. "Decision Dynamics in Two High Reliability Military Organizations." *Management Science* 40, no. 5 (May): 614–24.

Robinson, Paul H., Robert Kurzban, and Owen D. Jones. 2007. "The Origins of Shared Intuitions of Justice." *Vanderbilt Law Review* 60, no. 6:1633–88.

Robson, Arthur J. 1995. "The Evolution of Strategic Behaviour." *Canadian Journal of Economics* 28, no. 1:17–41.

Rogers, Everett M. 1995. *Diffusion of Innovations*. 4th ed. New York: Free Press.

Rogers, Everett M., and Floyd F. Shoemaker. 1971. *Communication of Innovations: A Cross-Cultural Approach*. New York: Free Press.

Rogoff, E., and Jean Lave. 1984. *Everyday Cognition: Development in Social Context*. Oxford: Oxford University Press.

Romanes, George John. 1893. *Darwin and After Darwin: An Exposition of the Darwinian Theory and a Discussion of Post-Darwinian Questions*. Vol. 1. 2nd ed. London: Longmans, Green.

Rose, Steven. 1997. *Lifelines: Biology, Freedom, Determinism*. London: Allen Lane.

Rosenberg, Alexander. 1992. "Neo-Classical Economics and Evolutionary Theory: Strange Bedfellows?" *PSA: Proceedings of the Biennial Meeting of the Philosophy of Science Association, 1992*, vol. 1, *Contributed Papers*, 174–83.

——. 1995. *The Philosophy of Social Science*. 2nd ed. Boulder, CO: Westview.

——. 1998. "Folk Psychology." In *Handbook of Economic Methodology*, ed. John B. Davis, D. Wade Hands, and Uskali Mäki, 195–97. Cheltenham: Edward Elgar.

Rosenberg, Nathan. 1982. *Inside the Black Box: Technology and Economics*. Cambridge: Cambridge University Press.

Rubin, Paul H., and E. Somanathan. 1998. "Humans as Factors of Production: An Evolutionary Analysis." *Managerial and Decision Economics* 19, nos. 7/8:441–55.

Ruggles, Rudy. 1998. "The State of the Notion: Knowledge Management in Practice." *California Management Review* 40, no. 3:80–89.

Runciman, Walter Garry. 1982. "Origins of States: The Case of Ancient Greece." *Comparative Studies in Society and History* 24, no. 3:351–77.

——. 2001. "From Nature to Culture, from Culture to Society." In *The Origin of Human Social Institutions*, ed. Walter Garry Runciman, 235–54. Oxford: Oxford University Press.

————. 2002. "Heritable Variation and Competitive Selection as the Mechanism of Sociocultural Evolution." In *The Evolution of Cultural Entities*, ed. Michael Wheeler, John Ziman, and Margaret A. Boden, 9–25. Oxford: Oxford University Press.

————. 2005. "Stone Age Sociology." *Journal of the Royal Anthropological Institute* 11, no. 1 (March): 129–42.

Ruse, Michael. 1979. *The Darwinian Revolution: Science Red in Tooth and Claw*. Chicago: University of Chicago Press.

Russett, Cynthia Eagle. 1976. *Darwin in America: The Intellectual Response, 1865–1912*. San Francisco: W. H. Freeman.

Ryle, Gilbert. 1949. *The Concept of Mind*. New York: Barnes & Noble.

Salamon, Sonya, and Jack Temple Kirby. 1992. *Prairie Patrimony: Family, Farming and Community in the Midwest*. Chapel Hill: University of North Carolina Press.

Sanderson, Stephen K. 1990. *Social Evolutionism: A Critical History*. Oxford: Blackwell.

Sarkar, Sahotra. 2000. "Information in Genetics and Developmental Biology: Comments on Maynard Smith." *Philosophy of Science* 67, no. 2:208–13.

Saunders, Peter T., and Mae-Wan Ho. 1976. "On the Increase in Complexity in Evolution." *Journal of Theoretical Biology* 63:375–84.

————. 1981. "On the Increase in Complexity in Evolution II: The Relativity of Complexity and the Principle of Minimum Increase." *Journal of Theoretical Biology* 90:515–30.

Saviotti, Pier Paolo. 1996. *Technological Evolution, Variety and the Economy*. Cheltenham: Edward Elgar.

Schaffer, Mark E. 1989. "Are Profit-Maximisers the Best Survivors? A Darwinian Model of Economic Natural Selection." *Journal of Economic Behavior and Organization* 12, no. 1 (March): 29–45.

Schotter, Andrew R., and Barry Sopher. 2003. "Social Learning and Coordination Conventions in Intergenerational Games: An Experimental Study." *Journal of Political Economy* 111, no. 3:498–529.

Schultz, Walter J. 2001. *The Moral Conditions of Economic Efficiency*. Cambridge: Cambridge University Press.

Schumpeter, Joseph A. 1934. *The Theory of Economic Development: An Inquiry into Profits, Capital, Credit, Interest, and the Business Cycle*. Translated by Redvers Opie from the 2nd German ed. of 1926 (1st ed. 1911). Cambridge, MA: Harvard University Press.

Schutz, Alfred. 1954. "Concept and Theory Formation in the Social Sciences." *Journal of Philosophy* 51, no. 9 (29 April): 257–73.

Schwartz, Shalom H. 1994. "Are There Universal Aspects in the Structure and Contents of Human Values?" *Journal of Social Issues* 50, no. 4:19–45.

Seagle, William. 1941. *The Quest for Law*. New York: Knopf.

Searle, John R. 1995. *The Construction of Social Reality*. London: Allen Lane.

Segerstråle, Ullica. 2000. *Defenders of the Truth: The Sociobiology Debate*. Oxford: Oxford University Press.

Semon, Richard. 1904. *Die Mneme als erhaltendes Prinzip im Wechsel des organischen Geschelens*. Leipzig: Engelman.

Senner, Wayne M., ed. 1991. *The Origin of Writing*. Lincoln: University of Nebraska Press.

Shannon, Claude E., and Warren Weaver. 1949. *The Mathematical Theory of Communication*. Chicago: University of Illinois Press.

Shapiro, Robert. 2006. "Small Molecule Interactions Were Central to the Origin of Life." *Quarterly Review of Biology* 81, no. 2:105–25.

Shaw, George Bernard. 1921. *Back to Methuselah: A Metabiological Pentateuch*. London: Constable.

Simon, Herbert A. 1955. "A Behavioral Model of Rational Choice." *Quarterly Journal of Economics* 69, no. 1 (February): 99–118.

———. 1957. *Models of Man, Social and Rational: Mathematical Essays on Rational Human Behavior in a Social Setting*. New York: Wiley.

———. 1979. "Rational Decision Making in Business Organizations." *American Economic Review* 69, no. 4 (September): 493–513.

———. 1981. *The Sciences of the Artificial*. 2nd ed. Cambridge, MA: MIT Press.

———. 1990. "A Mechanism for Social Selection and Successful Altruism." *Science* 250, no. 4988 (21 December): 1665–68.

Singer, Peter. 1999. *A Darwinian Left: Politics, Evolution and Cooperation*. London: Weidenfeld & Nicolson; New Haven, CT: Yale University Press.

Singh, Ajit. 1975. "Take-Overs, 'Natural Selection' and the Theory of the Firm." *Economic Journal* 85, no. 3 (September): 497–515.

Sipper, Moshe. 1998. "Fifty Years of Research on Self-Replication: An Overview." *Artificial Life* 4, no. 3:237–57.

Smith, Norman E. 1979. "William Graham Sumner as an Anti-Social Darwinist." *Pacific Sociological Review* 22:332–47.

Smolin, Lee. 1997. *The Life of the Cosmos*. London: Weidenfeld & Nicolson.

Sneath, P. H. A. 2000. "Reticulate Evolution in Bacteria and Other Organisms: How Can We Study It?" *Journal of Classification* 17, no. 2:159–63.

Sober, Elliott. 1981. "Holism, Individualism, and the Units of Selection." *PSA: Proceedings of the Biennial Meeting of the Philosophy of Science Association, 1980*, vol. 2, *Symposia and Invited Papers*, 93–121.

———. 1984. *The Nature of Selection: Evolutionary Theory in Philosophical Focus*. Cambridge, MA: MIT Press.

Sober, Elliott, and David Sloan Wilson. 1998. *Unto Others: The Evolution and Psychology of Unselfish Behavior*. Cambridge, MA: Harvard University Press.

Soderquist, Larry D. 2000. "Theory of the Firm: What a Corporation Is." *Journal of Corporation Law* 25, no. 2 (Winter): 375–81.

Somit, Albert, and Steven A. Peterson. 1992. *The Dynamics of Evolution: The Punctuated Equilibrium Debate in the Natural and the Social Sciences*. Ithaca, NY: Cornell University Press.

Spencer, Herbert. 1893. "The Inadequacy of Natural Selection." *Contemporary Review* 63:153–66, 439–56.

Sperber, Dan. 2000. "An Objection to the Memetic Approach to Culture." In *Darwinizing Culture: The Status of Memetics as a Science*, ed. Robert Aunger, 162–73. Oxford: Oxford University Press.

———. 2005. "Modularity and Relevance: How Can a Massively Modular Mind Be Flexible and Context-Sensitive?" In *The Innate Mind: Structure and Contents*, ed. Peter Carruthers, S. Laurence, and S. Stich, 53–68. Oxford: Oxford University Press.

Stadler, Bärbel M. R., Peter F. Stadler, and Günter P. Wagner. 2001. "The Topology of the Possible: Formal Spaces Underlying Patterns of Evolutionary Change." *Journal of Theoretical Biology* 213:241–74.

Steele, Edward J. 1979. *Somatic Selection and Adaptive Evolution: On the Inheritance of Acquired Characters*. Toronto: Williams-Wallace International.

Steele, Edward J., Robyn A. Lindley, Robert V. Blanden, and Paul Davies. 1998. *Lamarck's Signature: How Retrogenes Are Changing Darwin's Natural Selection Paradigm*. New York: Perseus.

Sterelny, Kim. 2000. "The 'Genetic Program' Program: A Commentary on Maynard Smith on Information in Biology." *Philosophy of Science* 67, no. 2:195–201.

Sterelny, Kim, Kelly C. Smith, and Michael Dickison. 1996. "The Extended Replicator." *Biology and Philosophy* 11:377–403.

Stewart, Ian. 2003. "Self-Organization in Evolution: A Mathematical Perspective." *Philosophical Transactions of the Royal Society of London*, ser. A, *Mathematical, Physical and Engineering Sciences* 361, no. 1807 (15 June): 1101–23.

Stich, Stephen P. 1983. *From Folk Psychology to Cognitive Science*. Cambridge, MA: MIT Press.

Stiglitz, Joseph E. 1991. "The Invisible Hand and Modern Welfare Economics." In *Information, Strategy and Public Policy*, ed. David Vines and A. Stevenson, 12–50. Oxford: Blackwell.

Stinchcombe, Arthur L. 1990. *Information and Organizations*. Berkeley and Los Angeles: University of California Press.

Stoelhorst, Jan Willem. 2008. "The Explanatory Logic and Ontological Commitments of Generalized Darwinism." *Journal of Economic Methodology* 15, no. 4:343–63.

Stumpf, Michael P. H., Thomas Thorne, Eric de Silva, Ronald Stewart, Hyeong Jun An, Michael Lappe, and Carsten Wiuf. 2008. "Estimating the Size of the Human Interactome." *Proceedings of the National Academy of Sciences (USA)* 105, no. 19:6959–64.

Suarez, Fernando F., and James M. Utterback. 1995. "Dominant Designs and the Survival of Firms." *Strategic Management Journal* 16, no. 6 (September): 415–30.

Suchman, Lucy. 1987. *Plans and Situated Actions: The Problem of Human-Machine Communication*. Cambridge: Cambridge University Press.

Sugden, Robert. 1986. *The Economics of Rights, Co-Operation and Welfare*. Oxford: Blackwell.

Sumner, William Graham. 1906. *Folkways: A Study of the Sociological Importance of Usages, Manners, Customs, Mores and Morals*. Boston: Ginn.

Szathmáry, Eörs. 2000. "The Evolution of Replicators." *Philosophical Transactions of the Royal Society of London*, ser. B, *Biological Sciences* 355, no. 1403 (29 November): 1669–76.

Szathmáry, Eörs, and John Maynard Smith. 1997. "From Replicators to Reproducers: The First Major Transitions Leading to Life." *Journal of Theoretical Biology* 187, no. 4:555–71.

Szulanski, Gabriel. 1996. "Exploring Internal Stickiness: Impediments to the Transfer of Best Practice within the Firm." *Strategic Management Journal* 17 (Winter): 27–43.

———. 2000. "Appropriability and the Challenge of Scope: Banc One Routinizes Replication." In *The Nature and Dynamics of Organizational Capabilities*, ed. Giovanni Dosi, Richard R. Nelson, and Sidney G. Winter, 69–98. Oxford: Oxford University Press.

Szulanski, Gabriel, and Sidney G. Winter. 2002. "Getting It Right the Second Time." *Harvard Business Review* 80, no. 1:62–69.

Teece, David J. 1976. *The Multinational Corporation and the Resource Cost of International Technology Transfer*. Cambridge, MA: Ballinger.

Thelen, Kathleen. 2004. *How Institutions Evolve: The Political Economy of Skills in Germany, Britain, the United States and Japan*. Cambridge: Cambridge University Press.

Thibault, Paul J. 2000. "The Dialogical Integration of the Brain in Social Semiosis: Edelman and the Case for Downward Causation." *Mind, Culture, and Activity* 7, no. 4 (January): 291–311.

Thomas, William, and Florian Znaniecki. 1920. *The Polish Peasant in Europe and America*. Vol. 2. New York: Octagon.

Tilly, Charles, ed. 1975. *The Formation of National States in Western Europe*. Princeton, NJ: Princeton University Press.

Todd, Emmanuel. 1985. *The Explanation of Ideology: Family Structures and Social Systems*. Oxford: Blackwell.

———. 1987. *The Causes of Progress: Culture, Authority and Change*. Oxford: Blackwell.

Tomasello, Michael. 1999a. *The Cultural Origins of Human Cognition*. Cambridge, MA: Harvard University Press.

———. 1999b. "Emulation Learning and Cultural Learning." *Behavioural and Brain Sciences* 21, no. 5:703–4.

Tulving, Endel, and Daniel L. Schacter. 1990. "Priming and Human Memory Systems." *Science* 247, no. 4940 (19 January): 301–6.

Tushman, Michael L., and Philip Anderson. 1986. "Technological Discontinuities and Organizational Environments." *Administrative Science Quarterly* 31:439–65.

Tushman, Michael L., and Elaine Romanelli. 1985. "Organizational Evolution: A Metamorphosis Model of Convergence and Reorientation." *Research in Organizational Behavior* 7:171–222.

272   REFERENCES

Tyler, Tom. 1990. *Why People Obey the Law*. New Haven, CT: Yale University Press.

Tylor, Sir Edward Burnett. 1871. *Primitive Culture: Researches into the Development of Mythology, Philosophy, Religion, Language, Art, and Custom*. 2 vols. London: John Murray.

Usher, John M., and Martin G. Evans. 1996. "Life and Death along Gasoline Alley: Darwinian and Lamarckian Processes in a Differentiating Population." *Academy of Management Journal* 39, no. 5 (October): 1428–66.

Utterback, J. M., and W. J. Abernathy. 1975. "A Dynamic Model of Process and Product Innovation." *Omega* 3, no. 6:639–56.

Vanberg, Viktor J. 1994a. "Cultural Evolution, Collective Learning and Constitutional Design." In *Economic Thought and Political Theory*, ed. David Reisman, 171–204. Boston: Kluver Academic.

———. 1994b. *Rules and Choice in Economics*. London: Routledge.

———. 2002. "Rational Choice versus Program-Based Behavior: Alternative Theoretical Approaches and Their Relevance for the Study of Institutions." *Rationality and Society* 14, no. 1 (Summer): 7–53.

———. 2004. "The Rationality Postulate in Economics: Its Ambiguity, Its Deficiency and Its Evolutionary Alternative." *Journal of Economic Methodology* 11, no. 1 (March): 1–29.

Vandermassen, Griet. 2005. *Who's Afraid of Charles Darwin? Debating Feminism and Evolutionary Theory*. Lanham, MD: Rowman & Littlefield.

van de Ven, Andrew H., and Marshall S. Poole. 1995. "Explaining Development and Change in Organizations." *Academy of Management Review* 20, no. 3:510–40.

Van Parijs, Philippe. 1981. *Evolutionary Explanations in the Social Sciences: An Emerging Paradigm*. London: Tavistock.

Veblen, Thorstein B. 1896. Review of *Socialisme et science positive*, by Enrico Ferri. *Journal of Political Economy* 5, no. 1 (December): 97–103.

———. 1897. Review of *Essais sur la conception matérialiste de l'histoire*, by Antonio Labriola. *Journal of Political Economy* 5, no. 3:390–91.

———. 1898. "Why Is Economics Not an Evolutionary Science?" *Quarterly Journal of Economics* 12, no. 3:373–97.

———. 1899. *The Theory of the Leisure Class: An Economic Study in the Evolution of Institutions*. New York: Macmillan.

———. 1909. "Fisher's Rate of Interest." *Political Science Quarterly* 24, no. 2:296–303.

———. 1914. *The Instinct of Workmanship, and the State of the Industrial Arts*. New York: Macmillan.

———. 1919. *The Place of Science in Modern Civilization and Other Essays*. New York: Huebsch.

Venkatraman, N., Lawrence Loh, and Jeongsuk Koh. 1994. "The Adoption of Corporate Governance Mechanisms: A Test of Competing Diffusion Models." *Management Science* 40, no. 4:496–507.

Verplanken, Bas, and Wendy Wood. 2006. "Interventions to Break and Create Consumer Habits." *Journal of Public Policy and Marketing* 25, no. 1:90–103.

Vincenti, Walter. 1990. *What Engineers Know and How They Know It: Analytical Studies from Aeronautical History*. Baltimore: Johns Hopkins University Press.

von Neumann, John. 1966. *Theory of Self-Reproducing Automata*. Edited and completed by Arthur W. Burks. Urbana: University of Illinois Press.

Vorzimmer, Peter J. 1977. *Charles Darwin: The Years of Controversy; "The Origin of Species" and Its Critics, 1859–1882*. Philadelphia: Temple University Press.

Vrba, Elizabeth S., and Stephen Jay Gould. 1986. "The Hierarchical Expansion of Sorting and Selection: Sorting and Selection Cannot Be Equated." *Paleobiology* 12:217–28.

Waddington, Conrad H. 1969. "The Theory of Evolution Today." In *Beyond Reductionism: New Perspectives in the Life Sciences*, ed. Arthur Koestler and J. R. Smythies, 357–74. London: Hutchinson.

———. 1976. "Evolution in the Sub-Human World." In *Evolution and Consciousness: Human Systems in Transition*, ed. Erich Jantsch and Conrad H. Waddington, 11-15. Reading, MA: Addison-Wesley.

Wade, Michael J. 1976. "Group Selection among Laboratory Populations of *Tribolium*." *Proceedings of the National Academy of Sciences (USA)* 73, no. 12:4604-7.

———. 1978. "A Critical Review of the Models of Group Selection." *Quarterly Review of Biology* 53:101-14.

Wallace, Alfred Russel. 1870. *Contributions to the Theory of Natural Selection: A Series of Essays*. London: Macmillan.

Walras, Léon. 1874. *Éléments d'économie politique pure; ou, Théorie de la richesse sociale*. Lausanne: Rouge.

Walter, Gordon. 1991. "Culture Collisions in Mergers and Acquisitions." In *Reframing Corporate Culture*, ed. Peter J. Frost, Larry R. Moore, Meryl Reis, Craig D. Lundberg, and Joanne Martin, 301-14. San Francisco: Sage.

Webb, Sidney J. 1889. "The Historic Basis of Socialism." In *Fabian Essays in Socialism*, ed. George Bernard Shaw, 33-61. London: Fabian Society.

Weber, Bruce H., and David J. Depew. 1996. "Natural Selection and Self-Organisation: Dynamical Models as Clues to a New Evolutionary Synthesis." *Biology and Philosophy* 11, no. 1 (January): 33-65.

Weber, Max. 1949. *Max Weber on the Methodology of the Social Sciences*. Translated and edited by Edward A. Shils and Henry A. Finch. Glencoe, IL: Free Press.

Wegner, Daniel M. 2002. *The Illusion of Conscious Will*. Cambridge, MA: MIT Press.

Wegner, Daniel M., and T. Wheatley. 1999. "Apparent Mental Causation: Sources of the Experience of the Will." *American Psychologist* 54:480-92.

Weikart, Richard. 1995. "A Recently Discovered Darwin Letter on Social Darwinism." *Isis* 86, no. 4 (December): 609-11.

———. 1998. "Laissez-Faire Social Darwinism and Individualist Competition in Darwin and Huxley." *European Legacy* 3, no. 1:17-30.

Weismann, August. 1893. *The Germ-Plasm: A Theory of Heredity*. Translated by W. Newton Parker and Harriet R. Ronnfeldt. London: Walter Scott; New York: Scribner's.

Weissman, David. 2000. *A Social Ontology*. New Haven, CT: Yale University Press.

Wells, Spencer. 2002. *The Journey of Man: A Genetic Odyssey*. London: Allen Lane.

Wenger, Etienne. 1998. *Communities of Practice: Learning, Memory and Identity*. Cambridge: Cambridge University Press.

Wheeler, Michael, John Ziman, and Margaret A. Boden, eds. 2002. *The Evolution of Cultural Entities*. Oxford: Oxford University Press.

Whitley, Richard. 1999. *Divergent Capitalisms: The Social Structuring and Change of Business Systems*. Oxford: Oxford University Press.

Wicken, Jeffrey S. 1987. *Evolution, Thermodynamics, and Information: Extending the Darwinian Paradigm*. Oxford: Oxford University Press.

Wilkins, John S. 2001. "The Appearance of Lamarckism in the Evolution of Culture." In *Darwinism and Evolutionary Economics*, ed. John Laurent and John Nightingale, 160-83. Cheltenham: Edward Elgar.

Willey, Malcolm M. 1929. "The Validity of the Culture Concept." *American Journal of Sociology* 35, no. 2 (September): 204-19.

Williams, George C. 1966. *Adaptation and Natural Selection*. Princeton, NJ: Princeton University Press.

———. 1992. *Natural Selection: Domains, Levels and Challenges*. Oxford: Oxford University Press.

Williamson, Oliver E. 1975. *Markets and Hierarchies: Analysis and Anti-Trust Implications: A Study in the Economics of Internal Organization*. New York: Free Press.

———. 1995. "Hierarchies, Markets and Power in the Economy: An Economic Perspective." *Industrial and Corporate Change* 4, no. 1:21–49.

Wills, Christopher. 1993. *The Runaway Brain: The Evolution of Human Uniqueness*. New York: Basic.

Wilson, David Sloan. 1980. *The Natural Selection of Populations and Communities*. Menlo Park, CA: Benjamin/Cummings.

———. 1983. "The Group Selection Controversy: History and Current Status." *Annual Review of Ecology and Systematics* 14:159–88.

———. 1999. "A Critique of R. D. Alexander's Views on Group Selection." *Biology and Philosophy* 14:431–49.

———. 2002. *Darwin's Cathedral: Evolution, Religion, and the Nature of Society*. Chicago: University of Chicago Press.

Wilson, David Sloan, and Elliott Sober. 1994. "Reintroducing Group Selection to the Human Behavioral Sciences." *Behavioral and Brain Sciences* 17, no. 4:585–608.

Wilson, David Sloan, and Edward O. Wilson. 2007. "Rethinking the Theoretical Foundations of Sociobiology." *Quarterly Review of Biology* 82, no. 4 (December): 327–48.

Wilson, Edward O. 1975. *Sociobiology: The New Synthesis*. Cambridge, MA: Harvard University Press.

———. 1978. *On Human Nature*. Cambridge, MA: Harvard University Press.

———. 1998. *Consilience: The Unity of Knowledge*. New York: Knopf.

Wimsatt, William C. 1999. "Genes, Memes, and Cultural Heredity." *Biology and Philosophy* 14, no. 2 (April): 279–310.

Winter, Sidney G. 1964. "Economic 'Natural Selection' and the Theory of the Firm." *Yale Economic Essays* 4, no. 1:225–72.

———. 1971. "Satisficing, Selection and the Innovating Remnant." *Quarterly Journal of Economics* 85, no. 2 (May): 237–61.

———. 1982. "An Essay on the Theory of Production." In *Economics and the World around It*, ed. Saul H. Hymans, 55–91. Ann Arbor: University of Michigan Press.

———. 1987. "Natural Selection and Evolution." In *The New Palgrave Dictionary of Economics* (4 vols.), ed. John Eatwell, Murray Milgate, and Peter Newman, 3:614–17. London: Macmillan.

———. 1988. "On Coase, Competence, and the Corporation." *Journal of Law, Economics, and Organization* 4, no. 1 (Spring): 163–80.

———. 1995. "Four Rs of Profitability: Rents, Resources, Routines, and Replication." In *Resource-Based and Evolutionary Theories of the Firm: Towards a Synthesis*, ed. Cynthia A. Montgomery, 147–78. Boston: Kluwer.

———. 1990. "Survival, Selection, and Inheritance in Evolutionary Theories of Organization." In *Organizational Evolution: New Directions*, ed. Jitendra Singh, 269–97. London: Sage.

Winter, Sidney G., and Gabriel Szulanski. 2001. "Replication as Strategy." *Organization Science* 12, no. 6 (November–December): 730–43.

Witt, Ulrich. 1997. "Self-Organisation and Economics—What Is New?" *Structural Change and Economic Dynamics* 8:489–507.

———. 1999. "Evolutionary Economics and Evolutionary Biology." In *Sociobiology and Bioeconomics: The Theory of Evolution in Biological and Economic Theory*, ed. Peter Koslowski, 279–98. Berlin: Springer.

———. 2003. *The Evolving Economy: Essays on the Evolutionary Approach to Economics*. Cheltenham: Edward Elgar.

———. 2004. "On the Proper Interpretations of 'Evolution' in Economics and Its Implications for Production Theory." *Journal of Economic Methodology* 11, no. 2 (June): 125–46.

———. 2009a. "Novelty and the Bounds of Unknowledge in Economics." *Journal of Economic Methodology* 16, no. 4 (December): 361–75.

———. 2009b. "Propositions about Novelty." *Journal of Economic Behavior and Organization* 70:311–20.

Wolf, Jason B., Edmund D. Brodie III, and Allen J. Moore. 1999. "Interacting Phenotypes and the Evolutionary Process II: Selection Resulting from Social Interactions." *American Naturalist* 153, no. 3:254–66.

Wolfram, Stephen. 1984. "Universality and Complexity in Cellular Automata." *Physica* 10D:1–35.

———. 2002. *A New Kind of Science*. Champaign, IL: Wolfram Media.

Wood, Wendy, and Jeffrey M. Quinn. 2004. "The Power of Repetition in Daily Life: Habits and Intentions Guide Action." Typescript, Duke University, Department of Psychology.

Wood, Wendy, Jeffrey M. Quinn, and D. Kashy. 2002. "Habits in Everyday Life: Thought, Emotion, and Action." *Journal of Personality and Social Psychology* 83:1281–97.

Wood, Wendy, Leona Tam, and Melissa Guerrero Witt. 2005. "Changing Circumstances, Disrupting Habits." *Journal of Personality and Social Psychology* 88, no. 6:918–33.

Woodburn, James. 1982. "Egalitarian Societies." *Man* 17, no. 3 (September): 451–71.

Wrangham, Richard. 2009. *Catching Fire: How Cooking Made Us Human*. London: Profile.

Wynne-Edwards, Vero Copner. 1962. *Animal Dispersion in Relation to Social Behaviour*. Edinburgh: Oliver & Boyd.

Yoffee, Norman. 2005. *Myths of the Archaic State: Evolution of the Earliest Cities, States, and Civilizations*. Cambridge: Cambridge University Press.

Zander, Udo, and Bruce Kogut. 1995. "Knowledge and the Speed of the Transfer and Imitation of Organizational Capabilities: An Empirical Test." *Organization Science* 6, no. 1:76–92.

Zental, Thomas R., and Bennett G. Galef Jr., eds. 1988. *Social Learning: Psychological and Biological Perspectives*. Hillsdale, NJ: Erlbaum.

Zucker, Lynne G. 1987. "Institutional Theories of Organization." *Annual Review of Sociology* 13:443–64.

Index